Filmmaking

Direct Your Movie from Script to Screen Using Proven Hollywood Techniques

Jason J. Tomaric

ELSEVIER

AMSTERDAM • BOSTON • HEIDELBERG • LONDON
NEW YORK • OXFORD • PARIS • SAN DIEGO
SAN FRANCISCO • SINGAPORE • SYDNEY • TOKYO

Focal Press is an imprint of Elsevier

Focal Press is an imprint of Elsevier
30 Corporate Drive, Suite 400, Burlington, MA 01803, USA
The Boulevard, Langford Lane, Kidlington, Oxford, OX5 1GB, UK

© 2011 Jason J. Tomaric. Published by Elsevier Inc. All rights reserved

No part of this publication may be reproduced or transmitted in any form or by any means, electronic
or mechanical, including photocopying, recording, or any information storage and retrieval system,
without permission in writing from the publisher. Details on how to seek permission, further
information about the Publisher's permissions policies and our arrangements with organizations such
as the Copyright Clearance Center and the Copyright Licensing Agency, can be found at our
website: www.elsevier.com/permissions.

This book and the individual contributions contained in it are protected under copyright by the
Publisher (other than as may be noted herein).

Notices

Knowledge and best practice in this field are constantly changing. As new research and experience
broaden our understanding, changes in research methods, professional practices, or medical
treatment may become necessary.

Practitioners and researchers must always rely on their own experience and knowledge in evaluating
and using any information, methods, compounds, or experiments described herein. In using such
information or methods they should be mindful of their own safety and the safety of others, including
parties for whom they have a professional responsibility.

To the fullest extent of the law, neither the Publisher nor the authors, contributors, or editors, assume
any liability for any injury and/or damage to persons or property as a matter of products liability,
negligence or otherwise, or from any use or operation of any methods, products, instructions,
or ideas contained in the material herein.

Library of Congress Cataloging-in-Publication Data
Application submitted.

British Library Cataloguing-in-Publication Data
A catalogue record for this book is available from the British Library.

ISBN: 978-0-240-81700-2

For information on all Focal Press publications
visit our website at www.elsevierdirect.com

SHEFFIELD HALLAM UNIVERSITY
WL
791.430233
TO
ADSETTS LEARNING CENTRE

10 11 12 13 14   5 4 3 2 1

Printed in the United States of America

Working together to grow
libraries in developing countries

www.elsevier.com | www.bookaid.org | www.sabre.org

ELSEVIER   BOOK AID
International   Sabre Foundation

This book is lovingly dedicated to my incredibly supportive family. Mom, Dad, Aimee, and Heather, thank you for all your support over the years. I couldn't have done it without you.

COMPANION WEB SITE ACCESS INSTRUCTIONS

Filmmaking is more than book…be sure to visit the companion site and utilize the multimedia included with the book.

To access the material, go to www.filmskills.com and log on at the top right-hand side of the page.

User name: filmmaking
Password: Enter the fifth word in chapter 18.

The companion site for *Filmmaking* includes:

- Over 30 minutes of high-quality video tutorials featuring over a dozen working Hollywood professionals
- Industry-standard forms and contracts you can use for your production
- Sample scripts, storyboards, schedules, call sheets, contracts, letters from the producer, camera logs, and press kits
- A 45-minute video that takes you inside the movie that launched Jason's career. Three thousand extras, 48 locations, 650 visual effects, and all made from his parents' basement for $25,000.

Contents

Acknowledgments

I would like to thank the many businesses and individuals whose helpful advice contributed to the completion of this book.

PHOTO CREDIT

Josh Romaine

Robyn Von Swank

Casey Slade

Peter Graves

SPECIAL THANKS TO

Elinor Actipis

Houston King

Ryan Carter

Brad Schwartz

Jim Lang

Steve Skrovan

Jerry Magaña

Andrew Huebscher

Stephen Campanella

John Henry Richardson

Apple Computer

Micheal K. Brown

Matthews Studio Equipment

Ed Phillips

Kino-Flo

Lowel Lighting

Arri

Panavision

Kodak

x   Acknowledgments

Audio-Technica

Screen Actors Guild

IATSE

Writers Guild of America

Directors Guild of America

. . . and, of course, to the cast and crews of *Time and Again, Fred and Vinnie, Currency* and all the productions I've worked on over the years.

I remember the moment as if it happened yesterday. It was a scorching summer afternoon in July 1984, and my fourth-grade friends and I stood anxiously in our spacemen costumes in the loft of my parents' Ohio barn. Surrounded by Christmas lights stuck through hastily painted cardboard boxes, we stared at the crayon-drawn view screen and yelled as the make-believe enemy ships fired their weapons at us. Throwing ourselves around the set, my Dad shook the camera as my friends threw pieces of cardboard debris on top of us. It worked perfectly. I stood up, called "cut," and we officially finished the first shot of my first movie. Looking around at the world I had created in the barn, I knew, in that moment, that I had found my calling . . . to direct.

In the following years, I learned to make movies through trial and error. I would shoot a movie, learn from my mistakes, and then move on and produce another one, hoping it would be better than the one before. Since then, I moved to Hollywood and have directed several award-winning feature films and international documentaries, dozens of national television commercials and music videos, and shot in over 34 countries, all while making a successful living doing what I love.

The first book I had written, *The Power Filmmaking Kit*, adapted the Hollywood-system for low-budget, independent movie production, focusing almost exclusively on my experiences as a low budget director in Ohio. When my publisher, Focal Press, asked me to write a second edition, I went a little overboard, doubling the amount of information and rewriting nearly every page with my experiences of working in Hollywood over the past seven years. The book you're now holding in your hands is the result – so much bigger and more comprehensive, we decided to publish it as a new book – one that encompasses the entire director's journey – one that doesn't look to redefine a century-old industry into a series of guerilla techniques, but one that paints it for what it is, helping you understand how the Film Industry works, and how you can get it to work for you. As a result, we renamed the book, more appropriately, *Filmmaking*.

Filmmaking systematically guides you through the process of making a movie through a collection of practical experiences, tips, and tricks I've learned over the years. As I wrote this, I thought about what I wish I had known 15 years ago when I was just getting started in this industry. Having the opportunity to talk with someone who had not only been through the process, but had done it successfully, would have been invaluable. With the right resources, information, and guidance, it is possible to make a great movie – you just have to know where to start.

Little did I know that that day in the barn with my dad, friends, and a cheap cardboard set was the first day of a journey that would eventually lead to a successful Hollywood career.

Be creative, persistent, and ambitious. Think big and get ready to live *your* dream.

Jason J. Tomaric

UNIT 1
Development

i. Begin with a strong idea, inspired by actual events, literature, personal experiences or historical occurrences.

ii. Set-up a comfortable, quiet workspace.

iii. Determine the genre, format and plot type of the story.

Developing the Idea

iv. Secure the rights from the author of a previous work, or from an individual whose story inspires your story.

v. Contact other writers with whom you may want to partner.

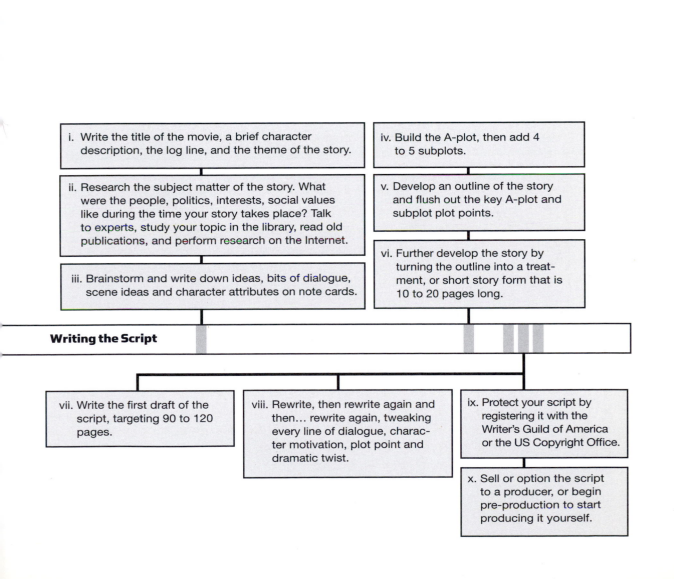

i. Write the title of the movie, a brief character description, the log line, and the theme of the story.

ii. Research the subject matter of the story. What were the people, politics, interests, social values like during the time your story takes place? Talk to experts, study your topic in the library, read old publications, and perform research on the Internet.

iii. Brainstorm and write down ideas, bits of dialogue, scene ideas and character attributes on note cards.

iv. Build the A-plot, then add 4 to 5 subplots.

v. Develop an outline of the story and flush out the key A-plot and subplot plot points.

vi. Further develop the story by turning the outline into a treatment, or short story form that is 10 to 20 pages long.

Writing the Script

vii. Write the first draft of the script, targeting 90 to 120 pages.

viii. Rewrite, then rewrite again and then... rewrite again, tweaking every line of dialogue, character motivation, plot point and dramatic twist.

ix. Protect your script by registering it with the Writer's Guild of America or the US Copyright Office.

x. Sell or option the script to a producer, or begin pre-production to start producing it yourself.

"The Yesterdays of Tomorrow"
by
Jason J. Tomaric

CHAPTER 1
The Script

5

INTRODUCTION

The script is the blueprint for the story and contains dialog, character movements, and scene descriptions. Like the old adage says, "If it ain't on the page, it ain't on the stage."

Every good movie is produced around a well-written script, and it doesn't matter how big the budget is, how good the actors are, how incredible the explosions are, or how dynamic the visual effects are if the story isn't moving, engaging, and believable. Films with high production values have been known to flop because the script was poorly written, and rarely has a bad script been made into a good movie. Writing a script is a craft that takes time to learn and requires a tremendous amount of discipline and understanding of story structure, psychology, human dynamics, and pacing.

Not only is writing a script is the *most important aspect* of making a movie; it's also the cheapest. Whereas Hollywood studios spend hundreds of millions of

A single shot on set can be very expensive to produce – from the cost of the cast and crew to the equipment and locations, it's cheaper to work through problems on paper than on set.

Filmmaking.
© 2011 Jason J. Tomaric. Published by Elsevier Inc. All rights reserved.

dollars on visual effects, great actors, explosions, and car chases, the materials involved in writing a script cost little more than a few dollars – the cost of a pencil and paper.

In embarking on the journey to the perfect script, there are three paths you can take. You can write the script yourself, you can option a script that has already been written, or you can hire a writer to write the script for you. This chapter will look at these three options and determine which may be the best choice for your production.

WORKING WITH A WRITER

Writers tend to be stronger in either structure or dialog and character, so finding a writing partner who complements your skills can lead to a much better script. Finding a competent writing partner can be as easy as contacting local writing organizations, colleges, or university programs with writing courses or seeking writers online or through industry contacts. When looking for a good writing partner:

- **Ask for a writing sample.** Read through the writer's past works to see if his style, ability to write dialog, pacing, dramatic moments, structure, and plot twists are on par with the nature of the story. To get an idea of the writer's ability, read the first 20 pages of one of his previously written screenplays and see if the script engages you. If so, keep reading. If not, consider finding another partner.

- **Find a partner whose strengths are your weaknesses.** If you are good at structure, then find a writer who is good at dialog and characterization. A good writing partner will bring additional talents to the table and balance your skill set.

- **Talk with your potential writing partner about the story and make sure she likes the genre, story, and characters before working with her.** For example, if you are writing a romantic comedy, look for partners who specialize or have an interest in writing romantic comedies.

- **Make sure your partner has the time and commitment to work on the script, especially if it's being written on spec (for free).** It's difficult to complete a screenplay if your partner has to drop out in the middle of the project or has obligations that may interfere with his ability to work on the project. Write and sign a contract that outlines the details of your working relationship together. Understand that when working with a writer, you both own 50% of the script, so if any problems occur during the relationship, the project may go unproduced.

- **Work out the credit your partner will receive as well as payment terms if the screenplay is sold, optioned, and/or produced.** It's vital to work out the details of

Bob Noll and I work through a scene of *Time and Again*. I found that collaborating with him was both inspiring and functional. We would often bounce ideas off each other if we were stuck, support each other if our ideas needed work, and ground each other if we felt our ideas were too good.

your business relationship before beginning work on a script, should any problems arise during or after the writing process.

Ultimately, a compatible partnership is as much about chemistry as it is about artistry: find a person with the same goals as yours, who compliments your vision but completes your skill set. A rewarding writing partner can be both inspiring and motivating, both traits that have a positive impact on the script.

WRITING YOUR OWN SCRIPT
Developing the Idea

The first step to writing a movie script is to have a solid idea, but before you settle on a concept for your film, it's important to decide what you want the project to do for you once it's finished. Are you going to make a movie for art's sake – to explore your vision and style, or maybe just to learn the process of filmmaking? Or are you looking to produce a commercially viable movie that can be sold and hopefully generate a profit?

Contrary to the popular belief of many filmmakers, these two options are almost always mutually exclusive. Most commercially produced movies tend to rely on a time-proven, revenue-generating formula designed to appeal to the widest possible audience. Because the marketing budget for most Hollywood movies is significantly higher than the production budget, the industry has to sell as many tickets as possible to cover not only the film's production and marketing costs, but also the costs of movies that fail to recoup their initial investment. Unfortunately, this commercialization tends to discriminate against artistic films that play to a smaller audience, leaving those productions to run, at best, in local art theaters and small film festivals.

Jason's Notes

So here's how Hollywood works. A young movie executive, whose job depends on the financial success of the movie he greenlights, has the choice between two scripts. The first is an emotional, awe-inspiring drama that captivates the reader with tales of entrancing human drama, riveting conflict, and heart-wrenching feeling. The second script is *Garfield: The Movie*. Which is he going to pick? The second one, of course – wouldn't you? With an existing fan base, practically guaranteed return on investment, and years of branding, *Garfield* is a sure shot. To this young executive, the choice was about the financial future of his next project and his career. This is how Hollywood works.

Making a movie is an expensive and time-consuming process, so think smart when choosing the type of story to tell. Carefully consider what you want the movie to do for you:

- **Do you want the movie to make money?** Then develop a concept around the industry standard formula, with marketable actors, clearly defined genre, a tight three-act structure, and high production values. This can be the most expensive option.

- **Do you want to make a movie for the educational experience?** If you want to learn filmmaking or practice your craft, produce a short film and know that you won't recoup your investment.
- **Do you want to make art?** Producing an artistic film that defies traditional Hollywood convention is risky because distributors tend to shy away from films they can't easily describe explain to viewers. If picked up for distribution, most art films will find homes in small art theaters and possibly on home video, although the odds of generating a profit are slim.

Jason's Notes

One of the biggest tricks to developing a strong idea is to work backward. Look at the types of movies that are selling in both the domestic and international marketplace, determine how much money you have, and list the resources you have access to before you settle on an idea for your movie.

The statistics are grim for filmmakers who produce feature films. I've read numbers that place the number of features produced in the United States every year at around 7,000. Less than 10% get picked up for distribution, and an even smaller percentage makes a profit. One of the biggest reasons is the lack of market research to determine the commercial viability of the film. Filmmakers often develop an idea and produce the movie without researching what distributors are looking for and what's selling in the international market, so they end up in massive debt with a movie that sits on the shelf.

The first real step of making a movie is to start at the end by contacting distributors and researching what types of productions DVD distributors and TV broadcasters are interested in buying. Find out what genres sell the best, the best format to shoot on, the ideal length, and which actors have the most international appeal.

Jason's Notes

Don't think of these boundaries as creative restrictions. Instead, use them as a guide to writing a marketable screenplay. Remember, the goal is to get your movie seen, and distributors are the gatekeepers that stand between you and the audience. They are looking for a product that can make them money, so give them what they can sell.

Writing What You Know

When it comes to developing a story, I find that it always helps to write what you know. The best piece of advice I ever received was to write what I've seen, what I have experienced, and what I've lived in life. Filmmaking is about truth, and writing scenes and moments that truthfully resonate with the audience can be a difficult task unless you are personally familiar with the material you're exploring.

One way of doing this is to dedicate your life to experiencing a variety of situations, cultures, and people so that when it comes time to write, you have a broad range of life experiences from which to draw. Many legendary filmmakers are older men and women who have put their life experiences on film, resulting in real, engaging moments that ring true to the audience.

Ultimately, ideas are everywhere – just be open to finding one that resonates best with you:

- Look at real-life moments for inspiration: childhood memories; interesting happenings at work; relationships with family, friends, and love interests. Think of family conflicts, your first job or your freshman year in high school, moving out on your own for the first time, and college experiences. Drawing on personal experiences leads to strong material because you've lived and experienced it.
- Read the newspaper, listen to the radio, and watch news stories that may captivate your imagination. The old cliché says that truth is often stranger than fiction, and in many instances, it is!
- Keep a journal of interesting things that happen every day: an engaging conversation, a funny moment, an unusual or interesting person you may have encountered in public. These moments can be the seeds not only of good ideas, but also of engaging characters, moments, and lines of dialog in the movie.
- Brainstorm and write down anything and everything that comes to mind. You'd be surprised what comes out. Listen to inspirational music, turn off the lights, let your mind roam free, and be ready to capture ideas as they strike.
- Study political history and the lives of dictators, emperors, famous people, and serial killers. All these peoples' lives involved extraordinary circumstances that are full of drama and conflict.

Jason's Notes

I have a concept called the 98% rule. When I come up with an idea, I need to be 98% happy and consumed with it before I agree to further develop and flesh it out. Too many times, I've tried to work on an idea I wasn't entirely enthusiastic about and ended up discarding the project, sometimes after investing hundreds of hours. I've learned to wait until I find an idea that really resonates with me before I commit to it.

- Be original and avoid copying concepts used in other forms of media, stories from movies or television shows, or major plot lines from popular books. Audiences want to see new, unique ideas, not rehashes of old ideas.
- Be careful not to infringe on copyrighted work. Copyright infringement can be an expensive mistake if the original owner of the stolen property chooses to sue.
- Surf the Internet. The knowledge of the world is at your fingertips and can provide outstanding ideas and motivation for a movie.
- Try reading the Yellow Pages, magazines, and even advertisements for inspiration.
- Get out of your house. Traveling to a new place, whether it's going out of town or visiting a local coffee shop, can help spur the imagination.
- Take breaks and don't force your imagination. A walk on the beach or through the woods can help clear your thoughts and open your mind to new ideas. I find that the less I think about my story, the more ideas pop into my mind.
- Write stories you're passionate about. Be excited and willing to explore the subject matter. Learn as much as you can about the world, people, and situations you're writing about.
- Ask "what if?" open-ended questions that help your mind wander – you may stumble onto a sharp idea.
- Read or reread classic literature and listen to operas. Stories of mythology, ancient romances, and tales of adventure and heroism are the root of storytelling. If in doubt, go back to see how authors of old tackled an idea.
- Research your idea by studying the time period, characters, customs, fashions, technologies, and values of the world in the story you're telling. Learning more about the actual events or motivation behind your story will help develop ideas.
- Learn from people who resemble or can provide insight into your character. If you're writing a crime drama, contact a local police station and ask to shadow an officer for a week. Listen to how she talks and acts, both casually and under pressure. Get a sense of the police environment so that when it comes time to create it into a script, you can write a realistic and believable world.

Concepts to Avoid

As you're developing the concept for your movie, be aware of several mistakes that independent writers often make:

- **Avoid writing a sequel.** Movie studios already own the rights to franchises like the Jason Bourne movies, *Spiderman*, and *Die Hard*, and develop sequels internally with staff writers. Studios will not even read your script if you choose to write a franchise-based story. You'll have a much better chance if you write an original idea, even on spec, and pitch it to production companies.
- **Don't follow the next trend.** Remember that movies take years to produce, and if you try to jump on the bandwagon of a hit movie by writing a

similar script, odds are that another movie will become the next big thing before you finish your script.

- **Develop an idea that is within your means to produce.** If you're looking to produce your own script, be attentive to your resources, both financially and materially. Don't write action or stunt scenes unless you can afford to shoot them properly. Be aware of the number of locations you create.
- **Know your market.** If you want to produce your script independently, know that distributors aren't looking for a low-budget attempt at a Hollywood movie, but rather an interesting, unique take that is usually possible only outside the studio system. If you choose to write a cheap version of a Hollywood film, know that your competition is huge … it's Hollywood itself. So make what Hollywood doesn't: character-driven, daring, uniquely told stories that go beyond the typical Hollywood storytelling formula.
- **Know your product.** If you're producing a low-budget movie, the audience can be forgiving of less-than-Hollywood-quality production values, as long as the story is strong and the performances engaging. The audience will expect an independent movie to look like an independent movie. Effects are expensive; a good script is cheap.

OPTIONING MATERIAL

As a writer, you can not only develop an original idea, but you can also develop a script around an existing work, such as a book, poem, short story, or even a personal account. However, to simply adapt the idea into a screenplay could violate copyright laws and expose you to increased legal liability.

One way of legally using this material is to option the rights to use it. An *option* is a short-term lease that grants a producer permission to adapt material into a screenplay and to either produce it or try to sell it to a production company. Once a story is optioned, you are free to market, sell, or produce the project as if you owned it during the term of the option.

The ability to option a book or story opens up hundreds of thousands of possibilities, so one way of finding a strong story is to go to the bookstore and start reading. If you find a book that you like, call the publisher and get the author's contact information. Explain how you want to use the book and how you will adapt it and ask if the author is willing to consider an option. The author may want money up front, a percentage of the profits, credit, or any number of deal points that would need to be negotiated. If the conversation gets this far, it's best to contact an entertainment attorney to help negotiate with the author on your behalf and draw up the necessary paperwork.

Never assume that your idea is freely available to be adapted into a movie. Although failing to secure an option to an idea may not hurt you during production, it will haunt you when you try to sell the project. Distributors require you to show documentation that you secured all necessary rights to the idea, actors, music, and third-party footage. If you can't, they won't distribute your film because the liability is too high for them.

Setting Up Your Space

Before writing your screenplay, find a comfortable, quiet space to work. Whether it's your office, your basement, or your workspace after business hours, designate this space as your "writing room," and remove any distractions. It's important to have a designated space so that when you enter it, your brain knows it's time to start being creative.

- **Find a quiet space that you use only for writing.** I like to work in a particular coffee house in Burbank. For some reason, this space, the constant rhythm of the people coming and going, and the quiet ambience help me focus and allow the creativity to flow.
- **Turn off the telephone and television.** These needless distractions will only draw your attention away from the script. Writing is a practice in the art of focus and discipline as much as it is about storytelling.
- **Be prepared with a pencil, paper, and computer.** Even though I use Microsoft Word and Final Draft when I write, I find that keeping a pencil and paper nearby is handy to write down notes and thoughts I have during the writing process.
- **Consider playing music from movie soundtracks or classical music that inspires you.** I find that background music, especially music without lyrics that supports the theme and tone of the story I'm writing, gets the creative juices flowing.

This is where I've been sitting for months now, writing this book – and that's the only thing I write when I sit here. Having a consistent workspace is a great way of helping my mind click into "book-writing mode."

STORY STRUCTURE

Whenever I begin a new story, I define the foundation first. Although the results seem obvious, it helps me narrow the focus to what I am really writing, why I am writing it, what my point is, and for what audience the story is intended.

I know it's impossible to thoroughly discuss the screenwriting process in one chapter, so I've included only the important points that you should understand – not to necessarily write a script, but to dissect, translate, and direct it effectively.

Step 1: Fiction or Nonfiction

Now that you have your idea both legally and conceptually established, you need to lay out the foundation for your story and make a few choices. The first is whether your movie is fictional or nonfictional.

Fictional stories involve made-up characters in made-up situations. Based on imagination more than fact, fictional stories allow the writer to evoke emotions and thoughts outside the realm of the audience's everyday world. Fiction provides a vehicle for the writer's creativity to blossom and take form in a nearly boundless format.

Nonfiction stories are true stories based on actual people and events. Nonfiction stories include documentaries, biographies, and stories based on history, politics, travel, education, or any real-world subject matter.

Always be aware of the rights involved in making a movie. Fictional stories grant you unrestricted access to the material, because you are creating it. Nonfictional stories may require you to secure the rights to an idea. Make sure you have permission to write about the subject matter you are writing.

Step 2: Genre

A genre is a category or type of story. Genres typically have their own style and story structure, and although there are several primary categories, movies can be a mixture of two or three different genres.

Some common genres include:

- Action
- Comedy
- Crime
- Drama
- Family
- Fantasy
- Horror

- Musical
- Romance
- Romantic comedy
- Science fiction
- Thriller
- War
- Western

When choosing the genre for an independent film, be aware of the costs and difficulties of shooting certain genres like science fiction or westerns, for which the cost of sets, costumes, and props may be prohibitive.

If you're making a commercial movie, horror movies and action films tend to sell better than other genres in foreign markets because the viewer isn't reliant on dubbed dialog to get into the story.

Jason's Notes

Traditionally, distributors tend to favor movies that are easily identified in a specific genre, making it easier for them to pitch and sell the movie to buyers. In the business, DVD rental stores, TV stations, and online distributors all know how particular genres like horror or action perform, basing these estimates on years of sales data. Movies that are not specifically genre-based can scare away distributors who aren't willing to invest the time and money needed to properly market and sell a film.

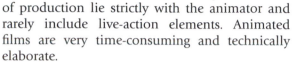

Commercials are mini-movies and are one of the most profitable types of production. With generally high budgets, short turnaround time and sometimes creative ideas, commercials are an outstanding way to be creative and pay the bills.

As attractive as feature films are to most filmmakers, they don't pay as well as other forms of production, require long hours on set, and make it difficult to have a social life.

Step 3: Format

Stories can be told in many different formats, each designed for a different purpose. Be mindful of your budget, the availability of resources, and time when you choose the format for your story.

The main formats include:

- **Animation.** Produced either by hand or using computer technologies, 2D or 3D movies still rely on traditional story structures, although the means of production lie strictly with the animator and rarely include live-action elements. Animated films are very time-consuming and technically elaborate.
  - **Commercials.** Designed to advertise a product or service, television commercials incorporate a wide range of styles, techniques, animation, narrative, and hard-sell techniques into 10-, 15-, 30-, or 60-second time lengths. Commercials are a great way for filmmakers to showcase their style, storytelling, and production capabilities, and are among the most lucrative, well-paying forms of production.
  - **Documentaries.** Documentaries are intended to study a subject, occurrence, theme, or belief in an attempt to either explore the subject or arrive at a conclusion about the subject. Documentaries can either take on an investigative approach, in which the filmmaker tries to answer a question or research a subject, or follow a subject and allow the story to unfold during the production. Documentaries can, in some instances, be inexpensive but time-consuming to produce.
- **Feature films.** The 90-minute narrative is the mainstay of Hollywood entertainment, and its production is the dream of millions of aspiring filmmakers. The riskiest style of production, feature films are expensive and time-consuming and rarely recoup the monies invested.
  - **Industrial/corporate.** These productions are typically marketing or how-to pieces for businesses. Although generally not very entertaining to watch or make, industrials are an outstanding way to make money.
  - **Music videos.** These highly stylized promotional videos for music artists are a great way for a filmmaker to explore unbridled creativity using any medium, any style of narrative or performance, and artistic editing.

A little-known secret in Hollywood is that pretty much everyone shoots industrial videos at some point in their career. Although you will probably not be making high art, industrials can provide consistent, lucrative work.

- **Short films.** Ideally under 20 minutes, shorts are a terrific way of learning the process of making a movie, showcasing your talents and generating interest from investors in future projects.

About Short Films

Many filmmakers produce short movies in an effort to help them move forward in the entertainment industry. You may use your short film as a tool to show investors your skills and abilities, but be careful: investors may assume that the quality of the feature you are asking them to fund will be same as the quality of the short you're using in your sales pitch. In most instances, it won't be, because the short was more than likely produced on a shoestring budget. This can potentially hurt you.

Every year around Christmas, when the film industry slows down, I produce a *spec project*: that is, a production that is completely self-financed and self-produced for the sake of improving my skills and my demo reel, and to get more work. This year's project was the short film *Currency*.

I've noticed that people have a tendency to acknowledge your abilities based on what you've already produced. For example, regardless of whether a cinematographer has shot three profitable horror movies, twenty commercials, and an action film, I know producers who would question his ability to light a person for a simple on-camera interview. The fact that the producer doesn't see an on-camera interview on the cinematographer's demo reel makes it difficult to trust that he can get the shot, even though he could do it very well.

Second, there is virtually no market for short films, making it nearly impossible to see a return on investment. It's very difficult for distributors to package a short film in a market that buys and sells 80- to 120-minute-long movies. Your movie may be screened in a film festival or included on a compilation DVD, but odds are good that you will never see a dime.

Despite the financial drawbacks of producing a short film, they are still outstanding ways to improve your skills as a writer, actor, director, or cinematographer by allowing you to practice the filmmaking process, learn new techniques, perfect your organizational abilities, and meet other filmmakers in your community.

Jason's Notes

If I could give you only a single piece of advice from my experience in the industry, it would be to produce several short films before tackling a feature. The process of learning how to make a movie is cyclical, meaning you have to go through the entire process at least once just to begin to understand the craft. For example, much of directing stems from understanding the editing process and the way shots work together to make a scene. Understanding just this one aspect will have a huge impact on your choices for camera placement and pacing when directing on set.

Don't turn your star idea into your first film; you'll regret it for your entire career. Start small and learn the process with a short film; then, with the second and third films, hone the craft of directing, working with actors, and directing the camera. You will know when you're ready to take on a feature.

Step 4: Plot Type

At the core of every great movie is a great idea, but an idea by itself is rarely unique. Every idea you can think of has already been written, produced, told, packaged, marketed, and reconstituted a thousand times throughout history. From Shakespeare to Spielberg, the core story elements are the same. So what makes a movie new and exciting to an audience? The *way* an idea is told.

Stories can be distilled to a very simple premise: the main character encounters a problem and is either successful or unsuccessful in solving it. The setting, supporting characters, and details are the padding that transforms this simple skeletal structure into a multilayered, interesting, and engaging story.

As you begin crafting your script, be aware of the simple plot structure that will become the backbone of the story. Here are some of the most common:

- **Overcoming the adversary.** The hero must find a way to overcome a threat presented by another person, society, nature, himself or herself, a supernatural force, technology, or religion. (*Terminator*, *Alien*)
- **The quest.** The hero undergoes a search for something, someone, or an idea. The perils he encounters and whether the hero meets his objective are up to the writer. (*Contact*)
- **The journey and return.** The hero undergoes a journey from home and experiences a change in character along the way. (*Lord of the Rings*, *The Wizard of Oz*)
- **Comedy.** This story type does not refer to comedy in the traditional fashion, but rather in a positive ending. Events in the story keep the characters apart until a happy reunification at the end. (*Casablanca*)
- **Tragedy.** Events in the story lead to the death of a character. This usually unhappy ending is not often seen in Hollywood movies. (*Braveheart*, *Passion of the Christ*)
- **Resurrection.** The hero is oppressed until events in the story free him. (*The Shawshank Redemption*)
- **Rags to riches.** The life of a character evolves from a life of nothingness to one of bounty, be it family, wealth, or fame. (*It's a Wonderful Life*)

Conflict

The single most important element to have in your story is conflict. Without a clearly defined conflict, the story will be weak, meaningless, and ultimately unfulfilling to the audience.

Jason's Notes

Conflict is *everything*. Without conflict, there is no story. The greater the conflict and the more pain you can inflict on your characters, the more emotion you can invoke from the audience, the more exciting the drama, and the more entertaining the story. In a way, you need to be somewhat of a literary sadist, willing to put your characters through as much dramatic agony as possible.

Conflicts can exist in many different forms, but as you may remember from way back in high school literature class, there are four basic classifications of conflict.

Develop the Idea
Consider marketability and affordability

↓

Develop the Premise
Determine the parameters of the story, style, and structure

↓

Write the Title
Think of a catchy title

↓

Develop the Theme
Make sure every scene supports the moral of the story.

↓

Write the Logline
Write a short paragraph of the story and remember to include the conflict.

↓

Treatment or Outline
Either will help flesh out the story into a fuller, robust tale.

↓

First Draft
Turn the outine into a 90-page rough draft.

↓

Rewrite
A good story is made in the rewrite process. Polish and rework the story until it's perfect.

↓

Protect
Register the script with the Writer's Guild and the U.S. Copyright Office.

↓

Produce or Option
Sell the script or produce the script yourself.

PERSON VS. SELF

Person vs. self is the theme in movies that places a character against his own will, confusion, or fears (*Jacob's Ladder*). It is an internal conflict that plagues the character. Person vs. self can also involve a character trying to find out who she is or coming to a realization or a change in character. Although the struggle is internal, the character can be influenced by external forces (*A Beautiful Mind*). The struggle of the human being to come to a decision is the basis of Person vs. self.

PERSON VS. PERSON

Person vs. Person is when the conflict exists between two similar but opposed people. This conflict, which usually occurs between the main protagonist and the main antagonist, may play a large role in the plot and contribute to the development of both characters (*Terminator, Die Hard, The Shawshank Redemption*). Throughout the story, there are usually several conflicts: emotional, physical, or intellectual.

PERSON VS. SOCIETY

The conflict in Person vs. Society is a theme in which the main character's source of conflict is social traditions, concepts, norms, and mores. Society itself is often looked at as a single character (*Milk*).

PERSON VS. NATURE/ENVIRONMENT

Person vs. Nature/Environment is the theme in movies that place a character against forces of nature. An example would be Tom Hanks' character in *Castaway*, or the marooned sports team in *Alive*. Many disaster films (*The Day After Tomorrow, Armageddon, Titanic*) focus on this theme, which is predominant within many survival stories.

PERSON VS. SUPERNATURAL

Person vs. Supernatural is a theme that places a character against supernatural forces. Movies about aliens, ghosts, or other unearthly antagonists fall in this category (*Jeepers Creepers*).

The Basics

Before we begin writing, we should first have a basic understanding of what our story is about. I realize this sounds trite, but one of the biggest problems of many scripts is the lack of a strong foundation, and one way we can avoid this problem is by going through the exercise of defining exactly what it is we want to say.

Step 1: Write the title (1–5 words). Name the film. This doesn't have to be the film's final title, but a strong working title can help maintain focus on what the story is about. When developing the title, it helps if it invokes a sense of the story's genre and plot.

Time and Again.

Step 2: Determine the theme (5–15 words). What is the "moral of the story"? Beneath the story, plot, characters, and genre, what is the message you want to convey to the audience after they finish watching the movie? Make sure that every scene, every moment, and every character supports this theme. If you ever encounter writer's block, or don't know where a scene should go, refer to the theme and write a scenario that supports it. I like to print the theme out on a piece of paper and tape it to my computer monitor for it to serve as a reminder as I'm writing.

A man's quest to find the truth supersedes everything, even love and death.

Step 3: Write the logline (15–25 words). Describe the good guy, the bad guy, the setting, and the conflict. The logline is the basic premise of what the movie is about. Think about what a movie reviewer would write up in the newspaper when trying to describe the premise of the film in a clear, concise manner. Describe the who, what, why, when, and where, and be sure to identify the conflict, or there's no story. A line like "problems arise when . . ." strongly sets up the conflict in the story.

Time and Again is the story of Bobby Jones, a convicted murderer, who has been sentenced to 30 years in prison for a crime he doesn't remember committing. Bent on finding the real killer, he escapes from prison only to be thrown back in time to July 14, 1958, the day of the murder. Problems arise when, with six hours to work, he must reconstruct a forgotten past to save himself. When he meets the sexy diner waitress, Awanda, his true priorities are tested.

STORY STRUCTURE

The A Plot

Stories have been told a certain way throughout history, and audiences have grown accustomed to this "formula." In a way, it's a language both the storytellers and audiences agree upon. First, stories begin by setting up the characters and setting in which the story will take place, then the problem or conflict appears. The drama of the story begins when the main character has to figure out how to cope with or solve the problem. These three components are considered the basic story structure; each can be divided into three distinct parts, called acts.

Act 1

Act 1 is the first 30 minutes of a 120-minute film and establishes the setting, time period, and technology of the world in which the story takes place. The audience is introduced to the main characters and their traits, personalities, likes and dislikes, problems, and challenges.

In short, Act 1 is about WHO the main characters are, WHERE the story takes place, WHEN the story takes place, WHAT is the story about, and WHY the problem is occurring; the drama begins when the characters figure out HOW to deal with the conflict. In a simplified example,

> Timmy is a ten-year-old boy walking home from school in the residential suburb of Highland Heights, Montana. He is a quiet and shy kid who is wildly imaginative, turning the most everyday items into play toys. He is well-dressed and lives in a typical middle-class neighborhood.

In Act 1, you have the most liberty in setting the stage for the rest of the story, and even though it may seem a little forced, the audience will accept and understand this.

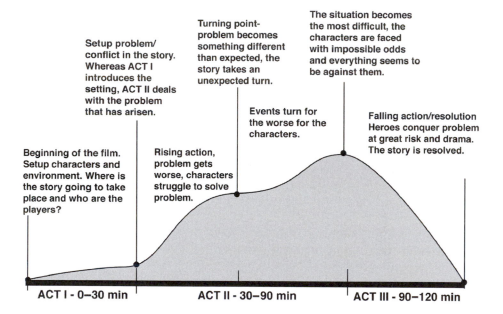

Setup problem/conflict in the story. Whereas ACT I introduces the setting, ACT II deals with the problem that has arisen.

Turning point- problem becomes something different than expected, the story takes an unexpected turn.

The situation becomes the most difficult, the characters are faced with impossible odds and everything seems to be against them.

Events turn for the worse for the characters.

Beginning of the film. Setup characters and environment. Where is the story going to take place and who are the players?

Rising action, problem gets worse, characters struggle to solve problem.

Falling action/resolution Heroes conquer problem at great risk and drama. The story is resolved.

ACT I - 0–30 min   **ACT II - 30–90 min**   **ACT III - 90–120 min**

The plot arc for a 120-minute movie.

Act 2

Act 2 is the next movement in the story, running an hour from the 30-minute point to the 90-minute point, and begins when the conflict is introduced.

> Timmy, while walking home from school, is approached by a vicious, ill-tempered dog. Scared and without anywhere to run, Timmy climbs up a tree, but the dog remains, barking and snarling at Timmy.

The dog is the conflict and now our story is about how Timmy deals with the dog. Be careful, however, because Act 2 is usually the most weakly written act in the entire script. A poor second act will bring the story to a screeching halt, so as you write, it's important to raise the stakes and increase the jeopardy against the main character. The more pain, agony, hardship, trial, and tribulation you can throw at the main character, the more the audience will root for him.

Timmy struggles to climb higher up in the tree, but he loses his grip
and begins to slide down the trunk, cutting his arms on the sharp bark.
The dog, now inches from his feet, snarls and snaps at Timmy's ankles.
Timmy struggles to climb onto a higher branch. He makes it and, for the
moment, is safe. It starts raining and Timmy opens his backpack and
pulls out his jacket. He loses his grip and the jacket falls to the ground.
The dog rips it to pieces.

Turning Point

The most important part of the second act is called the *turning point*, which
occurs at the middle of the story. The turning point is the instance in which the
story and plot line take a severe turn and the characters are forced to compensate for this twist.

As Timmy watches his jacket get torn to bits, the rain continues to pour
down. A car driving down the road hits a puddle, hydroplanes, and hits
the tree, knocking Timmy out of the tree and onto the roof of the car.

The story has changed direction drastically from the earlier plot of Timmy and
the dog to Timmy and the car. The latter half of the second act is about our
characters dealing with the new change in circumstances.

The man driving the car has been knocked unconscious in the accident.
The dog moves toward Timmy, while Timmy struggles to call for help
and assist the injured driver. Timmy is scared, wet, and alone as he
faces this new problem.

Act 3

Act 3 is the last quarter of the story, running from 90–120 minutes, wherein
the conflict becomes the most difficult for the character and he is forced to use
his skill, wit, and ability to resolve or escape from the problem with the maximum possible risk. Late in Act 3 is the point of no return, at which the character chooses a path that will lead to his ultimate success or failure.

Timmy struggles to pull the driver out of the car while throwing pieces
of his peanut butter sandwich to distract the dog. Timmy almost frees
the driver when he notices a gun, a mask, and a bag full of hundred-
dollar bills sitting in the back seat. The man wakes up and grabs the
gun and Timmy, holding him hostage, and threatens to kill him if he
escapes. All the while, the dog remains outside snarling at the two.

The third act ends with the conclusion of the story when the character resolves
the conflict. At this moment, the main character changes, either for the better
or for the worse, through redemption, understanding the importance of love,
learning to be kind and caring, or through any number ways.

Timmy, in the most dire moment, gathers up every last bit of courage
and stuffs the remaining peanut butter sandwich in the robber's face.
The dog jumps on the robber, giving Timmy enough time to grab the gun

and hold the robber at bay. The dog then turns on Timmy, and instead of attacking, licks Timmy's face, nuzzling him for more food. After having found the courage, Timmy waits for the police to arrive and arrest the robber. At the end of the ordeal, Timmy walks home, side by side with his new canine friend.

Subplots

We just created the primary or A plot of the story. Movies contain not only the primary plot, but also four or five smaller subplots that are interwoven throughout the movie, many of which help to develop character, pace the timing of the A plot, and give the story more depth. The subplots almost always tie into the A plot and feature four or five scenes apiece, with each subplot wrapping itself up in the middle of the third act.

In our example with Timmy, the A plot follows his plight with the dog and the robber. Some possible subplots could include:

- **The girl next door.** When he is in the tree, Timmy discovers he can see into a pretty girl's room from across the street. Reluctant to get her attention for fear that she will see him in this embarrassing position, Timmy tries hard to watch her while remaining unnoticed. At the end of the story, when the car crashes and Timmy holds the gun on the robber, the girl hears the commotion, calls the police, and finds Timmy to be a hero.
- **The report.** While Timmy is scrambling up the tree, the dog bites Timmy's book bag and his school report falls out. During the A story, Timmy attempts to use branches, even putting bubble gum at the end of a stick to try to save his report from being mauled by the dog. At the end of the story, the girl picks up the report and offers to put it in a fresh, clean binder, bringing closure to both this and the previous subplot.
- **The orphaned bird.** When Timmy climbs the tree, he finds a small bird left all alone in the tree, its nest about to crumble apart. Timmy tries to rebuild and support the nest with twigs and leaves. Timmy befriends the bird, and the dialog between Timmy and the bird afford us, the writers, the opportunity to hear Timmy's thoughts and feelings. At the end of the story, as Timmy is walking away with the girl, he looks back into the tree to see the mother bird return to her baby.

Every subplot ties in and supports the A plot, giving the writer several opportunities to write about during the story.

The Gasp Moment

Every good movie has four or five *gasp moments* in which the audience is startled or shocked by a turn in the plot. Be sure to write these gasp moments into the story. For example:

- **The car crash.** The biggest gasp moment in the story happens when Timmy's tree is struck by a car. This unexpected moment will certainly take the audience by surprise.

- **Timmy tries to escape.** Timmy, thinking the dog has left, tries to sneak out of the tree. He barely makes it down when he turns to look – the dog is inches from his face, ready to jump. Timmy scrambles back up into the tree.
- **The girl sees Timmy.** Timmy, while trying to build a support for the nest, pulls off his belt so he can use it to support himself on a tree branch. His pants, caught on a branch, start to slip off and he looks over to see the girl watching him. Trying to dismiss his actions and not look foolish, Timmy tells her everything is okay and he's saving a bird.

Jason's Notes

I've always hated writing. It requires discipline, focus, and a willingness to go back and rewrite something again and again. I know that I'm not the only person who feels this way. Lots of my writing friends agree that writing the script is one of the most difficult parts of making a movie; it's not fun, social, or exciting. Writing is a tough process that involves you, your computer, and your life experiences.

So how do you start writing? Well, the question has the answer built in . . . you *just start*. Follow the easy steps in this chapter to help you break into the first page. After that, it's up to you to find the motivation to write.

When I wrote *Time and Again*, I was really inspired by the idea of a man escaping from jail and appearing in the middle of an open field. I started writing down ideas I had had about where he ends up, who he meets, where and when he goes. All these questions helped me make a list of unconnected ideas that spawned additional ideas. As I kept writing down ideas, the plot eventually came into being. The more ideas I had, the more I was able to work the plot.

Once I had an idea of where the story was going, I called Bob Noll, a friend of mine at John Carroll University. We had discussed the idea for this story and he agreed to help me write it. We spent numerous nights at his office, brainstorming and developing the characters, fleshing out scenes, and ultimately developing an outline that was strong enough to begin turning it into a script.

I would think of the story in terms of how the audience would see it: one scene at a time, from the beginning to the end. As I verbally developed these ideas, Bob would type them into the computer in an outline form. Sometimes we would write dialog, sometimes just the character's actions. But whatever we wrote, our goal was to capture the spontaneous thoughts and ideas we had during our session so we could later go back and rewrite and tighten the story.

Bob Noll and I work on the script for *Time and Again*.

I always looked forward to these writing sessions because they helped me, as the filmmaker, deeply explore the world of our characters. I found that I really enjoyed the creative, brainstorming part of writing and Bob was really good at translating my ideas to the page. Our partnership began to take form, as I paced in his office and, following the outline of the plot points the story needed to hit, developed exciting scenes that would get our character from one plot point to the next in an exciting, unpredictable manner.

We usually worked for only a few hours a night. Beyond that, our brains would turn to clay and the creativity valve would shut off. Even if we tried to push longer, the material we wrote looked really bad when we came at it again with fresh eyes the next day. The lesson I learned was to listen to my mind. When it got tired, we quit for the night.

(Continued)

The process of writing the script from the outline was pretty simple. The more detailed the outline, the easier the process of writing the script. Completing the first draft, no matter how good it is, is the first crucial step in making a good story. Revising and rewriting the story to make it tighter and better paced, to make the characters stronger and the dialog more snappy, was a lot easier once we got past the hurdle of completing the first draft.

We went through several revisions of *Time and Again* before we were happy with the script and felt like it was time to go into preproduction.

Treatments and Outlines

Now armed with a strong idea and an understanding of the basic story format, you need to develop the idea into a literary structure, so your objective is to write two documents called the treatment and the outline to help you.

THE TREATMENT

A treatment is a short-story version of the movie that can be as little as two pages or as many as sixty pages long. Most treatments start out pretty short, and – as you develop the A-story line and subplots – get longer and more detailed. The purpose of the treatment is to establish the basic plot arc, the characters' journeys, and the essential plot points, all of which can change as you further develop the story. Although the treatment is a working document – a mixing palette for your story ideas – you should still know how the story begins and ends, and roughly what happens in the middle.

When you write the treatment, you can begin incorporating script-formatting elements that will eventually make their way into the finished screenplay. For example, each time a new character is introduced in your treatment, type the name of the character in capital letters followed by the character's age and a brief description. For example:

> AWANDA, 31, a lonely blond bombshell who hustles men in the hopes of finding true love.

The treatment can be as long or as short as the story requires. The more detail you can write into the treatment, the easier it will be to incorporate into the script. For example:

> The fog rolls across the prison yard, streaked by moonlight. Outside, three figures, BOBBY JONES, 32, a rugged young man whose face reflects his hard prison time, and two other convicts jump the fence. Landing hard between the perimeter fences, the three men take off running inside the courtyard, as guards and their dogs rush to intercept. Spotlights flick on and sirens pierce the night as Bobby turns a corner. BAM! A shot from one of the guards takes out one of the prisoners, but Bobby keeps running. Moments later, another shot rings out, taking out the second prisoner. Now Bobby, alone, picks up his pace, despite the guards' orders to stop. As he turns another corner, a vortex opens and, before he can stop, Bobby races through, landing in a golden wheat field on a sunny day. Tripping over a branch, he crashes to the ground as he tries to get his bearings.

The Other Side
Treatment – Version 3a

CRASH!
In a rural, Midwest town, six high school graduates excitedly head off on a camping trip before parting ways for college. They are CLINT (nature boy/boy scout, makes up in ingenuity what he lacks in the "cool" factor), MICHAEL (dim witted jokester, always on the lookout for a party), ALAN (straight-laced sports jock and the group's natural leader), AMANDA (shallow socialite and Alan's girlfriend), SUSAN (eager tomboy with an abundance of common sense), and JOHNNY (quiet outsider with a sharp sarcastic wit and not a fearful bone in his body).

The trip seems ill-fated from the beginning. Driving down the isolated dirt road through the woods to Clint's uncle's cabin, their SUV SLAMS into a pothole, SPINS violently and HITS a downed tree in the middle of a dirt road. The vehicle is totaled. Stranded in the middle of nowhere, with no cell phone reception, and still miles from the cabin, the group decides to cut their losses and head through the woods on foot. After all, according to Clint's GPS, the cabin is only about a mile straight through a forest he grew up in and knows well. With night looming, the group moves quickly, with Johnny, stopping periodically to snaps pictures of his friends as they argue over trip semantics.

Suddenly a great earthquake ROCKS the area. Shaken, but unwavering from their destination, the group continues toward the cabin, with little hope of turning back in the now dark woods. Soon they find themselves lost, and anxiety grows as dusk approaches. The GPS is acting up, their spirits are down, and scared. Then, in the middle of a small clearing our heroes stumble upon a floating doorway, just a few feet above the ground. The door is a portal opening into a room that can't be seen from the outside. The group ventures cautiously forward, and upon inspection, realize that it is the doorway to an enormous invisible spaceship, that stretches nearly a mile in each direction. This is the source of the earthquake.

They venture inside and find a pile of dead beings - aliens lying in front of a large passageway inside the ship. Accidentally stepping on a pad in front of the passageway, Alan inadvertently opens a portal, revealing an enormous ARMY of the same creatures that lie dead at their feet. The humans and the creatures stare at each other. Before Alan can react, one of the creatures reaches through the portal with a thin organic tendril and grabs him. The tendril lifts Alan off the pressure sensitive pad, forcing the doors to close shut, severing the tendril. The friends realize that this is NOT a place they want to stay, and with the door they originally entered now closed, they run off down a hallway to escape. With Alan in the lead, the group heads through the ship, and soon finds themselves in a laboratory. Aliens, Animals, and other known and unknown beings are strung up and dissected. Alan turns around to exit. "NOT THIS WAY!" Another hallway provides means to an exit, and the group tears out through the forest, praying for safety, with the hopes that they are not being followed. They desperately run for the cabin.

The cabin, however, is nowhere to be found. Spooked and tired, Michael trips and falls down a ravine, breaking his leg. Alan, Amanda and Johnny stay behind with Michael as Clint and Susan continue on for the cabin. With the only landline, and therefore means of communication for miles, the cabin is their only hope.

Use the treatment, written as a short story, as a tool to help you develop the plot points of the story.

Continue working and reworking the treatment until the entire story is fleshed out and reads smoothly from beginning to end. Keep the story and every plot point kinetic, with every moment leading the audience toward the next plot point. Make sure every scene supports and drives towards the theme of the overall story.

Some pointers to keep in mind when you are writing the treatment:

- **The treatment is a writer's tool.** It's not intended to be used as a selling document for investors or producers. Try to show only the final script and avoid releasing the treatment.
- **When writing the treatment, try writing the A plot and each subplot separately as if it were its own story.** This will help the story flow and ensure that each subplot is told in a logical, concise sequence. Once you finish writing each subplot, then you can begin intertwining the story lines to form the movie.
- **Good writers spend most of their time writing the treatment.** Remember that it's easier to rework a plot point, character, or event in the story at this stage than it is after the first draft has been written. The treatment is a short yet malleable document intended to help you work out story points.
- **The treatment should have the same tone and style as the story you are telling.** Treatments of suspense stories should keep the reader at the edge of his seat; comedic stories should be funny.
- **Build your story around sequences.** Remember that shots make up a scene, scenes make up sequences, and sequences make up a film. Sequences are moments and mini-stories within the larger story, and from an organizational standpoint, it's helpful to write portions of your movie in sequences.
- **Create setups and payoffs.** Situations, props, information, and people your characters encounter must lead to something or have some significance within the story. Remember, the audience is going to be looking for meaning in the elements you show them.

THE OUTLINE

Once the treatment is finished, further develop the story into an outline by writing a brief description of what happens in every scene, so that once it's complete, the reader understands every plot point of the story. Writing the first draft is then as simple as expanding each scene by adding dialog and developing each moment from the outline.

Begin outlining by taking a blank sheet of paper, and numbering lines 1–100. I prefer using Microsoft Word's numbering feature to add, remove, and change entries. With each number representing a scene, the goal is to ultimately describe the location where each scene takes place, the characters involved, and what happens in that scene, interweaving the A plot and each subplot. The more you detail you write into each scene, the easier it will be to write the first draft.

Start out by writing the plot points of the A story in the outline. I generally use the first five to eight scenes to set up the A story line, then add an A-story scene every two to three scenes throughout the outline, but this is only a guide and will certainly vary depending on the nature of your story. Toward the end of the story, reserve the last eight to ten scenes to resolve the A plot line.

Once the A-story points are listed out, begin adding subplots. There are usually four to six subplots in a movie that usually tie into the A story at some point and each run over four or five scenes. All subplots should resolve themselves by before the A plot resolves itself.

Here is the first page of an outline for a movie. Notice how each number is its own scene and how each story beat provides enough information for the reader to understand the action in each scene, without going into too much detail.

LOVE AND LOSS
Treatment

- Inside a makeshift plywood tree house, young JIMMY (12) and his best friend ERIC (11) carefully aim a slingshot. Eric takes bets that Jimmy won't hit him. Jimmy tests the rubber band, making sure it won't come off.
- Washing his car is 18 year-old KEVIN RUPLE, a skater-type with stringy long hair and an obscure high school rock band t-shirt. A beaten brown Pinto pulls up and JENNY JAMESON, a quiet, reserved goth type pulls out. She's carrying a tray of brownies.
- Back inside the tree house, Jimmy takes aim at Kevin and launches a small stone.
- The stone hits Kevin square in the middle of the forehead knocking him over. Jenny, tosses the brownies aside and rushes to his aid. Blood trickles from his cheek.
- Back in the tree house, the boys laugh, until. . .
- Kevin hears the laughter. Scanning the yard, he sees the two boys in the tree house. He jumps up and charges the tree.
- Jimmy and Eric panic and hide the slingshot under a loose board in the tree house floor. They quickly toss a rope ladder down the back and exit while Kevin scrambles up the front ladder. Barely missing Kevin's grasp, the boys jump to the ground and run to the fence, but it's too late. Kevin's already caught up to them. Kevin, careful to not let Jenny hear, confronts the boys as to why they always do this to him. They made a fool of him in front of Jenny. We learn that Kevin has a speech impediment.
- Inside the country-decorated kitchen, Kevin nurses his wound with an ice-filled dishrag while Jimmy's mother, ANN screams at Jimmy. Jimmy, crying, professes that he had nothing to do with Kevin's injuries. Ann doesn't believe him.
- Inside Jimmy's bedroom, the door slams shut, locking a sullen Jimmy in his room. Sitting on his bed, he hears Kevin, Jenny and his mother chatting outside as Kevin walks back to his car. Jimmy rushes up to the window to listen to their conversation.

- Outside, Kevin walks across the street to his car. Jenny yells out to him. He forgot the brownies. As Kevin turns to come back, he doesn't hear a car speeding down the road, which hits him, throwing him 25 feet in the air. Jenny screams.
- Inside, Jimmy recoils in shock. The phone rings, and without taking his eyes from the tragedy outside, he answers. It's Eric. He asks if Jimmy was grounded and wanted to see if he could come back out and play. Jimmy can't answer. Tears well up in his eyes.

Continue working and editing, adding and removing plot points and scenes until you are happy with the pacing and flow of the story. As you develop the outline, keep these points in mind:

- Every scene must push the story forward. If you can effectively tell the story without a particular scene, that scene should be removed.
- Every scene should support the theme of the movie.
- Know how the movie is going to end so you can write to a conclusion, instead of free-forming thoughts and ideas that may not go anywhere.

Ideally, the outline is where the most structural work is performed when writing the script. It's a lot easier to work and rework the story in the outline than once the first draft has been written.

Jason's Notes

I do the most work on my story in the outline phase. Usually, when working with a writing partner, we read through the outline and discuss each plot and subplot separately. Making changes is easy because we haven't written any dialog yet. The outline is about the broad brushstrokes of the story. As we continue to fine-tune the outline, we add more detail to each scene, even writing lines of dialog if we feel inspired. Once the outline is finished, the first draft of the script comes together very quickly.

Creating Characters

A movie is nothing more than a slice of a character's life, and his experiences dictate how he may respond to conflicts presented in the story. By developing each character's personal background, family history, personality traits, habits, and behavioral tendencies toward friends and family, you can make them become realistic, multidimensional people.

One of the strongest techniques for creating realistic characters is to base them on someone you know. Look to friends, family, or even yourself for inspiration and draw on their personal experiences, quirks, and idiosyncrasies. The more vividly you can picture each character in your mind, the easier it will be to write her dialog and behavior in each scene. For example, if you're basing a character on your neighbor Frank, think "What would Frank do in this situation? How would he act? What would he do?"

- **Create interesting names for your characters.** Try using a baby naming book or searching the Internet for random name generators.
- **Stories are about people, not explosions or car chases.** When writing your story, the dimension of your characters comes out when you show the audience how they react in different situations. Describe their strengths and weaknesses, attitudes and opinions, drives and ambitions, and what they want.

Characters fall into three primary categories, each having a specific role in driving the story forward.

PROTAGONIST

The protagonist is the central character or in the story: a person who either undergoes a personal transformation in a consistent environment, or who must remain steadfast in a changing environment and whose personality and motivations are explored more than any other character. The story is always about the protagonist, focusing on his journey of discovery and change. Although the protagonist is the focal point, the story may or may not be told through his eyes.

ANTAGONIST

The antagonist is the literary opposite of the protagonist, who presents obstacles, challenges, and situations the protagonist must overcome. The antagonist has her own goals and objectives that conflict with the protagonist's desires.

It is important to note that the antagonist, although the most fun to write, often ends up the most shallow and clichéd character in the movie. This is evident in cheesy action movies in which the overzealous Russian spy plans to blow up America unless $2,000,000 is wired to his Swiss bank account. The audience never learns what drives him to commit this crime, what his life is like, how his family is reacting to the situation, or what terrible circumstances in his life led to his devilish scheme. This lack of depth leads to a flat, boring character that simply does bad things. This character's impact on the audience is minimal and fleeting.

For an outstanding example of how a flawed character can be written sympathetically, watch Charlize Theron in *Monster*, in which she plays a murderous prostitute whose behavior is motivated by love and the need to preserve her self-identity. The character is so incredibly rich and well-written that the audience can't help but be drawn to her, despite her killing the men who hire her.

SUPPORTING CHARACTERS

Supporting characters are written to support either the protagonist or the antagonist, usually having similar objectives. Supporting characters work with the main characters, but never eclipse them, although supporting characters may have their own set of complexities.

In *Time and Again*, the main character is Bobby Jones, along with supporting characters Awanda, Sheriff Karl, young Bobby Jones, Martha Jones, and Robin Jones.

Although these primary characters carry the story, there are quite a few secondary supporting characters helping to provide a realistic backdrop for the story. These characters include the stickball players, the high school kids outside the theater, the deputy sheriff, and the diner waitress. Although they aren't aligned with either the protagonist or the antagonist, they are vital in providing information to the main characters and pushing the story forward. If the character cannot provide this function, they must be cut from the story. For example:

- **Stickball players.** By playing stickball, they provided the opportunity for young Bobby Jones to be in the middle of the street so that older Bobby Jones could see him.
- **Diner waitress.** She helped Bobby Jones when he ran into the diner, looking for Awanda, providing him with critical information that led him to his next course of action.
- **Students outside theater.** When Bobby Jones approached them, they also gave him critical information as to the whereabouts of young Bobby Jones.

MAKING ORIGINAL CHARACTERS

When designing and creating characters, I find it helpful to develop a character profile that lists the traits of each character. Consider running each character through this list to flesh him out to a fuller, more real person.

Describe the following traits and details for your character:

- Interests and hobbies
- Romantic successes or failures
- Family life
- Relationship with parents/siblings
- Financial situation
- Education
- Life goals
- Posture
- Musical tastes
- Culinary tastes
- Political views
- Travel experience
- Favorite vacation spot
- Worst habit
- Biggest fear
- Favorite occasion
- Reaction to criticism
- Television viewing habits
- Behavior while drunk
- Nickname

Another great way to create strong characters is to take a personality test as each character to identify his or her personality temperament. This will help you understand how the character will respond in different situations when problems arise in the story line. I highly recommend the book *Please Understand Me* by David Keirsey and Marilyn Bates (Prometheus Nemesis, 1984). It provides a short version of the Myers-Briggs Temperament Indicator with full descriptions of the 16 personality types.

CHANGES IN CHARACTERS

As you develop your characters, it is essential – especially for the main character – for them to grow and change by the end of the story. This change comes about through the situations the character encounters, the people he meets, and the choices he makes. In *Schindler's List*, Oscar Schindler often regarded Jews as cheap factory labor until the events of Nazi Germany changed his perspective and attitude. The atrocities he witnessed at the concentration camps and the Nazis he encountered changed his heart, and his love of money was replaced with respect for human life.

Characters can be defined by three traits: how they act, how they think, and their emotional state. Truly three-dimensional characters have a balance between these three traits, and the audience can see their behavior: we know what they're thinking and how they feel. To deprive your character of even one of these traits will result in a flat, clichéd character. Think about the blond supermodel who wants only an acting career. We never get to know what she's thinking, why she wants this, or what she's doing to achieve it. Her character is flat and lifeless.

Actor Brian Ireland plays Bobby Jones, the lead character in *Time and Again*. Remember that characters are real people with a complete history that helps shape their behavior in each scene. Know your characters, their motivations, what they want, and what they will do to get what they want.

Though these characteristics are accepted in ancillary roles, they are sometimes deadly in main characters. Consider James Bond. This character is largely defined by the actions he performs, so we rarely get a chance to see his emotional side. We never see him exhibit fear, anger, or sorrow. He is an action-driven character whose emotional disconnect adds a superhuman, although empty, quality to him. In much the same way, the Architect in *The Matrix: Revolutions* was so cerebral that he exhibited neither emotions nor behavior. The result was, again, a flat, lifeless character.

Conversely, the characters that truly move us are the ones who exhibit all three of these character traits, such as Tim Robbins's character Andy in *The Shawshank Redemption*, or Luke Skywalker in *Star Wars*. These characters felt like living, breathing people because we were able to see the good and the bad, the strengths and weaknesses, the fear and determination. The more vibrant an emotional palette you can paint, the richer the character.

Jason's Notes

I find it helpful to graph the character's emotional arc in much the same way I might map out a story arc. This helps me visualize the character's journey – her emotional state, her mindset, and her attitudes. I can see at what points of the story the character is most vulnerable, where the stakes are highest, and where she is at her breaking point. By looking at this chart, I can best pace the character's emotional journey across the scenes.

ABOUT DIALOG

Dialog is one of the most difficult elements to write. The quality of the dialog is a direct reflection of the characterization and the degree to which the audience identifies with the characters. Many times, strong dialog isn't about what the character says, but what he doesn't say.

There are a number of problems that plague many screenplays:

- **Dialog is cliché.** Cliché lines are common, overused words or phrases that don't reflect the character's true thoughts and feelings. When writing dialog, throw away any clichés in favor of sharp, original dialog.
- **Every character sounds the same.** Badly written dialog can be a symptom of shallow characters. As a writer, you cannot write strong dialog unless you know the character inside and out. Take the time to develop a strong back story, and understand what the subtext of the character really is in each scene. What does the character secretly want, and how does that reflect through the dialog? Remember that people rarely say what's on their minds.
- **Dialog is written in long speeches.** In reality, we speak in short phrases that are less than a few lines. Banter between two people is usually pretty quick and short. Many writers write long speeches that are difficult for an actor to perform realistically. In a well-written script, most lines of dialog are only a few lines long, at most. If you feel compelled to write big blocks of dialog, ask yourself what the character is trying to say, and how you can make the point most effectively.
- **Dialog is used to cover weak action.** In a well-written screenplay, the audience should understand the story by the action that's happening on the screen, not by what the characters say. Many novice writers use dialog as a crutch to help pull them through the plot, while their characters are often sitting idle. The result is a boring movie that loses the audience's interest. One of my favorite sayings is "show it, don't tell it": make sure the action is strong and the essence of the scene is conveyed in the scene before adding the dialog.

Dialog and Backstory

Backstory is a character's history up to the time the story takes place and directly affects the words he or she speaks. The events in the character's life from yesterday right up to a minute ago all have an impact on what the character thinks and says.

For example, if I were to write a scene about a teacher in a high school science class, it would be easy to write lines we expect teachers to say.

```
                    ALLEN
      Good morning, class. Today we're
      going to talk about natural
      selection and how viruses and
      bacteria are as much of the food
      chain as we are. Get out your books
      and turn to page 134.
```

The resulting dialog, although accurate, doesn't really take us into Allen's mind or help us understand what he is feeling – it's surface dialog. Instead, create Allen's backstory, possibly from events that occur in the movie, to create a multidimensional character.

Let's say that Allen didn't get any sleep the night before, because earlier that day, his eight-year-old son had just been diagnosed with encephalitis. This comes in the middle of a bitter divorce from his wife, so Allen is concerned that he won't be able to keep his house and pay for his son's medical bills. As a result, Allen was on the phone pleading with his wife to come back for their son's sake just before this science class began.

                         ALLEN
          Nature has a funny way of keeping
          life in check. Sometimes the smallest
          things can cause the most damage.
          Take a virus - it's small, simple,
          but it can kill something much
          bigger than itself ... it can kill
          its host - whether it's an animal
          in the forest or a little boy.

              (beat)

          Let's all turn to page 134.

The weight of what's happening in Allen's life directly affects his behavior in the classroom, especially when he begins teaching his class on natural selection. His dialog isn't simply educational rhetoric, but is also insight into his soul. His words are shaped by the events occurring in his life, which may be unknown to his students but resonates heavily with the audience.

Jason's Notes

One of my favorite exercises it to record a real-life conversation, then transcribe it so I can see how it looks on paper. It's amazing how fragmented the spoken word really is.

Dialog Tips

When writing dialog, keep these tips in mind:

- **Always remember the subtext.** Characters don't always say what they're feeling. A scene in which an angry married couple on the verge of separating are making breakfast may only talk about their plans for the day. Even though the scene is ripe with anger and discontent, none of these feelings need to be blatantly written – instead, their discussions of the husband leaving for work, indecisiveness as to when he's coming back, and telling the wife she's on her own for dinner can serve as a powerful metaphor for their relationship, dripping with subtext and deeper meaning for both the characters and the audience.

- **Dialog should be used when you cannot describe a character's motivations through action.** Be aware of what you want the audience to understand by the end of each scene and write only what is necessary to get this point across.
- **Be accurate and true to your character's heritage.** British people use different words and phrases than Americans. Research the language and culture so that the dialog sounds accurate and real.
- **Read the dialog out loud as you're writing it.** It should sound natural and conversational. Once you are happy with what you wrote, consider having a read-through of the script with actors. Hearing the dialog acted is an eye-opening experience and helps reveal cliché, forced, unnecessary or otherwise problematic lines.

THE FIRST DRAFT

By this point, you should have a strong treatment and a detailed outline that guides the reader, scene-by-scene, through the story. If you are confident in each plot arc, subplot and character arc, you're ready to write the first draft.

Before you jump in, it's time for a reality check - your first draft is going to be terrible. Don't fret about it too much though, because most first drafts are, even those penned by seasoned Hollywood writers. The goal is to simply get the story on paper and in the proper script format by expanding each scene, adding dialogue and crafting stronger scene descriptions than in the outline. It will take multiple rewrites to perfect the script before it's ready to be optioned or produced.

It's always good to plan daily or weekly goals when writing the first draft to help keep the writing process moving. Plan to write at least five pages a day, regardless of the quality, knowing that you will go back later to rewrite and polish each scene.

Formatting Guidelines

While it is entirely possible to write your screenplay in any number of word processing programs, Hollywood producers are extremely particular in reading a script, requiring it follow strict formatting guidelines.

Jason's Notes

One page in a properly formatted script roughly equals one minute of screen time. Consider that each department of a film crew from the line producer to the 1st assistant director relies on a standardized script format to properly budget and schedule the movie.

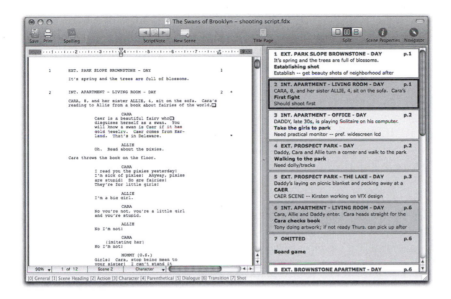

I recommend purchasing the program "Final Draft" (www.finaldraft.com) which automatically formats your script, produces limited script breakdowns, script reports and check for formatting errors.

Unlike novels and short stories which are formatted with text aligned margin to margin; scripts have a very specific format, and uses different margins to easily separate and identify location descriptions, scene descriptions, character names and dialogue – all intended to help the reader quickly read and break down the script.

The basics of a screenplay include:

- **Font** – Use 12-point Courier font (the typewriter font), the standard script font to ensure one page of properly formatted script roughly equals one minute of screen time.
- **Paper** – Print the script on standard white 8.5 × 11 paper. When a script is finished and ready to be produced, subsequent changes are made on specific colors of paper and distributed to the cast and crew, making it easy to track updates.
- **Margins** – The margins of a script are as follows:
  - **Top and Bottom Margins: 1″**
  - **Left Margin: 1.5″ (to allow space for the brads)**
  - **Right Margin: 1″**
  - **Header** – Each page should have a header .5″ from the top of the page that includes the date of revision and the color of the page.
  - **Scene headings:** margin starts 1.5 inches from the left edge of the paper.
  - **Stage directions:** margin starts 1.5 inches from the left edge of the paper.
  - **Character names** are centered on the page.

- ■ **Dialog:** left margin is at 2.5 inches and right margin is at 6.5 inches.
- ■ **Character directions:** left margin is at 3 inches and right margin is at 5.5 inches.
- ■ **Page Numbers** – Add page numbers in the upper right corner of each page, in the header.
- ■ **Length** – The average script is between 85 and 125 pages long. Most production companies are looking for 90-page scripts to maximize the shooting cost/page ratio.

FORMATTING A SCENE
Scene Header and Scene Descriptions

Each scene begins in capital letters and describes whether it occurs in an interior or exterior (INT or EXT), the location where the scene takes place in the story, and the time of day (DAY, NIGHT, DAWN, DUSK, LATER). For example:

```
INT. AWANDA'S TRAILER-DAY
```

Once the script is finished and each scene is numbered, the 1st Assistant Director will add numbers to the beginning and end of the scene header line. For example:

```
46.    INT. AWANDA'S TRAILER-DAY                    46
```

Screen directions always align in the same margin as the scene header, explain where and how the characters move and what is happening in the scene. Use the screen directions to describe to the reader what he will see on screen. For example:

```
46.    INT. AWANDA'S TRAILER-DAY                    46

       Awanda walks to the refrigerator and pulls out
       a pitcher of water, all the while watching Bobby
       from the corner of her eye. Bobby, unaware of her
       gaze, stares out the window.
```

When writing the scene header and scene descriptions, keep these tips in mind.

- ■ **Always write in the present tense.** Do not write, "We cut to Alan Blum who is walking down the street." Rather, write "Alan Blum casually walks down the street."
- ■ **Write with an active, not passive voice.** "The gun is picked up and fired by Howser" is an example of a passage written in a passive voice. Rewriting the same passage in an active voice would read "Howser picks up the gun and fires."
- ■ **Always use action verbs.** "John runs toward the supermarket doors." Although this description adequately describes what John is doing, there are more descriptive verbs we can use to paint a stronger picture of how John is moving. Is he sauntering? Sprinting? Doggedly running? The use of strong verbs will help more clearly convey your meaning to the reader.
- ■ **Write only what can be shown.** Scene descriptions describe what we can see in the scene, and what characters do. Avoid writing what the character

is thinking or feeling as there is no way to show this on screen. "Johnny slowly enters the room, remembering the memories of past Christmases with his wife and children." This is an example of a scene that can't be shot. Unless you cut to a flashback of Johnny's family, there is no way to show that he is thinking of last Christmas. Try approaching a scene in a more visual way.

- **Don't number your scenes while you write.** Scenes are later numbered by the first assistant director after the screenplay is finished. If you number the scenes in advance, rewriting the script will constantly change the scene numbers, throwing off the script breakdown and any department working off those breakdowns.

- **Don't use camera directions.** Camera directions indicate where the camera needs to be placed within the scene. This is not the writer's job, but that of the director and the cinematographer. Write the script as a story, focusing only on the characters and what they are doing and saying in each scene.

- **Don't break scenes up into shots.** A change in scene reflects a change in location in the story. Shots are individual camera positions within the scene that are designed by the director and cinematographer. Break up the script only into scenes.

- **Illustrations.** Never include illustrations, photos, diagrams or charts in your script. EVER.

Parentheticals and Dialog

When writing dialog, first write the name of the character speaking in capital letters and center it in the page. Each time a new character speaks, write his or her name. Directly below the character's name, add any parentheticals to indicate how a line should be interpreted. Use parentheticals sparingly and only if the character's intent is unclear from the subtext of the scene. Parentheticals must be aligned in a margin 3½ inches from the left side of the page. Directly below any parentheticals, or under the character name if there are no parentheticals, is the character dialog, which appears 4¼ inches from the left side of the page. For example:

```
46.    INT. AWANDA'S TRAILER-DAY                  46
       Awanda walks to the refrigerator and pulls out
       a pitcher of water, all the while watching Bobby
       from the corner of her eye. Bobby, unaware of her
       gaze, stares out the window.

                        AWANDA
                      (quietly)
              I heard you needed a place to stay.
```

Follow these tips when formatting dialog:

- **Character Description.** Although it is customary for theater screenplays to include a list of characters and descriptions, it is inappropriate for movie or television screenplays. Do not put a list of characters or character descriptions in the beginning of your script.

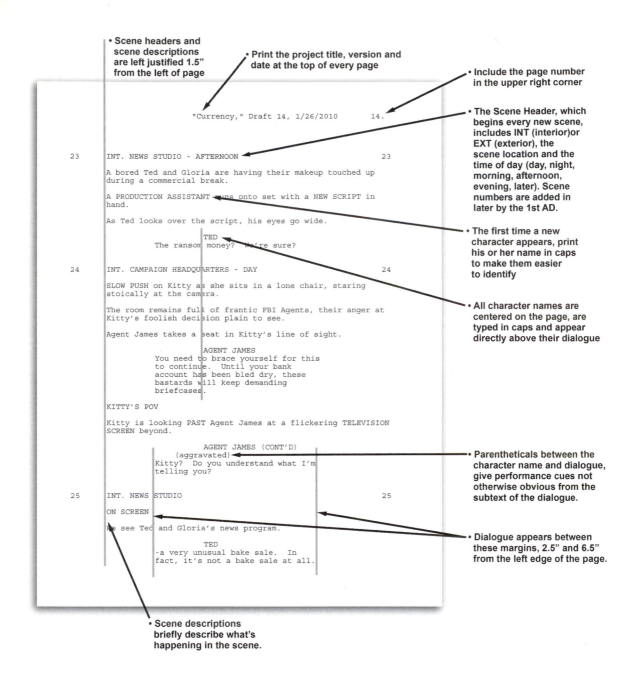

• Scene headers and scene descriptions are left justified 1.5" from the left of page

• Print the project title, version and date at the top of every page

• Include the page number in the upper right corner

"Currency," Draft 14, 1/26/2010   14.

• The Scene Header, which begins every new scene, includes INT (interior)or EXT (exterior), the scene location and the time of day (day, night, morning, afternoon, evening, later). Scene numbers are added in later by the 1st AD.

23   INT. NEWS STUDIO - AFTERNOON   23

A bored Ted and Gloria are having their makeup touched up during a commercial break.

A PRODUCTION ASSISTANT runs onto set with a NEW SCRIPT in hand.

As Ted looks over the script, his eyes go wide.

               TED
        The ransom money? We're sure?

• The first time a new character appears, print his or her name in caps to make them easier to identify

24   INT. CAMPAIGN HEADQUARTERS - DAY   24

SLOW PUSH on Kitty as she sits in a lone chair, staring stoically at the camera.

The room remains full of frantic FBI Agents, their anger at Kitty's foolish decision plain to see.

Agent James takes a seat in Kitty's line of sight.

             AGENT JAMES
      You need to brace yourself for this
      to continue. Until your bank
      account has been bled dry, these
      bastards will keep demanding
      briefcases.

KITTY'S POV

Kitty is looking PAST Agent James at a flickering TELEVISION SCREEN beyond.

           AGENT JAMES (CONT'D)
      (aggravated)
      Kitty? Do you understand what I'm
      telling you?

25   INT. NEWS STUDIO   25

ON SCREEN

We see Ted and Gloria's news program.

             TED
      -a very unusual bake sale. In
      fact, it's not a bake sale at all.

• All character names are centered on the page, are typed in caps and appear directly above their dialogue

• Parentheticals between the character name and dialogue, give performance cues not otherwise obvious from the subtext of the dialogue.

• Dialogue appears between these margins, 2.5" and 6.5" from the left edge of the page.

• Scene descriptions briefly describe what's happening in the scene.

There are many other formatting guidelines pertaining to transitions, montages, simultaneous dialog, intercutting, titles and credits, and abbreviations. I recommend logging onto the First Draft module at filmskills.com for a complete tutorial on proper script formatting.

Writing on a Budget

The secret to making a low-budget film is to write within your means and to be aware of the available resources. I know this probably sounds hypocritical because I tackled a seemingly expensive 1950s story on a budget of $2,000, but as I wrote the script for *Time and Again*, I knew I would have easy access to locations that could sell the time period. I also knew that in Ohio, antique cars are plentiful, vintage costumes were easily obtained, and cast and crew members would be willing to work for free. As I wrote the script, I thought carefully about how I would realistically produce each moment of every scene, so when it came time to go into preproduction, there were no unexpected surprises.

Understand that regardless of the budget, seemingly simple scenes can be very costly to produce, and whether you plan on producing your movie yourself or selling it to a production company, the costs of these scenes can potentially become an issue.

Smart writers know the rough cost of the scenes they are writing. Even though a conversation in a moving car may seem simple to shoot, in reality it can be a complex and expensive process — from renting a process trailer to hiring police and closing down the road, car interiors require a lot of time and money to do properly.

- **Minimize the number of locations.** When you write settings into the story, make sure the locations are accessible, available, and inexpensive to secure. Fewer locations mean fewer cast and crew moves, less setup and strike, and lower permitting and location fees. There's a reason that many low-budget movies take place in one or two primary locations.
- **Keep the number of characters to a minimum.** Even if your actors are willing to work for free, feeding them isn't, and working with professional paid

actors can quickly become very expensive. Keep the number of actors and extras to a minimum to keep budget cost low.

- **Avoid shooting at night.** HMI lighting, generators and the crew required to light large expanses of exterior locations and even interiors can become very expensive and time consuming. Daytime shooting allows the cinematographer to use bounce cards and reflectors to shape light faster and cheaper.
- **Write a story that takes place in the present day.** Avoid the need for expensive props, wardrobe, sets, or set dressing.
- **Avoid extensive special effects, stunts, makeup effects, and pyrotechnics.** The safety rigs, material costs, and price of hiring experienced personnel are minor compared to the time require to properly execute an effects sequence on set. If you're shooting a 12-day low-budget movie, spending half a day on a stunt or effect would place a strain on the schedule.
- **Keep the script to 90 pages.** As tempting as it is to write a 120-page script, remember that every page you write translates to a minute on screen. Think of it this way: if you have a $100,000 budget, you can afford to spend $833 per page on a 120-page script. But, you'll have $1,111 per page to spend on a 90-page script. Another way of approaching this is if a $100,000 budget will buy you 16 shooting days, you'll have to shoot 7.5 pages per day if your script is 120 pages. With a 90-page script, you'll only need to shoot 5.6 pages per day, allowing you to spend more time on performances and interesting camera moves.

Read the script for my short film "Currency" at Filmskills.com. See page vi for details.

Rewriting

Now that the first draft is complete, the real work begins: rewriting. But before you rewrite, I encourage you to set the script aside for a week or two so you can come back to it with fresh eyes. Many writers suffer from being so close to their script that they lose their objectivity. The endless days and nights spent pounding out each scene forces you into a creative box wherein your vision is limited by the scope of your work, so don't be afraid to back away from the project from time to time. It'll be better for you and certainly better for the script.

When I work with a writing partner, I let my partner develop the first draft of the script from the outline. When I sit down to read the draft, my objectivity allows me to notice problems that my partner may not have considered. I will do a rewrite, incorporating those changes while my partner takes some time off. When I finish, he can lend an objective eye to the story while I take some time away from the project. This technique of "leap frog" writing is invaluable in helping prevent creative burnout. It's also a great reason to advocate working with a writing partner.

Jason's Notes

Scripts written in the studio system often go through dozens and sometimes hundreds of rewrites. Writers are constantly reworking dialog, subplots, plot points, and pacing until the story is perfect.

Rewriting a script is a constantly evolving process that isn't really over until the movie is shot and in the can. Although rewriting can seem like a disorganized, organic process, there are ways to target your rewriting efforts to improve each pass and optimize your time.

Rewriting a script can seem like a daunting, overwhelming challenge, especially if you look at the story as a whole. Try approaching the rewriting process in smaller pieces by targeting specific aspects of the story such studying individual scenes, rewriting a specific character, or improving just the dialog. Focusing your approach will make your rewrites more effective and timely.

Jason's Notes

Production companies will often hire a writer to deliver a first draft and one rewrite. It's common for production companies to then hire a different writer to rewrite the script. Rewriting other people's scripts is a great way to get your foot in the door and work as a writer.

Individual Scenes

One common route to rewriting is to target each scene, one at a time. First, approach each scene as it fits into the bigger story and run each scene through a series of questions. Does it support the plot? Does it serve a vital purpose in the story? Will the story suffer if it is removed? Is the scene in the proper place in the script?

Then, look at the elements within each individual scene. Can the scene be more creatively written? Can it be tightened? Does the situation in each scene feel organic and natural?

As you're performing a scene rewrite, try these techniques to improving your story:

- **Separate the A plot and each of the subplots from the story to see if they stand on their own.** Does each plot line have a strong plot arc? Are the setup, middle, and resolution clear? Is each scene necessary? Does each scene serve to move the story forward? Is the story easy to understand? Can any scenes be cut or shortened? Can you better improve the flow of the movie by mixing scenes together? Do the scenes in each subplot help support the A plot? If not, how can it be rewritten to support the A plot?
- **Do scenes alternate between highs points and low points?** Do scenes take the audience on an emotional roller coaster in which an action scene is followed by a tragic scene followed by a scene of vindication followed by a scene of tension? A good screenplay intermixes scenes of varying emotional intensity to keep the audience engaged.
- **Look at the transitions from scene to scene.** Is there a more creative way to move the audience from one scene to another? Does the order of the scenes make sense? Can the dialog from one scene segue into the next scene?

- **Look at each scene and determine if it is as tight as it can be.** Does every line of dialog work to support the story? Is the action in every scene fully and concisely described? Are scene descriptions short and vivid? Do you use action verbs to describe the action that is happening in the movie? Is anything in the scene clichéd and is there a more creative way to let the action transpire?

Character Rewrite

The second type of rewrite focuses exclusively on each character and helps you improve each character's personality, temperament, motivations and dialog.

- **Follow each character's arc throughout the story.** Can his arc be strengthened? Can her high and low moments be higher or lower? Can you make a tragic scene more gut-wrenching or a tense scene more disturbing to the character?
- **Does each character have defining characteristics that make him or her unique?** If you were to hide all the character names in the script from a reader, would each character have enough personality for the reader to know who is speaking? If not, the dialog may not speak to the subtext and motivations of each character enough.
- **Does each character have a strong motivation or purpose in each scene, or is the character meandering through the story?** Characters should have a goal not only throughout the entire story, but on a scene-by-scene basis. Conflict and drama are created when the character tries to achieve this goal but is thwarted in some way. What does the character want in a scene, how does he go about achieving the goal, and what is the result?
- **Do the main characters change throughout the story?** They should undergo a transformation from rags to riches, from greedy to philanthropic, from bitter and jaded to optimistic. Is the main character's journey and change evident by the end of the story?
- **Do the characters actively engage in activities that push the story forward?**
- **Does each character have a clear objective in each scene?** In a good screenplay, the characters should have an objective they try to meet, although the scene completely reverses the situation on the character, throwing them into even greater peril.

Dialog Rewrite

Rewrites can also target dialog, arguably one of the weakest aspects of any first draft. As you work through the dialog, try some of these techniques:

- **Go through each line of dialog to determine whether it is sharp, original, witty, and concise.** Keep the dialog to the point by asking what the is character trying to say, how the character really feels, what the character wants, and how he is masking his true intentions through what he says.
- **Try to avoid long speeches.** If you encounter any lines longer than four or five lines, ask yourself how you can shorten or restructure the dialog. Remember that people do not pontificate: they speak in short, broken phrases.

- **Make sure the dialog *always* reflects each character's personality.** Look at every word a character utters and ask yourself if this *best* reflects who he really is.
- **Are there any clichéd lines you can delete or change?** Avoid clichés at all costs; they may cheapen the characters and hinder your efforts to sell your script.
- **Will a scene work without the dialog?** If not, consider revisiting the scene to strengthen the action, so the burden of storytelling falls on what the characters are *doing*, not on what they're *saying*.
- **Put yourself in the character's mind when you're writing the dialog.** Is she simply saying words, or do the words reflect a deeper meaning or motivation?

Subplot Rewrite

The next type of targeted rewrite focuses on the subplots. Although you may have looked through each subplot when rewriting the A plot, study each subplot even deeper to make sure each subplot fulfills its purpose.

- **Ensure the subplot story arc is strong.** Does each subplot have a beginning, middle, and end? Is it a tight, engaging story that invokes emotions from the audience? Do the subplots each have a purpose to drive the story, establish character, or create jeopardy for the main characters?
- **Ensure each subplot is tightly intertwined with the A-story line and pushes the story forward.** Do the subplots feel like they're thrown into the movie, or do they work to support the A plot?

Jason's Notes

A great example of subplots is in the Will Smith movie *The Pursuit of Happiness*. The A plot is his effort to get a job, and the subplots include: the landlord's eviction threat, the parking tickets, and the homeless woman who stole the medical device. As you may have noticed, each of the subplots is its own mini-story, but they all work to hinder Will's character from achieving his objective in the A plot.

- **Do the subplots resolve themselves within five or ten scenes from the end of the movie?** A good movie resolves the least-important subplots first, dedicating the end of the movie to the A plot. One reason the ending of *Lord of the Rings: Return of the King* felt long to some viewers was that Peter Jackson wrapped up the A plot first, then systematically resolved each of the subplots – the opposite of normal convention.
- **If the page count is running too long, can you delete one of the subplots?** To keep your script length between 90 and 120 pages, cutting one subplot is a great way to tighten a script.

Feedback

Odds are you've been working on your script either alone or with a writing partner. Either way, it's easy to get so caught up in the story that you lose sight of any problems the script may have. It's important to get feedback from objective, impartial readers who can identify problem areas of the script – pacing problems, plot points that don't make sense, and character flaws.

- **Check out local writing groups on college campuses.** Working with people interested in writing will not only improve the quality of the script critique, but can be a huge motivation to help push forward with the writing process.

Jason's Notes

Remember that you can't please everyone. Not everyone will like your script, and some advice you receive will be about changing the story itself. Beware of this advice, and don't be too quick to make changes until you're sure you need to.

- **Avoid friends and family.** Their feedback is usually worthless. Unless they are in the film industry, chances are that they don't know how to properly read a screenplay, let alone provide quality feedback. And remember, Mom will always love your work.
- **Beware the Hollywood reader.** There are thousands of scripts submitted to studios every month, and the studios employ professional readers to generate a detailed assessment of the script called *coverage*. Many readers are recent college graduates or just beginning their career, so their coverage may be rooted more in personal tastes than a professional business objective. Once readers cover your script, they will suggest that the studio pass or recommend it. Most scripts are passed on, with a record of that script being entered into a database and shared with other studios. Although coverage can be a valuable tool, it is not completely accurate, either. Many readers will opt to pass on a project simply because it places their careers less at risk were they to recommend a poor script.
- **Don't be too quick to adopt critical suggestions.** If three or more people make the same comment, the script has a problem. Some people may make a critique not because there is a technical or structural problem, but simply because they don't like the material. Learn how to sift through feedback to find the most accurate, objective suggestions.
- **Assemble a group of actors and organize a live table read of the script.** There is no better way to get a sense of the pacing of the story and quality of dialog than to hear it read out loud by professional actors. Take notes during the reading and be attentive to the actor's feedback and initial opinions. Scripts sound different when read and table reads are a great way of pinpointing weak dialog, shallow characterization, and plot problems.

FINISHING YOUR SCRIPT

- **Check your spelling**—Correct spelling and grammar are essential in presenting a professional screenplay for consideration by agents, managers, studios, and production companies. Always proofread your work before sending it out.
- **Quality Photocopies**—Make sure your script is copied as cleanly and legibly as possible on white, 20 pound paper.
- **Covers and binding**—Present the script with a white heavier-stock cover that states the title, the writer(s), writer(s) and/or agent contact phone numbers, WGA registration number, and copyright information. The script should be punched with three holes and "bound" with two gold clasps.
- **Keep it clean**—Do not use flowery fonts, quotes, artwork, or anything other than the industry standard for your title page. If you do, producers, agents and managers will peg you an amateur.

Jason's Notes

Producers, agents and managers receive sometimes hundreds of scripts a day. Since it is impossible to read them all, they usually discard any scripts that aren't properly formatted, have an inappropriate title page, or appear amateurish in any way. Before sending your script out, make sure it follows EVERY one of the formatting guidelines in this chapter.

- **Protecting your script** - Once complete, send your script to the U.S. Copyright Office and the Writers Guild of America for copyright protection. For a nominal fee and a simple application form, both offices will retain a copy of the script, so if you ever need to prove the date the script was written and its authenticity, submission to these agencies serves as evidence in court.

United States Copyright Office
Library of Congress
Washington DC 20559
Copyright forms hotline (202) 707-9100
Screenplays: Form PA
www.copyright.gov
Cost: $35 for electronic filing, $45 for paper filing

Writers Guild of America, West
WGAW Registry
7000 West Third Street
Los Angeles, CA 90048
(323) 782-4500
www.wgaregistry.org
Cost: $20 for non-WGA members, $10 for WGA members

Writer's Guild of America, East
East 250 Hudson Street
New York, New York 10013
212-767-7800
www.wgaeast.org

UNIT 2
Preproduction

i. Build a strong business plan and approach investors to raise money for the movie.

ii. Form a company and open a checking account.

iii. Build a budget.

i. Purchase insurance to protect you from liability. You'll need a Certificate of Insurance before renting equipment and securing locations.

Budgeting	**Scheduling**	**Insurance**	**Locations**	

i. Break down the script into categories.

ii. Determine the number of shooting days.

iii. Make the daily schedule.

i. Make contact with the local film commission.

ii. Scout locations and try to lock as many as possible 6 to 8 weeks before principal photography begins.

iii. Contact local government officials to secure shooting permits and coordinate with local police and fire departments.

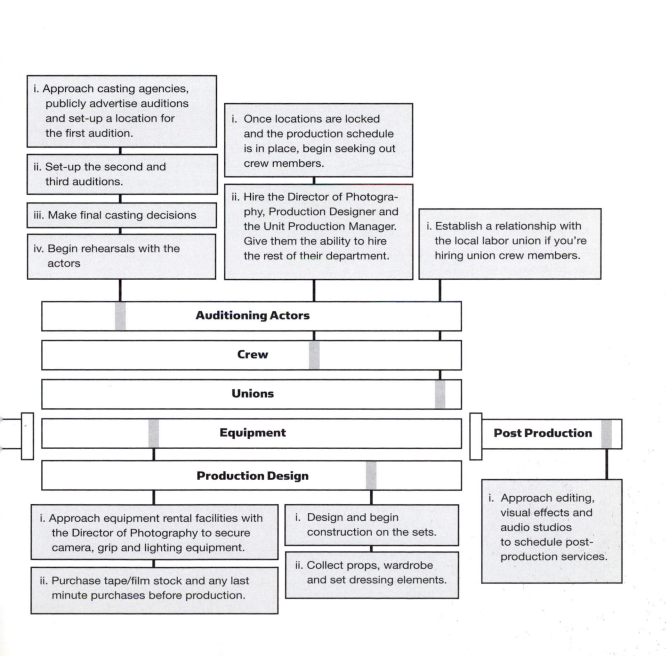

i. Approach casting agencies, publicly advertise auditions and set-up a location for the first audition.

ii. Set-up the second and third auditions.

iii. Make final casting decisions

iv. Begin rehearsals with the actors

i. Once locations are locked and the production schedule is in place, begin seeking out crew members.

ii. Hire the Director of Photography, Production Designer and the Unit Production Manager. Give them the ability to hire the rest of their department.

i. Establish a relationship with the local labor union if you're hiring union crew members.

Auditioning Actors

Crew

Unions

Equipment

Post Production

Production Design

i. Approach equipment rental facilities with the Director of Photography to secure camera, grip and lighting equipment.

ii. Purchase tape/film stock and any last minute purchases before production.

i. Design and begin construction on the sets.

ii. Collect props, wardrobe and set dressing elements.

i. Approach editing, visual effects and audio studios to schedule post-production services.

CHAPTER 2
Preproduction

INTRODUCTION

Once a script is finished and *greenlit*, which means it's ready to be made, the project moves into a phase called *preproduction*. Preproduction is the process of breaking down the finished script and preparing all elements of the movie for production, including:

- Breaking down the script
- Calculating the budget
- Securing the financing
- Scouting locations
- Casting
- Hiring the crew
- Securing equipment
- Scheduling the shoot dates

Preproduction is an extremely organized, methodical process similar to designing the blueprints for a house. Think about every aspect of the movie in advance and try to be as prepared as possible before arriving on the set. Remember, construction workers show up on a job site knowing exactly what must be done, because all the preparation was done ahead of time when the blueprints were being designed – not on the job site. The electrical contractors and plumbers are being paid to install the wiring and plumbing, not wait around while the architect decides how to build the house. The same is the case with a movie – every prop, every person, and every shot must be carefully thought out and planned so that you can make the best use of the time you have on set by focusing on the performances and not on logistics. Keep the following in mind:

- The quality of the production is directly proportional to the amount of time taken in preproduction. The more organized the project, the smoother everything will go on set.
- Preproduction is not complicated, but there are a thousand little jobs that need to be done. Although it may seem stressful, a careful and organized approach can help the process go smoothly.

Filmmaking.
© 2011 Jason J. Tomaric. Published by Elsevier Inc. All rights reserved.

- Even the best-planned shoots will encounter problems, so expect them. When they occur, don't get frustrated. Remember that if making a movie was easy, everyone would be doing it. Be prepared to deal with any problem that arises on set by thinking about possible solutions in advance.

SETTING UP AN OFFICE

Establish a home base where production efforts can be coordinated, phone calls can be made, meetings can be held, packages and equipment can be dropped off, and cast and crew can meet.

Make sure you have a comfortable workspace from which to work – and always keep it organized.

When setting up your workspace, be sure to have the following resources:

- Credit cards for use by office staff
- Coffee, copiers, fax machine
- Computers, printers
- Reliable Internet connection
- Extra paper, ink, envelopes, file folders
- Crew listings from the local film commission
- Current editions of local phone books
- Locations of office supply stores, USPS, FedEx, copier, rental car facility, hotels, restaurants (have delivery menus available)
- Meeting area with table and chairs for meetings and rehearsals
- Dry erase board with markers
- Production email accounts
- Accounts with a courier service
- DVD player and a television set
- Telephones (land lines and cell); set up a phone number for the production office
- Small refrigerator with beverages
- Copies of deal memos, script breakdowns, location agreements, and all pertinent production forms

Even if you're shooting a low-budget independent movie and can't afford an office space, be prepared to use your home for meetings and be ready for a lot of people to come and go throughout the shoot. You will probably be storing props, wardrobe, art direction elements, and production equipment in your home as well.

Research

This is a great time to begin conducting research to determine the best camera formats, explore the talent base in the area, and ultimately prepare to make not only a movie, but a product that distributors will want to pick up and sell.

- **Camera formats.** Although you should make the final decision with the director of photography, look into the current camera formats and best technology to shoot the movie. Research not only the cost of the cameras, but how a particular format will affect the process and cost of postproduction. Each week, there seems to be a new "hot camera" everyone is talking about, but look through the hype, call experienced local vendors, and learn what format is ideally suited for your project. Also contact distributors to learn what formats they prefer – many filmmakers invest time and money into completing a film only to learn that distributors won't accept a particular format.

- **Postproduction.** Don't be so focused on production that you forget about postproduction. The editing, sound mixing, mastering, color grading, visual effects, and music composition can easily be more expensive than the cost of shooting the movie. Begin contacting postproduction companies to discuss shooting formats, postproduction workflow, and costs. It's wise to get your postproduction companies involved early to ensure your production workflow is correct.
- **Marketing and advertising.** Movies are made or broken by the strength of their marketing campaigns, and it's not unusual for the marketing to begin well before a movie enters production. Consider finding a web company to begin work on a web site, write daily blogs detailing the drama behind the scenes, take pictures, and videotape the filmmaking process to build interest among potential audience members. It's a great feeling finishing a movie when you know thousands of people already know about and are interested in seeing it.
- **Contact other producers.** Don't be afraid to contact producers who have shot projects in the same city as yours. Learn from their mistakes – ask about quality vendors, crew member referrals, inexpensive and film-friendly locations, recommendations for office space, attorneys and casting directors.

HIRING AN ATTORNEY

Producing a movie involves a tremendous amount of paperwork, which makes it necessary to hire a qualified entertainment attorney to ensure that you are completely protected from liability, and that you comply with copyright law and adhere to union guidelines. Without proper legal protection, an accident or lawsuit can wipe out your savings and personal assets.

Although many boilerplate contracts and forms can be downloaded from the Internet, it's advisable for your attorney to look them over and customize the language to fit your production. Some of the many forms you'll need include:

- **Setting up the company.** An attorney can help you set up a new company, draw up the bylaws, register with the state, and manage all necessary paperwork to create and operate a functioning business entity.
- **Writer deal memos.** Whether you hire a writer to write the script or option an existing idea or script, writer deal memos guarantee your right to produce the work and define who owns the script and resulting movie. You will need to provide a Chain of Title, or proof that you hold the ownership to the script and movie to potential distributors upon completion.

- **Copyrights.** Secure necessary copyrights for the script by registering both the script and final movie with the United States Copyright Office.
  - **WGA registration.** Register the final script with the Writer's Guild of America for proof of date of completion and ownership.
- **Crew deal memos.** These agreements are drafted for each and every crew position and define the terms of their working relationship. From liability and nondisclosure clauses to hours, day rate, equipment usage, and mileage, all terms of employment should be included.
- **Actor deal memos.** For low-budget projects, actor contracts can be simple and universal, but if you plan on hiring recognizable actors, each agreement will need to be crafted specifically for each actor.

Jason's Notes

Film sets are high-risk environments – from trip hazards to risk of electrocution, people can be injured or even killed, even if all safety protocols are followed. In order to protect you from this liability, be proactive and liberal in posting warning signs and enforcing the signing of liability release forms to every person who steps foot on set. The bottom line is that you should do everything within your power to avoid being personally liable for anything that happens while making your movie.

- **Union agreements.** If your production is hiring Screen Actor's Guild (SAG) actors, then get ready for a massive amount of paperwork to be turned into SAG to prove the hours and work conditions for the cast. Even on low-budget productions, the SAG requirements can be daunting, so be prepared to research the requirements in advance.
- **Location agreements.** It's important to sign an agreement with each and every location at which you shoot. Location agreements address the date and time of site access, restroom access, power usage, parking, entrance and egress access, equipment staging, alterations and restoration requirements of the property, liability releases, insurance obligations, and the granting of general permission to be on and photograph the property.
- **Legal disputes.** Invariably, when people see a movie shoot, they equate it with wealth and money, regardless of the financial realities of low-budget film production. With hopes of a payoff, it's not uncommon for people to sue, threaten, or outright blackmail a production – all instances of which need to be promptly addressed by your attorney, usually with a simple cease and desist letter.
- **Distribution.** There are few phases of a film production that require an attorney's services as much as the distribution process. With complicated contracts, endless loopholes designed to financially favor the distributor and complicated licensing rights, having a strong, experienced attorney is critical.

Attorney fees can become very expensive very quickly, so when working with an attorney, negotiate an hourly rate, a flat rate for the entire production, or a percentage of the gross returns of the film. If you are working with an extremely limited budget, there are a number of organizations that offer free or discounted rates, especially in large production cities.

Jason's Notes

During the preproduction of *Time and Again*, I called a local attorney and asked if he would donate his time to assist our low-budget production in exchange for a credit. He gladly accepted and was an excited participant in the movie, so much so that he was even an extra in one of the scenes.

Preproduction

- Complete the final script, and copy and distribute it to the cast and crew.
- Set up production offices and hire necessary interns and staff. Secure office equipment such as a copier, computer, fax machine, and telephones.
- Set up insurance, bank accounts, and company structure. Hire a good attorney and accountant to help.
- Break down the script, create a production board, and make the production schedule.
- Begin location scouting.
- Schedule auditions for principal actors and extras. Contact local talent agencies to assist.
- Begin talking with crew members, focusing on main crew positions. Call the film commission for the production manual that lists all local crew members.
- Prepare agreements, deal memos, and contracts with cast and crew.
- Review budget with newly hired crew members to determine feasibility.
- Research and assemble props and wardrobe.
- Contact local film commission and establish relationship for permits and city services.
- Begin set construction and set decorating.
- Negotiate with vendors for camera, film stock, lighting, and grip equipment.
- Contact postproduction services, including editors, labs, composers, and visual effects artists.

CHAPTER 3
Budgeting

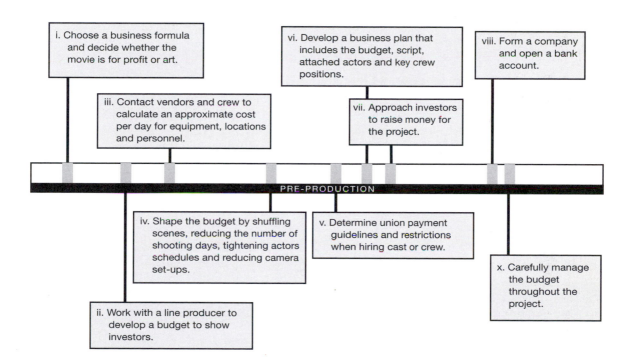

i. Choose a business formula and decide whether the movie is for profit or art.

iii. Contact vendors and crew to calculate an approximate cost per day for equipment, locations and personnel.

vi. Develop a business plan that includes the budget, script, attached actors and key crew positions.

vii. Approach investors to raise money for the project.

viii. Form a company and open a bank account.

PRE-PRODUCTION

iv. Shape the budget by shuffling scenes, reducing the number of shooting days, tightening actors schedules and reducing camera set-ups.

v. Determine union payment guidelines and restrictions when hiring cast or crew.

x. Carefully manage the budget throughout the project.

ii. Work with a line producer to develop a budget to show investors.

INTRODUCTION

Of all the art forms, filmmaking is the most expensive, and securing financing can be the most difficult aspect of producing a film. It's possible to produce a high-quality, low-budget movie by managing costs, but purchases, fees, rentals, and unforeseen problems can drive even the most modest budget into the tens of thousands of dollars.

As you read this chapter, know that the scheduling process (discussed in Chapter 4) and the budgeting process happen concurrently. One affects the other and each must change based on the other.

Filmmaking.
© 2011 Jason J. Tomaric. Published by Elsevier Inc. All rights reserved.

ACCOUNTING

Major Hollywood productions employ a production accountant whose responsibilities include assisting with the preparation of the budget, opening and managing checking accounts, overseeing petty cash accounts, entering accounting data, working with payroll companies, working with department heads to manage departmental budgets, and managing the outflow of every penny of the production. The production accountant answers to the producers, production manager, and production company, keeping them informed of the financial state of the production. Changes to the shooting schedule, artistic changes, overtime, and cost overruns keep the production accountant busy balancing the books and alerting producers to issues that may push the production into the red.

Larger productions will often employ an entire accounting department to oversee disbursement of funds to vendors, cast and crew, locations, and any person or company who does business with the production entity.

As an independent filmmaker, you not only have to do your own accounting, but must also raise money, form a company, and perform a number of very uncreative duties to set up a strong financial foundation for your project. Even though you may work without the benefit of an accounting department, it is still critical to maintain strict financial records of your production.

Raising Money

Raising the funds needed to produce your movie can be both challenging and frustrating. Like other industries, financiers will invest money into projects whose managers have demonstrated an ability to produce a profitable product. Unless you have already made and sold a movie, you have no track record, so approaching an investor for a million dollars is like a recent business school graduate asking for a million dollars for an upstart company. Most investors will laugh at him and tell him to build a company out of his garage and make a profit, and then come back and ask for investment dollars. The film industry works the same way: financiers flock to filmmakers with a proven track record, whose work has generated a profit in the past.

When producing a movie, as a line producer, you must account for every penny spent, regardless of whether it's tracking an investor's money, or for your own tax purposes.

So how do you secure the funds to make a movie? Start in the garage, so to speak, by producing a low-budget movie with local resources. If it's a good movie, then investors may notice and consider financing the second one.

The formula works like this:

> Make a good $2,000 movie and use it to raise the money to shoot a $20,000 movie.
> Make a good $20,000 movie and use it to raise the money to shoot a $200,000 movie.
> Make a good $200,000 movie and use it to raise the money to shoot a $2,000,000 movie.

Before you get frustrated, remember that there isn't a single filmmaker in the history of cinema who had a $100,000,000 budget for his first film. Not one. Every successful director started on small projects and grew from there.

- **Be very careful when spending your own money.** The odds of seeing your money back are slim to none, and unless you have expendable cash, know that investing in a movie is one of the worst investments possible. The first rule of independent filmmaking is to let someone else knowingly bear the financial risk of the project unless you are able to absorb the loss yourself.
- **Do not go into debt.** Although increasing your credit limit or securing another home mortgage are options for securing money for your film, avoid these at all costs. The likelihood of making your money back on the film is slim, leaving massive interest-laden credit card bills or the threat of having the bank repossess your house.

Budgeting

The first step toward securing financing for your movie is to calculate how much money you need. Remember that financiers respond better to a well-thought-out line-item budget, rather than a request for a general dollar amount. In preparing the budget, the first step is to break down the script (see Chapter 4 for a step-by-step guide on how to do this) to determine the number of shooting days, cast and crew requirements, production design, camera and lighting equipment needs, postproduction expenses, and so on. Once you have an idea of the resources needed to produce the film, contact vendors, cast and crew members, and locations to calculate the cost of each aspect of the movie. The result is a ballpark budget you can present to an investor.

Part of the fun of making a low-budget movie is to see how many elements can be found and secured for free. The more freebies, the more money-costing line items can be removed from the budget.

- **Be prepared to find actors who are willing to work for free.** Actors are interested in working on a quality project that will help their careers and may work for less than their normal rate if they like the script and their characters. Even Screen Actors Guild members may be willing to work under a Financial Core agreement, which allows them to work nonunion projects. When crewing up, seek recent college graduates or aspiring filmmakers in your community who are willing to work for the experience. Beware, however; although inexperienced crew members may be cheap, they may end up costing the production money in the long run because of their inefficiency on set. You ultimately want a competent crew so the set runs like a set – not a classroom.

- **Contact local equipment rental agencies and ask them if they can donate the equipment needed, or at least offer a discount.** Unless you're calling from a major studio, vendors are prepared to negotiate and often provide a higher rental rate in anticipation of reducing it. Don't be afraid to get the best possible deal – it's the way the film industry works.
- **Ask location owners if you can use their location for free.** It never hurts to ask, and in nonproduction cities, many people get excited about being involved in a movie. Asking for a location may seem like a favor to you, but the location owners look at it as an exciting opportunity. We didn't pay for a single location in *Time and Again*. I even negotiated to shut down a state prison, an entire town square, and an interstate for free, simply by presenting a professional proposal and having an open, honest conversation with the local authorities and a willingness to work with them.
- **Be creative with art direction, wardrobe, and props.** Think outside the box and go to places where you can get free or heavily discounted art pieces. From Goodwill stores to garage sales, there are veritable gold mines everywhere. We talked to people in town and borrowed props, wardrobe, and set dressing, mostly for free. Many of the 1950s costumes were rented for 75% off from a local costume shop, although some were borrowed from people involved with the production, like a police uniform for one of the main characters.
- If you live in a large city like New York or Los Angeles, leave the city and go to areas where film production isn't as abundant. The people and local officials will be more willing to help you because filmmaking is more of a novelty than an everyday occurrence. Some people in large production cities are bitter towards productions because of the inconvenience they cause – street closures, excessive noise, light pollution from night shoot, and parking problems are all some of the many annoyances.

Once the script is broken down and you have an idea of how much each department's needs will cost, begin typing the numbers into a budget form or use a budgeting program to calculate a final cost for the movie. If this cost exceeds the amount of money you have available in the budget, cut costs by reducing the number of shooting days, eliminating effects sequences, or simplifying scenes.

Keep in mind some factors that surprise filmmakers with unexpected costs:

- Look at the costs of shooting at each individual location and plan what elements will be needed, both in front of and behind the camera. Be sure to include location fees, permit fees, and costs of hiring city officials such as police or fire marshals. Does the location have restrooms? If not, it will be necessary to rent portable toilets. If you're shooting a night interior scene, will it be necessary to block out the windows if the location is only available during the day? How much will it cost to buy or rent black fabric to cover all the windows? Does the crew need a day to prelight the set? Remember that foresight is the biggest money-saver you have in your arsenal.

- Calculate the cost of crew members if they aren't willing to work for free. Most crew members will have a day rate for short projects and a weekly rate for longer projects. Several crew positions such as the director of photography, production sound mixer, and hair and makeup artists may have their own equipment that they bring to the set. Negotiate with them to rent their gear, as it may be cheaper than renting from a third party.
- If working with a union cast or crew, be aware of minimum payment requirements and overtime costs if the production goes over schedule. Remember that going nonunion is always a less expensive option.
- Ask the director of photography for a list of camera, lighting, and grip equipment needed for the production. With the list in hand, negotiate with equipment rental houses for discounts, especially for first-time, student, or independent productions.
- Consider all transportation costs, including vehicle rental, airport shuttles, and vehicles to transport set pieces or large props. Some cast and crew members may ask for gas money if they travel long distances to the set.
- Negotiate discounts or flat rates with postproduction facilities for editing, music composition, visual effects, and final mastering. These costs can be high, but begin negotiations early, as production costs may need to be reduced to allow budget money for postproduction. I know many filmmakers who spent their entire budget on production, expecting the film to magically edit itself. The footage sat on a shelf for years because they couldn't afford to finish it.
- Consider the cost of production insurance, including adjustments for stunts, pyrotechnics, water scenes, or any other potentially hazardous activity that could raise the cost of insurance. Insurance for film production is a very expensive yet very necessary part of making a movie. With premiums running into the thousands of dollars, insurance is required by most rental facilities and locations and is important to protect you from the cost of accidents, loss, or death.
- Know that it will be necessary to compromise some of the artistic vision in a film because of budget restrictions. Be creative and think of unique ways to maintain the artistic integrity of the film while keeping the budget low.
- Always stick to the budget, no matter what happens on set. Cost overruns in production will always carry through to postproduction. Running out of money in the postproduction process means the film won't be finished.
- Don't forget the small costs. Include all costs of copying, postage, telephone, and other office-related items.
- Budget for second meals. You may have already accounted for the cost of craft services and catering, but allow extra money for second meals – the required meals served at the 12-hour mark of a production goes over schedule.
- When budgeting the movie, allow an additional 10% on top of what you think you'll need. This "padding" will protect you if a problem occurs on set, such as a rainy day that requires you to add an additional day to the shoot.

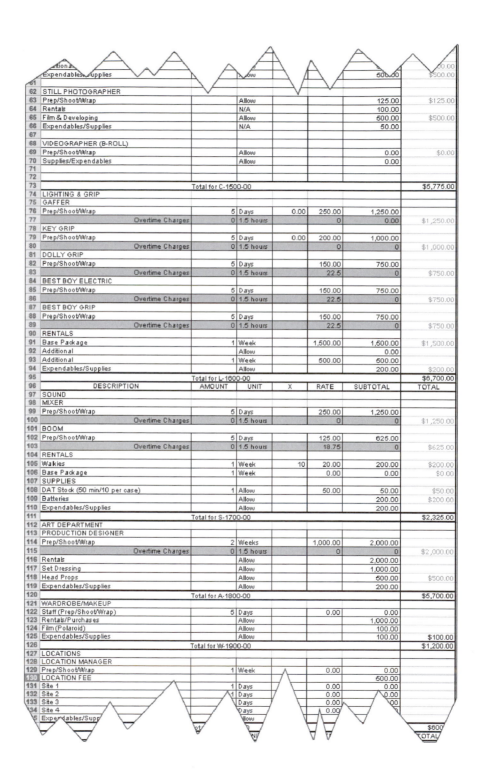

#	DESCRIPTION	AMOUNT	UNIT	X	RATE	SUBTOTAL	TOTAL
	...tional...					00.00	
	Expendables/Supplies		Allow			500.00	$500.00
61							
62	STILL PHOTOGRAPHER						
63	Prep/Shoot/Wrap		Allow			125.00	$125.00
64	Rentals		N/A			100.00	
65	Film & Developing		Allow			500.00	$500.00
66	Expendables/Supplies		N/A			50.00	
67							
68	VIDEOGRAPHER (B-ROLL)						
69	Prep/Shoot/Wrap		Allow			0.00	$0.00
70	Supplies/Expendables		Allow			0.00	
71							
72							
73		Total for C-1500-00					$5,775.00
74	LIGHTING & GRIP						
75	GAFFER						
76	Prep/Shoot/Wrap	5	Days	0.00	250.00	1,250.00	
77	Overtime Charges	0	1.5 hours		0	0.00	$1,250.00
78	KEY GRIP						
79	Prep/Shoot/Wrap	5	Days	0.00	200.00	1,000.00	
80	Overtime Charges	0	1.5 hours		0	0	$1,000.00
81	DOLLY GRIP						
82	Prep/Shoot/Wrap	5	Days		150.00	750.00	
83	Overtime Charges	0	1.5 hours		22.5	0	$750.00
84	BEST BOY ELECTRIC						
85	Prep/Shoot/Wrap	5	Days		150.00	750.00	
86	Overtime Charges	0	1.5 hours		22.5	0	$750.00
87	BEST BOY GRIP						
88	Prep/Shoot/Wrap	5	Days		150.00	750.00	
89	Overtime Charges	0	1.5 hours		22.5	0	$750.00
90	RENTALS						
91	Base Package	1	Week		1,500.00	1,500.00	$1,500.00
92	Additional		Allow			0.00	
93	Additional	1	Week		500.00	500.00	
94	Expendables/Supplies		Allow			200.00	$200.00
95		Total for L-1600-00					$6,700.00
96	DESCRIPTION	AMOUNT	UNIT	X	RATE	SUBTOTAL	TOTAL
97	SOUND						
98	MIXER						
99	Prep/Shoot/Wrap	5	Days		250.00	1,250.00	
100	Overtime Charges	0	1.5 hours		0	0	$1,250.00
101	BOOM						
102	Prep/Shoot/Wrap	5	Days		125.00	625.00	
103	Overtime Charges	0	1.5 hours		18.75	0	$625.00
104	RENTALS						
105	Walkies	1	Week	10	20.00	200.00	$200.00
106	Base Package	1	Week		0.00	0.00	$0.00
107	SUPPLIES						
108	DAT Stock (50 min/10 per case)	1	Allow		50.00	50.00	$50.00
109	Batteries		Allow			200.00	$200.00
110	Expendables/Supplies		Allow			200.00	
111		Total for S-1700-00					$2,325.00
112	ART DEPARTMENT						
113	PRODUCTION DESIGNER						
114	Prep/Shoot/Wrap	2	Weeks		1,000.00	2,000.00	
115	Overtime Charges	0	1.5 hours		0	0	$2,000.00
116	Rentals		Allow			2,000.00	
117	Set Dressing		Allow			1,000.00	
118	Head Props		Allow			500.00	$500.00
119	Expendables/Supplies		Allow			200.00	
120		Total for A-1800-00					$5,700.00
121	WARDROBE/MAKEUP						
122	Staff (Prep/Shoot/Wrap)	5	Days		0.00	0.00	
123	Rentals/Purchases		Allow			1,000.00	
124	Film (Polaroid)		Allow			100.00	
125	Expendables/Supplies		Allow			100.00	$100.00
126		Total for W-1900-00					$1,200.00
127	LOCATIONS						
128	LOCATION MANAGER						
129	Prep/Shoot/Wrap	1	Week		0.00	0.00	
130	LOCATION FEE					500.00	
131	Site 1	1	Days		0.00	0.00	
132	Site 2	1	Days		0.00	0.00	
133	Site 3		Days		0.00	00	
134	Site 4		Days		0.00		
	Expendables/Supp...		Allow				$600

Here are some tips on keeping the budget manageable:

- **The key to keeping the budget low is to restrict the number of shooting days.** Many low-budget features are shot in as little as 12 days with 12 working hours each day. If the script has 90 pages, that means that the crew needs to shoot 7.5 pages per day. This extremely tight shooting schedule and very ambitious approach won't allow for many extravagant camera moves, locations, pyrotechnics, stunts or large amounts of extras. With this type of shooting schedule, plan for two or three locations and mostly lock down (the camera is on a tripod) shots for most setups. Camera angles will be limited to a master shot, and in some instances, there may be time for close-ups and an insert shot or two.
- Remember that dolly, crane, steadicam, and even some handheld shots take a long time to set up and rehearse. These shots cost money and may require extra days if there are a lot of specialized shots in the movie.
- Special effects makeup, animals, children, car shots, night scenes, weather effects, and scenes in public areas, noisy areas, and hard-to-access locations always require a lot of time. Allow extra time when factoring in these elements.
- **Avoid working with children and animals.** Despite your best efforts, kids and animals will be both unpredictable and somewhat uncontrollable, adding to the time required to get the shot.

Download an Excel budget template for use on your production at Filmskills.com. See page vi for details.

CAST AND CREW

One important factor in determining the budget of a movie is assessing the costs of above-the-line talent versus below-the-line talent.

Above-the-line talent includes the director, producers, writers, and main actors. These positions involve negotiable salaries because of the substantial creative and marketing influence these artists have in selling the film. The more experience the above-the-line person has, the higher the negotiated salary and perks can be.

Because most independent filmmakers wear the hats of director, writer, and producer themselves, the only substantial above-the-line cost may be the actors. Nonunion actors may be willing to work for free, but union actors will certainly increase the cost of making the film, due to SAG requirements. In addition, casting a recognizable A-list actor for a few days of shooting can cost a significant percentage of the budget, but can greatly increase the chances of distribution.

Below-the-line crew members are people whose day rates are negotiable, locked amounts. These positions are typically much easier to budget in advance and are usually lower than above-the-line costs. Independent filmmakers working with little money can finesse the below-the-line category by soliciting free or discounted services; offering flat fees to crew members for the entire project instead of paying a daily rate; offering meals, a copy of the finished film, and credit in exchange for crew members' involvement; or offering deferred pay to slim down the below-the-line costs.

Many productions hire local below-the-line crew members from the city in which they are shooting.

This model works well with inexperienced crew members, but working professionals usually expect to be paid for their services, unless they have a personal interest in the movie. Don't be afraid to ask people to donate their time and services.

Unions and Guilds

Unions and guilds are long-standing organizations that protect the rights of, monitor the working conditions of, provide benefits for, and guarantee minimum levels of payment for their members. The primary unions and guilds in the American motion picture industry are the Screen Actors Guild, Directors Guild of America (DGA), Writers Guild of America (WGA), and International Alliance of Theatrical Stage Employees (IATSE).

- Producing a film with union cast and/or crew members can add to the cost of production, as minimum wages must be paid, payment to pension and health care plans must be made, and on-set work practices and restrictions must be enforced.
- Actors and crew members must demonstrate proficiency and experience in their crafts in order to be eligible for union membership. Although membership to a union or guild means the member met admission requirements, it by no means ensures their talents, work ethics, or abilities.
- There are dozens of unions and guilds for various crafts within the entertainment industry, such as the Motion Picture Editors Guild and the Writers Guild of America. Contact these guilds for lists of qualified artists for your production.
- Some locations may have contracts with a union or guild specifying that union members must be hired if a film crew is shooting on that location, regardless of whether it's a union film. Always be sure to ask before locking a location.
- Artists who join a union or guild are entitled to health benefits, guaranteed wages, controlled work hours, union representation in the event of a dispute with an employer, and many other benefits in exchange for dues, which are paid as a first-year entry fee and as annual fees. Producers hiring union crew members need to pay into their health and pension funds in addition to paying their daily rate. There may also be residual payment

requirements depending on the nature of the project. Contact your local union representative for more details.

- Using union actors in a nonunion film production violates the regulations of the union, but the U.S. Supreme Court established a principal called "Financial Core" that protects union members from being punished by their union for taking nonunion jobs. Financial core applies not only to actors, but also to unions for all industries in the United States.
- Actors and crew members have daily rates; however, working on a long-term production can be expensive, so the union offers weekly rates. Essentially, in guaranteeing the union member work for a certain length of time, the filmmaker can benefit from a slightly reduced rate.

As an independent filmmaker, the only union you need to consider involvement with is the Screen Actors Guild, especially if you're working with SAG actors. The other unions are not as influential in the production of your movie and although they can boycott your production, they may not have the power or ability to shut it down. If you choose to go nonunion, union members working on your movie may feel compelled to leave because of pressure and obligations to the union.

Don't be afraid to work with your local union or guild, but be sure to take the time to understand your obligations and requirements as a producer. Be aware that you do not need to enter into a long-term agreement as a signatory, but you can negotiate terms on a project-by-project basis. As is the case with any legal document, always read and understand any contracts you may be asked to sign. Most unions are happy to answer your questions.

Jason's Notes

When I produced *Time and Again*, I worked exclusively with a nonunion cast and crew for a number of reasons. First off, my budget didn't allow me access to professional union workers, and second, I wanted to make a film using local resources, in much the same way you would. I've worked on dozens of films as a director and cinematographer, and even on projects with budgets up to a million dollars, the only union members that we employed were the actors.

Be advised that even if you're working nonunion, it's still a good idea to honor the basic on-set work practices set forth by the unions:

- Keep shooting days to 12 hours unless you're able to pay overtime.
- Always schedule a turnaround time of 12 hours from the time the crew wraps to the call time the next day.
- Always feed the crew a meal every 6 hours.
- Always provide a safe working environment.

These practices will not only keep morale and dedication to your project up, but will also promote a safe, healthy, and productive work environment.

SCREEN ACTORS GUILD

The Screen Actors Guild is designed to protect the rights of actors and ensure that filming conditions, payment rates, and overall production conditions are professional. The guild also ensures that actors meet strict eligibility requirements upon entering, both professionally and artistically.

As an independent filmmaker, the union you are most likely to work with is the Screen Actors Guild. SAG provides a number of options for low-budget productions, allowing union actors to work on smaller independent and student films.

SAG actors have all met the guild's requirements for work experience and have paid the necessary dues to enter the union. Although there are many talented actors in SAG, SAG membership is not an endorsement of an actor's capabilities and talents.

Jason's Notes

My recommendation is to do everything possible to avoid working with SAG – work with nonunion actors, or SAG actors eligible for Financial Core, a status that allows them to work on nonunion projects. Although I fully support paying actors for their services, SAG requirements bind producers very tightly, often restricting what producers can do with their film. Even though a number of low-budget SAG contracts exist for indie filmmakers, carefully read the agreements and understand the restrictions SAG places on you and your film by signing.

Part of the SAG regulations specify minimum (or scale) payment requirements for SAG actors, depending on the budget of the film. Unfortunately, these requirements made it nearly impossible for independent filmmakers to use the high-quality, experienced actors in SAG until the guild created a multitier low-budget structure specifically designed for student and low-budget filmmakers. The following are the various options available to independent filmmakers:

Student Film Agreement

For students enrolled in film school. Performers may defer 100 percent of their salaries.

Short-Film Agreement

- Total budget of less than $50,000.
- 35 minutes or less.
- Salaries are deferred.
- No consecutive employment (except on overnight location).
- No premiums.
- Allows the use of both professional and nonprofessional performers.
- Background performers not covered.

Ultra-Low-Budget Agreement

- Total budget of less than $200,000.
- Day rate of $100.
- No step-up fees.
- No consecutive employment (except on overnight location).
- No premiums.
- Allows the use of both professional and nonprofessional performers.
- Background performers not covered.

Modified Low-Budget Agreement

- Total budget of less than $625,000.
- Day rate of $268.
- Weekly rate of $933.
- No consecutive employment (except on overnight location).
- Six-day work week with no premium.
- Reduced overtime rate.

Low-Budget Agreement

- Total budget of less than $2,500,000.
- Day rate of $504.
- Weekly rate of $1,752.
- No consecutive employment (except on overnight location).
- Six-day work week with no premium.
- Reduced overtime rate.
- Reduced number of background performers covered.

Diversity Casting Incentives

The Diversity in Casting Incentive applies to the Modified Low-Budget and the Low-Budget Agreements only. If the producer has demonstrated diversity in casting, the total production cost maximum may be increased to the following amounts:

Modified Low-Budget Agreement: from $625,000 to $937,500

and

Low-Budget Agreement: from $2,500,000 to $3,750,000.

The producer demonstrates diversity in casting by meeting the following criteria:

- A minimum of 50% of the total speaking roles and 50% of the total days of employment are cast with performers who are members of the following four protected groups: (1) women, (2) senior performers (60 years or older), (3) performers with disabilities, or (4) people of color (Asian/Pacific Islander, Black, Latino/Hispanic, and Native American Indian) *and*
- A minimum of 20% of the total days of employment are cast with performers who are people of color.

Background Actor Incentive

The Background Actor Incentive applies to the Modified Low-Budget Agreement only.

The total production cost maximum may be increased by an additional $100,000 if the producer employs a minimum average of three SAG-covered background actors for each day of principal photography, provided that the producer notifies SAG in writing of intent to utilize this incentive prior to the start of production.

Be sure to read the restrictions and requirements for working with SAG actors, including working within the eight-hour limit per day of production. These factors are important when you schedule and budget your movie, so contact SAG to make sure that you understand your obligations.

For additional information about SAG and the SAG independent filmmaker agreements, check out www.sagindie.com.

WRITER'S GUILD OF AMERICA

The Writers Guild of America is a labor union composed of the thousands of writers who write the television shows, movies, news programs, documentaries, animation, CD-ROMs, and content for new-media technologies that keep audiences constantly entertained and informed.

Their duty is to represent WGA members in negotiations with film and television producers to ensure the rights of screen, television, and new-media writers. Once a contract is in place, the WGA will enforce it. Because of the WGA's long-term efforts, writers receive pension and health coverage, and their financial and creative rights are protected.

In addition, the WGA is responsible for determining writing credits for feature films and television programs—a responsibility with far-reaching impact, both financial and artistic. Writers' livelihoods often depend on the careful and objective determination of credits.

The WGA monitors, collects, and distributes millions of dollars in residuals (payments for the reuse of movies and television programs) for writers each year. The Writers Guild also sponsors seminars, panel discussions, and special events for its members, as well as the public at large. For more information, check out www.wga.org.

INTERNATIONAL ALLIANCE OF THEATRICAL STAGE EMPLOYEES

IATSE is a union that services many of the behind-the-scenes crafts, including:

- Animation/computer-generated imagery
- Front of house
- Laboratory
- Makeup and hair

- Motion picture and television production
- Postproduction
- Projection and audiovisual
- Scenic artists
- Stagehands
- Television broadcast
- Trade shows/exhibitions
- Treasurers and ticket sellers
- Wardrobe

IATSE has local chapters around the world; see www.iatse-intl.org for more information. Working with IATSE crews can be very expensive and is generally an option only for productions with budgets over a million dollars. Once a production "goes union," a significantly higher portion of the budget must be apportioned to the union crews to cover higher rates and overtime and penalty pay.

Most low-budget filmmakers cannot afford to go union, but many IATSE chapters are interested in working with you to provide at least a few quality crew members, provided that you can pay union wages.

DIRECTORS GUILD OF AMERICA

In much the same way that SAG represents actors, the DGA represents directors. The DGA guarantees various creative and legal rights to its members as well as pension and health plans. Membership to the guild is possible when a director is hired to direct a film by a signatory company. Membership requires an initiation fee as well as yearly dues that are based on yearly earnings. For more information, visit www.dga.org.

THE BUSINESS PLAN

Now that you know how much money you need to produce the film, the next step is to create a strong business plan that describes the project, the target audience, how much money is needed, the results of similar projects, and all details of how the production will be structured. Remember that filmmaking is a business and that most investors, unless they're looking to fund the arts, want to generate a profit from their investment. Investing in a film is risky, so presenting a professional, well-designed business plan positions you as a professional.

The business plan should include:

- **The story.** What is the film about? Include a brief one-page synopsis of the story and include information on the characters, setting, and genre.
- **How well have other films in a similar genre done?** Reference the successes of projects similar to yours and demonstrate how your project may be able to achieve similar results. Look for projects with similar budgets, casts, genres, and production value.

- **What is the experience of the cast and crew?** Investors are looking for assurance that they will see a return on their investment. Listing the accomplishments of the key players, such as the cinematographer, producer, director, and actors, improves the perception that a professional, marketable product will be produced. Packaging a movie with experienced above-the-line cast and crew helps sell the marketability and viability of the movie.

- **Who is the audience?** Know the demographic data of the age, gender, education level, income level, and geographic location of the film's intended target audience. The demographics play a key role in which actors to cast, the cinematic and editing style of the movie, and to which distributors the movie should be marketed.

- **Try to secure distribution deals first.** Contact distributors to see how well films like yours have sold in the past and how well they are selling now. Have they made their money back? Have they taken a loss? Is the genre of your movie consistent in sales? How would a distributor approach the sales of your film?

- **The director's past credits.** What proof can be provided of the director's past successes? Film festival screenings, awards, and distribution contracts assure the investor that the director is qualified to produce a marketable film and that the odds of seeing a profit are greater.

- **How much will it cost?** Provide a detailed budget to show the investor on paper how his money will be spent.

- **What will the investor stand to profit from the film?** Discuss the investor's percentage of ownership in the project. Be aware, however, that it is illegal to guarantee a return. It is traditional for investors to recoup their investments from the first monies made from the sale of the film, before any profit sharing takes place.

- **Include any extra creative materials that may help sell the film.** Include storyboards, key art, photos of the actors, costume designs, set blueprints, and/or a mock-up poster to help the investor visualize the style and quality of the final production.

- **In addition to the business plan, create a web site that includes all the story information and people involved in the production.** If the cinematographer has a good demo reel, put his reel on the web site as an example of the potential quality of your movie. Also include actor bios and their previous acting experiences and successes. Make the business plan and script available in a secure area of the web site so investors can download and read them instantly. Consider using a password to keep the general public from accessing sensitive information.

Once the business plan is complete, have it professionally printed and bound using high-quality paper, or put it inside a high-quality presentation folder with your business card. First impressions are always critical when asking for investment dollars.

With the business plan in hand, begin approaching investors by making phone calls, researching family contacts, sending letters, and setting up meetings. This is a long, time-consuming process, so don't get frustrated. Believe in your project and there's a good chance you'll find an investor.

Here are some tips to finding potential investors:

- **Approach family members, friends, co-workers, local businesspeople, and wealthy contacts.** Try contacting professional business groups that are frequented by high-income occupations like doctors, lawyers, or business owners. Present the project with the business plan to generate interest.
- **Instead of finding one or two investors to finance the entire film, try approaching a number of people to invest small amounts.** Ten people willing to invest $10,000 will yield a $100,000 budget and may be easier to find than one investor for $100,000. The terms of the potential return on their investment are negotiable with each investor, but always consult an attorney to make sure these arrangements are set up legally.
- **Grants are free money provided to fund the arts that do not need to be paid back.** Applying for a grant is a difficult and competitive process and you may want to contact a professional grant writer to assist you if your project meets the requirements for the grant.
- **There are many corporations that fund the arts.** Begin researching corporations that have funded concerts, art exhibits, or even movies in your area.
- **Before you approach potential investors, shop the script around to distributors to see if they would be interested in buying the film when it is finished.** Having a letter of intent from a distributor will help assure investors that they may see their money back.

Business Formulas

There are a number of "formulas" used in the entertainment industry to produce movies on varying budget levels. The smaller the budget, the more creative producers need to be to maximize the money they have available.

FORMULA 1

The primary business formula in Hollywood is to generate enough money to pay each person and vendor the proper day rate. Although this can thrust the budget into the millions, creative control remains with the producers and all employees are happily paid. This is the ideal, but not the most practical approach for most independent filmmakers whose budgets prohibit them from paying each person on the production team.

FORMULA 2

One possible business plan for producing a low-budget movie is to pay everyone on the cast and crew, from the director to the production assistant, and the lead actors to the day players, $100/day. The twist is that each participant is awarded a percentage ownership in the movie. When the movie sells, 50 percent of the gross profits will go directly to the investor, and the other 50 percent is divided among the cast and crew based on their percentage of ownership. This back-end deal serves as an incentive for the cast and crew to work hard on the project and see it through to completion while minimizing out-of-pocket costs during production.

FORMULA 3

Offer the cast and crew deferred payment. Deferred payment means that there will be no up-front money, but the producer will pay everyone if the movie sells and makes money. Although repayment is extremely unlikely, many inexperienced cast and crew members will appreciate the effort and will be willing to donate their time and talent to the project up front.

Jason's Notes

"Copy, credit, meals" is a phrase often seen on Craigslist.org when cash-strapped filmmakers try to incentivize prospective crew members. This means if you agree to work on their movie, you will get a copy of the final movie, a listing in the credits, and food on set.

What this really means is that you will be working for free. Although this approach won't help you pay the rent, it can afford you experience and the potential to make valuable onset contacts. Remember: deferred pay really means no pay.

FORMING A COMPANY

When working with investment dollars, demonstrating proper management of the money will reassure investors that your production is legitimate. Consider forming a company to manage the accounting, provide legal protection for the producers, and keep clean tax records.

Forming a company will keep the movie's financing, legalities, and liability separate from your own. Even the large studios form smaller corporate entities for each movie and television show they produce; hence the occasionally humorous production company names that seem to be around for only one project. These companies serve as autonomous entities and protect the bigger company (the studio) from liability.

In the United States, there are seven major types of businesses that are recognized by law, each with its own advantages:

- A *sole proprietorship* is business conducted by an individual. None of the protections or tax benefits of a corporation carry to the individual, who is solely responsible for any liability, tax burden, and debt.
- A *general partnership* is an association of two or more people (partners) who have joint ownership in a company that is intended to generate a profit. A general partnership must be registered in the city or town it intends to operate in. The partners agree to share equally all the gains and losses that occur from the operation of the general partnership.

- A *limited partnership* is made up of two different types of partners: limited partners who provide the financial backing of the company, but have little say in the daily operation of the company, and the general partner who manages the operation of the company. The limited partners can't lose more than what they put into the company, but benefit from income, capital gains, and tax benefits. The general partner makes a percentage of the capital gains and income.
- A *corporation* is a business entity that exists completely on its own, as an individual does. Corporations protect their employees, shareholders, and partners' assets from lawsuit by making the corporation's assets liable, not the assets of the people who run the corporation. Corporations can own property, incur debt, sue, or be sued.
- A *limited liability company (LLC)* is a hybrid of a partnership and a corporation that shields its owners from personal liability, and gains and losses bypass the LLC directly to the owners without being taxed. The LLC is taxed as a partnership while offering the protection of a corporation.
- A *joint venture* is a partnership between two companies wanting to do business together. The principle of a joint venture is similar to that of a partnership, although instead of people partnering, it's other business entities partnering.
- A *nonprofit company* is an organization whose intentions are for noncommercial purposes only. Nonprofit companies require a lengthy application process and can be eligible for grants and other funding sources not normally available to for-profit entities.

Most upstart production companies choose the LLC, or limited liability company, because it offers the needed protection and tax benefits for movie production.

When forming a company, consider the following tips:

- Have a good corporate attorney draw up the paperwork. It is possible to file application papers yourself, but it can be a complicated process for the uninitiated. Generally, for a few hundred dollars, an attorney will file all applications and ensure that the business is properly set up.
- Open bank accounts in the company's name and specify who in the company is able to write checks.
- Open a checking account specifically for the film production to keep budget funds separate from your personal accounts. Keep the account strictly balanced.
- Open an *escrow account*, which is a neutral, monitored bank account for the investors' money, ensuring that the money is properly managed and dispersed at the correct time and place. The escrow account is managed by an escrow holder or agent who follows the agreement signed by the production company and the investors. An escrow account also protects the investors by prohibiting any inappropriate access to the account.
- If the project is large enough and the entire cast and crew is being paid, consider hiring a payroll company to handle disbursements of paychecks.

Approach an accountant or bookkeeper to assist with the handling of money for the production.

Managing the Budget

At this point, you've broken down the script, developed a rough budget, and secured the financing for your movie. One way of keeping the movie on budget is to keep the money carefully organized, so every penny is accounted for.

- **Only the line producer or unit production manager should have the ability to write checks.** In the independent world, only the producer should have this ability. This shifts the burden of accountability onto the shoulders of one person.
- **Keep all receipts.** As is the case with all businesses, receipts are necessary to maintain a balanced budget, track the spending of the budget, and maintain detailed records for tax purposes. Remember that you need to be able to prove each and every purchase to deduct it from your or your business's income taxes.
- **Purchase an accounting program to track expenses and maintain a balanced checking account.** Software solutions will make printing reports and filing taxes much easier than keeping handwritten spreadsheets.
- **If you're in the United States, issue W-9 forms to every paid employee.** You are legally obligated to report any payments to individuals above $600 to the IRS. Each cast and crew member with a paycheck greater than $600 must fill out a W-9 form.
- **Keep petty cash on hand, and keep careful track of who has been given money by signing out dollar amounts and putting receipts in the petty cash bag.** Make sure the total amount balances out at the end of each day.

Payroll

Many independent producers will pay the cast, crew members, and outside vendors from the production checking account themselves. Although this may be the best option for a low-budget production, you may need to manage withholding of federal, state, and local taxes if your rate of pay exceeds US$600 per year per person. To help manage this workload, you may want to consider hiring a bookkeeper or accountant to keep track of the payroll and ensure that the proper tax forms are filed.

If you are working on a larger production, there are a number of large payroll companies (Cast & Crew, Axium, Entertainment Partners, and All Payments) that can provide accounting software that will work in conjunction with your budgeting software. They will then handle disbursement of funds and manage any tax withholding. Hiring an accounting or payroll service can save you time and money in the long run.

- When you're beginning a production, make sure every cast and crew member fills out the following forms before they begin working:
    - U.S. Immigration I-9 form, verifying their ability to work in the United States.

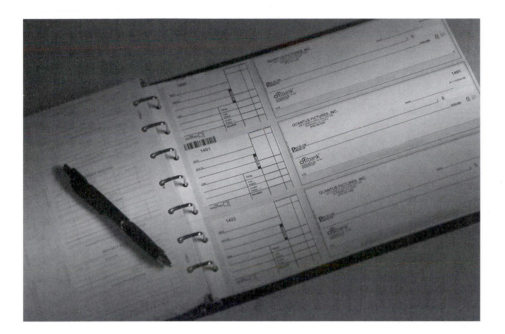

- Deal Memo that states the terms of employment, including start and stop dates, rates, overtime, kit or equipment rental fees, and any other terms of employment. Be sure to collect each employees' Social Security number or tax ID number.
- Contact information sheet with name, email address, and phone number.
- Accounting policies that detail procedures for issuing invoices, securing petty cash, payroll, mileage and fuel reimbursements, vendor accounts, and any other pertinent accounting information.
- Safety guidelines for the production.
- Some vendors who own or work through their corporation may request a loan out. A loan out occurs when a corporation or company "loans out" the services of its employees to the production company. Many subcontractors own their own corporations and prefer for a production company to pay the corporation rather than pay them as individuals. In doing so, the production company need not withhold federal, state, or local taxes, but will require proof of the corporation's ability to work in the state in which the production is taking place.

Petty Cash

Producers will often allocate a portion of the budget to be used as on-hand or "petty" cash. Petty cash should be used for small purchases such as parking fees, fuel, or small expendables. Although petty cash should not be used for salaries or to pay vendors, it must still be tracked.

Petty cash is usually controlled by the unit production manager (UPM). If a crew member requires petty cash, that crew member fills out a petty cash form that is also signed by the UPM. Once the purchase is made, the crew member must turn in every receipt as well as any leftover cash to the UPM. If the amount balances, the petty cash form is discarded. The UPM tapes the receipts to an 8.5×11" sheet of paper and writes what each purchase was for and turns them in to the Production Accountant.

- Petty cash purchases are usually capped at $300 per purchase.
- Petty cash purchase receipts must be clearly marked with the vendor's name, address, phone number, and a clear indication of what was purchased.
- Restaurant purchases must be itemized for each item ordered and who was eating.
- Any crew member turning in petty cash receipts for fuel or mileage must identify the purpose of the trip and log mileage logged for the vehicle driven.
- Any petty cash that is not accounted for is usually deducted from the signer's paycheck.

Mileage

If a UPM agrees to reimburse mileage for certain cast or crew members – usually production assistants, art department personnel, or other job positions that require a lot of driving for the production – he or she will determine whether to simply reimburse fuel costs or pay a flat rate/mile. The standard rate is $0.50/mile. The employee being compensated must maintain a log to track every mile driven, the beginning point and destination, and the purpose of the trip. This log must then be turned into the UPM for approval.

01	138, 140	INT	BEDROOM
			Nick returns morphing into old hag, hand of demon m...
03	143	INT	LIVING ROOM
			Lee confronts Nick, sees Helmut attack him; she ge...
04	A143	INT	LIVING ROOM
			Helmut pulls Nick by neck, attacks him w/ scissor...
07	138	EXT	DRIVEWAY
			Nick runs reflected in puddle with house

End Day # 5 Thursday, Decemb...

09	23	EXT	Deserted Road
			LEE drives away from Dr.'s surgery in car
4	45, 47	EXT	GARDEN
			Lee's hears conversation in head as she...
1	32	INT	KITCHEN
			Lee enters and drops dish startled- a...
2	111	INT	KITCHEN
			Helmut smashes open door te...

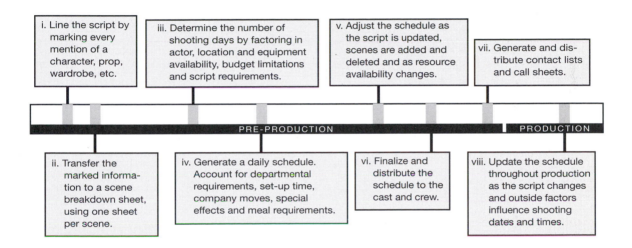

i. Line the script by marking every mention of a character, prop, wardrobe, etc.

ii. Transfer the marked information to a scene breakdown sheet, using one sheet per scene.

iii. Determine the number of shooting days by factoring in actor, location and equipment availability, budget limitations and script requirements.

iv. Generate a daily schedule. Account for departmental requirements, set-up time, company moves, special effects and meal requirements.

v. Adjust the schedule as the script is updated, scenes are added and deleted and as resource availability changes.

vi. Finalize and distribute the schedule to the cast and crew.

vii. Generate and distribute contact lists and call sheets.

viii. Update the schedule throughout production as the script changes and outside factors influence shooting dates and times.

PRE-PRODUCTION

PRODUCTION

INTRODUCTION

In order to properly schedule a movie production, you need to ensure that the script is properly set up. Many professional writers use software like Final Draft, mentioned earlier, which formats the script based on standard industry guidelines such as the "one page equals one minute" rule of thumb. It also makes it easier to change scenes, add or delete scenes, and alter the schedule.

Before you begin developing a schedule, make sure your script will pass the following tests:

- **The script should be properly formatted with 12-point Courier font.** If the script has been written in a program other than a script-writing program, consider importing the screenplay into Final Draft. The features in Final Draft will help you quickly break down the script and offer a multitude of tools to simplify the scheduling process.

Filmmaking.
© 2011 Jason J. Tomaric. Published by Elsevier Inc. All rights reserved.

Fred and Vinnie, Version 14   27.

40   EXT. FRED'S APARTMENT ROOF - DAY (C1997)   40

        Vinnie sits on an old abandoned fold-out chair and puffs on a
        cigarette while looking at his cards in his photo album. He
        turns a page, studies a card and turns the page again. We
        close in on one card and flip to another card.

                                                 MATCH CUT TO:

41   INT. BASEBALL CARD STORE - DAY (C1997)   41

        We pull back on the card to reveal we're at the card store
        the next day. The OWNER holds the card out. Vinnie nods and
        the owner puts the card back in the showcase.

        Fred stands in the background, not interested. When the
        owner goes to the back to retrieve another card, Fred walks
        over to Vinnie.

                                FRED
                        There a particular card you're
                        looking to buy?

                                VINNIE
                        I'm not buying any. I just like to
                        look.

        The owner comes back with a thick album of cards. Fred sighs.

42   INT. FRED'S APARTMENT LIVING ROOM - DAY (C1997)   42

        Fred and Vinnie sit on the couch with the TV on in the
        background. Vinnie looks at used instant lottery tickets, and
        then places them in a shoebox.

                                FRED
                        So you collect all your used lost
                        lottery tickets?

                                VINNIE
                        I got that and bags of everything
                        in the world stored back East.

                                FRED
                        And you got all your answering
                        machine tapes too? All the
                        classics?

                                VINNIE
                        I have every message from the last
                        fifteen years.
                                (MORE)

Always make sure the script is properly formatted before breaking it down. The formatting is calculated for one page per minute of screen time.

- **The script you receive from the writer should not have any of the scenes numbered.** Comb through the script and number each scene (a process that is automatically performed with professional script writing software). Once you are finished, the 1st assistant director (AD) will need to approve and sign off on the numbering of the script. Scene numbers, once applied, are permanent and cannot be changed because they are the foundation upon which all departments build their own breakdown of the script. If the writer writes a new scene, it is numbered with the previous scene number plus a letter. For example, if the new scene is inserted between scenes 12 and 13, the new scene will be numbered 12a. Scenes that are later deleted still retain the assigned scene number, but "OMITTED" is written next to it.
- **Number each page and lock the numbering.** Much like the scene numbers, page numbers should never change. If you add or lengthen a scene on page 52, instead of pushing all the following scenes forward, add a new page 52A to accommodate the new text, leaving page 53 untouched. Be sure to note any script pages that have scenes added or deleted by placing an asterisk (*) in the right margin next to the scene that has been changed.
- The script usually undergoes a number of rewrites and alterations throughout the course of production. To help keep track of these changes, updated

pages are printed on different color paper to help the cast and crew track updates. The order of colors is:

- 1st printing of the script: white
- 1st change: blue
- 2nd change: pink
- 3rd change: yellow
- 4th change: green
- 5th change: goldenrod
- 6th change: buff
- 7th change: salmon
- 8th change: cherry
- 9th change: tan
- 10th change: grey
- 11th change: ivory

If any given page undergoes more than 11 changes, you can return to white paper and begin the cycle again. By the end of production, your script will probably look like a rainbow, with many of the sheets having had been revised and replaced.

Always type the draft number and the date of revision in the upper-righthand corner of every page and mark lines of the script that have changed with an asterisk (*) in the right margin and quickly distribute changes to the department heads.

STEP 1: BREAKING DOWN THE SCRIPT

Lining the Script

Once the script is properly formatted and each scene numbered, you're ready to begin breaking it down. The first step is to go through the script and, using a pencil and ruler, draw a horizontal line across the page at the end of each scene.

The next step is to measure the length of each scene, enabling the 1st AD to later determine how long it will take to shoot. Begin by using a ruler to determine how many eighths of a page each scene is. When you factor in the size of the margins, an eighth of a page is roughly equal to an inch.

Increments are measured in fraction form: 1/8, 2/8, 3/8, 4/8, 5/8, 6/8, 7/8, and a full page. Scenes less than 1/8 of a page are still written as 1/8. If a scene spans more than one page, the scene is measured in terms of the number of pages, with any spillover in eighths: for example, $2\frac{3}{8}$ pages.

Write the length of each scene in the right margin of the page.

Breaking Down the Script

The next step is to comb through the script and identify every prop, location, character; every instance of extras; and every vehicle, stunt, animal, or any other person, place, or thing that needs to be acquired by each individual department.

Line the Script
Using different color markers, mark every category in every scene.

↓

Scene Breakdown Sheet
Transfer each category to a scene breakdown form, adding as much information as possible.

↓

Determine the Number of Shooting Days
Consider factors such as the budget, location, actor and equipment availability.

↓

Produce the Daily Schedule
Using a production board, determine the most logical order to shoot scenes in each day.

↓

Finalize the Schedule
Once complete, copy and distribute to the crew and continue pre-production.

↓

Contact List and Call Sheet
Assemble and distribute a contact list and generate a call sheet for each shooting day.

"The Day Bobby Jones Came Home" Draft 6/29   3.

Bobby, disoriented, runs away, trying to get his bearing.
He's sweaty, winded, tired and dehydrated.

7 2/8 EXT. COUNTRY ROAD - DAY   7

A car is coming down the road. Bobby can't make it out until
it's almost on top of him. Bobby sticks his thumb out. It's a
1957 Chevy that passes him up. Bobby continues walking down
road.

A van is coming down the road. Bobby again sticks his thumb
out. Van speeds past practically knocking him into a ditch.

8 1/8 EXT. COUNTRY ROAD - LATER   8

Another car flies by. Bobby continues walking down road.

9 4/8 EXT. COUNTRY ROAD - LATER   9

In the distance, he hears country music. Bobby looks up and
sees a thin form approaching. It is a bicycle.

The bike rider, AWANDA, a sexy blond in her mid-thirties,
wears a tight waitress outfit and has a radio strapped to the
back of her bike. She pulls up next to him and eyes him over.

                    AWANDA
             So where ya' headed?

                    BOBBY
             I don't know.

Bobby stumbles away. Awanda peddles to keep up with him.

                    AWANDA
             Yeah? Well, maybe I can help you
             get there. Here, hop on.

Bobby looks at the bike. There's no room for another person.

10 2 4/8 EXT. COUNTRY ROAD - MOMENTS LATER   10

Awanda struggles to peddle the bike with Bobby on the
handlebars. She doesn't seem to mind too much. Her hand is
right by his butt.

                    AWANDA
             So where ya' from?

                    BOBBY
             I'm just traveling cross country.

                © 2002 Robert T. Noll & Jason J. Tomaric

Using your lined script, get 10–12 different-colored markers, and read through each page of the script and mark each instance of the following categories:

- Actors—mark in red
- Extras—mark in green
- Props—mark in violet
- Wardrobe—circle every instance
- Stunts—mark in orange
- Special effects—mark in blue
- Vehicles/animals—mark in pink
- Special equipment—draw a box
- Makeup/hair—mark with an asterisk
- Sound effects/music—mark in brown

Also, take note of the following:

- The number of locations
- The time of day during which scenes take place (day, night, dusk, dawn)
- Any scenes that can be shot with a second unit crew to establish shots, stunts, special effects, or any shot that doesn't involve the principal actors

Identifying Characters

The next step of breaking down the script is to identify all of the characters in the story. Beginning with the most prominent character, assign each role a number, starting at 1. This number will represent the character in all scheduling documents and call sheets. Once a number is assigned to a character, it should never be changed.

On movies with a larger budget, the 1st AD usually lines the script. On independent movies with no 1st AD, or if that position hasn't been filled yet, the producer usually performs this task.

STEP 2: SCENE BREAKDOWN SHEETS

The next step is to print out a stack of blank scene breakdown sheets and transfer all the information you identified while lining the script to these forms. The scene breakdown sheet is broken down into a grid with one square designated for each category. Start at the beginning of the script and copy each marked item on the script to its corresponding category on the breakdown sheet, using one breakdown sheet per scene. If the script has 32 scenes, you will end up with 32 scene breakdown sheets.

Jason's Notes

Today, many line producers and 1st assistant directors use software programs like Gorilla Software or Movie Magic to automate this process. Working digitally makes it much easier to update information and adapt information to the various forms you'll use during production.

Scene breakdown forms include a multitude of information about the scene, including:

- Production company
- Name of the movie
- Breakdown page number (numbered sequentially from the beginning of the movie)
- Scene header
- Short description of the scene
- Scene location
- Time the scene takes place
- The cast for each scene
- Length of each scene
- Detailed list of the elements in each scene (you already marked these while lining the script)

As a way of helping keep the breakdown sheets and scenes organized, use multicolored paper to help differentiate between interior and exterior scenes and day and night scenes:

Day interior—white paper
Day exterior—yellow paper
Night interior—blue paper
Night exterior—green paper

Add additional prop, wardrobe, and extra information to the breakdown sheets, even though the script may not directly mention them. For example, in a scene that takes place in a car repair shop, even though the script may mention only the mechanic and the wrench he is holding, describe any additional wardrobe requirements like mechanics uniforms or set-dressing elements like tools, an air compressor, and work lights. The purpose of a breakdown sheet is to have as complete a list as possible of all the elements needed to film each scene in the movie, so the crew can look at the breakdown sheet and gather everything needed.

Once complete, the finished scene breakdown forms constitute the "bible," which should be copied and distributed to the head of each department. If the script changes, be sure to update immediately and issue a new scene update form.

BREAKDOWN SHEET

DATE: _____

PRODUCTION COMPANY	PRODUCTION TITLE	BREAKDOWN PAGE NO.
SCENE NO.	SCENE NAME	INT. OR EXT.
DESCRIPTION		DAY OR NIGHT
		PAGE COUNT

CAST Red	STUNTS Orange	EXTRAS/ATMOSPHERE Green
	EXTRAS/SILENT Yellow	
SPECIAL EFFECTS Blue	PROPS Violet	VEHICLES/ANIMALS Pink
WARDROBE Circle	MAKE-UP/HAIR Asterisk	SOUND EFFECTS/MUSIC Brown
SPECIAL EQUIPMENT Box	PRODUCTION NOTES	

Day Ext. - YELLOW   Night Ext. - GREEN   Day Int. - WHITE   Night Int. - BLUE

STEP 3: DETERMINE THE NUMBER OF SHOOTING DAYS

The third step toward building the shooting schedule is to determine how many days it is going to take to shoot the movie. The number of shooting days and the time frame for the production are dependent on a number of factors:

- **Budget.** The biggest determining factor in calculating the number of shooting days is how many days you can afford to shoot. Knowing how many crew members are needed, their day rates, the cost of equipment rental, the cost of hiring actors, the cost of craft services and catering, the location costs, and a number of other factors may limit the number of days in production. It's not uncommon for low-budget features to be shot in 10 or 12 days with a slimmed-down crew.

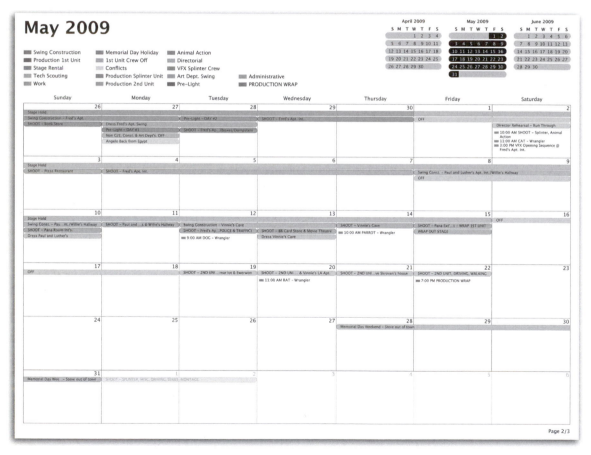

We mapped out each shooting day so we knew how to arrange in-studio days with location days, especially considering that the art department needed to rebuild every studio set while the crew was out on location.

- **Actor availability.** If you have a name actor, your production schedule may have to accommodate the actor's schedule. Be sure to work closely with the actor's agent or manager before locking in a schedule. It's not uncommon for productions to be placed on hold until even a few days before shooting is scheduled to begin because the actor hasn't committed.
- **Location availability.** Do the locations have restricted hours of shooting, limited hours for production, or other schedule conflicts you may need to schedule around?
- **Equipment availability.** If other productions are shooting in your area, will equipment availability be an issue? Consider scheduling your shoot so it doesn't coincide with other projects that may be shooting at the same time.
- **Weather.** Will the production need to be scheduled during a certain season? Would adverse weather affect the shooting schedule? How likely is the shooting area to be affected by changing weather?

Determining the number of shooting days can be tricky and is largely based on the experiences a first assistant director has had on set in the past. Be careful not to make the schedule overly ambitious, because if you begin falling behind, it's extremely difficult to catch up, scenes will need to be cut, and the quality of the movie will be compromised. Some tips to keep in mind when scheduling:

- **Hollywood movies shoot one to three pages of the script per shooting day.** Most independent movies must shoot upwards of five or six pages per day because of budget restrictions. Avoid scheduling more than six pages per day or the production value will begin to suffer – unless those pages are in one location for one or two dialog scenes. Six pages a day at multiple locations with company moves are nearly impossible to shoot. Three to five pages per day is a comfortable amount, allowing you and the actors time to work and giving the director of photography and other department heads time to do their jobs properly. The greater the number of pages, the faster the crew has to work, and the sloppier the work becomes.
- **When calculating the number of pages per day, look at the level of complexity in shooting each scene.** A three-page dialog scene between two characters in a restaurant can be shot much faster than three pages of an FBI agent combing through a building in search of a bomb. The various location changes, camera setups, and lighting setups will take much more time. Consider the number of setups and look at the director's storyboards to determine how much coverage is needed for each scene. Remember that simple 90-page scripts with limited cast and locations are easier and cheaper to shoot.

One of the biggest mistakes you can make is trying to cram too much into a shooting day. Even setting up a light like this 10k can take upwards of ten minutes, and without enough time or crew to help, you'll never make your day.

Jason's Notes

Ideally, we want to shoot our movies six days a week – the way it's done in Hollywood. The unfortunately reality of low-budget independent filmmaking means we need to shoot when we can, accommodating the cast and crew's 9 to 5 work schedules. Most often, we end up shooting on weekends and weeknights, squeezing shoots in when possible. But keep in mind that just because shooting days may be scattered around the calendar doesn't mean they can't be well organized and meticulously planned to optimize the time you have on set.

- **Allow six to eight weeks for the rest of preproduction before the first day of shooting.** This will allow enough time to hire the cast and crew, rehearse with actors, assemble equipment, dress locations, gather props and wardrobe, and attend to all the other details prior to shooting.
- **Schedule as many consecutive days as possible.** It's easier for cast and crew members to commit to "every weekend in July" or "the next eight days" than to scattered production dates over a long period of time. Keeping the schedule tight maintains the pace of the production and increases camaraderie among the cast and crew.

STEP 4: MAKING THE DAILY SCHEDULE
The Production Board

After you've determined the number of shooting days, it's now time to figure out what scenes to shoot during those days, and in what order. With so many variables to consider, such as location availability, actor availability, and multiple scenes within the script that take place in the same location, production boards are used to help simplify the process.

A production board is made up of a series of 1/2-inch multicolored strips of paper that each contain the information written on the scene breakdown sheets. Each strip represents one scene, and the colors each represent something different:

Yellow strips: day exterior
White strips: day interior
Green strips: night exterior
Blue strips: night interior
Black and white strips: day dividers
Solid black strips: week dividers

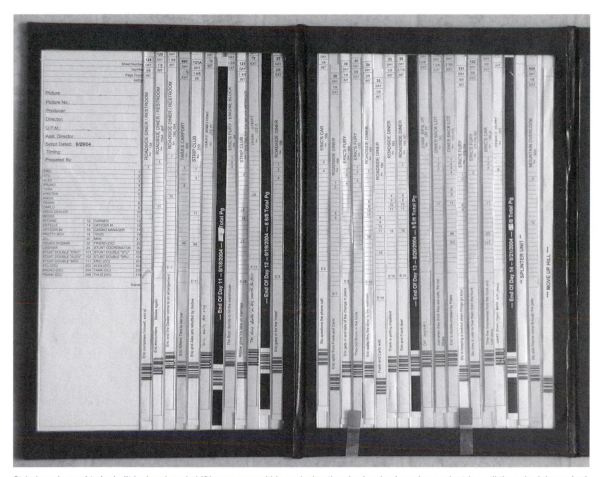

Strip boards used to be built by hand, and shifting scenes within each shooting day involved moving each strip until the schedule worked. Today, software programs automate certain aspects of the process, making even the most complex productions easy to schedule.

Referring to the scene breakdown sheets, create a traditional production board (or use a scheduling software program such as the one from www.filmmakersoftware.com to make one electronically) by writing the scene number, a brief scene description, the characters involved in each scene, the number of pages, the time of day, the location, and a description of the scene on each strip of paper. Scenes with the same actor, time of day, and location can be placed on the same strip.

Arrange and rearrange the strips to figure out the most logical way to shoot the scenes within each production day. Try to schedule scenes shot in the same location on the same day, and place scenes with the same actors together. Remember that because movies are not shot from the beginning of the story to the end, you can group locations together, or the days an actor is shooting together, to maximize the efficiency of the shoot. Use a black strip to identify the end of each day of production.

Breakdown Page #'s			1		9	10
Day or Night			N		D	N
Scene(s)			1,36		11,12,15	23
# of pages			6/8		2 1/8	1 2/8
			EXT. PRISON	2nd DAY - 6/8 Pages	INT. DINER	INT. DINER
Title: The Day Bobby Jones Came Home						
Director: Jason J. Tomaric						
Producers: Jason J. Tomaric & Adam Kadar						
Assistant Director: Kailyne Waters						
CHARACTER	**ACTOR**					
Bobby Jones	Brian Ireland	1	1		1	1
Awanda	Jennie Allen	2			2	
Sheriff Karl	Bob Darby	3				3
Martha Jones	Paula Williams	4				
Robin Jones	Rick Montgomery	5				
Teacher	Jeannie LaLande	6				
Young Bobby Jones	Andrew Zehnder	7				
Prisoners		8	8			
Stickball Players		9				
Extras		X			X	X
			1. Bobby and prisoners excape from jail 36. Bobby Jones is dead		Bobby discovers newspaper, looks at it in bathroom and talks to man at counter	Bobby rishes in, looking for Awanda

This is the strip board from *Time and Again*. Notice how each character has his own number, which makes scheduling around actor availability easier.

Scheduling Tips

- **It's easier to schedule each shooting day if you know the number of camera setups in each scene.** Give your shot list to the 1st assistant director prior to scheduling each day. Often, an overly ambitious shot list can be difficult to shoot within the budget and number of scheduled shooting days. Developing a schedule is the first way to see if you're able to acquire the shots, or if the shot list needs to be simplified.
- **Never underestimate the amount of time it will take to shoot a scene.** This is especially true with low-budget independent movies that employ inexperienced crew members. Hire an experienced 1st assistant director and line producer to build a realistic schedule based on the experience and size of the crew as well as the complexity of the shots required in the movie.
- **One great trick to scheduling based on the director's shot list is to assign a numeric value to the complexity of each shot.** For example, a crane shot will have a higher number than a static shot taken from a tripod, due to the amount of time it will take to unload, set up, rehearse and shoot the crane shot. When developing the schedule, if it becomes necessary to trim shots, look at cutting highest-rated shots first.
- **Allow more time to shoot scenes early in the day.** There is an interesting productivity arc that movie crews exhibit during the course of a day. Early in the morning, productivity tends to be high, although many productions tend to move slowly because of load-in and setup times. A good 1st AD will keep the crew on task and the schedule moving to ensure the schedule is met before lunch. After lunch, the crew regains energy for the first two hours. Then the food coma hits and the crew tends to slow down, feeling tired and sluggish. Provide coffee and a sharp attention to the schedule to help the crew work through this phase. If the shoot is running long enough for dinner to be served, the production is at the 12-hour mark and the crew will begin its downward slide as fatigue sets in. After 12 hours, the law of diminishing returns applies. Longer hours worked will not result in better work, but a diminished attention to detail will risk the safety of the cast and crew and potentially compromise the quality of the work.
- **If possible, shoot any establishing shots, nondescript insert shots, and special effects shots after you complete principal photography (shooting any shots that involve the main actors) with a second unit.** While you are lining the script, take note of any scenes or shots that can be shot by the second unit and develop a second schedule specifically for them. Often second unit crews are smaller, require less equipment and are able to shoot for less money that the first unit.
- **Be aware of any city or location events that could affect your production days, including holidays, fund-raisers, parades, or even road maintenance.** Always check your production dates to make sure they don't conflict with any other function and work closely with local authorities, especially if your production requires use of any public property.

Turnaround Time

Turnaround time is the amount of free time from the time a production wraps to the call time of the next shooting day.

Union guidelines and standard industry practice requires at least 12 hours turnaround. If you're working with a union crew, cutting into 12 hours will result in overtime and penalty fees; if you have SAG actors, they work on 8-hour days, with overtime rates applying thereafter. Contact your local guild or union for specific regulations governing turnaround time for the cast and crew.

Overtime

Common industry practice and crew day rates provide for 12-hour days, calculated from call time to wrap time, excluding meals. For example, if the call time is 7:00 a.m., and the production allows an hour lunch, the production must wrap at 8:00 p.m. If the production runs beyond the scheduled wrap time, the crew should be paid overtime.

Overtime is usually discussed and negotiated prior to signing on crew members to a film project. Although overtime rates vary based on the crew member and union affiliation, typical overtime rates are 1.5 times the prorated hourly day rate for the first two hours over the eight-hour work day, and double time beyond ten hours.

As you can imagine, running over schedule can get extraordinarily costly, even if you're working with a small crew. Be careful when developing the schedule to consider any factors that could result in overtime to avoid costly overruns.

Meal Time

Always allow time for the cast and crew to eat by scheduling a major meal every six hours. If call time is 6:00 a.m., then lunch needs to be served at noon. Assuming an hour is scheduled for lunch, the next six-hour time block begins at 1:00 p.m. Dinner should be served at 7:00 p.m.

If a production adheres to a 12-hour shooting day, it is not necessary to provide a second meal. If the crew runs into overtime, however, a second meal must be served. Catering costs, the addition of the cast and crew's overtime pay, and decreased productivity due to fatigue makes overtime expensive and impractical in most situations.

Company Move

A company move occurs when the production changes locations during the course of a shooting day. Company moves can be time consuming and costly, even if well-organized, taking time away from shooting time. If it becomes necessary to schedule a company move, be sure to allow ample time for striking the set, moving personnel and equipment to the new location, and setting the equipment up again. Allow even more time if the crew is inexperienced.

Shooting Exteriors

When filming exterior scenes, always have a backup interior scene to shoot if it rains or the weather prohibits filming. With the entire cast and crew present, don't waste a day just because of bad weather; shoot another scene.

STEP 5: FINALIZING THE SCHEDULE

One-Line Schedule

Once you organize the production strips into the most logical order and have a shooting schedule, you can develop a *one-line schedule*. This shortened version of the shooting schedule is distributed amongst the cast and crew.

Keep in mind that the schedule will change throughout the production process. Days will run over schedule, scenes will be cut, weather will interfere with the order of the scenes shot, or any number of other factors can affect the schedule. Be prepared to constantly change, rearrange, and move scenes to be able to complete the picture within the allotted time frame.

Now that you have the schedule prepared, it's time to move to the next step of preproduction:

- Begin scouting locations.
- Begin auditioning actors.
- Begin assembling props and wardrobe.
- Begin seeking qualified crew members.
- Approach equipment rental houses for camera, lighting, and grip equipment.

Try to secure locations before you schedule the cast and crew. With locked production dates, you can confirm the number of days each cast and crew member needs to dedicate to the production, making it easier for them to commit to the project. If locations are *not* secured and you try to lock cast and crew members for dates that keep changing, you will appear unprofessional and stand to lose the commitment from those volunteering their time.

Day-Out-of-Days

The day-out-of-days chart serves as a master calendar for all actors to assist them in understanding their daily schedules. Organized like a calendar, labeled with the number of shooting days listed along the top, each actor is assigned a status for each of the production days.

The various status indicators are:

S (Start): Identifies the first day the performer will work on the project. The Start date can be a travel day, a rehearsal or a shooting day.
R (Rehearsal): Identifies days the performer is scheduled to rehearse.
T (Travel): Identifies days the performer is scheduled to travel for the production.

Scheduled

***************SHOOTING ORDER***************

LOCATION DAY - BOOK STORE (BOOK SOUP) INTERIOR **PERMIT

Sheet #: 62	Scenes:	INT	THE WRITERS STORE (OR RETAIL EQUAL)	1, 14, 17, 18, 36	Est. Time
4/8 pgs	68	Day	Fred enters store, sees long line of cutomers, m		2:00
Sheet #: 63	Scenes:	INT	THE WRITERS STORE (OR RETAIL EQUAL)	1, 18, 25	Est. Time
1 6/8 pgs	69	Day	LATER...Fred after waiting in long line, is finally r		2:00

End Day # 1 Sunday, April 26, 2009 -- Total Pages: 2 2/8 -- Est. Time: 4:00

LOCATION DAY - MAILBOXES/FRED'S APT. COMPLEX INTERIOR

Sheet #: 65	Scenes:	INT	FRED'S APARTMENT COMPLEX MAILBOXES/FR	1, 6	Est. Time
2/8 pgs	71	Day	Fred is about to head upstairs when he hears so		:30
Sheet #: 23	Scenes:	INT	FRED'S APARTMENT COMPLEX MAILBOXES/FR	1	Est. Time
1/8 pgs	22	Day	Fred looks for mail and steps out.		:30
Sheet #: 110	Scenes:	INT	FRED'S APARTMENT COMPLEX MAILBOXES/FR	1	Est. Time
4/8 pgs	119 / 119A /	Day	Fred enters his apartment complex and goes righ		1:00

LOCATION DAY - FRED'S APT. COMPLEX DUMPSTERS

Sheet #: 66	Scenes:	EXT	FRED'S APARTMENT COMPLEX DUMPSTERS	1, 2, 12	Est. Time
2 3/8 pgs	72 / 72A	Day	Fred walks to where the rukus is coming from, at		3:00
Sheet #: 80	Scenes:	EXT	FRED'S APARTMENT COMPLEX DUMPSTERS	1	Est. Time
2/8 pgs	88 / 88A	Day	We see the only activity checked off the list, is I		2:00
Sheet #: 6	Scenes:	INT	FRED'S APT. BLDG. HALLWAY (OUTSIDE FRED'	1	Est. Time
1/8 pgs	5	Day	A PACKAGE sits in front of Fred's door, as Fred		:30
Sheet #: 27	Scenes:	INT	FRED'S APT. BLDG. HALLWAY (OUTSIDE FRED'	1, 2	Est. Time
4/8 pgs	26	Day	We see the back of Vinnie as he looks at the Ch		1:00
Sheet #: 73	Scenes:	INT	FRED'S APT. BLDG. HALLWAY (OUTSIDE FRED'	2	Est. Time
2/8 pgs	81	Day	Vinnie walks down stairs from rooftop and down I		:25
Sheet #: 75	Scenes:	INT	FRED'S APT. BLDG. HALLWAY (OUTSIDE FRED'	2	Est. Time
1/8 pgs	83	Day	Vinnie walks to door and begins to open.		:25

End Day # 2 Tuesday, April 28, 2009 -- Total Pages: 4 4/8 -- Est. Time: 9:20

STUDIO DAY - FRED'S BATHROOM INTERIOR (MORNING/DAY)

| Sheet #: 45 | Scenes: | INT | FRED'S BATHROOM DOOR/HALLWAY/FRONT D(| 1 | Est. Time |
| 2/8 pgs | 50 | Mornir | Fred paces outside bathroom door waiting for Vin | | :30 |

The one-line schedule displays the order of scenes within each shooting day. Once the schedule is finalized, distribute a copy of the one-line schedule to the cast and crew.

| Apr 3, 2009 1:19 PM | Fred and Vinnie Day Out of Days Report for Cast Members | | | | | | | | Page 2 of 4 |

	Month/Day	05/05	05/06	05/07	05/08	05/09	05/10	05/11	05/12	05/13
	Day of Week	Tue	Wed	Thu	Fri	Sat	Sun	Mon	Tue	Wed
	Shooting Day	7	8	9			10	11	12	13
1.	FRED	W	W	W			W	W	W	W
2.	VINNIE	W	W	W			W			W
3.	DAN (V.O.)		W							W
4.	FRED (V.O.)							W		
5.	PAUL							SW	WF	
6.	VINNIE (O.S.)			WF						
7.	LUTHER							SW	WF	
8.	THERESA									
9.	LEO									
10.	MR. BASIN						SW			
11.	VINNIE (V.O.)		WF							
12.	WILLIE							W	WF	
13.	LUTHER (V.O.)	SW	WF							
14.	CUSTOMER 3									
15.	DARLENE						SWF			
16.	FRED AS PIZZA DELIVERY GUY (O.S. from TV)									
17.	CUSTOMER 2									
18.	ADAM									
19.	ATTRACTIVE WOMAN								SWF	
20.	KAREN (V.0.)		SWF							
21.	MANAGER #2									
22.	CELEBRITY #2									SWF
23.	BARBARA									
24.	CHUBBY HISPANIC WOMAN									
25.	CUSTOMER 4									
26.	ANGELA									
27.	TV HUSBAND (O.S. from TV)									
28.	CASTING ASSISTANT						SWF			
29.	MANAGER #1									
30.	BARRY CARLSON						SWF			
31.	FRED'S MOM (V.O.)		SWF							
32.	INTERVIEWER						SWF			
33.	CELEBRITY #1									SWF
34.	STU (V.O.)		SWF							
35.	ANGRY GUY								SWF	
36.	CUSTOMER 1									
37.	DELIVERY GUY									
38.	RESTAURANT MANAGER									
39.	CELEBRITY #3									SWF

Script Dated: 2/13/09   **Jerry P. Magana, Richard Augello**

W (Work): Identifies days the performer is scheduled to perform on shooting days.

H (Hold): Identifies a day off for the performer. Although the performer is still being paid, she is not required to perform on set, rehearse, or travel.

D (Drop): Short for "drop/pick-up," this identifies a time frame between shooting days when a performer is not paid. For union actors working on movies produced in the United States, this time frame must be longer than ten consecutive days, and fourteen consecutive days for films produced outside the United States. "Drop" refers to the time an actor is not on the schedule.

P (Pick-Up): This refers to the date an actor resumes work on a movie after the drop/pick-up time period.

F (Finish): The last day of any obligations the performer has during production.

These designations can be combined, depending on the performer's status on the shoot. For example, an actor who is working on set for only one day will be labeled as SWF, meaning they are starting, working, and finishing their obligations on the same day. Actors who work more than one day will always begin their schedules with a two-letter designation; the first being S to identify their start date, and R if they are rehearsing that day, T if they are traveling, or W if they are working on the first day. The same applies to the final shooting day. TF and WF identify whether the last day is a travel day or a work day.

STEP 6: DURING PRODUCTION

Even though the schedule has been created in preproduction, it will always change and need to be updated throughout production. Two major documents that need to created, updated, and circulated are the contact list and call sheets.

Contact List

Assemble a contact list of each vendor, actor, and crew member and distribute to everyone on the project. Include phone numbers, email addresses, and physical addresses and keep the information updated frequently:

- If working with a well-known actor, do not distribute his or her personal contact information on the contact sheet; instead, use his or her agent's contact information.
- Circulate cast and crew phone lists as soon as possible. Make sure everyone on the production knows how to reach everyone else.
- Keep the contact list updated and distribute the list not only on paper, but also by email, to everyone in the cast and crew.

Call Sheets

Each actor and crew member needs to know where the location is for the next shooting day, the address, and the time he needs to be on set, as well as any information pertinent to the day. This information is relayed on a form called a *call sheet*.

(NAME OF MOVIE)	CALL SHEET		Date:	Tuesday, May 1st, 2007

(NAME OF MOVIE)

CALL SHEET

Date:	Tuesday, May 1st, 2007
Day:	1 of 13
1st Shot:	9:30 AM

Producer: (insert name)
(insert phone number)

Director: (insert name)
(insert phone number)

UPM: (insert name)
(insert phone number)

1st AD: (insert name)
(insert phone number)

Crew Call Time
8:00 AM

Craft Services At:
7:30 AM
Lunch Served
2:00 PM

DAY 1

Weather:	Partly Cloudy
SUNRISE:	6:08AM
SUNSET:	7:32PM
High:	69F
Low:	55F
Hospital	(hospital name)
	(hospital address 1)
	(hospital address 2)
	(hospital phone number)

I/E	SET DESCRIPTION	SCENE	CAST	D/N	PAGES	LOCATION
I	Jim's Office	13	1, 12	D2	3	**(Location name)**
	Jim receives "call to adventure"					**(Location address 1)**
						(Location address 2)
I	Alan's Office	17	2	D2	1 4/8	**(City, State, Zip)**
	Alan writes letter					
	SERIES: A-I					
						(Parking, loading info)
I	Hallway	8	2,3,4	D2	3 5/8	
	Alan and Jim meet	9				
		11				
						CREW PARKING
						free street parking
						always read all signs
						normal traffic laws in effect

				Total Pages:	8 1/8	

#	SWF	CAST/DAY PLAYERS	PART OF	RPT MU/WARD	ON SET	OUT
1	SW	(actor's name)	Jim	8:30 AM	9:30A	
2	SW	(actor's name)	Alan	12:00 PM	1:00 PM	
3	SW	(actor's name)	Sam	2:45 PM	3:30 PM	
4	SW	(actor's name)	Billy-Bob	2:30 PM	3:30 PM	
12	SWF	(actor's name)	Diva Mary	7:45 AM	9:15A	

			ADVANCE SCHEDULE			
DATE	DESCRIPTION	SCENE	CAST	D/N	PAGES	LOCATION
Thursday	Hallway	28	2		1/8	Location #4
May 3rd	Alan's house	29	2		1/8	1234 Main Street
	Alan's house	30	1		1/8	Suite N
	Restaurant	6	1,2		2 3/8	LA, CA 90046
	Green Screen	26	1,2		1/8	
	Green Screen	14	1		2/8	
	Alan leaves	2	1		6/8	

DIRECTIONS TO LOCATION:

FROM Westside Take 43 E to 101N to 112N
FROM Eastside get to 112N
FROM the Valley take 18 East to 5-South to 112N

US-112 NORTH
Take the AVE 40 exit- EXIT 20.
Turn LEFT onto S AVENUE 40.
Turn RIGHT onto Bloom RD.

The 2nd AD compiles call sheets for the next day, with input from department heads. Once approved by the line producer, the 2nd AD distributes the call sheets to each cast and crew member before she leaves the set. Call sheets are updated to reflect overtime, extended turnaround time, and any last-minute changes. The 2nd AD also emails the call sheets to everyone on the production.

Call sheets include:

- The name of the movie
- The date of production
- Day x of y days (day 12 of 16 days)
- Location of the shoot, including address and phone number
- Parking information: where to park and where not to park, including restrictions and time limits
- Contact information for key crew positions
- Suggested dress code (rain gear, cold weather, etc.)
- Scenes scheduled to be shot for the day as well as a brief five- to ten-word description of each scene
- Call times denoting what times cast and crew members need to arrive on set. The call times can be different for various departments, depending on how much work they need to do before the day begins. For example:
    - Hair/makeup: Is there any special-effects makeup that needs to be applied? Or does the hair stylist need to arrive early to create 1950s hairstyles?
    - Grip/lighting
    - Special effects department
    - Stunts
    - Rough schedule for the day
    - Call times for main crew
    - Makeup and wardrobe times
    - Scenes to be shot
    - Travel time, if there is a company move from one location to another
    - Breaks, including meals
    - Estimated wrap time
- Weather forecast for the day of production
- Directions and contact information for the nearest hospital
- Directions and contact information for the nearest police station
- Information on equipment to be used
- Contact information for the production company
- Vendors (companies from which equipment/services are being rented)

When determining what time each department needs to arrive the next day, consider the following:

- When making the call sheet, determine whether actors need to arrive early for makeup, hair, or wardrobe, and schedule the makeup, hair, and wardrobe departments accordingly.

- One of the biggest problems on independent film sets is that cast and crew members are scheduled to be on set all day, even if not needed. This just tires and frustrates the cast and crew, reducing the morale on set. Figure out which scenes are being filmed at what point during the day and schedule the necessary people to arrive half an hour before they are needed, unless special requirements require them to arrive earlier.
- Be sure to create a detailed map with directions to the location from the north, south, east, and west. Drive the directions before you pass them out to the cast and crew to eliminate the possibility of errors.
- Always include the name of a contact person and phone number on the call sheet in the event that cast or crew members get lost en route to the set.
- If traveling from a hotel or if cast and crew members live close to each other, consider carpooling to minimize the number of cars parked at the location.
- Include any parking permits that need to be posted on production vehicles along with the call sheet, if available. All parking details must be handled before the day of production.
- Always bring extra copies of the script, call sheets, deal memos, and all production paperwork on set. Cast and crew members and even the director will invariably forget theirs.

Download a script breakdown template, sample shooting schedule, and a call sheet template from Filmskills.com. See page vi for details.

CHAPTER 5
Insurance

99

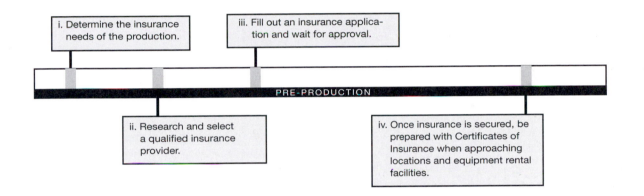

i. Determine the insurance needs of the production.

iii. Fill out an insurance application and wait for approval.

PRE-PRODUCTION

ii. Research and select a qualified insurance provider.

iv. Once insurance is secured, be prepared with Certificates of Insurance when approaching locations and equipment rental facilities.

INTRODUCTION

Anything can happen on a movie set: equipment can be stolen, cast or crew members can be hurt, or locations can be damaged. What happens if a light falls and burns the carpet or a grip trips and sprains an ankle? In each of these instances, you, the filmmaker, are personally liable. With the high costs of equipment replacement or repair, medical costs, and lawsuits, it is essential to have production insurance. In most instances, the production will be required to provide proof of insurance when you rent equipment or use a location.

- Purchase insurance policies for only the time period you need them. If you require a short-term policy, it may be cheaper to buy coverage for a week rather than for one day. If you plan on shooting often during the year, it may be even cheaper to purchase a year-long policy instead of on an as-needed basis.
- Some locations and rental facilities require that they be listed as "additionally insured" on the policy, which ensures that they are recognized and covered by the insurance agency, should a problem occur.
- Be prepared to present a certificate of insurance when approaching a location or rental house. Most will require that you have insurance and the

Filmmaking.
© 2011 Jason J. Tomaric. Published by Elsevier Inc. All rights reserved.

certificate is the proof. To obtain the certificate, simply call the insurance agency and request a copy.

- Be honest with the insurance agency about what you're planning on doing on set. If you're using pyrotechnics, tell them. Although this will raise your premium, the insurance policy *will* cover you should an accident occur. If, for example, you tell them that the entire film will be shot on land and you then do a scene in a boat on the ocean and someone is injured, then the insurance company will decline to cover the accident.
- When choosing an insurance company, make sure they provide production insurance. Homeowner's insurance is not enough and will not cover all incidents that occur on set. In addition, homeowner's insurance covers *only* the owner's home and will not protect the production outside of the home.

INSURANCE TYPES

There are several types of production insurance to choose from; it is best to discuss your needs with a qualified insurance company.

General Liability Insurance

The most common type of insurance policy, general liability insurance, protects you and your production in the event of property damage and claims for personal injury on set. The minimum accepted liability policy covers up to $1,000,000, although several factors will determine how much coverage the policy needs. For example:

- Will you be staging any stunts or other potentially hazardous activities that increase the risk of injury to cast or crew?
- Will you be shooting on or around water?
- Will you be using pyrotechnics, squibs, or explosives?
- Does your location add additional danger, such as shooting near a cliff or in an airplane?

Cast Insurance

Cast insurance reimburses the production company for certain expenses incurred due to the death of, illness, or accident to an insured artist or director.

Film and Videotape Insurance

Especially important when shooting film, this policy covers you if the film is ruined at the lab, there is a problem with the film stock, the film is lost in transit, and so on. The insurance will provide necessary funds to reshoot the footage.

Equipment Insurance

This protects your equipment from theft and damage. Most production companies require that you provide proof of coverage before they rent you equipment. Some rental houses require that you obtain your own insurance; others will add insurance for an additional fee. Be sure to check with the rental company before you arrive to pick up gear.

Worker's Compensation

Worker's compensation covers both employees and volunteers who work for you, should they be injured on the job. This insurance is calculated as a base percentage of the payroll and is required by state law.

Errors and Omissions Insurance

This insurance is generally needed only when a film is picked up for distribution. Distributors do not want to be liable for any legal issues you neglected to resolve. Errors and omissions insurance (or E&O for short) protects both you and the distributor from copyright infringement lawsuits, extras who may not have signed a release form and later sue, or placement of products in the film that you did not get permission to use. Typically, the E&O company will review all your documentation and, by awarding this insurance, confirms that your production has all legal documents in order and assumes responsibility should a law suit arise.

WHAT DO YOU REALLY NEED?

Insurance is an expensive and sometimes confusing aspect of moviemaking. When confronted with the list of potential insurance packages, understand that there are four types of insurance every production needs to purchase:

- **General liability insurance.** Purchase a $1,000,000 general liability policy. Most locations will require at least this amount of coverage, although use of stunts, pyrotechnics, or any other factors outside of what the general policy covers will require an increase in coverage. A one-year $1,000,000 general liability policy in Los Angeles costs around $2150. This premium may change depending on the city in which you live. Although there are short-term policies available, the year-long is the most affordable.
- **Equipment insurance.** Purchase the amount needed to cover the cost of replacement of all the equipment on set. If you're shooting with $100,000 worth of equipment, then purchase a $100,000 equipment insurance policy. All camera and equipment rental facilities will require you to provide proof of equipment insurance before giving you the gear.
- **Worker's compensation.** Any employer must, by law, have worker's comp insurance to cover any injuries to cast and crew on set.
- **Errors and omissions insurance.** Usually purchased when a film is about to be picked up by a domestic distributor, E&O insurance may be paid for by the distributor.

ACORD **CERTIFICATE OF LIABILITY INSURANCE** OP ID JE | DATE (MM/DD/YY)
ORACL-1 | 07/09/02

PRODUCER	THIS CERTIFICATE IS ISSUED AS A MATTER OF INFORMATION ONLY AND CONFERS NO RIGHTS UPON THE CERTIFICATE HOLDER. THIS CERTIFICATE DOES NOT AMEND, EXTEND OR ALTER THE COVERAGE AFFORDED BY THE POLICIES BELOW.
	INSURERS AFFORDING COVERAGE

INSURED	INSURER A:	Insurance
	INSURER B:	
	INSURER C:	
	INSURER D:	
	INSURER E:	

COVERAGES

THE POLICIES OF INSURANCE LISTED BELOW HAVE BEEN ISSUED TO THE INSURED NAMED ABOVE FOR THE POLICY PERIOD INDICATED. NOTWITHSTANDING ANY REQUIREMENT, TERM OR CONDITION OF ANY CONTRACT OR OTHER DOCUMENT WITH RESPECT TO WHICH THIS CERTIFICATE MAY BE ISSUED OR MAY PERTAIN, THE INSURANCE AFFORDED BY THE POLICIES DESCRIBED HEREIN IS SUBJECT TO ALL THE TERMS, EXCLUSIONS AND CONDITIONS OF SUCH POLICIES. AGGREGATE LIMITS SHOWN MAY HAVE BEEN REDUCED BY PAID CLAIMS.

INSR LTR	TYPE OF INSURANCE	POLICY NUMBER	POLICY EFFECTIVE DATE (MM/DD/YY)	POLICY EXPIRATION DATE (MM/DD/YY)	LIMITS	
	GENERAL LIABILITY				EACH OCCURRENCE	$ 1000000
A	X COMMERCIAL GENERAL LIABILITY		04/22/02	04/22/03	FIRE DAMAGE (Any one fire)	$ 50000
	CLAIMS MADE X OCCUR				MED EXP (Any one person)	$ 5000
					PERSONAL & ADV INJURY	$ 1000000
					GENERAL AGGREGATE	$ 2000000
	GEN'L AGGREGATE LIMIT APPLIES PER:				PRODUCTS - COMP/OP AGG	$ 2000000
	POLICY PRO-JECT LOC					
	AUTOMOBILE LIABILITY				COMBINED SINGLE LIMIT (Ea accident)	$
	ANY AUTO					
	ALL OWNED AUTOS				BODILY INJURY (Per person)	$
	SCHEDULED AUTOS					
	HIRED AUTOS				BODILY INJURY (Per accident)	$
	NON-OWNED AUTOS					
					PROPERTY DAMAGE (Per accident)	$
	GARAGE LIABILITY				AUTO ONLY - EA ACCIDENT	$
	ANY AUTO				OTHER THAN EA ACC	$
					AUTO ONLY: AGG	$
	EXCESS LIABILITY				EACH OCCURRENCE	$
	OCCUR CLAIMS MADE				AGGREGATE	$
						$
	DEDUCTIBLE					$
	RETENTION $					$
	WORKERS COMPENSATION AND EMPLOYERS' LIABILITY				WC STATU-TORY LIMITS OTH-ER	
					E.L. EACH ACCIDENT	$
					E.L. DISEASE - EA EMPLOYEE	$
					E.L. DISEASE - POLICY LIMIT	$
	OTHER					

DESCRIPTION OF OPERATIONS/LOCATIONS/VEHICLES/EXCLUSIONS ADDED BY ENDORSEMENT/SPECIAL PROVISIONS

CERTIFICATE HOLDER	N	ADDITIONAL INSURED; INSURER LETTER: ___	CANCELLATION

SHOULD ANY OF THE ABOVE DESCRIBED POLICIES BE CANCELLED BEFORE THE EXPIRATI
DATE THEREOF, THE ISSUING INSURER WILL ENDEAVOR TO MAIL __10__ DAYS WRITTEN
NOTICE TO THE CERTIFICATE HOLDER NAMED TO THE LEFT, BUT FAILURE TO DO SO SHAL
IMPOSE NO OBLIGATION OR LIABILITY OF ANY KIND UPON THE INSURER, ITS AGENTS OR
REPRESENTATIVES.

AUTHORIZED REPRESENTATIVE

ACORD 25-S (7/97) © ACORD CORPORATION 1988

CERTIFICATE OF INSURANCE

When securing a location or renting equipment, you may need to provide proof that the production is insured. The official form that is used is called a "certificate of insurance." You can obtain one for free simply by calling your insurance company and requesting a certificate of insurance. They will ask you the name, address, and phone number of the company or individual you are providing the certificate to and whether you want that company or person to be listed as additionally insured. This will place their name on the policy, so that in the event of a claim, they can call it in and collect for themselves.

CHAPTER 6
Locations

105

| i. Make a list of locations required by the story. | iii. Visit each potential location to make sure both artistic and technical needs are met. | v. Make sure there are no other public events or activities that may interfere with the shooting dates. | vii. Perform a technical walk-through with all department heads to work out artistic and logistical issues. | ix. Return the location to the same condition as when you found it. |

PRE-PRODUCTION | **PRODUCTION**

| ii. Contact the local film commission or a location scout to assist in finding potential locations. | iv. Contact local authorities to secure required permits. Work with police and fire officials if necessary. | vi. Provide a Certificate of Insurance and sign a location agreement with the owner. | viii. Treat the location with respect during production. |

INTRODUCTION

Movies can be filmed either on a soundstage, where sets are constructed and the environment is completely controlled, or at an existing location that meets or can be altered to meet the requirements of the story. Shooting on location can add to the realism of the scene, but can also increase costs and complicate logistics.

Shooting on location presents innumerable challenges that, if unaddressed, can significantly hinder the production process. Remember that locations were built to be functional, not to serve as movie sets, so they often need to be altered to fit the needs of the production. Find locations that require minimal alterations to save money on set construction or dressing.

FINDING LOCATIONS

Scouting locations is the process of researching and looking for places that fit your vision of the setting of the story. Convincing a location owner to allow you to shoot on his property is a lot like selling a product or service, in that you

Filmmaking.
© 2011 Jason J. Tomaric. Published by Elsevier Inc. All rights reserved.

The larger picture is the photo taken during the location scout, and the smaller inset is the actual frame as it appears in the movie "Currency."

have to persuade the owner to accept the inconvenience of having a movie crew present for little or no money. The trick is to sell the story and vision behind the project. Make the owner feel like he is a valuable part of the production process and that his contributions will help make the project successful.

In high-production cities like Los Angeles and New York, the frequency of big-budget movie and television show productions has raised location owners' awareness of location fees, and it's not uncommon for studios to pay thousands – if not tens of thousands – of dollars a day for the use of a location. This is problematic when an independent, low-budget movie producer asks to use the same location. If you can't write a check, then the owner will probably decline your request.

Once secret to finding cheap locations is to get out of the major cities, into smaller, neighboring communities, where movie production isn't as common. The novelty of having a movie made is still an enticing factor that may sway a location owner to allow you to shoot.

Professional productions generally hire a location scout whose job is to look for potential locations that match your vision. Ideally returning with three or four options for each setting, the location scout also makes contact and establishes a relationship with each location owner, should you decide to shoot there. Armed with a still and video camera, the location scout will thoroughly document each location, noting sun position, parking situation, and any other pertinent information that affects the production. You can then choose which locations you like and organize a visit with your department heads.

Jason's Notes

The very first feature I directed, *Clone*, was a locations extravaganza. We shot our low-budget, post-apocalyptic movie in more than 48 locations, including NASA, a nuclear power plant, cathedrals, underground caverns, train stations, high schools, the county courthouse, and many others. The rich look of these locations helped us create a truly expansive world, and the best part was that all the locations were free. Why? We shot in Cleveland, where the community rallied around the project and offered support – something I would have had difficulty finding in Los Angeles.

Some states even offer tax incentives and rebates for productions that shoot in their state. Contact the film commission in each state for more information.

Before you begin searching for prospective locations, list all the locations mentioned in the script, whether they are interior or exterior, and whether the scene needs to be shot during the day or at night. Once the list is complete, you can begin the search.

- Contact the local film commission and send them the list of locations you're looking for. Many film commissions have a file full of production-friendly locations, complete with contact information.

- Patronize businesses you're considering shooting at. Use this as an opportunity to get to know the owner, so that when you approach her with the request to shoot, you're not walking in cold off the street.
- Always scout locations and secure them in writing *before* scheduling cast and crew members. Determining the shooting schedule is largely dependent on location availability, and it's difficult to reschedule people if a location falls though. Location availability will often affect the production schedule.

Jason's Notes

Locations are vital to providing a realistic backdrop for the characters, especially in producing a period movie like *Time and Again*. We used numerous locations, from diners and trailers to prisons and town streets – locations that we never paid a penny for, but were legally allowed to use.

The secret to securing locations is to establish a relationship with the owner of the location and show that you are serious and your production is organized and professional. When we needed a 1950s street for the stickball scene, I looked at several towns before we found Chagrin Falls, Ohio, a quaint country town with the charm and appeal the story needed.

I spent several hours looking at streets and houses, trying to find not only the look I wanted, but also an area that would work logistically. The area we selected was within an eighth of a mile of a municipal parking lot, which the local residents could use to park their cars, allowing us to populate their driveways with our 1950s period cars. Also, there was a clean shot at either end of the street, so I couldn't see modern buildings or freeways from the set.

After I drew up a map of the area, I called City Hall and asked to speak with the mayor. She was very polite, listened to my request, and asked me to submit a proposal. Because I had already done the location scout, I had all the information I needed: not only where I wanted to shoot, but how the logistics could be worked out.

The proposal went well and we were approved for the shoot, but I was asked to pay a $1,000 location fee to shoot. Knowing that that was half the budget, I called the mayor and explained to her that we weren't a Hollywood production, but independent filmmakers making a no-budget movie. All of our locations, props, and wardrobe were donated and the cast and crew were all local volunteers. Once she understood this, she reconsidered and waived the location fee.

We then approached the police chief with our request and began the process of working with local officials to coordinate the closure of four city blocks for the shoot.

When the day of the shoot arrived, everything worked like clockwork and the shoot went without incident. We couldn't have done it without the help of the Chagrin Falls officials, who were exceptionally helpful and accommodating. The moral of the story is that we were able to shut down four residential blocks with the assistance of local officials for free, just by asking.

Film Commissions

When a production company is looking for a city in which to shoot, there are several factors to consider. Permits, local laws regarding film production, tax incentives, and coordination between police, fire, and other city departments will affect the budget and shooting schedule. Because the production company may not be aware of the local regulations and procedures, each state has set up a film commission to work with the production company.

No one knows a location like someone who lives there. Every film commission has a library of photos of production-friendly areas. Call them and ask for help finding the best location for your project.

In addition to state film commissions, large cities may have their own. Film commissions serve to provide the following services to filmmakers:

- **Production manual.** Film commissions usually produce a yearly directory of all the film production personnel, equipment rental houses, casting agencies, hotels, travel accommodations, and postproduction services in the area. This directory is usually free to filmmakers and is a tremendous resource. Get one.
- **Locations.** Film commissions often maintain a database of thousands of photographs of locations available in the region and can assist filmmakers in finding and securing locations. Locations in high-production cities may be broken up into those that are available for free or for a slight fee and those with larger rental costs for bigger budget productions. When shooting in another state, that state's film commission may mail location photos to the producer to assist with finding locations.

- **Coordination with city services.** Film commissions work with the city to help secure permits, coordinate police and fire officials, shut down streets, or perform any other service needed to ensure a smooth production. Without the film commission, filmmakers would need to apply for each of these services separately and could encounter needless delays.
- **Coordination with local residents and businesses.** Film commissions help the filmmaker work with local businesses and residents, especially if production activity interferes with traffic or access to stores and businesses. Film commissions can also help deal with local complaints and concerns over the production.

Film commissions are responsible for increasing film business in their state by promoting and marketing their state's resources to film producers. Tax breaks, state rebate programs, free permits, and other incentives help cities attract productions that could bring in millions of dollars of revenue to businesses, restaurants, and hotels, not to mention the fame a city receives from being the setting for a big Hollywood film.

Film commissions are also sensitive to independent filmmakers whose projects may not carry the financial backing of a Hollywood blockbuster. Independent filmmakers who are successful may just want to come back when they are Hollywood moguls, so film commissions see a low- to no-budget independent film as a possible investment in future business.

Contact your local film commission to arrange details for your next production. Remember, they are a resource: use them.

SCOUTING LOCATIONS

When you visit prospective locations, consider the logistical feasibility in additional to the artistic merit of each location. Unless the space can accommodate the cast and crew, equipment and technical needs, it is worthless, regardless of how perfectly it may match your vision.

Typically, the 1st AD, director of photography, gaffer, key grip, production designer and location scout all visit prospective locations together, with each department head looking to see how they need to alter or work within the space to fulfill the storytelling requirements.

Be aware of the following when scouting a location:

- Bring a digital camera, flashlight, tape measure, electrical outlet tester (available from a hardware store for $5), business cards, a notebook, and a pencil.
- Take pictures or videotape the location during the scout so you can reference it later in preproduction meetings.

- Check for parking availability. Are you permitted to use parking lots? Are there restrictions on parking on the street? What days are designated for street cleaning? Will your parking affect the neighboring residents or businesses? Are certain streets permit-only parking past a certain time? Do you need the police to reserved metered spaces? When issuing call sheets, be sure to include parking restrictions.
- Note where and when the sun rises and sets and where on the location it shines throughout the day. Factor in the sun's position when scheduling the shooting schedule.
- Check to see where the crew can load equipment into the location. Is there a loading dock or cargo elevators you can use? If you're using the regular elevators, do you need protective padding for the walls or floor?
- Determine where you can stage the equipment during the shoot so that it is close to the set, yet secure.

Make sure there is ample parking for production trucks and check clearance heights of trees and building awnings.

- Where can you park the production vehicles? Cast and crew vehicles? Equipment trucks? Is the area secure, or do you need to hire a security guard or assign a production assistant to watch the vehicles?
- Check the breaker box to determine the number of circuits and the electrical load that can be drawn from each. If you cannot identify all the outlets or circuits, consult the building manager or maintenance department for assistance in finding other breaker boxes. Map out the circuits to determine power load.
- Check for anything that may make noise and figure out how to disable it, especially refrigerators and air conditioning units. When turning off a refrigerator, put your keys inside to remind you to turn it back on at the end of the day.

Always take your gaffer, key grip, production designer, 1st AD, and producer with you to locations to work through artistic, technical, and logistical problems.

- Locate the restrooms. If you are shooting in a park or an area without restroom facilities, identify a location to place a portable toilet.
- Determine where you can set up craft services and catering and determine refrigeration, heating, and power requirements.
- Measure the room, including ceiling height and door width. (Can the dolly track fit in the door?) Note the number of windows and doors and what the switches on the wall control.
- Listen for outside sounds, such as nearby airports, trains, freeways, sirens from hospitals, police or fire stations, and schools, that may disrupt the audio. List the times throughout the day that are the busiest: for example, when school lets out, or when air traffic stops for the night. Understanding these schedules will help plan the shooting schedule to compensate for these uncontrollable audio sources.
- If shooting in a public area, make sure that precautions are taken to secure the set. Place warning signs around the perimeter notifying the public of the shoot. Use production assistants to control pedestrian traffic flow, and use caution tape to close off restricted areas. Work closely with the authorities or location owner when coordinating shoots that could potentially affect the public.
- Make sure when shooting in a location such as a restaurant or store that the owner is able to close the business during the shoot. On-set production is difficult enough. Dealing with customers and the associated liability could seriously affect the production.
- Be aware of any art, photographs, posters, logos, or any other copyrighted images on the walls or surfaces that may need to be replaced with approved artwork. Using copyrighted work without permission in the movie increases your liability and exposure to a lawsuit.

Quantus Pictures Inc.

Motion Picture Production Company

July 9, 2002

Dear Chagrin Falls, Water Street Resident,

On Saturday, July 13, 2002 from 1:00pm-6:00pm we will be closing Water Street between West Washington and Center Street for a film shoot. The scene is from a short subject we are producing for international film festival release, tentatively titled, "The Day Bobby Jones Came Home."

"The Day Bobby Jones Came Home" is the story of convicted murderer Bobby Jones who has the chance to exonerate his name by jumping back ten years earlier to the day before he allegedly committed the murder that sentenced him to a lifetime in prison. Falling in love with the sexy diner waitress Awanda in his old home town, Bobby uncovers the true murderer, only to learn that Awanda is the victim. Framed by the very evidence he left during his relationship with Awanda, the police arrest and convict the innocent 15-year-old Bobby Jones, creating a paradox that will haunt Bobby Jones to his death.

The scene we are shooting on Water Street involves several high school kids playing stickball when, for the first time, Bobby Jones sees his younger self.

Because this story takes place in the summer of 1958, we will be bringing in several period cars to park both on the street as well as in various driveways up and down Water Street. We are kindly requesting that, from 1:00pm-6:00pm, you park your cars in the Municipal Lot. Although we will allow local access for residents of Water Street, the street will be closed to public traffic. We would also ask for your support in allowing us to park a period car in your driveway. All shooting and equipment setups will be on the street, so cast and crew will not be on your property for the shoot.

Thank you again for your kind assistance and we're looking forward to making Water Street look terrific! If you have any questions, feel free to call our offices at 216-299-1690.

Warmest regards-

Jason J. Tomaric
Director

This document is intended for reference only and is not intended as a legal binding contract.
©2004 Quantus Pictures, Inc.

- Check to see if you need any special permits from the city or if you are required to have a police officer or fire marshal present during the shoot. Many cities, especially high-production towns, require a fire marshal on set, regardless of whether the shoot occurs on private or public property.
- Locate local hospitals and prepare directions and emergency information for the cast and crew in the event of a medical emergency on set.
- Locate local hotels if the location is distant. Negotiate reduced rates for extended stays.
- Confirm directions to the set and double-check to make sure call sheets and maps are correct. Do not trust online mapping web sites without driving the directions given before the shoot.

When working with location owners, understand that from their perspective, a film crew is like a military invasion – lots of people, equipment, art departments moving furniture and set dressings, grips building rigs around the location – which can be overwhelming. Take the time to thoroughly explain what you are planning to do and always restore a property to its original state.

- Be honest and open with the location owner in terms of what you want to do at the location, the number of people involved, parking needs, power consumption, food usage, if any stunts or pyrotechnics will be required, and if you need to change or move anything. It's better to work out the details in advance than for the location owner to arrive the day of the shoot and be surprised by elements he didn't expect. He would be within his rights to kick the crew off the property.
- Most locations will require you to provide proof of insurance. Insurance will protect you, the cast, the crew, and the location owner in the event that an accident occurs that results in damage to the location or injury. Be prepared to discuss the type and amount of coverage of your insurance policy.
- If you approve of a location, check to see if you need further approvals from neighbors, nearby businesses, or other entities. Some cities require an approval form from neighboring residents and businesses.

Locations to Avoid

Avoid white-walled locations like apartments, classrooms, or offices, unless the white walls are the desired look. These locations are extremely difficult to light and shoot in because preventing the walls from overexposing takes valuable production time. If you have total control over a location, consider repainting the walls a light gray. The walls can be lit to appear brighter, but under normal lighting conditions will read much better on camera than white.

- Be wary of locations with low ceilings that restrict the placement of a microphone boom over the actors or the height at which lights can be rigged.
- When the script calls for a small room, consider shooting in a larger set. It's easy to make a large room appear small by shooting in a corner and creatively dressing the set. It also makes it much easier for the production team

to work by allowing room for placement of lights, camera, and production personnel.

- Avoid any locations that you cannot reasonably control during the shoot. Important factors include shooting in public where people can trespass on set, locations that restrict alterations or moving furniture, noisy locations, and locations that are subject to the weather.
- Be careful when shooting in public – sidewalks, parking lots, and malls expose you to greater liability and require additional production assistants and security to guard equipment and prevent public access to the set.

Securing a Location

If a location serves both the artistic and the technical needs of the production and you and the owner agree to terms of access, payment, and time and date of usage, then you can submit a contractual package to the owner. The package usually includes:

- **Location agreement.** This contract confirms the use of the location, the dates and time of use, what parts of the location the crew is allowed to use, parking, restroom access, craft service/catering setup location, load-in/load-out location, permission to move furniture or rearrange the location, and definition of use of pyrotechnics or stunts. The location agreement also includes the waiver of liability, which protects the owner in the event of an accident on set, acknowledgment of insurance, and any special permission to use the location. Always have a signed location agreement before scheduling and locking that location.
- **Certificate of insurance.** This document, obtained from your insurance company, serves as proof to the location owner that you have production insurance. The certificate also identifies the amount of coverage and can list the owner as additionally insured, essentially placing the owner on the policy.
- **Production schedule.** Give the location owner a schedule for the shooting day so she understands what will be happening at her location. This allows the owner to prepare and know what to expect the day of the shoot.

Once a location is secured, call the local city hall or the film commission to file for any necessary permits.

Download a Location Release Form for use on your production at Filmskills.com. See page vi for details.

COMMUNITY RELATIONS

Permits

Many cities require filmmakers to secure a permit. These permits – which are sometimes free – help the local authorities coordinate with filmmakers to ensure public safety, coordinate traffic and parking, provide necessary police and fire personnel, and schedule public events around the shoot.

- Contact city hall or the chamber of commerce of the city you are shooting in to see what the permitting and insurance requirements are. Be sure to begin the process at least a month before the proposed shoot date.
- Although there may be a fee for the permit or a cost of hiring city officials such as police or firemen, avoid shooting guerilla-style. Permits alert the city of your presence and prevent any other city services from interfering with your shoot. Besides, it is difficult to manage a production when you're always hiding from the police.
- In many instances, shooting in public parks is free, although you still need a permit. Contact the parks and recreation department for details.
- Some cities may require you to hire an off-duty police officer or fire marshal for the duration of the shoot, especially if it involves pyrotechnics, fire, and/or the operation of a generator. Some cities may allow you to negotiate these rates with the individual officers.
- Always carry a copy of the shooting permit with you on set at all times. If the police visit the set, they will ask to see the permit. Have it handy to minimize any delays to shooting. If you choose to shoot without a permit, the police can shut down the production, issue a fine, or even arrest the location manager or producer.
- The local or state film commission may be able to assist in getting city permits through faster or may be able to help get a discount for independent film productions. Most city governments work with filmmakers through the film commission.

Working in a Community

Many people have a rosy view of the film production industry until a production comes to their town. Trucks clogging the road, bright lights and noise at all hours of the night, pushy production personnel, and the general inconvenience of having to work around the film crew often taint this view.

You can take steps to ensure the production experience is pleasant for both the community and the film crew:

- When approaching city council or local authorities, present a professional, organized proposal of what you want to do. Include a letter of introduction, maps and diagrams of the areas you want to shoot in, a list of the number of people involved, insurance information, and any other materials that would make it easier for the city to approve your request.
- If shooting exteriors, alert nearby businesses and residents in writing as to the nature of your shoot and how it will affect them. Be open to addressing any concerns they may have.
- If you require public parking, work with the police to see if they can reserve parking spots for your production vehicles. You may need to pay for the revenue the parking meters could have generated for the city during the time they were reserved for you.

During Production

Once a location has been secured, it's important to respect the location, owners, neighbors, and general public while shooting:

- Be mindful of the behavior of the cast and crew, keep the location clean and neat, and always make sure you put everything back the way you found it.
- Make sure set dressers take detailed photographs around the set to ensure that if something is moved it will be put back in its proper place at the end of the shoot.
- Post signs, especially in public areas, notifying passersby of your activities and alert them that they are potentially in the shot. Consider having a production assistant present at sidewalks to stop pedestrians temporarily while the crew is rolling during a take and manage foot traffic safely around the set.
- If shooting in the owner's home, place cardboard or furniture pads on the floor to avoid dirtying or scratching the floor, especially if setting up dolly track and heavy light stands.

FILMMAKERS' CODE OF CONDUCT

The Los Angeles film production office has compiled the following guidelines for all movie crews shooting on location. Abiding by these unofficial guidelines makes it easier for productions in our industry to shoot in communities, homes, and businesses. Consider distributing these guidelines to all crew members at the beginning of production.

Remember that you are invading someone's personal space when you take over a location. Behave in a way that leaves a good impression of film crews and the industry overall. Don't ruin it for yourself or for the next film crew that comes after you.

- Production companies arriving on location in or near a residential neighborhood should enter the area no earlier than the time stipulated on the permit and park one by one, turning engines off as soon as possible. Cast and crew must observe designated parking areas.

- When production passes that identify employees are issued, every crew member must wear the pass while at the location.
- Moving or towing vehicles is prohibited without the express permission of the municipal jurisdiction or the vehicle owner.
- Production vehicles may not block driveways without the express permission of the municipal jurisdiction or the driveway owner.
- Meals must be confined to the area designated in the location agreement or permit. Individuals must eat within the designated meal area. All trash must be disposed of properly upon completion of the meal.
- Removing, trimming, and or cutting of vegetation or trees is prohibited unless approved by the owner or, in the case of parkway trees, the local municipality and the property owner.
- Always clean up garbage, water bottles, construction materials, food, and paperwork at the end of the shooting day. Try to leave the location in better condition than when you found it, and always haul your own trash away from the location. Do not use public trash containers.
- All signs erected or removed for filming purposes will be removed or replaced upon completion of the use of the location, unless stipulated otherwise by the location agreement or the permit.
- When departing the location, all signs posted to direct the company to the location must be removed.
- Noise levels should be kept as low as possible. Generators should be placed as far as practical from residential buildings. Do not let engines run unnecessarily.
- All members of the production company should wear clothing that conforms to good taste and common sense. Shoes and shirts must be worn at all times.
- Crew members must not display signs, posters, or pictures that do not reflect common sense and good taste.
- Cast and crew are to remain on or near the area that has been permitted. Do not trespass onto a neighboring resident's or merchant's property.
- Cast and crew must not bring guests or pets to the location, unless expressly authorized in advance by the production company.
- Designated smoking areas must be observed, and cigarettes must always be extinguished in butt cans.
- Cast and crew must refrain from using lewd or offensive language within earshot of the general public.
- Cast and crew vehicles parked on public streets must adhere to all legal requirements unless authorized by the film permit.
- Parking is prohibited on both sides of public streets unless specifically authorized by the film permit.
- The company must comply with the provisions of the permit at all times.

Michael K. Brown

Actor - SAG

HM(818) 558-4043
C(818) 416-1699
Actormkb@yahoo

DVD DEMO
2 Minutes

Tara Radcliffe

CHAPTER 7
Casting the Roles

121

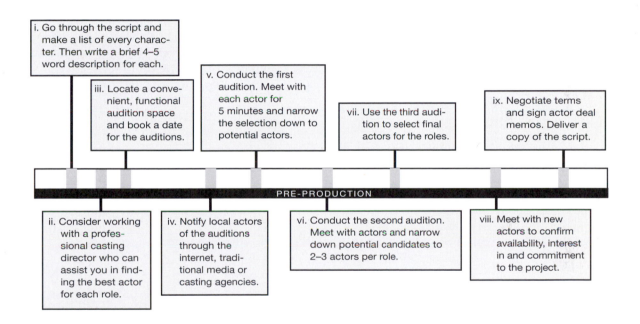

i. Go through the script and make a list of every character. Then write a brief 4–5 word description for each.

iii. Locate a convenient, functional audition space and book a date for the auditions.

v. Conduct the first audition. Meet with each actor for 5 minutes and narrow the selection down to potential actors.

vii. Use the third audition to select final actors for the roles.

ix. Negotiate terms and sign actor deal memos. Deliver a copy of the script.

PRE-PRODUCTION

ii. Consider working with a professional casting director who can assist you in finding the best actor for each role.

iv. Notify local actors of the auditions through the internet, traditional media or casting agencies.

vi. Conduct the second audition. Meet with actors and narrow down potential candidates to 2–3 actors per role.

viii. Meet with new actors to confirm availability, interest in and commitment to the project.

INTRODUCTION

Actors are the life blood of your story. Their portrayal of the characters they play is more engaging to the audience than virtually any other aspect of the moviegoing experience. Actors are also essential in helping to sell the movie to distributors.

An actor, much like a stock, has a perceived industry value that changes from day to day and week to week depending on the success of his past projects, media visibility, and overall industry interest. Producing a movie that features a strong, marketable name actor is one of the biggest determining factors in negotiating a profitable distribution contract.

Filmmaking.
© 2011 Jason J. Tomaric. Published by Elsevier Inc. All rights reserved.

FINDING ACTORS

Casting Directors

Much like other departments in a film production, the casting process is managed by its own team. Led by the casting director, this department is responsible for finding the best possible actors for each role in the script.

Many independent filmmakers working on a budget are hesitant to spend the money on a casting director – a mistake that is rarely made twice, as the casting process is time-consuming, resource-intensive, and requires an intimate knowledge of the regional acting base. For the uninitiated or neophyte filmmaker, casting a film without the aid of a casting director usually yields poor results.

Well-connected casting directors often have a history with recognizable actors, both personally and professionally, and may be able to help get your project in front of the right people. Beware of casting directors who promise access to A-list actors. Unless you're walking to the negotiating table with tens of millions of dollars, a high-powered agent, and a studio deal, odds are they are lying to you.

Breakdown Services

Once you hire a casting director, she will either go through the script herself and generate a list of all the characters in the story, or send the script to Breakdown Services, a Los Angeles–based company that specializes in creating a detailed breakdown of the plot and every character in the movie. Breakdown Services will write a brief character description for each role before submitting the breakdown to agents and managers throughout the industry, who will then refer the actors they think match the breakdown to your casting director to audition. Although this process will cost a little more money, it saves you a lot of time versus finding actors on your own.

Casting Name Actors

The first step to hiring a name actor for your independent film is to develop a script that actors are interested in. Most working actors are hired to play stereotypical roles in major studio films, like Angelina Jolie playing the tough woman in *Tomb Raider*, or Will Smith as the jaded cop in *I, Robot*. Although these are extremely profitable movies and wise business decisions for the high-profile actor, they often provide limited options to the play rich, multifaceted characters most often seen in independent cinema. As an independent filmmaker, your script should be different than the typical Hollywood story, driven by engaging, unique characters more than special effects, explosions and car chases. Such character-driven stories are often attractive to successful actors, giving them an arena to be creative and delve much deeper into the characters they play than do the corporate-tailored, studio-processed, mass-market films you see in the multiplex.

Although you may not have a large budget to work with, many successful working actors may not need money as an incentive to work on your film. They make their money from large studio ventures, television shows, and commercials, and may be enticed by a strong story and a role that challenges their artistic and creative sensibilities.

Jason's Notes

If you have to hire SAG actors, try to hire actors who are Financial Core, a status that allows union workers to work on nonunion projects. This will help you avoid the pitfalls of the SAG low-budget process and free you to screen and market your film any way you wish.

After you've developed your script, create a list of name actors you could envision playing the principal or supporting roles. Don't be afraid to think big – you never know who may say yes to you. As you're generating your list, divide your actor choices into two categories: actors you have a good shot at signing, and the dream list. Although you shouldn't hesitate to approach the management of all the actors on your list, be realistic about who may respond and always have a backup plan.

Benefits of packaging actors:

- **Casting recognizable actors can help attract investors to your project.** Investing in a film project is an extremely risky venture, and having a bankable actor in your film increases distributor interest. If you have already produced a successful, distributed film, some distributors may be willing to write a letter of intent stating their nonbinding interest in distributing your current project. This commitment can help allay some of your investors' fears by increasing the likelihood of distribution and thus offering a higher potential return on investment.
- **Name actors can increase the profit margin of your movie.** Distributors are not only more likely to pick up a movie, but have a greater chance at selling it, if there are marketable names attached. Think about it from the audience's perspective. You're looking for a movie at your local video store on a Friday night. Are you more likely to rent a movie with a recognizable actor on the box than an unknown? Most people are. This form of product branding helps assure, sometimes incorrectly, the customer of a high-quality product. In both domestic and foreign markets, audiences will often watch a movie strictly because one of their favorite actors is in the film. As a result, distributors are willing to pay you more money for the right to distribute your movie because they know they will make more money.
- **Name actors help attract other name actors.** There is a phenomenon that occurs in Hollywood wherein people suddenly become interested in a project if everyone else is interested. It can be tremendously challenging to attain this critical mass of interest, but once you sign one name actor, the second name actor is even easier and the third yet easier still to sign. Having the commitment of several successful actors brands your project as being worthy and of interest, making it attractive to others. If there is a hot project in town, everyone wants to be a part of it.

Jason's Notes

Distributors will ask you five questions about your film. yeah ... what's it about?
Who's in it? Who's in it? Who's in it? Who's in it? And oh

Director Steve Skrovan, Fred Willard, and I are on the set of *Fred and Vinnie*. Even though we hired Fred for only one day of shooting, his presence in the film helped us negotiate a better distribution deal.

■ **Name actors are often good actors.** But not always. One challenge in casting name actors is that although they may help sell your movie, they may not be the best performers, or the right actor for the role. This is often a cause for argument between directors and producers. Producers want marketable names, regardless of their acting ability to help them close a profitable distribution deal. Directors often want the best actors to realize their vision for the characters in their story. In some instances, these two goals are mutually exclusive, so work closely to settle any casting conflicts by erring on the side of marketability. A good film isn't worth much if audiences don't have the chance to see it.

Name actors can certainly help increase the value of your movie in the eyes of distributors. Unfortunately, they can be both cost-prohibitive and a scheduling challenge.

■ **Consider casting a name actor in a small role that may require only a day or two of shooting.** The shorter the time requirement, the easier it will be to sign a name actor. If you're shooting a feature film, limit the actor's schedule to two weeks. Productions longer than two weeks will likely scare people away as bigger, more profitable jobs may come up.

■ **Shoot near the actors' home city.** Name actors are more likely to participate in a low budget movie if the shoot is close to where they live. Asking an actor to travel will force you to incur travel and accommodation costs, higher fees, higher per diems, and a higher day rate.

Once you have your list of potential actors, you need a way to reach them. One option, if they have representation, is to contact their agents or managers directly. You can find this information, and a variety of other pertinent business information, on www.imdbpro.com. For an inexpensive yearly membership, you can access one of the Internet's most comprehensive industry online directories. Search for any actor or crew member to find a list of career credits, box office statistics, contact information, representation, photos, and inside industry information.

Contact each agent and manager and request the procedure for submitting your script. Keep in mind that agents and managers make their money by earning a percentage of every job they bring in for their clients. In California, state law allows licensed agents to take 10% of the gross earnings of their clients; managers, who are unlicensed and unregulated by the state, typically take 15% of their client's gross earnings. This can pose a problem for the low-budget producer: without a substantial budget, many agents and managers won't even consider your project because it is unprofitable for them.

The workaround is to take advantage of personal relationships you have with name actors. This can be difficult if you haven't worked in Hollywood or don't know many people in the industry, so use your contacts and connections to help get your script in the right hands.

Jason's Notes

Although casting name actors will make it more difficult to schedule your movie, the end results are usually worth the effort.

Casting name actors is a delicate balancing act that requires special skill to appease the actor's agent or manager, enough space in the actor's schedule, and the actor's willingness to work on a low budget project, especially with a neophyte director or producer attached. The more organized and professional your approach, the greater your chance of landing a meeting with the actor to pitch your project.

Actors, especially those who are already established, want to feel confident that the directors they work with are going to make them look good and help them play a character different than they have played before. Actors are looking for projects that will help improve their careers, marketability and industry exposure. Agents and managers will always ask to see a sample of your work and your resume. If you don't feel that either of these are strong enough, consider shooting a short film to highlight your strengths and abilities before pursuing your feature. Remember that this actor is approached by producers and directors of all levels of the industry, and to get the actor to consider your project, you need to demonstrate the ability to produce content on par with other directors.

Be smart about the type of project you choose to produce and which actors you approach. Your timing and approach is everything.

Casting Unknowns

Casting directors can be incredibly helpful in finding undiscovered talent. These "unknown" actors are abundant, especially in Los Angeles, but despite the sheer numbers of people who dream of Hollywood stardom, very few are both technically equipped and talented enough to convincingly play the intricacies of a character on screen.

To sift through the thousands of actors, a casting director will set up auditions to methodically test each person, eventually whittling the potential finalists down to a mere handful. This daunting and exhausting task is best handled by an industry insider who knows the agencies, the agents, the managers, and any accomplished, talented working actors.

Jason's Notes

The casting process is all about finding the one diamond among thousands of pieces of coal. There are some amazing unknown actors in the world. The challenge is finding them.

Neither Brian Ireland nor Jennie Allen had ever acted before, making *Time and Again* their debut movie. Despite their inexperience, both Jennie and Brian delivered exceptionally strong performances, helping us secure distribution for the movie.

The cost of hiring a casting director can save you a lot of time and aggravation and will yield better actors than if you were to take on the task yourself.

Although it takes time to find them, there are a number of extremely talented actors, any of whom could play any role of your film brilliantly. It's simply a matter of time, money, and resources to find them. Be aware, however, that although unknown actors may be perfect for the role, their marketability to distributors is extremely low.

- **Avoid casting friends and family.** Although your close acquaintances may be ready and willing, the quality of your movie will undoubtedly suffer. Acting is a skill that requires years of training and mastery to be effective, invisible, and moving. Unless your family or friends are professional actors, avoid the potential for damaging performances.
- **Stage actors.** Many towns and cities have local theatre groups full of talented stage actors. Think twice before hiring stage actors, especially in critical roles. They are trained to give big performances to the audience members in the back row of the theatre and often lack the experience to render the subtleties required of a convincing on-camera performance. You may find that when you are directing a scene, you are constantly trying to "pull back" a performance. Instead of directing the subtext and nuances of a performance, you will be spending your time reigning in the actor's over-the-top rendering of the role.

Casting on Your Own

If your budget doesn't allow the hiring of a casting director, you can cast the movie yourself, using one of two approaches. The first is to post a general audition notice in newspapers, acting magazines such as *Backstage West*, classified

"Time and Again" Character and Casting Information

MAIN CHARACTERS:

Bobby Jones - Built white male mid-late 20's, escaped prisoner convicted for murder who maintains his innocence.
Awanda - Late 20's early 30's buxom 1950's diner waitress. She knows what she wants and can play men like cards. Has strong sexual presence.
Karl the policeman - 40's white stocky male, small town Sheriff, knows everybody and his very presence keeps the peace.

SUPPORTING CHARACTERS:

Prison Escapees (2) - 30's-40's stocky males (race unimportant), prison convict type
Prison Guards (4) - Men 30's-40's
Teacher - Early 30's pretty white female school teacher
Man in Diner-60's-70's an old timer who probably started eating in the diner when it first opened
Diner Waitress - White female, mid-late 20's high school student?
Policemen (2)- 30's-40's white male
Adam and teenage friends(5) - High School students mixed races and sexes
Young Bobby - 15 year old built white boy, is younger version of Bobby Jones
Bobby's Mother - early 50's white housewife.
Bobby's Father - early 50's white blue collar man

About the Story:

"Time and Again" is the story of convicted murderer Bobby Jones who has the chance to exonerate his name by jumping back ten years earlier to the day before he allegedly committed the murder that sentenced him to a lifetime in prison. Falling in love with the sexy diner waitress Awanda in his old home town, Bobby uncovers the true murderer, only to learn that Awanda is the victim. Framed by the very evidence he left during his relationship with Awanda, the police arrest and convict the innocent 15-year-old Bobby Jones, creating a paradox that will haunt Bobby Jones to his death.

About the Director:

Jason J. Tomaric has directed several productions including television commercials and music videos for clients such as McDonald's and RCA Records. Having recently won five national Telly Awards, Tomaric's most well-known work is the feature-film, "Clone" that premiered in Cleveland's lavish Palace Theatre.

About the Writers:

Written by Jason J. Tomaric and internationally-renowned writer Bob Noll, Bob Noll now teaches script writing at several venues including John Carroll University and the Cleveland Film Society. After working in Los Angeles for several major studios, Bob Noll is the recipient of dozens of international awards and enjoys worldwide publishing success of hundreds of scripts.

The Purpose of this Project:

"Time and Again" is being produced for two purposes: to produce an educational DVD for independent filmmakers to teach the filmmaking process, and to provide content for the international film festival market as a way of increasing the filmmakers' exposure in the industry.

ads in the newspaper, web sites like www.craigslist.org, and announcements on the local news. The benefit is that hundreds of people may show up; the downfall is that the general notice will also attract a lot of unqualified actors who will take a lot of time to sift through. Casting a wide net will collect a lot of fish both talented and untalented.

- When you are publicly promoting the auditions, list each role you are casting and a brief description of the character. For example, Edward is a 32-year-old single slacker who lives with his mom and edits at the local news station. This should help roughly narrow down the actors who come to the audition.
- Post an audition notice on www.craigslist.org. This free online worldwide bulletin has grown increasingly popular and is an outstanding way of reaching the masses.
- Contact local community theatres, theatre guilds, and university acting programs to spread the word of the upcoming auditions.
- Get a copy of the local film commission production manual and look up the casting agencies in your area. Often times, these agencies sign on talented actors with little experience, so the agency may be willing to direct those actors to your audition.

The second approach to finding qualified actors is to use online casting resources like www.actorsaccess.com, www.nowcasting.com, and www.LAcasting.com. Actors pay a small yearly fee to list their head shot, resume, and demo reel, and producers can view these profiles for free.

Jason's Notes

Remember these sites:

- www.actorsaccess.com
- www.backstagewest.com

- www.craigslist.org
- www.LAcasting.com
- www.nowcasting.com

When casting a project, producers or casting directors enter descriptions for each character – physical attributes, abilities, and personality information. All the actors whose profiles match your posting are immediately contacted and have the opportunity to respond to you. Within hours, you will have hundreds of responses from interested actors. Comb through the responses and look at the actor's head shot. If you think the actor has the right look for the part, invite him or her to the audition.

This approach to selecting actors will help ensure that the actors that arrive to the audition at least have the right look for the part, saving you time and money in the audition process.

Working with Casting Agencies

If you're planning to shoot in a smaller city where there isn't a lot of film or video production, contact local casting or modeling agencies. Casting agencies represent actors and models and assist filmmakers in finding the right actor for the part, provided that the actors will be paid. For a percentage of the actor's wages, the casting agency negotiates terms on the actor's behalf, finds work by soliciting production companies looking to cast, sets up auditions, and negotiates pay wages. Although casting agencies look for paying productions, independent films are a terrific opportunity for new, inexperienced actors to build a demo reel and add credits to their resumes, so don't be afraid to contact casting agencies and propose your project to them. The more professional the presentation, the greater the likelihood that the agency will assist you with your casting needs.

Casting agencies not only help cast lead and supporting characters, but also extras. We relied heavily on Stone Talent and Model Management for the extras casting in my feature *The World Without US*.

Many agencies only represent print models – people with extensive posing and modeling experience but little acting experience. Although this talent will certainly look good on camera, you may have difficulty getting a strong, natural performance.

AUDITIONING ACTORS

Auditions are the process of finding the best actor to play each role in the film. It can sometimes be complicated because as a director, you're forced to select strangers with whom you will be working for possibly months on a project.

When a movie is finished, the believability of the story hinges on the quality of the acting, so it's important to find actors who can convincingly play the role while working professionally on the set.

Finding an audition space

The goal of auditioning is to systematically meet and cast your actors from a vast pool of acting talent. Finding an audition space that is easily accessible, well laid out, and allows for the organized processing of actors will not only help the auditions run smoothly, but also let prospective actors know that the movie is being produced by professionals.

Casting facilities vary from project to project and budget to budget. In major production cities, there are spaces available for rent specifically designed for auditions. With rental rates averaging $15 to $50/hour, these facilities offer a waiting area for actors and a private room to conduct the audition.

If professional casting facilities are not available, consider booking a school classroom on a weekend or a library conference room. Both of these facilities can be inexpensive, are centrally located, are easy to find, and provide a large holding and private auditioning area. Be sure to select an area that will afford you privacy. Avoid booking your auditions in a functioning business like a coffee shop or restaurant, because the influx of actors may disrupt the business' normal clientele.

- **Don't hold auditions in your house or apartment.** Not only will your home be unable to accommodate the sheer number of people who will show up to the audition, but it is also unprofessional and dangerous. Casting strangers and members of the opposite sex from your home can increase your liability. Always cast in a public facility.

Jason's Notes

When producing an independent film, you are auditioning for the actors as much as they are auditioning for you.

Present a professional, organized appearance, beginning with the auditions.

- **Find a large, central, easy-to-get-to location** like a library, office building, school gym, or classroom to hold the auditions. It will make publicizing the audition easier and establish you as a professional. Most public buildings with meeting rooms will allow you to use them for free if your project is not-for-profit. The more recognizable and easy to find the audition space is, the better your turnout will be.
- When setting up the audition space, designate a large waiting room for the actors to wait in and a second room to for conducting the individual auditions. Station a production assistant in the waiting area to distribute the audition forms, collect headshots and resumes, lead the next actor into the audition area, and manage the incoming actors.
- Consider setting up a television in the waiting area to show clips from previous films you've worked on to excite the actors as they wait.

Jason's Notes

For *Time and Again*, I contacted a local independent casting agency, North Coast Central Casting, which used the top floor of a martial arts dojo for meetings and auditions. Because most actors in Cleveland knew where it was, it made sense to hold the auditions there.

I spoke with the owner, Ray Szuch, and he let us use the space for free for six hours on a Saturday afternoon. We had over 300 people show up to audition and everything worked out without a problem.

Preparing for the Audition

It is important that you and your casting director are clear on what will happen in the auditioning room in advance. Be prepared with everything you need for the auditions to run smoothly.

- **Check-in sheet.** Create a check-in sheet with a space for the actors' name, phone number, and the role for which they are auditioning. Every actor should sign in upon arrival. The casting assistant will then use this sheet to call each actor into the audition.
- **Audition schedule.** If you are expecting a large turnout, consider providing an audition schedule so actors can choose a one-hour time window to return to audition. This will prevent actors from having to wait for hours on end for their turn, allowing them to run errands instead of sitting in the waiting room. You can reasonably schedule 15–20 actors per hour for the first audition. Be aware that not every one will show up to the audition. I usually find that we have 60–75% turnout based on the number of actors who accept the audition. In professional auditions, actors are given a specific time to audition. If they fail to show up on time, they usually lose their opportunity to audition.
- **Information sheet.** Ask each actor to fill out an information sheet that contains their contact information, personal statistics, acting experience, union affiliation, representation and availability. Leave a space so the casting director can make notes about each actor during the audition. Staple this sheet to her head shot and resume.
- **Sides.** Sides are selected scenes from the script you want each actor to read. When choosing the sides, find three scenes of varying emotional intent and intensity. You want to see each actor's range and ability to deliver an array of interpretations of the character. Post the sides online so actors can download the material in advance and always have extra copies in the waiting area. Remember, the more prepared the actors are, the better the performance and the better of an idea you will get of their abilities.
- **Video Camera.** Consider video taping the auditions so you can compare performances later. You will see a lot of actors, and it's easy to forget who's who. Be sure to have adequate lighting and a good microphone.
- **Reader.** Many casting directors will hire a reader to read opposite the auditioning actor. This will help you focus on the actor's performance, and not worry about reading the other part.
- **Water.** Auditions can be a long and grueling process. Be sure to bring plenty of fluids and a snack. Never eat during an audition: this is extremely unprofessional and inconsiderate to the actors.

Download a blank Audition Form for use on your production at Filmskills.com. See page vi for details.

AUDITION FORM

You are auditioning for (title of project) which will be shooting in (list dates). Please understand that this project is a low-budget, non-paid production. Please print clearly and include your headshot and resume with this audition form. Thank you.

Personal Information

Name _____

Age _____ Sex _____ Ht. _____ Wt._____ Hair Color _____ Eye Color _____

Address _____

_____

Phone _____ Cell _____

E-Mail Address _____

Professional Experience

Film/Television Experience _____

_____

Are you available during these dates and times?:

(list production dates)   YES   NO

                                                         YES   NO

Are you affiliated with an agency or union? _____

Understanding that, due to budget restrictions, you will not be paid, why are you interested in participating in this production?

_____

For Office Use Only

NOTES

The First Audition

Auditioning is a nerve-wracking experience for the actor, and it's your job to make them feel as comfortable as possible. The more comfortable the actor, the better the performance, and the better the performance, the more of their skill level you will see.

■ **Beginning the audition.** When you're ready for the first audition, have one of the production assistants from the waiting area bring the first actor to the audition room. When the actor enters, greet him, take his audition form and headshot, and thank him for coming. Always be polite and courteous; these actors are taking time out of their schedules to come to your audition with the hopes of helping you and getting a role. Be appreciative and respectful of that.

■ **The monologue.** After the introductions, if you require a monologue from the actors, ask the actor to begin and watch for body language and believability. In major cities like Los Angeles and New York, experienced actors rarely, if ever, use monologues for auditions and are accustomed to performing a dry read of the script. Monologues are valuable for seeing an actor perform a piece with which he is comfortable.

Sometimes you just know when the actor is the right choice the moment she walks through the door. This certainly was the case with Angela Nicholas, whom we cast in the lead role of Kitty Drysdale in my film *Currency.* Her poise, range, and depth of character were apparent in both the auditions and on set.

■ **The first read.** After about 30 seconds, stop the actor, even if he's not finished with the monologue, and give him a two-page scene from a script other than from the movie you're casting for. Some directors don't like to use the script from the movie, as this may give the actor they're auditioning a premature idea of the character. Character development should happen between the director and the actor in a rehearsal setting, not the audition. Instead, use a script from another movie with a similar tone, characters, and dialog similar to those of the film you're casting for. Briefly introduce the scene and explain what is happening: "You are playing the role of the factory worker, Joe, who just left work after finding out he's been laid off. This scene takes place in the diner across the street from the factory between Joe and his old friend, Jean, the waitress." After the actor briefly reads over the script, have him perform the scene. Watch for realism and spontaneity in the performance.

- **Give direction.** After the scene is finished, ask the actor to perform the scene again, this time changing the approach to how he accepts direction: "Try it again, but this time, instead of being laid off, you just received a $5,000 bonus." Watch carefully to see how well the actor takes last-minute direction, how he changes his approach, and if he successfully incorporates your new direction into the scene. This is an important skill for the actor to have – there are often directorial changes on set to which the actor must quickly adjust.
- **Wrap up.** After the second read, thank the actor and, if you feel he may be right for the part, give him a flyer for the callback, or second audition, the following week. Be sure to have the second auditions already scheduled so that you can invite actors to it during the first audition. If you don't like his performance, thank the actor for coming in and politely let him know that you will be notifying him of the audition results. Have a production assistant draft a friendly email and send it to the actors you did not choose. Be sure to thank them for their time, as you may work with them in the future and you shouldn't burn any bridges. In Los Angeles and New York, producers hardly ever notify actors who are not called back.
- **The next actor.** Once the actor leaves, the production assistant from the waiting area should bring in the next person. Each audition should last about five minutes and is designed for you to quickly determine whether you could see each actor as one of the characters.

Auditions are mentally and physically draining for the director and the casting director. Being prepared will help you make the best choice for each role after the auditions conclude.

- In nonproduction cities, few auditioning actors may have headshots. Be prepared by bringing a digital camera to photograph each auditioning actor as a reference. Attach the photo, headshot, and resume to the audition form.
- If videotaping the auditions, have each actor face the camera and state her name before beginning the audition to help you keep track and identify each actor.
- When auditioning an actor, and before casting her for a role, look for the following attributes during the audition.
  - **Physical traits.** Does the actor look the part? You have a vision for what each character should look like, and this mindset can be both a strength and a drawback. Keep an open mind if an actor delivers a terrific performance but might not look the way you envisioned. It's better to have a good performance than a good look.

- **Vocal traits.** Does she sound real and convincing? You shouldn't see a big difference between the actor's persona when she enters the room and when she begins to act. Acting is very much being an extension of yourself. Acting should sound natural, believable and convincing. If an actor jumps into "actor" mode for the audition, then you may have a problem on set trying to get a realistic performance.

- **Personality.** Is the actor easy to work with and friendly? Avoid prima donnas – egocentric and self-absorbed actors. They are difficult to work with and often put themselves before the material.

- **Directability.** Does the actor respond well to your direction or is there resistance or no change in performance? On set, last-minute changes to the script happen often and actors need to respond accordingly. Some actors lock into an approach or motivation for their character and have a difficult time changing. The ideal actor is malleable, open to change, and willing to experiment with different approaches to their character.

Good actors like Julian Starks from my film *Currency* are easy to work with – they know their jobs, and they do them well.

- **Technical skills.** Does the actor understand technical acting: finding the key light, hitting his mark, opening his body to the camera? You may be able to coddle inexperienced actors through the ups and downs of an individual performance, but it is more difficult teaching them how to find their mark or work off a key light. Experienced actors, however internal their performance, know how to balance their art with the technical requirements of shooting the scene.

- **Professionalism.** Will she be on time and remain dedicated to the production? Is she reliable? Will she have done her homework: developing the back story, understanding her character's arc, arriving on set with all the lines memorized?

- **Acting ability.** Can he deliver a convincing performance? Is it real, believable, and engaging?

- **Experience.** What has the actor done before? Has she worked on movies or television shows before? How can this experience help her play the part?

Audition Warning Signs

The audition process is a short period of time relative to the length of a film shoot, so selecting the right actor for a role is critical, from both a creative and a professional standpoint.

Use the casting process to find an actor who fits the role, has a good work ethic, is excited about the project, understands the financial limitations of a low-budget project, and acknowledges the intense schedule and the need to sacrifice outside activities for the sake of shooting the film. If an actor has even the slightest reservation about any of these points in the audition, no matter how small, then chances are good that these problems will reoccur later in production when it's too late to recast.

There are a number of warning signs to look out for during and after the audition:

- Beware the actor who questions the lack of pay and expresses concern about his financial ability to get involved. If he behaves as though he is doing you a favor by being in your movie, recast the part immediately.
- An experienced actor who patronizes you, especially if you're new to film-making, is an immediate warning sign that can develop into a major problem on set. It is difficult for you to do your job when the actor constantly questions your experience and skill set.

Jason's Notes

It's better to recast a problematic actor at the audition phase than in the middle of production when it's too late. Be hypersensitive to any early warning signs you may see.

- Actors who question the project's time requirements or mention a job schedule that may be difficult to work around may not show up on set if their boss schedules them to work.
- Actors with no prior experience may seem excited at first, but the time demands and intensity on set may turn them away from the project later.
- Actors who want rewrites of the script before learning and understanding their characters are not interested in your vision but their own.
- An actor who shows up late to the auditions may have difficulty committing to the scheduled production times.
- Actors who show up to auditions without memorized monologues, head-shots, or resumes. Be especially wary of people who arrive "off the street" with only a Polaroid or family picture. They are not professionals.

If you notice any of these warning signs, no matter how subtle, seriously consider casting a different actor. It's better to recast in the audition phase then halfway into production.

The Second Audition

The second audition is similar to the first; however, this time you know that the attending actors meet your initial physical requirements of the characters, they have an acting ability that you would be content with, and you could see them playing a character in your story. The purpose of the second audition is to work further with each actor so you can whittle down the potential actors to a very short list of two or three actors per role.

The first audition is a cold read; this time, allow the actors more time to go over the sides to build a character, understand the scene, and even memorize the lines. Some directors avoid using scenes from their movie, instead choosing similar scenes from other scripts from which the actors read.

Angela Nicholas and Kelley Robin Hicks auditioned together for the roles of Kitty and Dana, which gave me a chance to see their chemistry together – a chemistry that was critical to the plot of the movie.

Begin the audition by having the actor perform each scene three different times, prompting him with different emotional subtexts for each performance. Watch for the range of his performance, believability, and realism, and, most importantly, how he responds to your direction. Be aware of how the chemistry is shaping between you and the actor. If he is invested in the part and agreeable to your direction, the relationship should feel very easygoing and kinetic.

If you like an actor and can envision her playing one of the roles, chat with her about why she wants to do the movie, her availability, and what her interests are. Learn more about her personality and what it would be like to work with her for months on set.

Each of the second auditions can last ten to fifteen minutes and should result in two or three finalists for each main role. Within a couple of days, call the actors you'd like to see a third time and invite them to the third and final audition.

The Third Audition

The third audition is the last round, in which you choose the actors for the roles. At this point, you should know the individual capabilities of each actor but not yet the chemistry between actors.

I have a pretty unorthodox approach to the third audition, in which I put all the actors in the same room, pair them up, and have them act out scenes together to see how they relate, who works well with whom, and what the chemistry is like between them.

Jason's Notes

It's all about the chemistry. Casting actors is like play-   click with each other – especially if there's a love inter-
ing matchmaker. You want to find the people who really   est between characters.

What's interesting about this approach is that all the actors become much
more comfortable with each one another and the material, so they feel more
confident, their personalities come out, and you get a sense of who they are as
individuals.

You can immediately tell who will get along with whom, which actors are the
scene hogs, the introverts, the sensitive types, the pranksters, and the intellec-
tuals, so take advantage of this by pairing up different people to see how the
dynamics of the scene changes with each actor. This is a great way of casting
the lead roles.

By the end of the audition, you should have a pretty good idea of which actors
you want to cast. Be sure to thank all the actors and tell them that you will
notify them of your final casting decision in a week.

After the Auditions

After the third audition is complete and the final contenders have been nar-
rowed down to one actor per role, meet with each actor and discuss the project
in greater detail. Explain the production requirements, on-set demands, possibility of shooting pick-up shots even after the film is edited, Automated Dialog
Replacement (ADR) and voice-over requirements, and all other expectations
before signing the actor deal memo. This is especially important with inexperienced actors and will reduce the likelihood of them dropping out of the project in the middle of production.

If you are dealing with professional actors, work with their agents and managers to negotiate pay, project time requirements, hours worked, on-set
perks, travel and hotel accommodations, pick-up shoot schedule, residuals or
deferred pay schedules, and any number of deal points before the actor's management will recommend accepting the project. Some of the deal points actors
may want to negotiate:

- **Restricted days or hours of shooting.** Actors may only offer their services
  during a small window of time and want to be contractually held to that
  window.
- **Specific hotel and travel accommodations.** Actors may require to be flown
  first class and housed in five-star hotels. They may want a driver or a limou-
  sine for transport to and from set.

Quantus Pictures Inc.

Motion Picture Production Company

To the cast of "Time and Again"

Dear Sirs and Madams,

Congratulations on winning your role in the short film tentatively titled, "Time and Again." I thank you most sincerely for your interest and willingness to work on this project and hope that this will be a mutually-beneficial venture for everyone involved. The purpose of this project is twofold: practice our art form so as to improve our story-telling abilities as director, actors and crew members and to create a piece to run the worldwide film festival circuit in an effort to circulate our work in the mainstream.

My team and I pride ourselves on crafting top-quality productions in a time-conscious and budget-sensitive manner. We respect your time as much as your talent and will maximize our efforts in the allotted time. Therefore, by the end of June when I return from my trip, we will have a final call sheet and shot breakdown for you. Our goal is always to minimize the on-set surprises by properly preparing every detail beforehand.

Enclosed, please find a copy of the shooting script as well as an Actor Deal Memo. This legal document is a standard form that acknowledges our working relationship on this project. If you should have any questions about this form, do not hesitate to contact me. If you agree to all the terms, please sign it and return it to the address on the letterhead. Be sure to make a copy for yourself.

Please plan on a cast meeting on Saturday, June 29, 2002 in the evening. I will contact you about a location when I return. The purpose of this meeting is to read through the script, discuss the characters, plan on the look and feel of the project, discuss schedules, shooting dates and times, and how our sets operate. This is a critical meeting that everyone is strongly requested to be in attendance.

Although there is written dialogue, the success of "Time and Again" will come from your characterizations through the dialogue. MEMORIZE your lines and know them well. Then we can play with delivery and create some memorable moments.

Thank you again for your participation and I am honored and very excited about working with you. Happy reading and feel free to call me at any time if you have any questions.

Most sincerely,

Jason J. Tomaric
director

- **Specific hair/makeup artists.** Many actors require a production to hire their personal makeup artists and hair stylists.
- **Food requirements.** Specific menus or food items may be required on set.
- **On-set accommodations.** Many actors may require a trailer or private area set aside for them to review their lines during set-ups. Generally the bigger the actor, the bigger the trailer.
- **Credits and billing.** Name actors may specify in a contract where in the credits their names appear and whether they get single credit billing or the screen is shared with another actor's name. Co-producer or associate producer credits can also be given to further incentivize actors.
- **Any other demands.** From gyms on set to agreements that the crew never talk or make eye contact, actors often provide seemingly outlandish requirements, but it is your job as producer to satisfy these requirements if you really want a particular actor in the movie.

Often, professional actors have numerous conflicting project offers and will take whichever project pays the most or is of the most interest. This can make scheduling the movie difficult for the producer, but is an unfortunate part of the business. I have known actors to hold off producers until the day before production was to begin before calling to accept or decline the role. Be prepared for this and have a backup actor if you're not able to cast your primary choice in a timely manner.

Do not release your second and third casting choices until the primary choice has accepted the role and signed a deal memo. Once you are confident, be sure to call each finalist and thank him for his time.

After you congratulate the actors on winning their respective roles, present them with a packet that includes a letter of introduction and welcome, a production schedule, an actor deal memo, a rehearsal schedule, a character description, and a list of contact numbers for key crew people.

Now that the auditions are finished and your actors are cast, schedule the first rehearsal and script read through within the first week following the final audition.

CHAPTER 8
The Crew

i. Your shot list and the budget determine what crew positions are needed to fill on the set.

iii. View demo reels and resumes. Set up interviews with potential candidates.

v. Grant the director of photography, production designer and unit production manager the ability to hire department heads.

vii. Department heads will hire subordinate crew members. Hires must be approved by the line producer.

PRE-PRODUCTION

ii. Solicit potential crew members online or through a film commission.

iv. Hire the director of photography, production designer and unit production manager first.

vi. Approve hires of department heads.

viii. Once hired, crew members must sigh a crew deal memo that outlines the terms of their employment.

INTRODUCTION

From cinematographers, boom operators, costume designers, and production designers to property masters, hairstylists, grips, and assistant directors, there are many creative people involved in providing the technical and creative support to help you realize your vision.

I had a crew of more than 50 people for a national commercial I directed in Los Angeles. Although it may seem difficult to manage, a properly run film set is very similar to a military operation, where each person knows his specific role and to whom he reports.

Filmmaking.
© 2011 Jason J. Tomaric. Published by Elsevier Inc. All rights reserved.

Although the number of people listed in the credits of a Hollywood movie may seem extreme, each crew position is essential in the moviemaking process.

CREW POSITIONS

A movie crew comprises numerous departments, with each department having its own staff. The number of people within each department is dependent upon the complexity of the production and the size of the budget. For example, a period film is going to require a bigger art department than a present-day romantic comedy.

Listed here are the main crew positions in a Hollywood movie shoot. Although it might not seem like it, even small independent productions can benefit from having a similar crew setup. Take a look at the crew graphs later in this chapter for a better idea of what crew positions you really need on your set.

The Producers

- The **executive producer** oversees the entire production, sometimes multiple productions, but is not involved in the daily operations of the film, deferring those duties instead to the producer. The executive producer is typically the financier of the production, providing most, if not all, of the funding. Often, the executive producer has distribution ties or can actually be the distributor. Executive producers are usually the general partner of a limited partnership whose role is to raise financing for the project. The ideal executive producer is a businessperson who recognizes good commercial material and has an understanding of how to package and sell it.
- The **producer** is responsible for finding a script, attaching a director and actors, securing financing, coordinating the hiring of cast and crew, supervising the production and postproduction processes, and assisting with the sales and distribution of the film. The producer is in charge of all business components of the production. In the independent film arena, the director may actually hire the producer to manage the business duties of the production.
- The **associate producer** is an associate to the producer who is able to bring some resource, be it financial or technical asset, to the film. In recent years, however, this title has been diminished, as the "associate producer" credit is handed to people who may not actually fulfill the duties of a producer, as a bargaining tool at the negotiating table.
- The **line producer** is responsible for the daily operations of the film production and approves any and all expenditures for locations, cast, and crew. Whereas the producer handles the overall production, the line producer is in charge of daily tasks, working closely with the unit production manager, first assistant director, director, art director, editor, and composer to prepare the production budget and shooting schedule. The line producer is aware of local resources and knows the below-the-line personnel in a region and can manage these resources to ensure a cost-effective, timely production. The line producer is the ultimate liaison between the production team and the producers.

The Production Department

- In independent movies, the producer/writer is, more often than not, the director. If this is not the case, finding the right director for a project is of key importance. As the **director**, you are responsible for translating the script to the screen by working with actors to achieve the ideal performance and collaborating with creative departments to build a convincing world in which the action takes place. The producer will bring you in early and, while the production manager hires the majority of the below-the-line crew members, you will select the key creative personnel. You are also involved in every aspect of the filmmaking process, from casting actors and choosing locations to working with editors, composers, and digital effects houses. You can also be writers and producers on the same production.

- The **production manager**, also known as the unit production manager (UPM), is in charge of the daily details of planning and managing the business side of the production. The production manager prepares the budget, may work out the preliminary shooting schedule with the 1st assistant director, negotiates with and hires the below-the-line crew, and works with locations by organizing the scouting of, traveling to, and securing permissions from the location before giving these responsibilities over to the location manager. The production manager is responsible for ensuring that the production runs as smoothly and efficiently as possible, staying on schedule and on budget. The production manager also helps manage the daily budget by managing salaries, equipment rental, and other production costs. Even though the department heads can choose the crew positions below them, all hires and rates must be approved by the UPM.

- The **production coordinator** is in charge of booking all personnel and equipment. From cast to crew, equipment, and transportation, the production coordinator ensures that equipment and materials are at the right place at the right time, that crew members are in place and have all the necessary materials to perform their jobs, and that the actors have their contracts and are on set.

- The **assistant director** (or 1st AD) is not so much the assistant to the director as much as he is in charge of running the set, much like a stage manager's duty in theatre. The 1st AD's primary duties include creating the shooting schedule, coordinating the crew departments on set, ensuring the production remains on schedule, scheduling locations and actors, scheduling the day's shooting, serving as a buffer for the director, and solving on-set logistical problems so you can work with the actors. The 1st AD is also in charge of directing extras, freeing you to focus on the principal actors. The director and director of photography are the only positions that supersede the 1st AD's authority on set.

- The **2nd assistant director** assists the 1st AD with preproduction and production tasks, signing actors in and out as they arrive and depart each day, completing on-set paperwork, and managing production assistants.

1st assistant director Casey Slade manages every department to ensure the day comes in on schedule.

Script supervisor Dennis Marrell tracks continuity from shot to shot and keeps track of camera coverage – ultimately creating an organized index of shots for the editor.

- The **script supervisor** is in charge of the continuity of each scene and logs dialog spoken, number and duration of takes, lenses and filters used, actor's movements, camera coverage, and positions of props and set pieces, so that scenes and shots can be perfectly reproduced.

- The **casting director** is responsible for finding, auditioning, and ultimately, with the your and the producer's approval, casting the actors and extras for a film.

- The **production assistants** are the runners and general assistants, both in the production office and on set. They are responsible for assisting in whatever matters are asked of them, including making copies, running errands, getting coffee, keeping the public away from the film set, standing in for an actor, and transporting actors to and from set.

- The **location scout** is responsible for finding locations that meet your vision and production requirements. You and the creative team assemble lists of possible locations, and the scout will travel to these locations and photograph and videotape each one, bringing the photos back to you for consideration.

- The **location manager** is responsible for coordinating the use of a location with its owners; coordinating logistics between all departments to ensure the location meets all production needs; working with local officials to secure permits and approvals; securing parking, changing rooms, restroom facilities, and other support services; and making sure the location is in clean, working condition before the film crew leaves.

- **Craft services** provides noncatered food and beverage services on set. Craft services usually maintains a table with snacks and beverages during each day of production.

- A **stand-in** is a person who bears a resemblance to the actor in height, skin, and hair color and who replaces the actor while you and director of photography light and set up the shot, so as not to fatigue the actual actor. Once the technical setup has been completed, the real actor is brought on set for final lighting tweaks.

- The **still photographer** takes behind-the-scenes photos of the production, cast, and crew for use in press kits, marketing materials, and DVD features.

- The **storyboard artist** works closely with you and production designer to map your ideas into rough drawings called storyboards that help the creative team previsualize the film, either on paper or using storyboarding software.

- **Talent agents** represent actors, voice artists, and models in an effort to generate work for them on film, television, radio, or print projects.

The Director of Photography and the Camera Crew

The **director of photography** (DP) is responsible for the photographic look of the movie. For more about the role of the director of photography, check out Chapter 13.

I frame up the next shot on the set of the feature *Fred and Vinnie*.

The Camera Department

- The **camera operator** operates the camera during blocking, rehearsals, and takes. As the highest position in the camera department, the camera operator is present when you block the scene, while the rest of the camera crew moves and preps the camera. The camera operator also instructs the boom operator of the top of frame and helps tweak small elements in the frame to improve the overall composition. In the days before digital video and video tapes on film cameras, the camera operator was the only person to see what was happening through the lens, making his contributions invaluable.

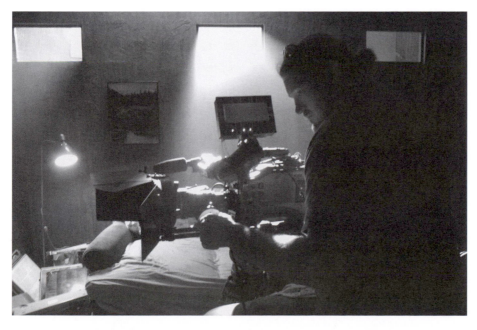

Camera operator Drew Lauer frames up a shot.

- The **assistant camera (or 1st AC)** is responsible for setting up, maintaining, cleaning, and repackaging the camera and camera accessories, including lenses, magazines, eyepieces, filters, and other camera parts. The 1st AC will set and pull focus for each shot. This is one of the most demanding and thankless jobs on set – if the shot's in focus, no one notices; if it's not, the 1st AC takes the heat.

1st assistant cameraman Nick Savander watches the camera between setups. Besides setting up, cleaning, maintaining, and moving the camera, the 1st AC is also responsible for the most critical job – keeping the shots in focus.

- The **2nd AC** is responsible for loading the unexposed film stock in the magazines, threading film through the camera, assisting with lens changes, marking each shot with the clapboard and maintaining camera logs. The DP will typically hire the 1st and 2nd ACs.

2nd AC Mark Grabianowski marks a shot on set.

- **Video assist** sets up and operates a video feed from the camera that is recorded and can be played back per your request.
- The **media manager** is a newer position that has developed with the advent of non-tape-based formats in which footage must be downloaded from cards or hard drives, backed up, and organized. This near full-time position is critical to ensuring that footage is properly copied before media cards are erased and re-recorded onto.

The Grip Department

- The **key grip** is the department head and is in charge of all grips. The key grip supervises the setup, moving, adjustment, and teardown of green screens, lighting, and camera support equipment (C-stands, flags, nets, silks, reflectors, and so on), creature comforts (dressing rooms, craft services tables, tents, and so on), operating dollies and cranes, and pulling cables on set. The key grip answers to the director of photography and issues orders to the best boy grip.

Key grip Tom Hunt makes a final adjustment to a shiny board.

- The **best boy grip** is the main assistant to the key grip and usually remains on the grip truck to prepare and issue equipment to the other grips.
- The **dolly grip** is responsible for setting up the camera dolly and dolly track as well as operating the dolly during a take. In larger productions, the dolly grip answers to the camera crew, although he may play double duty between the camera and the grip departments.
- **Grips** are responsible for moving, setting up, and tearing down camera support and light equipment. They are the movers on the set and do much of the carrying, lifting, and rigging.

Gaffer David Sheetz adjusts a 5k tungsten light on set.

The Electric Department

- The **gaffer** is the chief lighting technician on the set and is responsible for designing and rigging the lighting per the director of photography's vision. The gaffer supervises the electrical crew and answers directly to the director of photography. The gaffer is an expert at lighting and sometimes plays a more creative role, if permitted by the DP.
- The **best boy electric** is the primary assistant to the gaffer and works on the grip truck, preparing, maintaining, and repairing equipment.
- The **electrician** is responsible for rigging, wiring, and plugging in electrical cables and answers to the best boy and the gaffer.
- The **generator operator** is responsible for the transportation, maintenance, and operation of the generator on set.

The Art Department

The **production designer** is responsible for designing the overall look of the world in which the story takes place, including the look of the sets, props, and costumes. The production designer works closely with the director and is involved early on in the preproduction process, developing drawings, plans, and models around the director's storyboards. Often working with a large budget, production designers have many responsibilities to the producer and work closely with the director of photography and costume designer to ensure that all departments create a compatible look for the film.

The art department on *Fred and Vinnie* makes last-minute adjustments to the set dressing of Fred's apartment – a set they built at Panavision.

When shooting an independent movie, look for a production designer with experience on a number of features. Experienced production designers also have numerous contacts in the industry and will be able to help identify and locate art elements at a discount or for free.

Ask the production designer to hire the following crew positions:

- The **art director** works under the production designer and supervises the art department crew, coordinating the implementation of the production design.
- The **set designer** is the lead architect, who drafts tangible blueprints and designs of the sets based on the direction and guidance of the production designer.
- There can be several **assistant art directors**, or assistants to the art director, based on the complexity and amount of work involved. Assistant art directors are responsible for daily duties, including measuring set spaces, assisting in set design, and serving any of the art director's needs.
- The **set decorator** works under the production designer or art director and is responsible for coordinating the furnishings on set that are not touched by the actors. The set decorator researches, acquires, places, and then strikes any artistic element that helps improve the look and design of the sets.
- Working directly under the set decorator, the **buyer** is responsible for finding, buying, and renting set-dressing elements.
- The **lead man** is the foreman of the set decorating crew.
- The **set dresser** works on set and physically dresses, alters, updates, maintains, and removes the set dressing. Set dressers are responsible for any creative elements on a set, from doorknobs and windowpanes to furniture and drapery. Although most of the set dressing work is done prior to shooting, an on-set dresser remains on set in case any changes are required.
- The **key scenic** is responsible for all set surfaces, from wood and marble to stone. The key scenic works closely with the production designer and oversees a team of painters to create the exact look of each set.
- The **construction coordinator** oversees the construction of set pieces, orders materials, schedules tradesmen, and manages the construction crew.
- The **head carpenter** is the foreman in charge of the carpenters.
- The **greensman** is responsible for setting and dressing any plants, trees, and foliage, both real and fake. The greensman usually works for the set decorator except in productions in which greens are an integral aspect of the set, in which case he reports directly to the production designer.

The Prop Department

- The **property master** is in charge of identifying, acquiring, and maintaining all props used in the film. Props are handled by the actors and fall under the control of the property master. Elements not handled by the actors are considered set dressing and fall under the responsibility of the set decorator.
- The **props builder** designs and builds original props for the movie.
- The **armorer** works exclusively with firearms and weaponry and has the necessary licenses to do so.

The Hair and Makeup Department

- The **hairstylist** creates and maintains the actors' hairstyles on set. From working with the actors' natural hair to employing wigs, the hairstylist will style the actors' hair at the beginning of the day and be on set to touch it up between takes. There may be several hairstylists on set, depending upon the number of actors and the complexity of the hairstyles in the film.
- The **makeup artist** is responsible for maintaining the cosmetic look of the actors. With duties ranging from applying the initial makeup at the beginning of the day to touching up the makeup between takes, makeup artists can create everything from realistic, natural looks to special effects makeup such as blood or wounds or prosthetics using foam latex, rubber, or bald caps.

Key makeup artist Donna Sexton touches up Angela Nicholas on the set of *Currency*.

The Wardrobe Department

- The **costume designer** designs and oversees the creation of the costumes, working closely with the director to create a look that matches her vision of the story.
- The **wardrobe supervisor** is responsible for maintaining the costumes and accessories for the actors and extras. Working closely with the costume designer, the wardrobe supervisor ensures that wardrobe is ready, prepped, and cleaned for the actors each day and that continuity is maintained from scene to scene by taking Polaroid photos of the actors.
- Always present on set, the **costume standby** is responsible for helping dress the actors, if necessary, and maintaining the continuous look of the actors' costumes from take to take by tweaking and adjusting as necessary.
- When wardrobe needs to be worn, torn, or altered, the **art finisher** comes in to distress new garments.
- The **buyer** locates and purchases fabric and material for costumes.

The Audio Department

- The **production sound mixer** is responsible for setting, monitoring, and recording the audio on set. She is responsible for choosing and placing the proper microphones, monitoring the sound levels during a take, and coordinating with the camera and lighting crews to ensure that the microphone is out of the frame and not casting shadows. She will notify the director of any problems with the audio during a take, such as background noise or poor audio levels.

John Churchman monitors the sound levels while positioning the boom over the actors.

- The **boom operator** places the microphone in the optimal position over the actors without breaching the camera frame or casting a shadow on the actors or set.

The Stunts/Special Effects Department

- **Special effects** is responsible for all mechanical and/or physical effects that occur on set, such as glass breaking, furniture breaking, weather effects, and gags.
- **Stunt coordinators** create, rig, and execute the stunts for a scene, ensuring maximum safety while creating spectacular stunts.
- The **stunt people** replace actors for any shots that require potentially dangerous physical actions. Stunts include everything from freefalls, fights, running, and trips to car stunts, including any activity that could potentially cause injury.
- Licensed and experienced in explosives, **pyrotechnicians** are responsible for building, rigging, detonating, and securing explosions, gunshots, sparks, and any chemical-based reaction that causes an explosive effect. Pyrotechnicians need state and federal licenses.

The Transportation Department

- The **transportation captain** is responsible for getting the cast and crew to the location, as well as vehicle movement and parking. All drivers report to the transportation captain.
- **Drivers** transport talent and key crew members to and from the set.

Postproduction

- The **composer** will write the score for the film, using a live orchestra or a MIDI computer setup. Working closely with the director, the composer is usually the last person to work on the film and has a strong understanding of music styles, instrumentation, and composition.
- The **editor** is responsible for taking the rough footage shot on set and assembling it into a linear, sensible story. Editors, because they're not on set, can provide an objective viewpoint for the director, ensuring that the film is well paced and makes sense.

Mike Farona mixes the dialog tracks at Neon Cactus Studios.

- The **sound designer** is responsible for editing the soundtrack for a movie. In the independent world, the sound designer can also record ADR and Foley and mix the final soundtrack of the movie.
- The **Foley artist** is a sound effects artist who is responsible for recreating and recording the normal, everyday sounds in a scene, such as footsteps, clothing movement, doors opening and closing, items being picked up or handled, and any sounds an actor would make when interacting with the environment.
- The **animator/compositor** is a digital effects artist who can either create or supplement existing footage with 2D or 3D animation or composites to accentuate the look of the movie. Often working on shots immediately after they are shot, animators are involved in the creative process from the beginning, helping to ensure that footage to be altered is properly shot.

HOW TO HIRE THE CREW

It's easy to get overwhelmed by the long list of crew members that need to be hired for a production. Instead of worrying about each position, hire the department heads, then give them a budget and the freedom to hire the rest of their crew.

The producer should hire for these four positions:

Director
Director of photography
Production designer
Unit production manager

Crew Structures

If you've ever watched the closing credits of a Hollywood movie, the seemingly endless list of people who worked on the film may seem like overkill, but in reality, the logistics and demands of a large production require each one of the artists, technicians, and coordinators.

To get an idea of the complexity of a Hollywood production, here's a simplified structure of an average-sized Hollywood crew.

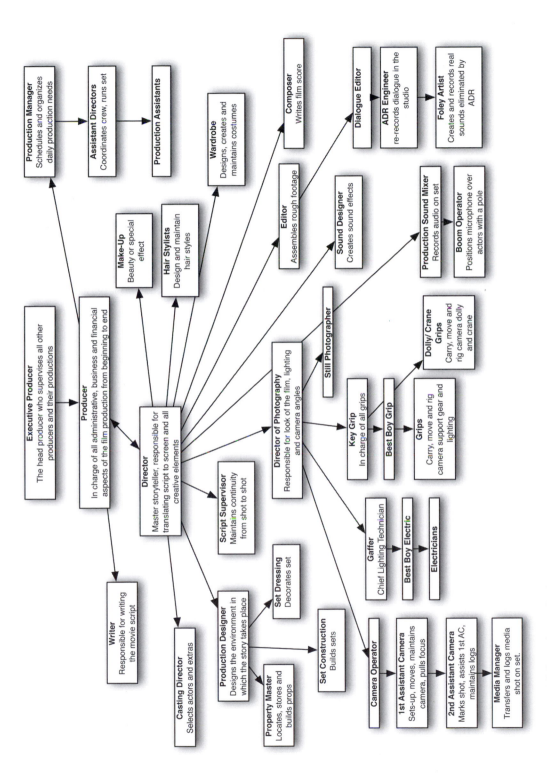

Traditional small Hollywood crew structure.

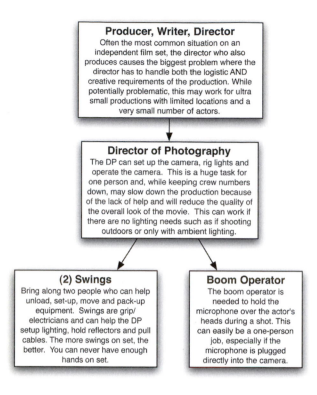

Producer, Writer, Director
Often the most common situation on an independent film set, the director who also produces causes the biggest problem where the director has to handle both the logistic AND creative requirements of the production. While potentially problematic, this may work for ultra small productions with limited locations and a very small number of actors.

Director of Photography
The DP can set up the camera, rig lights and operate the camera. This is a huge task for one person and, while keeping crew numbers down, may slow down the production because of the lack of help and will reduce the quality of the overall look of the movie. This can work if there are no lighting needs such as if shooting outdoors or only with ambient lighting.

(2) Swings
Bring along two people who can help unload, set-up, move and pack-up equipment. Swings are grip/electricians and can help the DP setup lighting, hold reflectors and pull cables. The more swings on set, the better. You can never have enough hands on set.

Boom Operator
The boom operator is needed to hold the microphone over the actor's heads during a shot. This can easily be a one-person job, especially if the microphone is plugged directly into the camera.

In an independent film, elaborate Hollywood crews are not only unnecessary, but unaffordable. As an indie filmmaker, who do you really need to have on set? If you could compile a wish list for your productions as they grow in size and complexity, what positions would you need and which ones could you do without?

THE ULTRASMALL CREW STRUCTURE

This crew structure is the most basic and is ideal for small scenes involving one or two actors in a location that doesn't require significant lighting and needs virtually no major props, wardrobe, hairstyling, or makeup. This ultrasmall crew can be very fast and mobile, but when taking on larger scenes, can become quickly overwhelmed.

The cost of hiring an ultrasmall crew is around $750/day, provided you're hiring crew members new to film, out-of-work professionals, or crew members looking to work in another position. These rates are based on a low-budget, nonunion production. The cost of hiring professionals may be significantly higher, so remember that productions this small may be better served with aspiring filmmakers and film students to keep costs low.

> **Producer, writer, director**—$0. This person is probably you.
> **Director of photography**—$300/day
> **Swings** (two)—$150×2 = $300/day
> **Boom operator**—$150/day

THE BASIC CREW STRUCTURE

The basic crew has the basic crew departments, often run by only one person, but is structured so that each major component of the production is addressed. Although it seems like a lot of people, this 15-person crew is an ideal size for small- to medium-sized productions. The number of bodies on set is low, but no one department is overwhelmed. Most independent films with a modest budget should try to build this type of crew.

The average cost of the basic crew is approximately $2,175 per day.

> **Producer**—variable; negotiate this price.
> **Director**—$0. This person is probably you.
> **Production designer**—$200/day
> **Director of photography**—$300/day
> **First assistant camera**—$150/day
> **First assistant director**—$200/day

Script supervisor—$175/day
Gaffer—$200/day
Electrician—$150/day
Key grip—$200/day
Grip—$150/day
Boom operator—$125/day
Hairstylist/makeup artist—$175/day
Craft services—$150/day

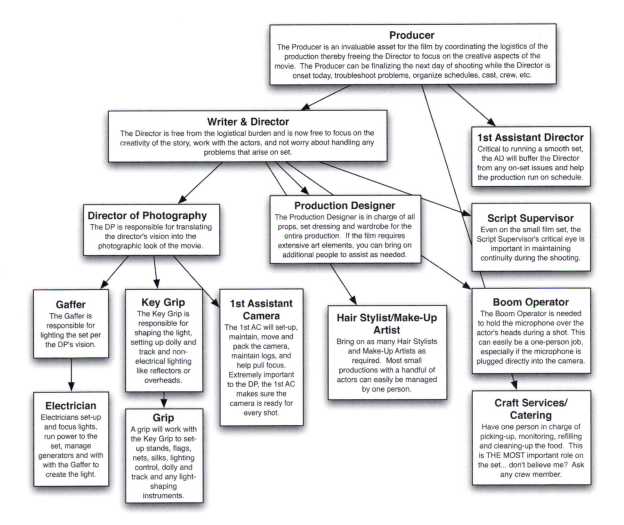

Finding Qualified Crew Members

When beginning a new movie, having a strong crew is critical to a smooth-running production. Avoid the temptation of doing everything yourself. You'll get burned out and won't turn out quality work. Instead, surround yourself with people who know their individual responsibilities, are professional, have experience, and have a strong work ethic. Finding crew members is as easy as looking at your local resources:

- **Film school graduates.** Use the phone book to find local film schools or colleges that have a communications program. They may be willing to let you speak with a class, contact local graduates, or otherwise solicit students to work on your crew. The benefit to using film school students or graduates is their hunger to learn and willingness to work for free and shoot for long hours. The drawback is their lack of experience. Film students are a terrific asset as production assistants or grips (if they know how to use professional production equipment), but should never be employed in key positions. Also beware the "film school attitude," which is the tendency to think that they know better than anyone else on set.

- **Internet.** Posting crew calls on web sites like www.craigslist.org, www.mandy.com, and www.productionhub.com is a great way of reaching potential crew members, especially in large cities. Craft a professional posting that describes the production, the dates, and approximate rates. A good online post will read: A feature film being shot in Chicago in July is hiring the following crew positions: Gaffer, Grip, [and so on].
  - Production will span 14 days and 3 nights, will be fully catered, and will be paying. If interested, please email your resume, link to an online demo reel, and your contact information. Our production office will be in contact with you within the week. Thank you for your interest.

An experienced crew is worth every penny – not only will they do an outstanding artistic job, but it will be done right, on time, and on budget.

- **Film commission.** Contact the local film commission and ask for a copy of their production directory. This directory includes the names, credits, and contact information for most below-the-line crew members, equipment vendors, stages, postproduction facilities, and rental facilities in the state.

The people in the directory range from recent film school graduates to experienced production personnel. Don't be afraid to call them and ask if they are interested in working on the movie. Even if they aren't available, they may be able to refer you to someone else in the area.

Every state produces a production manual that lists local freelance crew members.

- **Film festivals.** Attending local film festivals is a great way of networking with other independent filmmakers. Be sure to bring plenty of business cards. After screening a movie, seek out any crew members in attendance. Many of these people are willing to work for low or deferred payment just for the experience.

When hiring creative positions, ask to see a demo reel of past projects the person worked on, as well as a resume that lists all past projects, awards, film festival credits, and educational experience.

- **Demo reel:** When looking at this collective sample of a candidate's work, look only at what her contributions were, not at elements out of her control. For example, if you're looking to hire a cinematographer, look at the quality of the camera work and the lighting, but don't let bad sound or bad acting affect your decision. When looking at the quality of work on the reel, think about whether you'd be happy with that quality on your movie.
- **References:** Ask for references from past producers and directors with whom this person has worked. Ask about his work ethic, attitude, and involvement in the film.

- **Interview:** Finally, meet with the candidate and talk about the film and what you're willing to offer in exchange for her services, and generally get a feeling about or her personality. Remember that – much like auditioning actors – you have only a few short meetings to determine whether you want to spend hours working in a stressed environment with this person.

Above all, remember that the candidate is also interviewing you, trying to determine the type of working relationship he will experience, how organized you are, how passionate you are about the project, and your attitude. Good teamwork and successful productions are a result of solid relationships with a strong team of people. Build a good one.

- It's a good idea to have the production schedule in place *before* you start contacting crew members. It will be easier for them to commit to the project if they know specifically when you need them. You will also appear professional and organized, which may help attract more experienced people to your production.
- Be aware that working with inexperienced crew members like volunteers or film students may require more time on set for them to learn how to use the equipment. It's a good idea to have an orientation before the shoot to show the crew how to use the equipment and your set policies and procedures. The equipment rental company may be willing to host this orientation.
- When scheduling students or crew members new to production, it's a good idea to schedule more people than you need, because not everyone will show up. Consider a crew member reliable if he has proven, through action, his reliability. Don't go on someone's verbal commitment alone. It's better to have too much help than not enough.
- When selecting crew members, beware of people who appear even the least bit hesitant about the time requirements or who aren't enthusiastic about the project. They not only will be difficult to work with on set, but may not be reliable, often coming up with excuses to leave early or miss shoots entirely.
- Crew members, especially those who are working for free, are giving two very important elements: their talents and, more importantly, their time. Be appreciative and supportive of their efforts, and always be sure to thank them profusely for their dedication to the production.
- Schedule a meeting with the crew before the first day of shooting to go over the script, storyline, schedule, and what is expected of them. You want the crew to be as prepared as possible when they arrive on the set the first day.
- If necessary, schedule an equipment review with the crew, possibly at the equipment rental facility, to make sure that everyone knows how to set up, use, and pack up the gear.
- Avoid scheduling the crew too far in advance. Experienced crew personnel may be hesitant to book a job too far in the future. A good rule of thumb is to begin booking crew members within about three weeks of production.

PAYING CREW MEMBERS

Compensating crew members can be an expensive process, but consider that many new, aspiring filmmakers would be willing to work for other types of compensation.

Working with inexperienced crew members can be more expensive than hiring professionals in the long run. Novice crew don't work as fast, because they are learning on the job, resulting in fewer camera setups per day. Safety can become an issue if grips don't know how to safely and properly build various rigs; a improperly flown 20 × 20 silk can easily topple over and seriously injure or kill someone. An inexperienced 1st AD who doesn't understand the demands of each department may not be able to keep the production running smoothly and on time. An inexperienced DP will spent more time experimenting with lighting and camera settings than simply getting on set and doing it right the first time. Inexperienced production designers may not have the necessary set dressing on the day of the shoot. Any one of these setbacks can cost significant time and money, but more importantly, many novice crew members lack the experience in translating the creative and artistic components of the story to film because they are so focused on learning the process.

Money

Paying crew members is the best form of compensation, although in most cases your budget may prohibit you from paying the crew. Typical crew wages are based on a daily basis for short projects and discounted weekly rates for long-term projects. Crew wages are dependent on the length of the project, if travel is required, how experienced the crew member is, and how many potentially qualified people are available for the job. Talk with each potential crew member and work out a deal for her day rate and offer to rent her equipment or kits as an incentive for her to accept a lower daily rate.

If you are paying the crew, it is customary to issue a check either at the end of the production, if it is a short project, or every two weeks if the production is a feature.

Discuss the rate in advance and include the rate in a crew deal memo. The crew deal memo is a contract between the production company and the crew member that states the terms of employment. Other factors to include are:

- **Overtime.** When crew members work on a full-paying or union job, their daily rate usually covers a 12-hour day. It is customary to pay two times the hourly rate for any time over 12 hours. However, this can get costly, especially on a low-budget independent film, so negotiate a standard day rate regardless of the number of hours worked.

Always hire people who know the filmmaking process, understand current techniques, and are well-versed in the latest technology.

- **Per diem.** If the production spans distant locations, cast and crew members are given a per diem, or additional daily money to cover food purchases. Per diems are always negotiated before the production begins and range from $30 to $75 a day. Each crew member is given the per diem amount in cash at the beginning of the day.
- **Expenses.** If the budget allows, offering to pay for travel expenses such as gas may attract higher-caliber crew members. Even on low-budget movies on which crew members may be working for free, offering gas money is a powerful and inexpensive incentive that will help bring and keep people onboard.
- **Time of payment.** Most cast and crew members expect to be paid by the last day of production. Write checks for the full amount and have them ready for the crew on their last day of work. Paying crew members late will tarnish your reputation in a community and make it difficult to crew up your next production.
- **Payroll.** Most independent movies will pay the cast and crew as subcontractors, meaning the production is not responsible for taking out taxes. In projects that involve a large number of cast and crew members, or ones that span a long period of time, consider hiring a payroll service to cut checks and take out taxes, making the cast and crew members employees of the production. Be sure to consult your accountant.

There are several factors that determine the rate of pay for crew members:

- How experienced is the crew member? In most instances, the more experienced crew member will request a higher daily rate, unless she is excited about the project. Try to sell each person and get them excited, and you may be able to negotiate a lower rate.
- How many qualified crew members are there in the production area? In major cities where the crew pool is large, it's easier to negotiate lower rates because of increased competition.
- Are there any other productions that are hiring crew members at the same time? In cities where there isn't a large crew pool, competent crew members will go to the production with the higher rate, making it difficult to staff your movie. Consult with the local film commission before making the shoot schedule, so as not to conflict with another production.
- Is there a nearby film school that can provide students or recent graduates willing to work for free? If so, then professionals may be willing to lower their rates to compete with the free labor.
- Are the crew members union or nonunion? Nonunion crews are often willing to work for more reasonable rates, longer hours, and fewer creature comforts than experienced union crews.

Deferred Payment

Another method of paying crew members is to pay them from the money a film makes after it is sold. Deferred payment is risky for the crew because they will get paid only if the movie makes money, which is not a guarantee. Most seasoned crew members consider this arrangement "working for free" and will accept the job because they like the project, not because of the promise of back-end money.

Some productions will pay crew members a percentage of their usual rate up front and defer the balance.

Credit

If you can't afford to pay crew members up front, or do not foresee your film making a profit, offer what you can: credit. Credit is the listing of the crew member's name and job title in either the opening credits or the film's closing credits. Oftentimes, first-time film crews are excited at the prospect of gaining the experience of working on a film and seeing their names in the credits, which may lead to future jobs.

Contracts and Deal Memos

Deal memos are contracts between the production company and the crew members, which identify the crew member's job, working dates, daily/weekly rate, overtime pay, per diem, credit, travel allotment, and any additional factors that you negotiate with the crew member.

The crew deal memo is signed before production begins. A copy is given to the crew member, whereas the master is kept on file in the production office. Once signed, the arrangements of the contract are sealed, alleviating any possible future conflicts over the terms of the agreement.

If paying the crew in the United States, have each crew member fill out a W-9 form for tax and accounting purposes before the production begins.

Download a blank Crew Deal Memo for use on your production at Filmskills.com. See page vi for details.

Crew Wages

It is often difficult to determine appropriate crew wages for a film production, because rates are dependent upon where in the country the film is being shot, the number of qualified crew members available, the number of shooting days, and the format on which the movie is being filmed. The following is a list of average crew rates for a $1 million, nonunion film production shot in a major metropolitan area in 20 days. Understand that there is no standard rate chart for nonunion productions, so the following scale is a starting point for negotiating crew wages on your production. These rates have been calculated for a 6-day week, 12 hours/day, with a 12-hour turnaround shooting schedule.

Position	Rate
Production manager	$300–$400 per day
First assistant director	$300–$400 per day
Second assistant director	$200–$300 per day
Production assistant	$0–$150 per day

Most production assistants are interns willing to work for free for the experience.

Position	Rate
Production designer	$1,500–$1,700 per week
Art director	$1,200–$1,500 per week
Assistant art director	$1,000–$1,200 per week

Art department positions are usually hired on a per-week basis.

Position	Rate
Script supervisor	$200–$250 per day or $800–$900 per week
Director of photography	$500–$800 per day or $2,000–$3,000 per week
First assistant camera	$200–$250 per day
Second assistant camera	$175–$225 per day or $1,000–$1,100 per week
Camera operator	$175–$225 per day
Film loader	$150–$175 per day or $850–$950 per week

Film loader rates are dependent on film vs. video. If shooting film, this position requires a much more experienced person, which can increase the rate.

Position	Rate
Script supervisor	$200–$250 per day or $800–$900 per week
Key grip	$200–$250 per day or $1,000–$1,200 per week
Best boy—grip	$175–$225 per day
Grip	$125–$175 per day or $800–$900 per week
Dolly grip	$175–$225 per day

The dolly grip rate is usually the same as that for the best boy position.

Position	Rate
Gaffer	$250–$300 per day or $1,000–$1,200 per week
Best boy—electric	$175–$225 per day or $900–$1,000 per week
Electrician	$150–$200 per day

Usually, the 1st assistant cameraman, key grip, and gaffer make the same scale. The second assistants/best boys in those categories make the same, and the third tier/film loader make the same scale. Grips and electricians make slightly less.

Position	Rate
Production sound mixer	$275–$350 per day or $1,200–$1,400 per week

The production sound mixer usually has his own equipment, which can raise the rate.

Position	Rate
Boom operator	$125–$175 per day or $500–$600 per week
Makeup	$225–$275 per day or $1,000–$1,100 per week

(Continued)

Position	Rate
Assistant makeup	$200–$250 per day or $900–$1,000 per week
Prop master	$200–$250 per day or $900–$1,100 per week
Assistant prop master	$175–$215 per day or $800–$900 per week
Body makeup	$150–$200 per day or $750–$850 per week

Makeup artists may also charge a kit fee, which includes all the makeup materials necessary for the film shoot. When negotiating rates, some makeup artists will be willing to work for free but may charge the kit fee to cover the costs of materials.

Position	Rate
Key hairstylist	$200–$250 per day or $900–$950 per week
Hairstylist	$175–$215 per day or $800–$850 per week

Hairstylists may also charge a kit fee to cover materials and equipment.

Position	Rate
Wardrobe	$200–$250 per day or $900–$950 per week
Costume designer	$400–$500 per day or $1,900–$2,200 per week
Key costume	$175–$225 per day or $800–$850 per week
Stunt coordinator	$900–$1,100 per day or $3,800–$4,100 per week
Stunt person	$600–$700 per day or $2,400–$2,600 per week

Hollywood stunt people are also paid each time they perform a stunt, making complicated stunts with multiple takes very expensive. This is in addition to the base daily or weekly pay.

Position	Rate
Construction foreman	$190–$220 per day or $800–$900 per week
Craft services	$175–$225 per day
Editor	$50–$55 per hour
Assistant editor	$28–$32 per hour
Music editor	$40–$45 per hour
Sound editor	$40–$45 per hour

In many instances, postproduction positions may charge for the project or on an hourly basis. Some studios will sell "blocks" of time at a discounted rate. The rates charged are dependent on the size and experience of the studio, the studio's current workload, or how involved your project is.

WORKING AS A FREELANCER

There are traditionally two ways of working in the film industry. The first is as a paid employee, and the second is as a freelancer. Unless you're working at a production or postproduction company, odds are that as a DP, director, gaffer, key grip, electrician, grip, PA, production coordinator, sound mixer, production designer, or any of the other on-set positions, you're working as a freelancer. This means that you are hired on a particular job and whether it's a one day commercial or a six week feature, you are paid for your services, then you wait to hear where your next job is coming from. Sometimes work is so plentiful that you will leave one project and roll right into the next one, and other times weeks and even months can go by between projects.

Just about every crew member in Hollywood works as a freelancer.

Although this may sound like a great way to work with lots of free time, the free time between jobs can be stressful and is usually spent searching for the next production.

There are several benefits and drawbacks to working as a freelancer:

- **Freelancers can make more money.** Because freelancers are hired on a daily rate, with overtime and meal penalties added on, it's easy to make significantly more money that a salaried person who does not enjoy such perks. Several freelancers may also own equipment and rent it out for an additional kit fee. Whether it's the production sound mixer's audio gear, or a gaffer's lighting truck, or the DP's camera, these equipment subrentals can sometimes exceed the day rate.

- **Feast or famine.** One challenge of working freelance is the unpredictable nature of the work, and as nature would have it, work always seems to be either in abundance or in complete scarcity. Typically, especially in Hollywood, you will either be so busy, there's little time to sleep or you'll sit around for weeks, waiting for the phone to ring with the next job.

- **No health insurance.** Unfortunately, you're responsible for your own health insurance, as employers are not hiring you as a salaried worker.

- **New boss every time.** One significant unknown is who you're going to work for. You never know from one job to the next how the working relationship will be with the producer, director or production company. There are some productions which are poorly managed and terribly directed, and every minute is painful. These days are sometimes balanced with wonderful production where the chemistry amongst the cast and crew make it a pleasure to go to work. In an industry with a myriad of creative personalities, there are always conflicts and challenges.

- **Taxes aren't taken out.** Salaried employees enjoy the benefits of being on payroll, which means employers pay for half each employee's Social Security and Medicare. As a freelancer, you are responsible for paying all these taxes yourself, reducing your overall take-home pay.
- **Unpredictable schedule.** Most freelancers will get the call for a job within a week or even a couple days of the project, making it difficult to have a social life. Often, plans with friends and family, trips, and even vacations are always kept tentative pending an upcoming work. Living the freelance production life makes it difficult to maintain a personal life, yet it's important to be available for work lest your client find someone else in the future.
- **Unpredictable rates.** Each production pays a different day rate based on the budget, so even the rate of pay varies and cannot be relied upon. Benefits like overtime, meal penalty, and mileage compensation also vary. It's important to negotiate your rate in advance, and always sign a deal memo with an employer to ensure a verifiable paper trail, should you have trouble collecting once a project is complete.
- **Develop a good reputation and work ethic.** Your reputation is the single most important hiring tool you have. Clients will hire you or not solely based on your reputation. The film industry is ultimately a very small community and people always talk. Having a good attitude, strong work ethic, showing up early and leaving late to set, never complaining, always being resourceful, knowing your craft, and being fun to work with will help establish you as a valuable member of any team.
- **Always develop and improve your skills.** In an industry where technology and the latest techniques change almost daily, learning and keeping on top of the latest trends improves your value for potential clients. Subscribe to trade journals, attend conferences, and visit local equipment companies to be the best in your field.
- **Get in with a good DP or director.** One way of working successfully as a freelancer is to find a team of filmmakers who work a lot. If you are able to get on the crew of a successful working director or DP, then you will go with him from one job to the next. People tend to work with people they know and like, and every DP has a crew he trusts and relies on.

CHAPTER 9
Equipment

169

i. Determine shooting format.

ii. The director of photography uses your shot list to determine the equipment needed to shoot each scene.

iii. Contact local vendors and negotiate the best rental price.

iv. The line producer provides vendors with a Certificate of Insurance.

v. The 1st assistant cameraman, gaffer, and key grip make lists to keep track of rental equipment on set.

vi. Upon return of rented equipment, be prepared to pay for lost and damaged gear.

PRE-PRODUCTION   PRODUCTION

INTRODUCTION

Getting the right equipment is essential to producing a high-quality movie. Because purchasing the camera, lights, and other production equipment is an expensive proposition, there are a number of rental facilities that rent gear for the duration of your shoot.

I make sure my grip and lighting truck, the Mobile Movie Studio, is fully stocked with a wide array of grip and lighting equipment. It's important to be prepared on set for any creative challenge that may arise.

Filmmaking.
© 2011 Jason J. Tomaric. Published by Elsevier Inc. All rights reserved.

One common misperception filmmakers have is that they can use existing light, handheld cameras, and onboard microphones to achieve a "natural" look. This disastrous approach results in an unwatchable film; the audience can't hear the actors; the image is dark, grainy, and shaky; and the focus shifts constantly during a shot.

Both film and digital media react to light in a way much different from that of the human eye, so often, large quantities of light are required to light a scene, even if you're striving for a natural look. In addition, camera support equipment gives filmmakers the flexibility to move the camera in artistic and creative ways, without distracting the audience with shaky camera moves. Investing in the proper equipment is the first step in crafting controlled, creative shots that will not only increase the production value of the movie, but also help engage the audience deeper into the story.

The first and most important decision is which camera on which to shoot. Although your camera choice is partially determined by distribution requirements, several other factors such as resolution, compression algorithms, ASA – or chip sensitivity – and noise factors all affect the types of lighting and camera support equipment you may need.

CAMERAS

Choosing a camera and a format on which to shoot is one of the most important decisions you'll make when selecting gear for your production. There are many different options among video and film formats. If you choose to shoot film, you could use the inexpensive Super8 format, but the image quality will be poor; or you could choose high-quality 35 mm film and pay tens of thousands of dollars on the camera rental, film, and processing. Video offers the same array of choices, from inexpensive HDV to professional-quality high-definition video, each with an equal array of benefits and drawbacks. Consider all the factors of cost, quality, and even distribution requirements when choosing a format.

Video versus Film

Filmmaking has always been an elitist medium that costs a massive amount of money, and unless you have a rich uncle or a spare quarter-million dollars, it is next to impossible to produce a professional-looking 35 mm or even 16 mm feature film at the independent level. This financial requirement kept many people from realizing their dreams . . . until the digital revolution. In the late 1990s, a digital format called DV (digital video) was developed, which forever altered the way movies are shot. By producing broadcast-quality imagery, the average person could easily afford technology that in past years would have cost ten times the amount. Digital video opened the doors and empowered the masses to explore, produce, and tell stories through the visual medium.

But the debate as to whether film or video is superior still rages. Both media have their pros and cons. Film is much more expensive to shoot when one considers the cost of film stock, processing, and equipment rental. However, the look of film, to many, is vastly superior to the look of video by providing greater contrast range, depth of field, and image resolution. A movie shot on film is also easier to sell to foreign distributors than a movie shot on video, as video has a reputation of looking cheap and amateurish. Film can be easily adapted and transferred to one of many broadcast and exhibition formats around the world. Many high definition formats available today, from traditional HD to RED camera footage, is capable – when properly lit and shot – of very closely mimicking the look of 35 mm film, providing a cheaper and more flexible shooting option.

When you begin your filmmaking career, consider shooting your first few projects on digital video so that you can focus on the process of making a movie (directing, working with actors, and working with the crew) instead of the technical challenges of shooting film. Once you feel comfortable with the process and have a few short films under your belt, then consider shooting a project on film. Too many people invest thousands of dollars into film stock and processing on their first movie, and because they are inexperienced in the process, the movie ends up being shelved due to bad acting, poor script, loose directing, sloppy editing, and so on – and the money spent on film is wasted. Focus on the process, then shoot on film.

Shooting Film

Film is a strip of plastic composed of several chemical layers, the most important being a layer of light-sensitive silver-halide crystals, made up of silver nitrate and halide salts. In the manufacturing process, the size, shape, and composition of the crystals can be modified to produce film of varying sensitivities. Once the chemical layers of film are exposed to light, the film must be processed for the image to be visible.

During the developing process, the image appears as a negative of the original image, with blacks and whites inverted, and in the case of color film, the colors inverted. The lab then produces a positive from the negative, which displays the images as they are supposed to appear.

FILM FORMATS

Film is available in a variety of sizes and resolutions. Each film stock is measured diagonally, corner to corner, in millimeters and the larger the frame, the more "resolution" and detail the film is able to capture.

- **8 mm.** 8 mm and Super8 formats were the predominant formats before video cameras became standard in the home. You can purchase the film and process it for around $10.00 per minute. Although this is the cheapest film stock, it is also the poorest quality.
  - The film is eight millimeters wide and has perforations on only one side.
  - The aspect ratio is 1.33:1, the same as NTSC television.
  - Super8 includes an oxide stripe, which allows sound to be recorded onto the film.
  - All 8 mm and Super8 cameras run at 18 frames per second, and many cameras can run at 24 frames per second.

Regular 8mm film

Super 8 film

16mm silent film

16mm film with audio

- Super8 is sold in 50-foot lengths and is rolled in a plastic cartridge that is inserted into the camera. The camera automatically loads the film. This amounts to 3:20 of shooting time if you roll at 18 frames per second, or 2:47 if rolling at 24 frames per second.
- Due to environmental legislation regarding manufacturing, Kodak no longer makes film stock with sound recording capabilities.
- Super8 film costs around $25 per roll to purchase and about $15 per roll to develop.
- **16mm.** Capable of capturing excellent image quality, especially when viewed on television, 16mm film is used for low-budget projects and documentaries. Beware however, the resolution of 16mm film may be sufficient for television broadcast, but may not be adequate for viewing on a large movie screen. A common film format is Super16, which eliminates the perforations on one side of the film, allowing a greater area to be exposed. Super16 film features a wider aspect ratio and is a format of choice for filmmakers who are looking for a lower-cost option to 35mm film.
  - Measuring 16 millimeters from corner to corner, 16mm film is perforated either on one side (single-perf) or on both sides (double-perf), although single-perf, one sprocket hole per frame, has become the standard.
  - The aspect ratio of 16mm film is 1.33:1.
  - Super16 film has an aspect ratio of 1.66:1 and is always single-perf.

Arriflex 16mm camera.

Table 9.1	Film vs Video

Film	Video
Costs $55 to buy and process 1 min of 35 mm film	Solid-state media is much cheaper over time
Minimal number of takes, dependent on budget allotted for film stock	Unlimited number of takes, tape stock is cheap and solid-state media pays for itself over time
Cameras are heavier and bulkier	Cameras can be smaller and easier to handle
Requires more time to light and set up each shot	Can set up shots quickly
Cannot see footage until the film is processed	Can see the image immediately and on playback
Very high resolution, images are crisp and defined	Lower-quality formats have limited resolution and won't hold up well on the big screen, but higher-quality formats rival 35 mm film quality
Requires a separate sound recording device, because you cannot record audio onto film	Can record audio directly to the camera audio remains in sync with the video image
Film needs to be processed and transferred to tape before editing	Footage can go immediately into an editing suite
Distributors are much more likely to pick up a movie shot on film, especially in the foreign market	Distributors are much less likely to pick up a movie shot on lesser-quality formats especially in the foreign market
Has significantly shallower depth of field with larger film formats	Has significantly deeper depth of field, unless cameras with 35mm or 4/3″ chips are used
Has a greater contrast ratio (10–12 f-stops, depending on the film stock) and handles overexposure much better	Has a narrower contrast range in lower-quality formats and does not handle overexposure as well; high-quality formats have contrast ranges that equal that of film
Is much more complicated in postproduction, especially if the final result is to go back to film	A much simpler postproduction process, although costs of printing video to film are high
Film generally has a more aesthetically pleasing look	Video generally has a harsher look, can appear "too perfect."
Film is able to capture an infinite range of colors, making images vivid and deeply saturated	Lower-end video formats must compress color information, so saturation and the chroma range are limited
If film is underexposed and pushed in processing, film is subject to granularity and graininess	If underexposed and gain is used, the video image is subject to noise
Film is very expensive to duplicate and loses quality with each generation	Video is inexpensive to duplicate at a high quality

- **35 mm.** The primary format of choice in professional filmmaking, 35 mm film captures sufficient detail for projection onto a movie screen. The only drawback is its $55 per minute cost for film stock and processing.
  - The film measures 35 millimeters across.
  - The 35 mm full camera aperture aspect ratio is 1.33:1, but is typically matted to 1.85:1.
  - There are a number of variations of the 35 mm format, including Super35 and 35 anamorphic; talk with your film supplier about which format is the best choice for your project.
  - This film can hold SDDS, Dolby Digital, analog optical, and DTS time code tracks.
  - This film runs at 16 frames per foot, 24 frames per second, 90 feet per minute.
- **65 mm.** This is the primary format for IMAX presentations, for which the frame must contain enough visual information to hold up on the big screen. This film format is generally not used for traditional moviemaking. The aspect ratio for 65 mm film is 2.20:1.

Table 9.2	Running Time of Film Rolling at 24 Frames Per Second	
Length of Film	**16 mm (36 ft/min)**	**35 mm (90 ft/min)**
100 ft	2.77 min	1.11 min
200 ft	5.55 min	2.22 min
400 ft	11.11 min	4.44 min
800 ft	22.22 min	N/A
1,000 ft	27.70 min	11.11 min
1,200 ft	33.30 min	N/A
2,000 ft	55.55 min	22.22 min

BUYING FILM

Approach the purchase of film as you would buying a car: be prepared to *negotiate*. First, when preparing a budget for a movie, you need to know how much film you will need to shoot the movie:

- Assume you are shooting a 90-minute movie. If 35 mm film at 24 frames per second at 90 feet per minute is pulled through the camera, you can calculate that a 90-minute movie has about 8100 feet of film.
- Calculate the ratio between footage shot and the amount of footage used in the final movie. This is called the shooting ratio and generally isn't more than 6:1. This means that for every setup, the director will shoot six takes with the intention of using one take. So 8100 feet × 6 = 48,600 feet. For the sake of discussion, round the number up to 50,000 feet. You will need

to buy 50,000 feet of film to produce a 90-minute feature with a 6:1 shooting ratio.

- 35 mm film comes in two lengths: 400-foot rolls that are used for handheld and steadicam shots and 1,000-foot rolls for everything else. Go through the script and determine how many pages are to be shot handheld or Steadicam. The number of pages you count equals the number of minutes of the movie that will be shot handheld. Multiply by 6 for your shooting ratio, and you have the number of minutes you need to buy in 400-foot rolls. For example, if your script has eight pages of handheld setups, one page in the script equals one minute in the movie. Eight minutes of movie time times 6 (the shooting ratio) equals 48 minutes of footage. Forty-eight minutes of footage equals 4,320 feet, which, if purchased in 400-foot rolls, comes to 11,400-foot rolls of film. The remaining 45,680 feet will be purchased in 46 1,000-foot rolls. Next, calculate which scenes will be lit with daylight or tungsten lighting and calculate how many feet of daylight film and how many feet of tungsten-balanced film you'll need.

Panavision 35 mm camera.

- The retail cost of 35 mm film is around $0.65 per foot. Negotiate the cost down to around $0.40–$0.50 per foot by talking with both Kodak and Fuji.
- Instead of buying new film from the manufacturer, you can save money by purchasing:
  - **Buybacks.** If a production purchases film but doesn't use it, they sell the unused, factory-sealed film to resellers. Purchase buybacks for approximately $0.35–$0.40 per foot.
  - **Recans.** When a production company purchases film, loads it into magazines, and doesn't use it, they repackage it, tape it up, and sell it to film resellers. Recans sell for around $0.25 per foot.
  - **Ends.** When a 400- or 1000-foot roll is loaded in a magazine and the filmmakers expose only part of the roll, the remaining film is cut, unloaded, and recanned. Purchase ends of more than 700 feet (long ends) for $0.18–$0.20 per foot and short ends of less than 400 feet for $0.10–$0.12 per foot.
- Once you've chosen the film size, you can now choose the sensitivity, or ASA of the film stock, which determines how fast or slow the film is. Faster film has a higher ASA number and is more sensitive to light. Although this may seem like a good thing, faster film stocks are often grainier because the silver-halide crystals in the film are much larger. Larger crystals are more light-sensitive, but because they are larger, there are also fewer of them in one film frame, lessening the image resolution. Talk with the director of photography to determine the amount of lighting of each scene and the optimal required film speed before purchasing film stock.

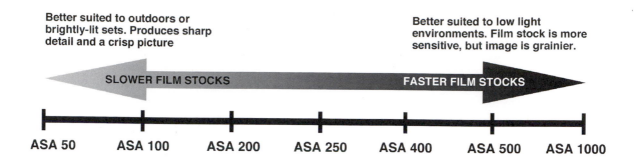

Another factor in shooting film is the cost of camera and support equipment, purchasing the film stock, processing, and postproduction. The options and choices of format, amount of footage, and camera gear are dependent on many factors including:

- **What the final exhibition format of the movie will be.** Do you want to print the movie back to 35 mm film for a theatrical screening or is the final movie going to be exhibited on video or DVD? The cost of creating a 35 mm film print is extremely expensive and can cost thousands of dollars, depending on film format and length of the movie. Today, many theatres are equipped with digital projectors, negating the need to project on film.
- **How bright the locations will be.** Cleaner images require a slower film, which requires more lighting and production equipment for proper exposure. Will the budget support the additional lighting equipment and the crew to rig it?
- **Increased crew requirements.** Can the production afford qualified crew members who know how to load and operate a film camera?
- **Whether there will be any digital effects.** If shooting on film and there are a lot of visual effects, the cost of printing these effects will add to the postproduction costs.
- **Availability of labs and rental facilities.** Not all labs can handle all types of film, nor are all rental facilities able to support all formats. Renting or processing in another city or out of state can be costly.

FILM WORKFLOW

Traditional Postproduction

- Once the film is shot on location, the exposed film stock is taken to a film processing lab to be developed, generating a *workprint*. Also called *dailies* or a *rush print*, the workprint is the footage used to edit and assemble the movie.
- Once the edit is complete on a lower budget film, the editor will then physically cut the original film negative so that the edits match the edit performed on the workprint. On higher budget films, a copy of the negative is edited to preserve the integrity of the original negative and create different cuts of the film. This process is called *conforming* or *negative matching*.
- This newly cut negative is the actual film that was exposed in the camera and the only master of the movie, so if something happens to it, the film

could be irreparably damaged. That's why filmmakers make a copy of the negative to make an *interpositive,* also called a *master positive.* It's at this stage that titles, transitions, and special effects are spliced into the movie.

- Once the master positive is complete, the movie can be transferred to video using a telecine process. Or the lab can duplicate the interpositive to make an *internegative* (or "dupe negative"). Prints for theatrical screenings are made from the internegative.

Digital Postproduction 1

- Film is exposed on set and then delivered to a lab for processing. The cost of processing varies depending on the format you're shooting on.
- If you want to edit the footage digitally using a nonlinear editor like Avid or Final Cut Pro, you need to telecine your film footage, which is the process of cleaning the film and running it through a high-resolution scanner to convert it into a digital format. Once scanned in, the lab will sync your production audio to the digitized film.
- The scanned footage is then recorded to one of many HD video formats.
- Once the footage has been digitized into the editing system, the editor can begin assembling the footage.
- Color correct; add digital effects, titles, and music; mix the sound; and complete through the final cut.
- Render and output to a format of choice. You can hire a film lab to transfer the movie from its current digital format back to film using high-resolution printers that prints each frame, one at a time. Although the price has dropped significantly, you can still expect to pay upward of $30,000 for a 90-minute feature. This option is rarely used, as many theatres are equipped with digital projectors. The quality of an HD projection is just as good and costs a fraction of 35 mm projection.

Digital Postproduction 2

- Film is exposed on set and then delivered to a lab for processing.
- The film is run through a telecine process and delivered on a video format of your choice.
- The video version will be digitized into a nonlinear editor and an editor will edit an offline version of the movie.
- Once the edit is complete, the editor will provide an EDL, or edit decision list, to a negative cutter who will physically cut the negative so it conforms to the offline edit. Digital effects, titles, and transitions can be performed optically, or digitally generated, and then printed back to film.

Film processing labs can brighten or darken the exposed film if the film wasn't properly exposed, there was too much or too little light used on set, or a special look is desired. When the lab brightens the film by lengthening the time of development, this is called **pushing** or **forcing** the film. Pushing by a stop won't adversely affect the image quality, but pushing more than a stop will begin to degrade the image by increasing grain and washing out shadows. Conversely, **pulling** is the process of darkening overexposed film.

Benefits of Shooting Film

- Film's rich, organic look is due, in part, to the random mosaic of silver-halide particles that makes each frame unique. Unlike video, which captures light and converts it using a grid of light-sensitive sensors, film's chemical process mimics the way the human eye operates. Its high resolution is similar to an eight-mega-pixel still image, compared to HD's two-megapixel image quality. Be aware that after film has been processed and undergone copying, generation losses degrade the image projected in theaters to the same resolution quality as HD.
- Film offers a greater contrast range, color saturation, and resolution than digital video. Film is more sensitive to light and is able to capture low-light scenes and high-contrast scenes much better than most video sources. Film is also more forgiving in over- and underexposed areas of the image.
- Film cameras are able to offer a wide range of shooting speeds of 400 frames per second, although several HD digital cameras are capable of shooting thousands of frames per second for ultra-slow-motion shots.
- Film is the most universally accepted distribution format. Any country will accept a film-based movie, in part because of the ease of transferring it to other mediums.
- Larger film formats offer a shallower depth of field than some digital formats due to the larger film plane size.
- Film lasts longer than video formats.

Drawbacks of Shooting Film

- The cameras are heavy and may require additional camera personnel to operate them.
- Film is expensive to purchase and process.
- You cannot see what you've shot until the footage is processed at the lab.
- Audio needs to be recorded separately and then synced in postproduction, which is an expensive, time-consuming process.
- Film is susceptible to dust, scratches, and debris that may damage the coating.

Early HD cameras like the Panasonic HVX200 brought true HD capabilities to independent filmmakers for a fraction of the cost of larger cameras.

SHOOTING DIGITAL VIDEO

Video has been an evolving format over the years, coming close to – and sometimes equaling – the quality of film, especially with newer camera systems. Recently, high-definition and uncompressed formats as well as advanced CCD and CMOS chips have begun leveling the playing field between video and film, allowing filmmakers to tell their stories like never before. From low-budget independent movies to Hollywood movies like *Superman*, *Star Wars: Episode II (Attack of the Clones)* and *Star Wars: Episode III (Revenge of the Sith)*, *Collateral*, and *Miami Vice*, the digital acquisition format has gained significant traction as a viable production medium.

There is a significant difference in the image quality, resolution, contrast range, and color space between the old analog formats such as VHS, Hi8, 8 mm, and VHS-C and the new digital video formats of MiniDV, DV, DVCPRO, RAW, XDCAM, and DVCAM. If you are serious about producing a commercially viable movie, consider investing in or renting a high-quality HD camera system.

Jason's Notes

When making the decision whether to shoot standard-definition or high-definition video, high-definition formats should warrant careful and serious consideration. The recent proliferation of HD content has made consumers more willing to invest in HD television sets, prompting media providers to create more HD content.

Any filmmaker willing to invest money in a movie should be using a format that meets current and near-future broadcast and distribution specifications. Most distributors will no longer accept standard-definition product because of the limited resolution, poor aesthetic quality, and inability to sell it to HD-savvy audiences.

Fortunately, HD has been a working format long enough that rental and purchase prices of HD cameras and postproduction solutions have dropped significantly, making them more affordable than ever.

Standard Definition

The NTSC (National Standards Television Committee) color television signal, which has only recently been phased out, was the main television format in North America from its inception in the late 1940s. Termed "standard definition," televisions, DVD players, tape players, and broadcasters all utilize the same signal specifications:

720 × 480 RESOLUTION

This refers to the number of horizontal pixels to the number of vertical pixels in the television image. Sometimes referred to as the **lines of resolution**, the NTSC signal contains 525 lines of resolution with several lines reserved for closed captioning, time code, and other data hidden in the signal. Nonlinear editing systems digitize NTSC video at resolution of 720×480. Not all televisions display all lines of data, so although televisions have improved in picture quality over the past half-century, the signal itself hasn't changed.

The majority of the productions I'm hired to shoot are shot on HD cameras. The workflow and postproduction costs make it an ideal format for most commercials, movies, and documentaries.

4:3 ASPECT RATIO

The aspect ratio refers to the ratio of the width of the frame to the height. All NTSC television signals are 4:3, which equates to four blocks wide by three blocks high. The NTSC aspect ratio is sometimes described as 1.33:1.

29.97 INTERLACED FRAMES

The NTSC signal operates at 29.97 frames every second. Color televisions use cathode-ray tubes (three, to be exact – one for each primary color), or CRTs, which operate like a gun that shoots a stream of electrons at a photosensitive screen, causing it to glow. Electromagnets surrounding the CRT pull the electron stream across the screen systematically scanning each and every of the 525 lines of the frame. The engineers who created this system discovered that they could fit more lines of resolution into the frame if the electron beam were to scan every *even* line first and then jump back to the top of the frame and scan every *odd* line. Each of these passes is called a **field**, and two fields together make one frame. This is why NTSC television is called **interlaced**. So the NTSC television standard consists of 29.97 frames per second and 60 fields per second. Elsewhere in the world, the European television standard, PAL (Phase Alternating Line), has 25 interlaced frames per second consisting of 50 fields.

Let's say that you're watching an action movie on VHS and pause the tape to get popcorn out of the microwave. When you come back, you notice that in the frame you paused at, the action hero, who is running in front of a bus, is jumping back and forth. Even though you paused the *frame*, you're seeing the interplay between the odd and even *fields*.

BENEFITS OF SHOOTING VIDEO

- Video is much cheaper than film, doesn't need to be processed, and can be viewed instantly for playback on set or in the editing room.
- The postproduction workflow is much easier when shooting video. It's even possible to transfer the footage to a laptop on set and assemble a rough cut before finishing a day of shooting.
- What you see is what you get. There is no need to wait for the developed film to come back from the lab to determine if there were any mistakes made in exposure, framing, or coloring. The image you see on a properly-calibrated monitor is the image that has been recorded.
- The cameras tend to be smaller and lighter, making it easier to set up the camera for a new setup.
- It's possible to schedule more setups in a day, shortening the number of days needed to shoot a film and keeping the budget lower because it's easier to set up the camera.
- The audio can be recorded directly to tape, eliminating the need to sync the sound in postproduction.
- HD video cameras are rapidly producing images of the same quality and resolution as film, making it a vastly superior choice for low budget movies.

High-Definition Video

High-definition video is the long-awaited replacement to standard definition and offers huge improvements in resolution, variable frame rates, detail, and

DRAWBACKS OF SHOOTING VIDEO

- Video is an electronic process that forces the image into a grid of pixels that can result in aliasing, or jagged distortions in curved or angled lines.
- Shooting a movie on video may hurt its chances for distribution, as many distributors still prefer movies shot on 35 mm film.
- Shooting video has a limited contrast range and much less sensitivity to light than film.
- Video cameras are limited in their ability to overcrank and undercrank. Certain HD cameras can shoot only up to 60 frames per second, although specialized cameras are capable of capturing thousands of frames per second for ultra slow motion.
- Compression, especially in consumer formats like DV and HDV, eliminates a lot of color detail, causing artifacts, blockiness, and flat colors in favor of smaller file size.

color. Designed as the new worldwide standard, there are two primary high-definition formats that are used.

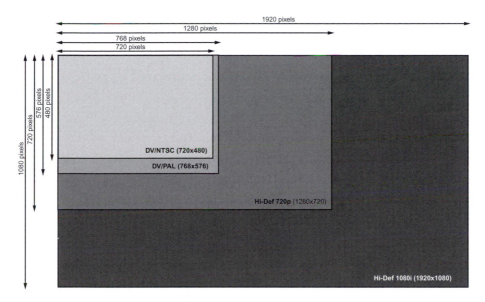

Compare the size and aspect ratios of common standard definition and high definition formats.

720P

The smaller of the two HD formats has a resolution of 1280×720. Used for television broadcasts where the larger HD format is too big for current broadcast carrier waves, the 720 format boasts an impressive array of features.

The 720 format has a 16×9 aspect ratio. Like its 1080 HD brother, it has a frame shape similar to 35 mm film. Much wider than standard definition, HD offers a much more aesthetically pleasing shape and image.

The 720 format supports a variety of frame rates as well as progressive and interlaced frames.

TELEVISION STANDARDS

Television standards are like languages. Each is unique and incompatible, but can be translated to another format. Following are the major television formats of the world.

NTSC
- Used in most of North and South America
- Screen aspect ratio is 4:3
- 525 lines of horizontal resolution
- 29.97 frames per second
- Each frame is made of two fields
- Roughly 30 MB per second uncompressed

PAL
- Used in western Europe and Australia
- Screen aspect ratio is 4:3
- 625 lines of horizontal resolution
- 25 frames per second
- Each frame is made of two fields

Secam (Sequential Couleur Amemorie)
- Used in France and various parts of the Middle East and Africa
- Screen aspect ratio is 4:3
- 819 lines of horizontal resolution
- 25 frames per second
- Each frame is made of two fields

High Definition
- Screen aspect ratio is 16:9
- Resolution is either 1280×720 or 1920×1080
- The frame rate is 23.98, 24, 25, 29.97, 30, 50, 59.94, and 60 frames per second
- HD can be recorded in either interlaced or progressive modes
- Roughly 300 MB per second uncompressed

1080I/P

The larger of the two high-definition formats, 1080 boasts a resolution of 1920×1080 pixels in either interlaced or progressive mode. With a 16:9 aspect ratio, the progressive format 1080p provides the highest resolution and image quality of the two formats, although 720p still offers approximately 30% greater resolution than the interlaced 1080i format.

Choosing the Right Camera Equipment

It's easy to get caught up in the hype surrounding the latest and greatest camera on the market, but before you jump on the bandwagon, consider whether the camera is right for your project:

- **What is the style of your movie?** Renting a high-end 2 k or 4 k camera may be great for an action movie or a sprawling epic with lush vistas and sweeping visuals, but is it the best choice for a character drama in which you'll be framing close-ups of the actors for most of the movie? Acquiring in 4k resolution may sound like a great idea until you realize that you can see every pore, wrinkle, and imperfection on your actor's face in astonishing clarity. Will you need to spend money in the editing room softening or reducing the resolution of the image? Can you afford to build sets to the degree of detail necessary to look good in 4k?

- **What is the exhibition format?** I am constantly surprised by how many filmmakers chose high-end camera formats when the final product is output to standard-definition DVD or streamed over the Internet. If you're planning on a theatrical release or distribution on Blu-ray, then higher-resolution formats are perfect. For lower-resolution deliverables, 720p or 1080p are outstanding and much less expensive formats with which to work.
- **What does the DP think?** All too often, directors of photography are hired based on the type of camera they own. In actuality, hire a DP for his or her skills, and rely on his expertise in choosing the proper camera.
- **What is the postproduction cost?** Consider the costs of data storage, transfer, and editing costs when choosing a camera format. The costs of working with Panasonic's P2 DVCPro HD format are merely the price of an off-the-shelf hard drive and a basic home computer, whereas working with footage from uncompressed formats requires editing systems powerful enough to handle the data workflow. These professional systems can cost hundreds of thousands of dollars to buy and tens of thousands of dollars to rent.

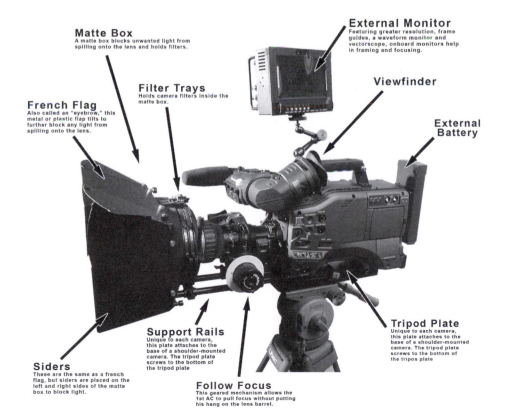

From top to bottom:
35 mm film, 35 mm
CMOS chip, 2/3″ CCD,
and 4/3″ CMOS.

Professional CINE-style digital cameras are designed to provide the greatest degree of support and flexibility over the image, and although they look intimidating, all the accessories and components that make up the camera system are vital on a film set.

- **Camera body.** Most professional camera manufacturers sell only the camera body, giving the cinematographer the ability to customize the body with lenses, monitors, and accessories appropriate to each production. The most important three components to keep in mind when choosing a camera for your project is what type of light processing chip you want, what type of video signal is captured, and how it is recorded.
  - **The chip.** In much the same way that film "records" light that falls on it, CCD or CMOS chips are light-sensitive sensors that convert light into an electrical signal that is then encoded and recorded onto the recording format. There have been significant advances over the years, producing chips that capture a higher resolution in lower light, producing a result that is closer to film. There are two basic types of chips available in professional cameras:
    - **CCD.** Short for "charge-coupled devices," CCDs have been the primary technology used in digital video cameras for years. CCDs feature two types of sensors built onto each chip, one that is sensitive to the color of the light, and the other to brightness. Inexpensive consumer cameras use only one CCD, whereas professional cameras feature a prism that breaks the light into its red, green, and blue components, focusing each color onto one of three CCDs mounted in the camera body. 3-CCD cameras produce a much sharper, cleaner, and more color-saturated image than single-CCD cameras. In general, CCD cameras produce less noise (or grain) in the image, tend to be more sensitive in low-light scenarios, and generate less heat. The only drawback of CCDs is their size. It's difficult to create a depth of field close to 35 mm film due to physical limitations of the optics and CCD size in a 3-CCD camera body. CCDs range in size from 1/3″ to 2/3″, with the larger chip size capable of producing a shallower depth of field and less noise. Although the image can still look like film, the difference between a 2/3″ CCD and a 35 mm film plane is significant.
    - **CMOS.** Recently, digital camera manufacturers started using the same chips used in still cameras. These CMOS chips are 35 mm and are capable of mimicking the depth of field of 35 mm film cameras. Although very popular with filmmakers, CMOS chips tend to generate a lot of heat, which is picked up as noise by the sensors. As a result, CMOS chips can be very grainy in low-light scenarios and are not as light-sensitive as their CCD counterparts. Conversely, CMOS chips offer greater latitude, better response to highlights, better color range in flesh tones, and smoother overexposure curves than CCDs.

Jason's Notes

The size of the CCD or CMOS chip has a direct relationship to the lens width. The smaller the chip, the narrower the field of view. Shooting on 2/3″ chips will yield a much wider field of view than when working with a 1/3″ chip, and this can make all the difference when shooting in small, confined spaces. Although you can use a wide-angle adapter, you will achieve a crisper image by choosing a larger-chip format.

- **Video signal.** The number of sensors on either the CCD or the CMOS chip help determine the resolution of the final video image. There are a number of standard resolutions that can be acquired by digital cameras:
  - **720p (1280×720).** This is the smallest of the HD resolutions and is used mostly in broadcast productions. Recorded as a progressive frame, 720p is an outstanding choice for TV commercials, feature films, and programs designed for broadcast.
  - **1080 (1920×1080).** The larger of the two HD formats, 1080 is available either as a progressive format (1080p), meaning each line of the frame is captured concurrently to create a more "film-like" look, or as an interlaced format (1080i), meaning the odd lines are captured first, then the even lines. The resulting image has a more "video" look. 1080p is a much better format for shooting motion pictures, although the data management requirements are much higher. Generally, 1080p-capable cameras are significantly more expensive than their 720p counterparts.
  - **2k (2048×1080)/4k (4096×2160).** Both 2k and 4k image formats are used in digital cinema and are not bounded by the same resolution, frame rate, and aspect ratios as 720 and 1080 HD broadcast specifications. The level of detail in a 2k or 4k frame is so good that the resulting image comes very close to matching the look of film. Although the image looks incredible, the drawback of working with 2k and 4k images lies in the cost of storage and the postproduction workflow.
- **Recording format.** Once the image has been captured by the CMOS chip or CCD, the camera will compress the image so that it can be stored on the supported recording format. Some cameras need to heavily compress the video so it can be stored on a solid-state device like Panasonic's P2 card or a Sony ExpressCard or directly to tape like HDCAM or HDV formats, whereas cameras like Panavision's Genesis camera or the RED camera can capture an uncompressed signal directly to hard drive. Know in choosing your camera that less compression equates to a better image but also results in much larger file sizes.
- **Lens.** The lens is the single most important component of the camera system, and choosing a good lens can significantly improve the overall image quality of your production. Interchangeable lenses used in professional

Interchangeable lenses, like this Canon lens, allow you to choose the right glass for your project.

camera systems are made of glass, reducing image artifacts and ensuring a sharp image. Although glass is vastly superior in quality to the plastic lenses found in low-end consumer camcorders, it is also very expensive, so manufacturers have begun using lenses made of fluorite – a composite plastic material that although inexpensive still offers a high picture quality and low-light sensitivity. See Chapter 13 to learn more about lenses.

- **Lens types.** There are several types of lenses to choose from, each suited to the specific demands of your production.
  - **Fixed vs. interchangable.** Many consumer cameras feature built-in, non-removable lenses. Although not the highest quality optics, fixed lenses are designed for each camera body and generally produce a crisp clean image. You can purchase a wide angle adapter or a telephoto lens to increase or decrease the focal length, but adding additional pieces of glass will slightly soften the image and require you to open up the iris to compensate for slight light loss.
  - **Zoom vs. prime lenses.** Professional lenses come in two varieties: zoom lenses, which allow the operator to change the focal length, and prime lenses, which are of fixed focal length. Prime lenses come in sets of five or six lenses and need to be physically changed in order to change the focal length. Although zoom lenses are more convenient to work with, prime lenses offer crisper images with less light loss because there's less glass through which light is refracted.
  - **Fast vs. slow lenses.** The "speed" of a lens refers to the maximum opening of the iris and how much light it lets through to the film plane. Fast lenses are able of opening to a T1.4 or T1.3, whereas slow lenses open to only a T5.6 or a T8. Fast lenses are generally more expensive, although they may not be necessary when shooting outdoors or in environments are well-lit.
- **Lens problems.** Cheap lenses can degrade the quality of the image, resulting in any number of visual defects:
  - **Vignetting.** Occurs when the corners and outer edges of the frame are darkened.
  - **Loss of contrast.** Black objects appear lighter or slightly milky.
  - **Softening or blurring.** Inexpensive lenses may not transmit light as cleanly as glass lenses, causing enough light refraction to soften the image, reducing the clarity and overall sharpness.
  - **Distortion.** Inexpensive lenses can cause spatial distortion, causing objects to be disproportionately portrayed at various parts of the frame.
  - **Chromatic aberration.** This occurs especially at the long end of the lens (zoomed all the way in), wherein the refraction through the

glass creates a color separation, essentially turning the lens into a prism. Most noticeable around high-contrast objects like a tree branches against the sky, you can see a red halo around one side of the object and a blue halo on the other side. Some professional cameras have a feature that detects and minimizes the effects of chromatic aberration, but nothing will completely solve the optical problem like a good quality lens.

Vignetting

- **Viewfinder.** Single-unit video cameras feature built-in viewfinders and in many cases flip-out LCD screens. Professional cameras offer viewfinders as an added accessory, giving the operator a choice between color and black and white, 4×3 or 16×9 aspect ratios, and overall image size. Many camera operators prefer to use the viewfinder, as it focuses their attention on the image and their closeness to the camera offers better panning and tilting control. The one drawback to a viewfinder is its inability to display the full resolution of HD 720/1080 images, making focus difficult to accurately gauge.

Softening

- **Onboard monitor.** Onboard monitors are capable of displaying a higher resolution than the camera's viewfinder, making them a great tool for framing and setting focus. Often, the 1st assistant cameraman will use the onboard monitor when pulling focus to ensure the image is sharp, or the operator can use the monitor for framing complicated moves for which using the viewfinder is difficult. Advanced monitors incorporate a number of features that allow the operator to adjust and control the picture.

Distortion

  - **Waveform monitor and vectorscope.** These overlaid graphs display the brightness and color values of the image and are used to help determine proper exposure and color balance.

Loss of Contrast

  - **Frame mask.** Although you may be shooting in 16:9 HD video, you may want to mask or letterbox the image later in postproduction to a different aspect ratio. Professional monitors can mask the frame so the camera operator can properly compose the shot.
  - **Frame guides.** Many HD productions still need to be broadcast on standard definition 4:3 TVs, meaning the left and right sides of the frame will be cut off. Monitors are capable of overlaying frame lines of different video formats to ensure the subject is properly framed.

Professional monitors provide more image calibration features than consumer monitors, helping ensure that what you see is what you're getting.

- **Blue mode.** Professional monitors can be set to display only the blue color channel so you can adjust the monitor to ensure what you're seeing is really what you're getting. For more information on calibrating a production monitor, refer to Chapter 13.
- **Multiple formats and inputs.** Professional monitors can accept a wide variety of inputs from different video sources, including analog composite signals and HD-SDI signals sent from professional cameras.
- **Follow focus.** If the 1st assistant cameraman tries to pull focus with his hand on the camera lens, he can easily move or shake the camera, ruining the shot. Follow focus units are geared instruments that shift manipulation of the focus knob to a large dial that is much easier to access and control. Follow focus units feature a dry-erase ring that enables the 1st assistant cameraman to write focus marks for a shot.
    - **Whips** – If the camera is mounted on a steadicam or during a complicated dolly shot, it's difficult for the 1st assistant cameraman to keep his hand on the follow focus, so a whip is used. A *whip* is an extension that plugs into the follow focus and allows the 1st AC to pull focus from a distance.
- **Matte box.** The matte box is supported in front of the camera lens on support rails and is designed to block extraneous light from reaching the camera lens and to hold camera filters in front of the lens.
    - **Filter trays.** Most matte boxes use filter trays to hold camera filters in front of the lens. With one or more of these trays capable of rotating 360 degrees, filters such as polarizers or streak filters that need to be rotated to an optimal position can be easily set and locked in position. Both matte boxes and filter trays can be purchased in different sizes depending on the camera format, usually 4″×4″ and 4″×5″.
    - **French flag.** Sometimes lights on set can create lens flares, especially rim or hair lights that are focused towards the camera lens. French flags are metal flaps that are mounted on the front of a matte box used to block this light from hitting the camera lens. Typically, the term "French flag" is used only to describe the top flag.
    - **Siders.** Siders are French flags used on the left and right sides of the matte box.
- **Filters.** Filters are pieces of glass placed into a matte box intended to affect the image. There are hundreds of types of filters, but the most critical to add to your toolkit affect the exposure. The effect of softening and other specialty filters can be added and altered with much more control in the editing room.
    - **Neutral Density (ND) filter.** ND filters are used to reduce the light entering the camera lens. Think of them as sunglasses for the camera; by using an ND filter, you must open the camera iris to compensate for the light loss, which yields the desired result of a shallower depth of field.

Graduated ND filters are used when shooting outside to darken the sky to within the camera latitude without affecting the subject on the ground.

- **Polarizers.** Windows and windshields can reflect so much light that it's nearly impossible to shoot the subject sitting behind them. Polarizers, when properly rotated in front of the camera lens, can all but remove these reflections. In addition, polarizers will bring out colors, making the image much more saturated. One trick to using polarizers: shoot as close to a 45-degree angle to optimize the polarizer's effect. Using a polarizer when shooting perpendicular to a reflective surface has virtually no effect.

Photograph without polarizer

Photograph with polarizer

Polarizers are ideal for removing reflections in glass, especially when shooting vehicles.

- **Softening filters.** There are a variety of filters that can soften the subject and are especially valuable when shooting documentary subjects or close-ups on actors. From Tiffen Pro-Mist filters, which take the sharp edge off an HD image, to specific Diffusion FX filters, which soften only flesh tones, softening filters can add a lot to the image. Be careful, however, because if you shoot through a softening filter and the effect is too strong, it's impossible to remove the effect later in post. It's best to be conservative when using a filter on set, especially when software plug-ins in the editing room can mimic most softening and tinting filters.

- **Battery.** The battery is one of the most underappreciated components of a camera system. Ranging from a few hundred dollars for consumer and prosumer camera batteries to a few thousand for battery systems for larger cameras, batteries need to be able to provide the necessary power and be able to handle the rigors of on-set production. Bring at least three batteries with you at all times, so while you're shooting with one battery, the second one can be charging and a third can be ready, should you deplete the first one.

PRODUCTION MONITORS

Decades ago, when film was the predominant medium for shooting movies, the only person able to see the frame was the camera operator. The director and DP placed tremendous trust in this person, and if he said another take was needed, another take was shot. If he said the shot looked good, the director would move on. This reliance on the camera operator is no longer the case.

With the proliferation of digital video cameras and video taps for film came advanced monitoring which enables the director and DP to see what is actually being shot, pixel for pixel. The benefit is that there are no surprises in the editing room. The director can actually see what is being shot live on set, making adjustments as needed.

Always work with good monitors so that you know the image you're seeing is accurate.

There are two types of production monitors available:

- **CRT (cathode ray tube).** Although these monitors use the same older technology as home TVs from the past 50 years, the image is arguably better than newer LCD screen. With a better contrast range and more saturated colors, CRTS are still a favorite on set. The only down sides are the bulky size of the monitors and the expensive cost of HD CRT monitors.

- **LCD (liquid crystal display).** A more common and inexpensive monitor is the flat LCD screen. Different from the flat screen you may have at home, production monitors feature better resolution, wider contrast range for accurate image display, and a host of controls to properly calibrate and adjust the image.

Using a production monitor can cause just as many problems as it solves:

- **Accuracy of picture.** Be careful to not set the exposure or determine the colors of your shot based on how it appears on the monitor. They are notoriously inaccurate – no two monitors in the world will give you the same image. Use a light meter, waveform monitor, and vector scope to ensure that you are properly capturing the footage, and always calibrate the production monitor before you begin shooting.
- **Opinions.** One problem with a monitor is that a lot of people can see it and on set, and everyone has an opinion. When I'm directing or DPing, I prefer to tent off the monitor area known as "video village" to prevent unnecessary people from chiming in with opinions.

CAMERA SUPPORT

Camera support equipment helps stabilize the shot by moving the camera in a smooth, controlled manner. There are a variety of different types of support tools, including tripods, dollies, and cranes, that you can use to improve the production value of your movie.

Tripod. The biggest problem with independent movies is that the camera is handheld too often, drawing the audience's attention to the shaky camera and away from the story. Although the handheld technique has its place in action sequences and point-of-view shots, nothing can beat a steady camera, carefully panning and tilting on a tripod through each shot. A tripod is made of two different parts: the legs, which are the three supports, and the head, which is the pan/tilt mechanism the camera sits atop. There are several types of tripod heads:

- **Friction head** ($50–$100). These tripods are the least expensive and are designed for still cameras and lightweight camcorders. The tension controls on the head increase and decrease pressure on two metal plates. Although ideal for lockdown shots in which the camera doesn't need to move, panning and tilting actions are not smooth because of the two plates grinding against one another. These tripods are also very lightweight, so even the steadiest camera operator will have a difficult time getting a stable shot, especially if the camera is zoomed in on the subject.
- **Fluid head** ($250–$8,000). Fluid-head tripods rely on a thick oil to increase and decrease tension in the head, resulting in a smooth panning and tilting movement. The cost of fluid-head tripods is dependent on their size. Bigger cameras need bigger heads. Because fluid-head tripods are used mostly in professional applications, they can be configured in many different ways to suit the needs of the production. Legs and heads can be purchased separately so you can build your own tripod.

A fluid head.

Matthews Studio
Equipment Doorway Dolly.

Matthews Studio
Equipment Intel-A-Jib.

■ **Gear head** ($10,000–$20,000). Used to support large 35 mm cameras, the *gear head* is used to precisely control the camera, whose weight may make it difficult to handle on a conventional fluid head. The gear head has two wheels, one on the side that controls tilt and one on the back that controls the panning movement. These wheels have gear settings that control the responsiveness of the wheels so the operator can, by moving the wheels the same speed, pan and tilt quickly or very slowly, depending on the requirements of the shot. Rarely used in video, gear heads are usually seen on shoots utilizing larger film cameras.

■ **Dolly** (free–$500/day to rent). A *dolly* is a platform with wheels that moves the camera in a smooth, controlled manner. Always pushed by an operator, the dolly can be used with oversized tires if the ground is smooth, or can operate on a track, which gives the dolly grip precise control over the camera's movements. Dollies can be cheaply constructed by mounting skateboard wheels parallel to each other on an angled piece of steel and then attaching them to the bottom of a piece of plywood. Track can be made out of PVC pipe, cut to whatever length you need. Professional dollies, like the Matthews Doorway Dolly, can be rented for $50–$70 a day with eight-foot pieces of track renting at around $15–$25 a day. Using professional equipment will be much easier when setting up controlled shots. Large, pneumatically controlled dollies like the Super PeeWee or the Chapman are heavy, sophisticated dollies that can raise and lower the camera and are designed for heavy motion picture cameras. They can be rented for $300–$500 a day.

■ **Crane** ($400–$1000/day to rent). Cranes are camera support devices with long arms that can raise and lower the camera or arm the camera over a crowd or set. Some cranes are able to support only the camera; others can support the camera and two people. Always counterbalanced with weights, a crane grip will raise, lower, and arc the crane around for the shot. Cranes usually come with an operator who will set up, operate, and tear down the crane because of the unit's complexity and risk.

- **Steadicam** ($400–$1000/day to rent). Steadicams are counterbalanced devices, either handheld for small cameras or worn on a vest for heavier cameras, that absorb the shock of the operator's movements, allowing the operator to walk and run. The result is a smooth shot much like that from a dolly, but it frees the operator to walk up and down stairs, run on rocky terrain, or secure a smooth shot impossible to get with a dolly or crane. Smaller Steadicams can be purchased for around $1,000, whereas the bigger rigs cost around $15,000–20,000.

LIGHTING

In order to meet the exposure requirements of the shooting medium and the artistic requirements of the story, be sure to have access to a wide range of lighting instruments. From inexpensive lights available from the hardware store, to practical lights seen in the shot, to professional high-wattage fixtures, professional tools are the key to creating and manipulating light.

There are a variety of light fixtures, including halogen metal iodide (HMI), fluorescent, and tungsten lighting, that can be configured into harsh, soft, direct, and diffused sources of different color temperatures to provide filmmakers with varying degrees of control.

Two basic categories of lights are open face and Fresnels:

- **Open-face lights** feature an exposed lamp placed in front of a focusing reflector. Using nothing more than a wire scrim in front of the lamp and a lever to focus or spot the light, the basic functionality of the fixture makes them inexpensive and versatile.
- **Fresnels** are lights with a built-in lens that focuses the light. Generally sturdier and more easily controlled, Fresnels provide greater, more focused light output and more flexibility for the user than open-face fixtures.

Tiffen Company Archer 2 Steadicam.

Lowel open face tungsten light.

Arri tungsten Fresnel light.

Although inexpensive solutions may provide the light output needed to light a scene, the lack of control over the light will ultimately create a problem. Some features to look for in a light fixture include:

- **Barn doors.** These four metal flaps help shape the light roughly. Completely configurable, barn doors are the first line of flagging, shaping, and reducing the spill of the light. Gels and diffusion can be clipped to barn doors.
- **Flood and spot.** A dial or lever on the side of the light will move the lamp closer to and farther from the reflector, focusing the light beam into a narrow beam or spreading the light across a greater area.
- **Lamps.** Professional lights accept industry-standard bulbs. Although expensive, these bulbs are designed to generate light at a specific color temperature and wattage.
- **Lenses.** Some Fresnels, such as HMI Pars, come with interchangeable lenses that give the user greater flexibility in shaping the pattern of light emanating from the fixture.

Remember that the secret to good lighting is about controlling the attributes of the light, a capability delivered only by professional-grade motion picture lights.

Tungsten

Using the same element found in most household light bulbs, tungsten light fixtures produce a warm orange light (3200 K). These fixtures are among the least expensive and provide a wide range of flexibility and control.

At the cheap end, you can purchase construction work lights from a hardware store or use the clamp on pie-tin utility lights that use standard lightbulbs. Whereas these lights are inexpensive, they lack the control that you have with professional fixtures.

Professional lights produced by companies like Lowel (www.lowel. com) or Arri (www.arri.com) are much more expensive, costing anywhere between $100 and $2,000 per light fixture, depending on the wattage and output of the light. These fixtures offer a much greater degree of control over the light by allowing the user to flood or spot the light, shape the light with barn doors, and reduce the light by adding scrims. Professional lighting equipment can also be rented from a local rental company.

Fluorescent

Tungsten light fixtures require a lot of electricity and generate a lot of heat, making them ineffective in small, tight quarters, so filmmakers often use fluorescent lights instead. Ideal for creating a soft wraparound, these fixtures are cool and energy-efficient, although a single fluorescent lamp does not produce as much light as a tungsten lamp. Light kits of two or three fixtures cost around $3,000 and can be purchased from Kino-Flo (www.kinoflo.com) or Videssence (www.vides-sence.com).

Kino-Flo.

The lamps can be easily switched in fluorescent fixtures between daylight (5600 K) or tungsten (3200 K) lamps so the color temperature matches the ambient light.

Professional fluorescent lights differ from consumer fluorescents in a number of ways:

- **Flicker.** Professional fixtures utilize a special, flicker-free ballast. Unlike consumer fluorescents, which flicker when recorded on a 24-frame-per-second camera, professional lights will not flicker on screen.
- **Dimmability.** Professional fluorescents can be dimmed from the ballast to reduce the light output.
- **Color temperature.** Professional fluorescent fixtures can be outfitted with special bulbs that match the color of either tungsten or daylight, allowing them to be used in either lighting condition.
- **Durability.** Professional fluorescents are designed and built to withstand the rigors of film production and provide a number of controls, from barn doors to egg crates, to craft and focus the light.

LEDs

A popular new light used in small, confined spaces or when the only power available is from the camera battery is light panels. Light panels are arrays of high-output LEDs that generate a substantial amount of heat with minimal power requirements and are idea when used as an interview light atop the camera or as a standalone light in small locations like bathrooms or car interiors. LED light fixtures are generally dimmable and can be gelled and diffused like any other light head.

Lite Panels LED light.

HMI

Halogen metal iodide lights are fixtures that use a gas globe instead of a tungsten bulb and produce roughly five times the amount of light as a tungsten lamp at the same wattage. HMIs produce a blue light that matches the color temperature of sunlight and cost around $8,000 for one light. A 1,200-watt HMI, which is the largest HMI that can run off a household circuit, can be rented for around $120/day from most rental companies.

- **High light output.** HMIs generate five times the light of a similar wattage tungsten light and run much cooler in temperature.
- **Cost.** HMIs are expensive to purchase and maintain. A 1,200-watt globe costs about $200 to replace. HMIs can also be very finicky and fail to strike if power conditions aren't perfect. Repairs and maintenance of HMIs can also be costly.
- **Work outdoors.** The primary light fixture of choice when shooting during daylight, the color temperature of an HMI matches the color of sunlight, eliminating the need to add gels.
- **Dimmable and timed.** HMIs have both dimming controls and the ability to work in flicker-free mode, making them ideal when working with film.

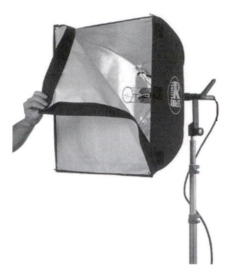

Lowel Rifa-Lite softbox.

Lowel Light Kit.

Softboxes

Softboxes are tungsten or HMI lights with a black fabric housing mounted on the light fixture with a soft white diffusing material that softens the light. Ideal for filming people, the softbox smoothes the light, making much softer shadows. Softbox lights can be purchased or rented as an all-in-one unit that also includes the light fixture, or you can obtain a Chimera (www.chimeralighting.com), which is a separate softbox that can be added to virtually any light fixture.

One outstanding softbox is the Lowel Rifa-Lite. This all-in-one-unit contains a hardwired lamp mounted inside a collapsible umbrella, leaving a very small storage footprint.

Light Kits

Lights can be purchased or rented individually or in a kit. Kits generally include two to four light fixtures, light stands, barn doors, and accessories in one case. This is, in most instances, the best option for filmmakers. A light kit with a 1,000-watt light, a 500-watt light, and a 250-watt light should be sufficient for most small-sized indoor scenes.

Shiny Boards

One of the most common tools used to shape sunlight are shiny boards. These 40"×40" hard reflectors feature a shiny side for harder reflection and a feathered side for a softer bounce. Mounted on a yoke, shiny boards can be used either on a combo stand, or placed on the ground to create an up-light. Shiny boards should be treated like a light in that they can be focused through 4×4 frames of gels or diffusion to create the necessary look.

Matthews Studio Equipment Shiny Board.

Jason's Notes

Never underestimate the power of reflected light. In some situations, all you need is a bounce board to reflect sunlight or provide a little return from your key light. One of the best and most affordable reflectors is one you can make yourself. Visit your local home improvement store and buy a 4′×8′ sheet of bead board (styrofoam insulation), then go to your local craft store and buy a 4′×8′ sheet of white foam core. Cut each piece in half and tape the piece of foam core to the back of the bead board. You now have a 4′×4′ reflector with a harder (foam core) side and a softer side (bead board). Run white gaffers tape along the edges to secure it, and you can now either rig to a stand with a platypus clamp or hand hold it.

Overheads

Overheads are large metal frames used to stretch a variety of special fabrics designed to reduce, reflect, or soften light. Overheads can be rigged over a set to reduce the harshness of the sun, rigged on stands to serve as a large reflector, or even be stood upright for use as a backdrop. The most commonly used overheads come in 6′×6′, 8′×8′, 12′×12′ and 20′×20′ sizes, although larger sizes are used for custom of large-scale rigs.

I used a 20′×20′ green screen behind dancers for a commercial campaign I shot. Notice the 12′×12′ overhead skinned with silver lamé to bounce the sunlight to create the key on the performers.

The fabrics, also called "rages," used on overheads can be broken into three distinct categories:

- **Nets.** Nets are see-through fabric screens used to reduce the light. Using the same material as a scrim, single nets reduce the light by 1/2 stop and a double net reduces the light by a full stop.

- **Reflectors.** These fabrics are designed to reflect sunlight with varying degrees of intensity and specularity, all of which depend on the distance of the actors from the overhead, the quality of sunlight, and the desired look. Some common reflectors include:
  - **Ultrabounce.** A hugely popular reflector, Ultrabounce creates a soft pleasing source with low specularity. Ideal for shooting people, Ultrabounce makes a soft, even light, and when used in conjunction with a shiny board to create a more intense edge or key light, Ultrabounce is the best choice for medium reflectivity and soft wraparound.
  - **Microwave.** A silver, ultrareflective material, microwave is extremely specular and best used when a lot of light is needed on the subject. Generally too harsh for lighting actors, microwave is great for lighting the outside of buildings, creating large highlights on the set, and reflecting light into a dark alley or the interior of a box truck.

Microwave is an ultrareflective material intended for bouncing harsh, direct light.

  - **Lamé.** Lamés come in silver, gold, and silver/gold checkerboard and are more reflective than ultrabounce, but not as specular and harsh as microwave. Often used to light actors, especially from a distance, lamés are a great choice when a lot of reflectivity is needed but you still want a softness on the face.
- **Silks.** Silks are used to soften and diffuse light and are often flown in a frame above the set to soften harsh, overhead sunlight that causes heavy, unflattering shadows under the actor's browline. DPs choose the type of material based on the degree of diffusion of the light.
  - **Full silk.** The most common type of silk, full silks take the majority of the edge off the sunlight while retaining a little bit of the specularity and

direction of the light. Ideal for most purposes, full silks are part of the standard package of rags that come with an overhead.

- **Gridcloth.** This material features a light grid that more heavily diffuses the light along the grid, creating a softer light than a standard silk. Gridcloth will spread the light across its entire surface, creating a larger, more uniform light.
- **Muslin.** Muslin is a heavier material that comes either bleached (white) or unbleached (beige). As a heavier material, it does not diffuse across the entire area of the overhead, but provides a beautiful, soft look. Perfect for lighting people at a close range, muslin requires a lot of light for a very soft, pleasing look.

Safety

Overheads of any size are large sails that pose a huge danger in windy situations. Always hire an experienced key grip to properly rig, fly, and secure an overhead.

Jason's Notes

The grip will "shake up" a shiny board or reflector, which simply means refocusing the light after some time to compensate for the movement of the sun.

LIGHTING SUPPORT

Anyone can set up a light and turn it on, but the real craft of lighting a scene is in controlling the light. Lighting control tools, called *grip equipment*, include flags, nets, silks, and C-stands, which are used to shape, craft, reduce, and diffuse light.

Nets are netted fabric material stretched across a metal frame that, when placed in front of a light source, reduce the amount of light. A single net will cut the light by one-half of an *f*-stop. A double net will reduce the light by one *f*-stop and a triple by almost two *f*-stops. Nets come in a variety of sizes and are often held in front of the light source with a C-stand.

Silks are similar to nets, but instead of a netted material that reduces the light, a silk has a solid white material that softens the light. Silks are used to reduce the harshness of a light source and, like nets, are available in a variety of sizes.

Flags are frames with a solid black material that completely blocks the light. Used to cast shadows, flags are a good tool to help shape the light so that it falls only where you want it.

C-stands are multipurpose stands with a grip head and an extendable grip arm that can hold flags, nets, silks, and even lights.

Flags, nets, and silks are common tools for reducing and softening light.

There are hundreds of different stands, clamps, and rigs that you can use to mount lights and lighting control instruments.

Gels

In addition to controlling the quality of light, it is also important to control the color of light by placing thin films called *gels* in front of the lights. Gels are multicolored pieces of film that will tint your light a certain color, sometimes for aesthetic reasons and other times to balance the color of the light to match the color of other lights within the scene.

The two most common types of gels are CTO (color temperature orange), which is designed to convert the color of sunlight to match the color of tungsten light, and CTB (color temperature blue), which converts tungsten light to match sunlight. To learn more about color temperature, refer to Chapter 13.

You can get a free sample book that includes a variety of gels by contacting Lee Filters or Rosco Filters. Gels can be purchased from a local rental company for around $6 per 2'×2' sheet.

Diffusion

Whereas gels will tint the color of the light, diffusion will soften the light. There are several types of diffusion, each with varying intensities. A gel sample book will also include samples of diffusion.

Both gels and diffusion can be cut with scissors and attached to a light's barn doors using C-47s (the fancy technical term for clothespins).

Matthews Studio Equipment C-Stand with rocky mountain leg and 40" gobo arm.

MICROPHONES

Good audio is critical to a movie, so it is important to have a high-quality shotgun microphone, a boom pole to suspend the mike over the actors, a shock mount to suspend the mike at the end of the boom pole to minimize extraneous sounds, several XLR audio cables, and a good pair of headphones.

Do not use the built-in camera microphone, because the distance from the microphone to the subject will vary from shot to shot, introducing too much ambient sound. Instead, by placing a microphone at a constant distance over the actors, regardless of the camera position, the dialog will be strong and noise-free.

Audio-Technica makes high-quality on-set microphones. See Chapter 14 for more information on microphones and on how to make an inexpensive boom pole.

For more information on microphones and audio recording equipment, please refer to Chapter 14 – Audio Recording.

WHAT DO YOU REALLY NEED?

The list of equipment necessary to shoot a scene can be really complicated and intimidating, so here are some guidelines for the basic must-haves on every film shoot:

- The camera
- A tripod
- A portable television monitor
- Shotgun microphone with a boom pole, XLR cable, and headphones
- Reflector
- Basic lighting kit (one 1000-watt light, one 500-watt light, one 250-watt light)
- White foam core reflector
- Extension cords

In addition, every filmmaker should have a production bag with the following items:

- Screwdrivers, both flat head and Phillips
- A small crescent wrench
- Pliers and needle-nose pliers
- Tape measure
- Small level (used to level pictures and posters hung on set)
- Walkie-talkies
- Light meter
- Volt meter
- Pens, pencils, dry erase markers, and permanent markers
- First-aid kit
- Lens cleaners, camel hair brush
- Can of compressed air
- Small and large flashlights
- Clapboard
- Gaffer's tape, two-inch black and one-inch white
- Video cables and adapters
- C-47s (springed clothespins)
- Book of sample gels
- Swiss Army knife
- Utility knife
- Camera filters
- Spare fuses
- Leather work gloves
- Bug spray
- Dulling spray (reduces glares on reflective surfaces)

LOW-BUDGET ALTERNATIVES

For cash-strapped filmmakers, here are some low-budget options for building an inexpensive equipment package. Understand that by using cheaper tools, you're reducing the amount of control you would normally have by using professional fixtures.

- **Work lights.** When I started shooting my movies, I purchased several construction work lights from the hardware store. Costing $25 each, these lights are switchable between 500 and 1,000 watts and included a light stand and power cable. Although they put out a lot of light, the color of the lights is really warm – much more so than tungsten. Consider buying some one-half CTB gels to correct the light to a standard tungsten light. Also be careful about putting gels or diffusion too close to the lamp. The heat will burn the gels and cause a fire hazard. One major drawback of construction work lights is that the light they generate is very broad and extremely difficult to control.
- **Clamp light.** Available for around $8 each from your local hardware store, these clamp-on lights accept standard tungsten light bulbs and feature a screw-on pie-tin shape reflector. These lights are extremely versatile and the lip of the reflector is perfect for attaching diffusion or gels using C-47s.
- **China lanterns.** China lanterns feature a standard light socket with an expandable two-foot paper globe that dramatically softens the light. Used on major movie sets, China lanterns are a great way of creating a soft ambient source. You can purchase these for under $10 at discount home furnishing stores.
- **Microphone boom pole.** Boom poles are used to suspend a microphone over the actors on set. Real boom poles cost nearly a thousand dollars. For a hundred dollars, you can make an effective boom pole yourself. Purchase a paint roller extension handle and a nice paint roller from the local hardware store. Make sure the paint roller handle will screw onto the end of the extension pole. Next, buy a $50 microphone shock mount from a music or instrument store. Remove the wire and roller from the paint roller handle and screw the shock mount in its place. The result is a retractable boom pole with a removable shock mount that even has a handle.
- **Diffusion.** A frosted shower curtain or a bedsheet, placed a safe distance from a light source, can create a really great diffused light. Also try using tracing paper as diffusion on low-wattage, 100 watts and below, clamp lights to soften the light. Always maintain a safe distance between the diffusion and the light source to avoid a fire.
- **Reflectors.** Professional shiny boards used to reflect sunlight can cost hundreds of dollars to purchase. For an inexpensive alternative, visit the hardware store and purchase a sheet of Tyvek insulated foam. This inch-thick foam has shiny paper on either side and serves as a rugged reflector. Also try white foam core for a softer reflector and foam core wrapped in aluminum foil for a harsher reflector.

Approaching a Rental Facility

Go online or to the phone book and look up "video production," "stage and lighting rental," or "equipment rental," or contact the state film commission for a list of rental houses in the area. Most major cities will have some type of rental company that rents lights and grip gear, although much of their equipment may be for theatrical productions. There's a big difference between movie production equipment and theater equipment, so be sure to ask which they stock. Renting cameras may require contacting a rental facility in a larger city, especially if it's specialized equipment like a 35 mm or high-definition camera.

Once you find an equipment rental house near you, call them up and ask them about their services and get to know the rental agent. Talk about your project and be excited, but don't talk about prices or discounts yet. Use this as an opportunity to build a relationship.

Schedule a time to visit and bring the script, storyboards, and production schedule. This will show that you are serious about your project. Remember that rental companies have dozens of filmmakers walking in off the streets asking for free stuff. They say no, because the filmmakers are never organized and don't have a plan. Show them you're organized and know what you're doing. Talk to them about the dates of production and ask them for advice on what equipment you may need.

Once you assemble an equipment list, talk to them about your budget and ask if they would be willing to cut you a deal on the rental costs of the gear. Always show your excitement and conviction for the project. This is your best sales tool.

Many rental houses will have a daily rental rate or a three- or four-day rental week. This means that if you rent the gear for a week, you will pay for only three or four days. This is an incentive for companies to rent gear for a week at a time. Negotiate this rate down to two-day weeks or even one day a week.

A lot of rental houses will let you use the equipment for free, but if a paying client comes in and wants the same gear, you will have to give it up. This can cause major problems, especially if you have an entire shoot scheduled, cast and crew arriving, and locations secured. You don't want to find out the day before that your gear is suddenly unavailable. Paying a little money may be a solution to this problem.

- Look in the phone book or local film production manual (available from the local film commission) for equipment rental facilities and schedule a tour and demonstration of the types and variety of lighting and grip equipment they carry.
- A rental facility can help you select the proper equipment for your production and even show you how to use the gear if you're not familiar with it. Many of the people who work at rental facilities crew on movies, so they know the ins and outs of how the gear works. In addition, rental companies are very uncomfortable renting their equipment to people who don't know

how to use it. Such rentals could result in costly repair or replacement bills. Having educated renters is in the equipment rental house's best interest.

- When shooting a film, approach a rental company with a plan. show them how serious you are about your production, and prove to them why they should let you have their equipment at a discounted rate or for free.

- Most rental facilities give student discounts if you can prove your project is school-related. Get a letter from the school on school letterhead as proof. Don't be afraid to ask for a discount or for free equipment.

- Always check the equipment at the rental facility to make sure it works properly. If you don't check the gear until you're on set, problems with equipment can cause costly delays.

- Make sure you have the proper insurance to cover the rental of the equipment. Many rental agencies will require a certificate of insurance before letting you leave with the gear.

- Make sure you have a list of every piece of equipment you're renting so you can check off each item when returning it to the rental facility.

- If you're not sure how to use a piece of equipment, ask. The rental agents will be happy to help you.

- Think about how you're going to transport the equipment from the rental house to the set. Will you need to rent a van or truck?

- Bring along a friend to help load and unload gear. The more hands, the easier the work.

- *Never* leave equipment in an unattended parked car, especially cameras and lenses. If any items are stolen, you are personally liable and will be responsible for the cost of replacement.

CHAPTER 10
Production Design

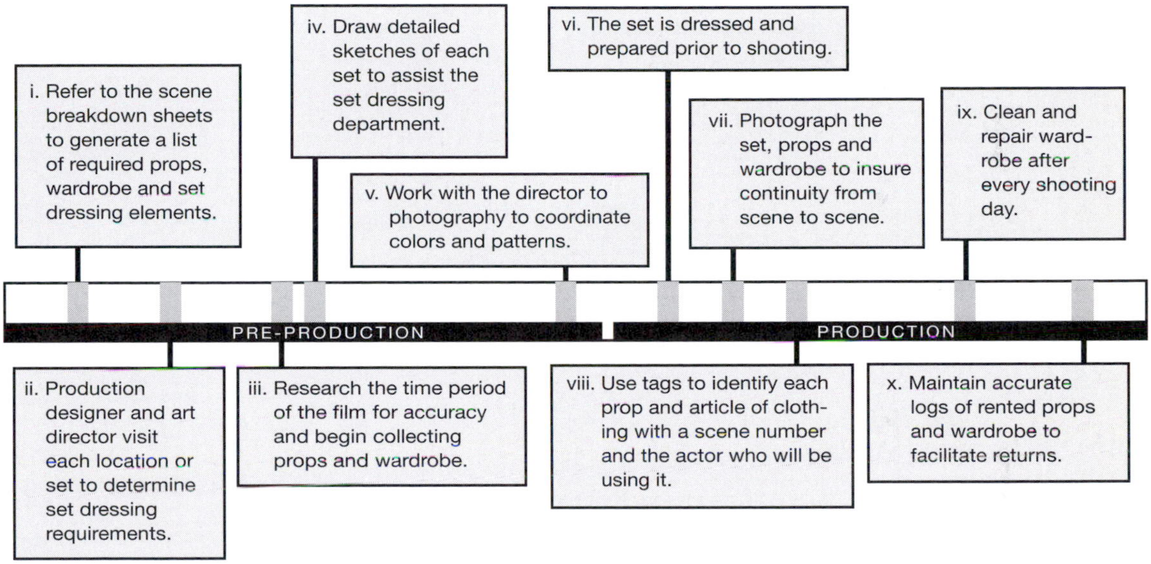

i. Refer to the scene breakdown sheets to generate a list of required props, wardrobe and set dressing elements.

iv. Draw detailed sketches of each set to assist the set dressing department.

v. Work with the director to photography to coordinate colors and patterns.

vi. The set is dressed and prepared prior to shooting.

vii. Photograph the set, props and wardrobe to insure continuity from scene to scene.

ix. Clean and repair wardrobe after every shooting day.

PRE-PRODUCTION

PRODUCTION

ii. Production designer and art director visit each location or set to determine set dressing requirements.

iii. Research the time period of the film for accuracy and begin collecting props and wardrobe.

viii. Use tags to identify each prop and article of clothing with a scene number and the actor who will be using it.

x. Maintain accurate logs of rented props and wardrobe to facilitate returns.

INTRODUCTION

The production design of a movie involves designing and constructing sets, collecting and building props, designing costumes – essentially, creating the environment in which the characters interact. Made up of the production designer, art director, assistant art director, set designer, set construction crews, set decorator, and prop and wardrobe departments, this department works closely with the director to help realize his vision for the story.

The art department can command the largest percentage of the budget and usually has the most scalable crew, especially in set-heavy genres like sci-fi or period films. Good production design in a movie is virtually invisible to the audience, but yet is influential in weaving subtext into the characters and story.

Filmmaking.
© 2011 Jason J. Tomaric. Published by Elsevier Inc. All rights reserved.

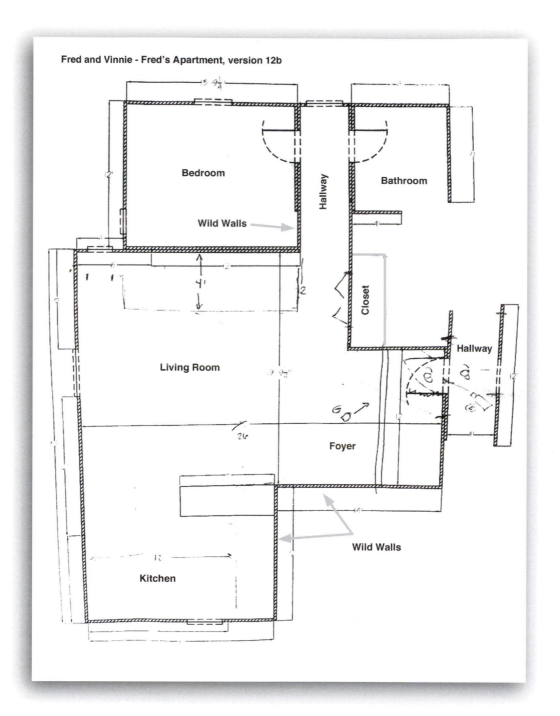

Fred and Vinnie - Fred's Apartment, version 12b

Bedroom

Wild Walls

Hallway

Bathroom

Closet

Living Room

Hallway

Foyer

Wild Walls

Kitchen

We spent a lot of time designing and redesigning Fred's apartment set for the feature *Fred and Vinnie* to ensure it would work both artistically and technically within the budget and space limitations of the Panavision soundstage on which we shot.

WORKING WITH THE PRODUCTION DESIGNER

Whereas the director is in charge of translating the script to the screen through the actors' performances and the cinematographer determines the cinematic look of the film through lighting and camera movements, the production designer is in charge of the visual appearance of the environment in which the story takes place.

The set of *Fred and Vinnie* was carefully designed to subtly give the audience clues about Fred's life while being easier to shoot than a practical location.

As a department head, the production designer answers to the director and manages several departments, including:

- **Set construction and dressing.** The production designer oversees the design, construction, and dressing of all the sets and locations in the movie. Depending on budget and artistic requirements, he may have a large or small crew that includes construction coordinators, painters, greensmen (in charge of plants and greenery), and construction foremen. The production designer works closely with the director and cinematographer to ensure that any sets that are built meet both artistic and technical needs. Sets may be designed with wild, or moveable, walls to accommodate lights and the camera during shooting, removable ceilings, raised floors, even sets mounted on motion control rigs to simulate motion. When shooting on location, the production designer is responsible for the crews that paint, alter, and dress each location so it creates the appropriate environment for the story.
- **Wardrobe.** The production designer oversees the wardrobe department. Whether the wardrobe is purchased, rented, or custom-designed, he ensures that the clothes the actors wear work with the visual style of the sets, locations, and the overall world he is creating.

Watch a video detailing the relationship between the director and the production designer at Filmskills.com. See page vi for details.

- **Props.** The production designer manages the props department, ensuring the look, authenticity, and believability of any objects the actors hold in a scene.
- **Hair/makeup.** The production designer also manages the hair and makeup departments, especially in period films or productions that require a specific look for the actors.

Jason's Notes

When you're shooting on a real location, you are forced to work inside the boundaries of the four walls, floor, and ceiling – so the camera, cast, crew, and equipment all coexist inside a box. The beauty of building a set on a soundstage is that most everything can be set up outside the box – lights can be set up behind set walls, softboxes can be hung where a ceiling normal goes, and even walls can be repositioned to accommodate a camera move. This unprecedented control provides you with an even greater number of options when shooting a scene.

BUILDING SETS

Finding an uncommon location such as a laboratory or space ship interior can be both challenging and cost-prohibitive, so in many instances, building a set piece is the most reasonable course of action.

The back of Fred's apartment is nothing more than plywood flats. Designed to look good on camera, movie sets are built as inexpensively as possible and intended to last for only a very short time.

Constructing a set gives you unprecedented control over the layout, design, and style of the set, including the ability to design the placement, style, color, and texture of walls, the ceiling height, floor plan, and architectural elements, while creating a camera friendly environment with removable walls to allow better camera access, gimbaled windows to remove reflections from light fixtures, predesigned points for light sources and support for special effects. Production designers create sets that complement the actors' blocking, and provide you and the director of photography much more flexibility than working at a traditional location. Open-ceiling sets allow the director of photography to rig lights from behind and over the top of set walls, granting a greater degree of control over the look of the movie.

One factor in crafting realistic sets is the need for believable set dressing. Small details such as furniture, aging the walls, and details in photos and artwork on set will all help sell the realism of the set.

Jason's Notes

When director Steve Skrovan, line producer Jerry Magaña, and I began looking at the script for *Fred and Vinnie*, we faced a big decision: whether to shoot the apartment scenes in Fred's real apartment in the heart of Hollywood or to build the sets on a soundstage.

Although it seemed cheaper to shoot in Fred's actual apartment (an idea which made sense, because the true story of Fred and Vinnie took place in this apartment), we realized there were several problems that would have actually cost the production more money in the long run. The first of these issues was sound. Since Fred's apartment is located on a busy intersection, we had no way of controlling the sounds of traffic from outside, and because the script is largely dialog-driven, we would have incurred significant costs in postproduction to ADR, or re-record, the audio afterwards.

The second big issue was the amount of space required for crew support services. Hair and makeup departments would need their own area, we would need to find space for equipment staging, crew parking was a huge problem in Hollywood, finding a space for craft services and catering ... the footprint taken up by a production like this was bigger than the location could have allowed.

If we shot at Fred's apartment, we would have to pack up and remove the vehicles every night, then repark, unload, and re–set up the equipment every day for both security and permitting reasons. Conversely, shooting on a soundstage would net an additional two hours of shooting per day by allowing us to walk away, or soft-wrap, at the end of each shooting day. When the crew arrives each morning, all we would need to do is flip a switch and start shooting.

In addition to the logistic problems, I had a serious problem with the eight-foot-high ceilings. Low ceilings make it challenging to rig lights, place boom poles and working *within* the four walls and ceiling of a practical location. Shooting on a soundstage would have alleviated these problems by allowing us to build removable ceilings and wild walls to accommodate the lighting.

Working with ceilingless sets makes it much easier to rig lights than on practical locations with ceilings. On the set of *Fred and Vinnie*, we prerigged lights above every room to create standard ambience and accent lighting, which helped reduce overall lighting time from scene to scene.

When considering all these factors, the nearly $30,000 it would cost us to rent Panavision sound stages and build a complete working set of Fred's apartment would give us much greater flexibility. We will be able to design the set to meet Steve's vision, craft a set that was production-friendly, and have complete support services of a full-blown studio.

When building a set, keep these tips in mind:

- When budgeting for set construction, consider the cost of truck rental, cost of materials, helping hands to load and unload the materials, rental of the property where you'll be building the sets, utility bills, flooring, cleanup, portable toilets if needed, dumpster rental, and possibly a generator for power.
- Consider hiring a local construction contractor to assist in building the sets. Although you may want to try it yourself, a professional touch will make the set believable on camera. If the scene requires an elaborate set piece, consult a local architect for help. Don't be afraid to ask these professionals to donate

Set walls are built several feet away from the studio walls to provide both an open fire lane and to allow the director of photography to set up lights outside windows.

their time if you're on a tight budget. You may be surprised at their willingness to help.

The Anatomy of a Set

Hollywood sets look vast and amazing on screen, but in reality, they are built as minimally as possible to achieve the look. What appears as stone, marble, wood, glass, and brick may in reality by plywood flats, Styrofoam, textured façades, and exquisite paint jobs that give the illusion of richer materials.

Most sets utilize the same basic components to ensure rapid, inexpensive construction and easy manipulation.

- **Flats.** At the heart of every set are 4′×10′ or 4′×12′ flats. A flat is a piece of plywood with two-by-fours used to brace and hold the flats vertically. Flats can be aligned side by side, taped and spackled to create a smooth wall, then painted or wallpapered. The flats can be moved during production to allow placement of the camera in places otherwise impossible in a real location.

- **Safety.** Always make sure the set is safe and secure. Use sandbags to weigh down flats and safety cables when rigging lighting, and be sure the set can withstand the rigors of film production.

It's easy to build a square room, but difficult and boring to shoot. Try these easy tips to help make your set architecturally interesting:

- **Soffits.** Soffits are the finished underside of a structure. Inside homes, soffits are built around air conditioning ductwork or under stairs and add dimension to a set wall or ceiling.

- **Dormers.** Instead of building windows into a flat wall, try building the window out vertically, as if it were sitting out on a sloped roof. The space inside a dormer is usually large enough for a desk, couch, or even a bed, making it easy for the camera to dolly around a dormer corner to "reveal" the character. Although they can be expensive to build, dormers add a tremendous amount of depth and artistic opportunities to a set.

- **Recessed walls.** If you have to build a long stretch of wall, consider offsetting a section of the wall back 4 or 5 inches. For example, if a wall is made up of five 4′-wide flats, consider sliding the three middle flats back several inches to break up the wall.

Once walls are built and safely rigged, you can apply virtually any surface to the walls – from simple paint or wallpaper to fake brick facades.

- **Avoid white walls.** Because they reflect almost all light, white walls are very difficult to expose and limit the cinematographer's ability to tint or add patterns of light. Instead, paint walls a light to medium gray so they fall off in the background. The cinematographer can easily add light to brighten up darker walls or throw a colored light to break up the background much easier than with white walls. And remember, the walls can still be photographed to appear white. Although it depends on your vision, it is often better to have a background that is slightly darker than the actor's flesh tones. Remember: it's easier to light a dark background to make it brighter than it is to work with a bright or white background.

- **Facades.** Some hardware stores stock 4′×8′ sheets of textured lauan plywood surfaced with a thin molded and painted veneer. These surfaces include brick, marble, stone, or wood paneling and are an easy way to create large surfaced areas without purchasing and installing the real materials.
- **Fabric.** Fabric is a cheap way of dressing drab walls, floors, furniture, and windows. Purchase inexpensive material from a craft store, or buy ends at a discount. Be sure to coordinate the fabric's color and pattern with the actors' wardrobe and production design.
- **Windows.** Windows can be mounted into flats. Although regular windows can be used, special windows on gimbals are often installed so that the glass can be rotated on either the horizontal or vertical axis to avoid glare from the lights. There are a number of techniques to creating or blocking the view out of a window.
  - **Sheers or curtains.** Using light sheers are a great way to allow light in through the window while keeping the audience from seeing that nothing exists outside the window.
  - **Frost or diffuse the window.** Ask the grip department to render a window translucent by applying diffusion to the outside of the glass. By focusing a light onto the diffusion, the window will glow without being see-through. On screen, the window appears overexposed.
  - **Translight.** Bigger budget productions use massive photographs printed on a translucent, backlit surface that, when placed outside a window or door, looks like a realistic exterior environment. Most often used on sitcom sets, translights are an ideal although expensive solution.
  - **Plants.** Place plants or thick tree branches outside the window to give the illusion of greenery. Combining light diffusion, sheers, and greenery is the most cost-effective way to dress a window exterior.
  - **Flats to create another building.** If the window is supposed to look out at another building, consider building a small wall dressed with a brick façade. Place the wall several feet away from the window, so the view is of the neighboring building.
- **Floors.** Flooring can really make the set, and it doesn't have to be expensive. Building only walls will limit the potential camera angles, so consider buying carpet remnants, tile, linoleum, or inexpensive wood laminate from a local home improvement store.
  - **Baseboards.** Install inexpensive baseboards to conceal the space between the flats and the flooring.

- **Crown molding.** Whereas baseboards are installed on a wall at floor level, crown molding is installed at ceiling height. Although most movie sets are built without a ceiling to accommodate overhead lighting, crown molding not only serves as a nice architectural touch, but also gives the camera operator a visual indication as to when the frame is nearing the top of the sets.
- **Ceilings.** Some sets may require either a complete or a partial ceiling, which can be expensive and ultimately limit the cinematographer's ability to rig overhead lighting and grip equipment. In virtually all cases, ceilings should be built in removable sections to accommodate the technical needs of the shoot.
- **Fixtures.** It's the small details that add realism to the set. Wall-mounted light fixtures, doorknobs, window casings, heating vents, electric outlets, light switches, and even overhead lights suspended from the grid are all important additions. When working with light fixtures, consult the director of photography for the best type of fixture, position, and style on the set.

Set Building on a Budget

Building a set doesn't have to be expensive – creative thinking and utilizing available resources are the best way to start. Ideal movie sets are built on soundstages equipped with sound-reducing walls, a light grid for rigging lights and set pieces, ample power, large doors for loading and unloading, dressing rooms, production equipment, and even a kitchen. Unfortunately, many low-budget productions cannot afford proper production facilities, but with some creative thinking, you can adapt an existing building into a makeshift soundstage.

The first step is to find a large facility in which you can build a set but which also meets the technical needs of your production:

- **Vacant buildings.** Landlords of vacant commercial properties may be willing to give you a space for free or for a heavily discounted rate if you plan on using it for a short time. Make sure the building still has utilities such as power and running water. Empty grocery stores, shopping malls, strip centers, and factory buildings provide plenty of room to work, spacious parking, loading areas, and sufficient power.
- **Accessibility.** Make sure that the rental space has a loading dock or is otherwise accessible to trucks so that you can bring lumber, set dressing, and production equipment. If you plan on building flats, make sure there are large doors called *elephant doors* that can accommodate 8' or 10' tall flats.
- **Power and utilities.** Check the power and circuit configuration in the building to ensure that it can support the electrical draw of the lighting gear. Also make sure the water and toilet facilities are in good working order and there is heat, especially in the winter.
- **Ambient noise.** Listen to the ambient sound outside the building. Warehouses or gymnasiums aren't designed for the acoustics needed for film production. Avoid buildings near freeways or heavily trafficked areas.
- **Parking.** Make sure there are ample parking spaces for the cast and crew and any equipment trucks.

Remember that sets can be dismantled once filming wraps and the materials reused and built into another set. This is an economical and cost-effective way to getting the most set for your money.

Jason's Notes

In designing the sets for "Fred and Vinnie," there were thee major set pieces: Fred's apartment, Paul and Luther's apartment, and Vinnie's cave. In the interest of time and money, production designer Coree Van Bebber's team built Fred's elaborate 1,200-square-foot apartment, complete with kitchen, living room, hallway, bedroom, bathroom, and closets. After spending six days on shooting on this set, the production crew went on location for two days while Coree's team repainted and redressed part of the set, turning it into Paul and Luther's apartment. The production crew returned for one day to shoot in the new set, then left for another few days of location work. During this time, Coree completely dismantled the apartment set and built Vinnie's cave. By coordinating the shooting schedule, carefully designing the shots and expertly crafting the sets, we were able to build three completely different environments with the same materials.

SET DRESSING

Set dressing is the decoration of a studio set or location with any objects or furnishings an actor does not touch during the scene. Set dressing is important in establishing the tone of the scene and establishing the realism of the setting.

The set dressing in *Time and Again* helped establish the 1950s time period, right down to the old radio young Bobby Jones was building on his desk.

There's a big difference between dressing an existing location, which may only require a few elements to alter its look and a constructed set on a soundstage, which needs to be completely dressed from scratch.

Jason's Notes

When designing Fred's apartment in the feature *Fred and Vinnie*, the set dressers needed to create Fred's apartment from scratch. Although this cost a little more money and took a bit more time than if we were to shoot on location, this control gave us the ability to truly craft the space appropriate to Fred's character.

When you're dressing a set, keep these tips in mind:

- **Permission.** Always ask the location owner's permission before moving or using any furniture or object at the location.
- **Planning.** Design the set dressing during the location scout and work everything out on paper. Once you get to the set on the day of production, the set dressers should simply unload the truck and set everything up, not figure out what to do ten minutes before it's time to roll the camera.
- **Artwork.** It is a violation of copyright law to shoot artwork without the permission of the artist. This includes paintings, photographs, movie posters, and contemporary art. Bring replacement artwork you have permission to use to avoid legal liability.
- **Products.** Much like artwork, shooting products like cereal boxers, soda cans, and any logo can be construed as a corporate endorsement of the movie and can open you to legal liability. Always mask or greek (alter the logo so it's not recognizable in its original form) logos that appear in the frame. You can also purchase fake rights-free products specifically created for use in movies and television shows. Designed to look like recognizable brands, these movie props are unique but completely authentic designs.
- **Plants.** One of the least expensive ways to break up a background is with fake ficus trees or floor plants. Adding a little greenery can make a big difference against monochromatic walls.
- **Hanging pictures on walls.** If you can't hammer nails or use regular push pins on the walls of a location, try using straight pins. They are so small that the hole isn't noticeable, yet strong enough to hold up material or set dressing.
- **Photograph.** Especially when working on location, it's critical to photograph and document the location before you begin working so the crew can restore the location to its original look upon completion of filming.

Creating an Emotional Subtext

The production design of a movie has as much of an impact on the audience as the actor's performances, however subliminal it may be. The character's surroundings, the possessions they own, and even the clothes they wear give the

The final set dressings – from furniture to wall coverings – help make the set believable. Note how the recessed walls on either side of the window and couch add interesting angles to the set.

audience information about the background, personality, and taste of the characters. Although this depth of character isn't necessarily identified in the script, it is up to the production designer to create this added layer through extensive preproduction meetings with you. Think carefully about what you want the set to say about the characters.

The emotional content of the sets can be conveyed through a variety of ways, each carefully controlled to best augment the character's emotional arc:

- **Colors.** In as much the same way as the cinematographer's lighting can create an emotional subtext within a scene, so too can the colors chosen for the set by the production designer. Reds can invoke the feeling of power, green and earth tones can represent serenity, and purples can represent wealth. Think carefully about the color palette of each set, what the colors may represent, and the information the audience may get from your choices.

Jason's Notes

In the feature film I shot, *Fred and Vinnie*, the main character Fred is a middle-aged loser, unable to score a date and always in pursuit of an acting career. In order to portray the drab stagnation of his life, production designer Cory Van Bebber built Fred's Los Angeles apartment at Panavision soundstages with textured beige walls, water stains, and chipped corners. This worn, LA look perfectly reflected the very nature of Fred's life. We continued this look throughout the film, deliberately avoiding bright colors, choosing instead drab, earth tones: browns, beiges, darker reds ... depressing, monotonous colors for the sets, props, and most importantly, Fred's wardrobe.

- **Texture.** Construction crews often use inexpensive materials to build movie sets, which are then discarded or reused once filming is complete. Although the materials may be cheap, the only part that really matters to the audience is what the camera sees – the texture and paint. Incorporating textures on walls, floors, and even ceilings helps make the set walls interesting and visually engaging. Even the most subtle textures will create a sense of depth and dimension from the lighting. Techniques such as aging and distressing set walls can invoke feelings of isolation, despair, and fatigue, and faux marble, granite, and stone can convey wealth and grandeur. Texture on walls and set surfaces adds a touch of realism and visual appeal to the set.
- **Set dressing.** Furniture, paintings on walls, and items placed around the set convey a lot of information about the character, adding depth and dimension not necessarily mentioned in the script. For example, in a scene that takes place in a garage, the production designer can tell a lot about the character – are there tools scattered around? Is the garage neat and tidy or is it full of boxes left over from when the character moved two decades ago? If the character enjoys fixing cars, are there car parts stored in a corner? If the character has kids, are their bikes stored in the garage?
- Even though the script might not describe the character as clean, messy, mechanically inclined, or into cars, the look of the garage can convey this information to the audience, making it important to work with the production designer early in preproduction to create environments that accentuate and add to each character.

THE PRODUCTION DESIGN PROCESS
Production Design During Preproduction

During the early phases of preproduction, the director of photography and the production designer work closely with you to craft the look of the sets, wardrobe, hair, and makeup. From a creative standpoint, the production designer will take your creative input and develop sketches or visual composites as to how the sets should look, while keeping the designs within the budget limitations of the production. Whether scenes are to be shot on a soundstage or on location, there are a number of factors to keep in mind:

- **How much does each set need to be dressed?** When working on a location that requires furniture, rugs, wall art, paint or wallpaper, the production designer works with the line producer to ensure that the budget can support additional art department personnel to dress and restore a location before and after the shooting day. In addition, the cost of renting or buying, storing, and transporting the furnishings to set can significantly add to the cost.
- **How many crew members are needed?** The art department can scale up or down in size depending on the needs of the scene – often when dressing or tearing down a set. On low-budget movies, the art department may be overwhelmed and need additional help for larger scenes, so be sure to budget accordingly.

Jason's Notes

When we were scouting theatre locations for *Fred and Vinnie* in Los Angeles, our budget prohibited us from shooting in a proper theatre lobby. With movie theatre owners requesting upwards of $5,000 for an afternoon of shooting, we quickly began searching for less-expensive alternatives: building lobbies, community theatres, even school buildings. Although the cost of renting these location was lower, we would have had to have spend much more money on renting the set dressing needed to turn a boring corporate lobby into a movie theatre: counters with popcorn makers, rope and stanchions, red velvet curtains, movie posters, ticket counters, and movie displays. The added cost of securing parking on the street so our 5-ton art truck could deliver the dressing added even more to the budget. After looking at the budget, the amount of work and the added costs of furnishing a cheaper location, we decided to spend the money on a proper location and shot at the Egyptian Theatre in Hollywood – a location that required no work at all and played beautifully on screen.

- **Where will furnishings be stored?** Factor in the cost of storing furniture and set dressing when it's not being used on set. If the dressing is only needed for one location, it may not be possible to store furnishings in the truck, or at other filming locations throughout the shoot. Consider a rental space, or hire an art PA to pick up and drop off furnishings before and after each shooting day.
- **Consider building models of each set.** For productions with elaborate sets, the production designer will often create foam core miniatures, which allow you and the DP to determine camera angles and lighting requirements. This process helps the production designer build a production-friendly set as cost-effectively as possible.
- **Storyboard each shot.** It's helpful to draw storyboards for scenes requiring sets so the production designer knows exactly how much of each set to build. Building an entire kitchen if the audience is only going to see the sink and one adjoining wall is a waste of both time and resources. On low-budget productions, you may need to work with the production designer to compromise on certain shots, scale the scope of certain set pieces down or minimize set dressing to accommodate the budget.
- **Research is sometimes required to accurately recreate a time or place.** The production designer should use all available resources to create as convincing an environment as possible so the audience believes the setting of the story. And this is even more the case with period films, or movies taking place in a foreign country. Although these settings may be unknown to the film crew, invariably some audience members who are familiar with the subject matter will notice inconsistencies in the production design if time is not taken to accurately and faithfully create the setting.

The Production Designer and the Director of Photography

The production designer must make sets that not only look good, but also meet the technical needs of the production. Working closely with the director of photography throughout preproduction, the production designer designs set elements like wild (removable) walls, secret holes covered by paintings, and removable windows to allow unrestricted placement of the camera and lights – all based on storyboarded shots. Sets that incorporate lighting, such as control panels in a submarine or lighting under kitchen cabinets, are carefully planned with the DP's input to ensure that the lighting fulfills his photographic requirements.

If a set is to be used for only one or two scenes, you and the DP may determine that there will be five camera angles used to cover that scene. For each of the five camera angles, the production designer determines how much of the set to build, and how the set needs to move to accommodate the camera and lights.

Production designer Coree Van Bebber and I discuss the set dressing of a NASCAR race track for a commercial I directed and shot.

Jason's Notes

A large percentage of *Fred and Vinnie* takes place in Fred's apartment. Although described in the script as a small, old Hollywood apartment, we build the set a little larger to accommodate the camera and lighting equipment. We had also decided early on that the set didn't need a ceiling, allowing the grip and electricians to build a light grid above each room, from which we hung large softboxes and light fixtures. Furthermore, each wall could be detached and removed if we needed room to set up a dolly and track, or for a more expansive wide shot. The flexibility of the set was determined early, which saved us a lot of time and effort on set by determining our technical needs in advance.

Production Design On Location

Most productions shoot at existing locations and it is the production designer's responsibility to transform these real-world places into the movie's fictional environment. Sometimes all it takes is some basic set dressing – add new curtains, pillows on the couch, a few plants, and you're done. Other times, however, these changes are more drastic – repainting walls, removing existing walls or building new walls, tearing up and replacing flooring, or adding interesting architectural elements like soffits or dormers to create visually appealing lines and angles on the set.

We built an entire shuttlecraft cockpit for less than $60 for my feature film *Clone* from several cardboard boxes, Christmas lights, spray paint, good lighting, and a lot of ingenuity.

Many creative decisions surrounding the production design of a location are decided upon during the initial location scout attended by the director, director of photography, gaffer, key grip, and production designer. Although the goal is to find a location that perfectly matches your vision, it's more likely that a location will need to be altered.

The severity of these changes depends on the allotted time, budget and willingness of the location owner to allow these changes to take place. For significant changes, the producer has more than likely engaged in long discussions and offered to pay a sizable location fee to the owner, understanding that the art department will restore the location to its original state – a time consuming and expensive process.

Production Design on a Budget

The art department is one of the most important departments on a film crew, and the one that is most often overlooked or understaffed on low budget independent movies. Although the creative contributions of the art department are vitally important to the fabric of the story, they are often restricted by the size of the budget, requiring novel and creative approaches to making a set work. Here are a few tips to effectively designing the look of your movie on a budget:

- Production design will make the difference between an amateurish film and a professional film. Invest time in dressing sets and locations so they are not only appropriate to the story, but also visually interesting. Make backgrounds as realistic as possible by incorporating visually interesting items, shapes, and colors. Many of these items can be picked up inexpensively from thrift shops or pawn shops, or simply borrowed from neighbors.
- Avoid shooting against white walls *at all costs*. They are boring and flat, look cheap, and are very difficult to shoot. If you have to shoot in a small apartment or a location with white walls, consider adding plants, fake trees, or posters (make sure you have the rights to use them in your movie).
- Contact local interior designers for decorating advice and suggestions on where to get inexpensive furnishings. Also call local construction companies and ask them who decorates their model homes. They might not only be up for the challenge of dressing movie sets, but also have great contacts to get inexpensive furniture and set dressing elements.
- Think out of the box. Good production design doesn't have to be expensive. Use local resources like garages, attics, thrift shops, and even stores looking to get rid of old inventory to dress the set, clothe the actors, or provide props.
- Contact local artists who may allow you to use their artwork on set in exchange for credit. You will need a signed release form from the artist granting you permission to use the artwork, or risk a copyright-infringement lawsuit.

The contributions of the production design and art departments are both vastly underrated and underappreciated on most independent films, until the day of the shoot arrives and the director realizes how sparse the background looks. When producing a low-budget film, bring the proper art department people on board early, communicate your vision, and give them a budget to go out and begin collecting what they need to make a set look great on screen.

Jason's Notes

The production design of a movie is incredibly important in creating a realistic environment for the characters, especially in a period film like *Time and Again*. We spent a lot of time making sure that everything in every shot was of authentic 1950s look and feel. In some instances, like the diner, we didn't have to do too much work, but other sets, like Awanda's trailer, were dressed from the ground up.

Often, simple things like old dishes, a blanket, and old pots and pans work wonders. We tried to find a few authentic items like radios and clothes to put in the background that really sold the time period.

Ultimately, we spent less than $250 on all the props and set dressing in the movie, finding free or really cheap objects in thrift shops, borrowing from friends, and sometimes making our own props. Doing the production design for *Time and Again* wasn't difficult; it just involved a little research, seeking out good deals, and having fun in the process.

PROPS

Props are objects or items that an actor physically touches or handles. This department, overseen by the property master, is responsible for breaking down the script to develop a list of props needed in each scene. Whereas some props are basic, everyday elements like glasses, books, or kitchenware, other props may require significant research to ensure accuracy to the time period or location of the scene. In some instances, props need to be custom made.

There is a difference between props and set dressing. If an object is ever touched by an actor, it is the responsibility of the props department to locate, manage, maintain, and return the object. If the object is not touched but is part of the set dressing, it is the responsibility of the set dresser. For example, if the script mentions that a character picks up an apple in the kitchen and begins to slice it, the prop department is responsible for the apple and the knife. But the set dresser is responsible for both objects if they are merely sitting on the countertop to add realism to the set.

What types of objects fall under the responsibility of the props department?

- **Food.** If an actor is required to eat, the props department must locate and prep the food, plates, glasses, and utensils. In scenes in which the food needs to look attractive, such as in a banquet scene or a hamburger commercial, a professional food dresser must be hired to carefully cook and display the food in the most appealing manner.
- **Magazines and newspapers.** Any printed materials are the responsibility of the property master. Designing and printing newspapers can be a costly and time-consuming process, especially when featured in a shot.
- **Photographs or videos.** If a character takes a picture or video that reappears in the movie, the props department is responsible for organizing, staging, and shooting the photo so that it can be used on the proper day of shooting.

We recreated a 1950s newspaper for *Time and Again* by printing our design on newsprint, giving authenticity to the prop.

Jason's Notes

In the feature film *Fred and Vinnie*, lead character Fred Stollar takes several photographs of restaurants for a book he's writing, *Restaurants You Don't Feel Self-Conscious Eating Alone At*. Production designer Coree Van Bebber spent an afternoon traveling around Los Angeles to photograph various restaurants and then printing the photos so they were ready on each shooting day.

- **Weapons.** Most movies that require the use of weapons have a dedicated armorer to manage guns, knives, swords, or any other type of weapon. If your budget cannot afford an armorer, the responsibility falls on the shoulders of the property master. When handling weapons on set:
    - Weapons must *always* be in the property master's possession at all times except for the exact moments of rehearsal and shooting.
    - Weapons are *not* toys and should *never* be used as such on set.

- *All* weapons must visually inspected prior to arriving on set and immediately before being handed to an actor to ensure that they are not loaded. Always check the chamber to make sure that a round is not loaded.
- Ideally, all weapons should be disabled and nonfunctional.
- *Always* have a meeting with the entire cast and crew notifying them of safety protocol when working with weapons.
- Weapons should *never* leave the set and must *always* be stored in closed containers when not being used in a scene.
- Whenever blanks are used, they must always be visually inspected and verified as blanks.
- *Never* point a weapon at another person unless required by the scene.

- **Computer monitors.** If an actor is physically working on a computer, the property master may be responsible for the information displayed on the screen. Sometimes a prerecorded video feed is sent to the monitor so the information appears live on set. Other times, the screen is photographed blank and the information is composited in digitally in postproduction.

PROPERTY MASTER

The property master's primary responsibility is to comb through the script to generate a list of all the props required in the film. Working with her team, she will then supervise the acquisition, design, construction, and/or rental of the props. Throughout the film, each prop will be catalogued and be available for the appropriate scene.

During Preproduction

The types of props needed for each film varies wildly. For simple present-day dramas, the props are mostly everyday objects that are easily acquirable, but for fantasy, period, or science fiction movies, every object held by the actors must be either meticulously researched and gathered, or designed and hand-crafted to create a realistic environment for the story.

On big-budget productions, the props department can be made up of a number of craftsmen, but for low-budget productions ,you may need to begin the prop hunt yourself.

- Once the property master receives the script, he breaks it down and creates a list of the props mentioned in each scene. Many times, props may be needed that aren't called out specifically. For example, for a scene in which the characters are talking in the kitchen, although there may be no mention of food or utensils, the property master should talk to the director and gather fresh vegetables, cutlery, a cutting board, a dishrag, and several bowls to give the actors something to do during the scene.

- Label each prop with the scene in which it's needed and keep a detailed list of where each prop was obtained – this will make returns much easier at the end of the shoot.
- In some instances, multiple sets of each prop may be required – perhaps a champagne bottle needs to be uncorked or an apple eaten. Enough should be provided in case you want to do multiple takes with a given prop.

LOCATING PROPS

Finding props can be a fun and adventurous hunt. Especially when looking for obscure or unusual props, using your local resources can be a great help to find the perfect object for the scene:

- **Garage sales.** Keep an eye out for garage or estate sales. It's amazing what people are selling, usually for pennies on the dollar.
- **Prop houses.** In large production cities, you can rent practically anything from prop houses – massive warehouses that collect, catalog, store, and rent everything from the everyday to the unusual for use in productions. Although prop houses feature an enormous inventory, the rental prices can be high. If you're on a budget, try to find props in more traditional locations before visiting a prop house. Be aware that prop houses and owners of expensive props usually require proof of insurance and may request a deposit to ensure the safe return of the props. Contact the production department for a certificate of insurance.
- **Internet auctions.** Auction sites like eBay or Craigslist are invaluable resources. Especially in large cities, it's possible to find virtually anything on the sales boards, and usually for a reasonable price.
- **Family and friends.** Don't be afraid to ask the people you know if they have any leads on a particular prop. Many people have a lifetime of things stored in their garages and attics and may be willing to lend you what you need for the shoot.

During Production

During production, the property master must provide each prop when it is needed for a scene. Sometimes props are damaged and need to be repaired or preplaced instantly to avoid slowing down shooting, so it's a good idea to keep tools and spray paints ready on set.

- **Props are not toys.** No one should handle props at anytime unless it is for a rehearsal or actual take.
- **Photograph props.** For scenes in which a prop changes – for example, a plate of food is partially eaten, or the characters are assembling a motorcycle engine during the scene – the property master must photograph and document the prop to ensure continuity from one scene to the next.
- **Always include a line item in the budget for damaged or lost props.** Anything can happen on a movie set, and despite being cautious, props can be lost or damaged. Be sure to allow a portion of the budget to compensate the owners of lost or broken props.

Always photograph the set between setups to ensure continuity of props and set dressing.

WARDROBE

Wardrobe is the clothing that actors wear in the movie, and can be as simple as jeans and a T-shirt or as elaborate as an 1800s French ball gown. Except for movies in which the wardrobe really stands out, like period or sci-fi movies, the clothes the actors wear tend to be overlooked. In reality, a character's wardrobe provides an important glimpse into her life and persona. In a society where people are judged by the clothes, colors and styles they choose to wear, so too does the audience judge the characters. Designer brands, specific colors, textures, layering, and age of the clothes can all provide contextual clues into the character's life. Is the character wealthy or poor and attempting to look wealthy? Does the character use a particular piece of clothing as a security blanket? Does a drug addict not care about her clothes, which always appear mismatched, or rather is her clothing perfectly planned to avoid arousing suspicion? Does a boy always wear hand-me-downs from his older siblings that never quite fit right?

Not only does style play a key role in helping create the character, but so does the color. Choosing strong reds can convey a sense of power, whereas browns and earth tones can help a character appear less intimidating.

Jason's Notes

I recently directed the film *Currency*, in which the main character – the wife of the mayor of Los Angeles – goes from being a crime victim to finding herself in a position of power. In designing her wardrobe, I wanted her to always wear an off-white dress or blazer when she was suffering, but as she began taking control, she would wear a red scarf. In a plot where nothing is as it seems, I used the colors in her wardrobe to give the audience a subliminal clue as to when she was being played and when she was the player.

COSTUME DESIGNER

The costume designer, who answers directly to the product designer, is responsible for the acquisition, rental, design, maintenance, cleaning, delivery, and sometimes even making the wardrobe. Depending on the budget and demands of the movie, the costume designer may be staffed with a wardrobe supervisor to ensure that the wardrobe is prepped and ready for each scene; a costume standby, who is always on set monitoring the wardrobe for continuity; an art finisher, who distresses wardrobe; or a buyer, who purchases clothes and materials.

During the preproduction phase, the costume designer works closely with the production designer to comb through the script and create a list of all characters and their wardrobe requirements for each scene. After listening to the director's artistic ideas for each character and each scene, the costume designer designs a wardrobe that not only serves the time and setting of the story, but also helps convey the personality of each character.

Much time is spent coordinating the wardrobe choices with the set design, lighting, and makeup, making the costuming process an important collaboration.

During Preproduction

RESEARCH

Do your research on the Internet, at the library, or simply by talking to people knowledgeable about the time period your story is set in, and then select a wardrobe that is appropriate to the time. You can almost always find experts to help you find the appropriate costumes for the movie. For medieval, Civil War, or World War wardrobes, try contacting a reenactment group, whose attention to details sometimes even rivals that of the most meticulous costume designer. In some instances, the members of a reenactment group may be willing to appear as extras – in costume!

Jason's Notes

When I shot my sci-fi feature *Clone*, I had to shoot a very elaborate scene in which the U.S. National Guard infiltrates a refugee camp in the postapocalyptic future. Instead of hiring actors and renting the military uniforms, I contacted the National Guard directly and worked with more than a dozen men, all of whom were too happy to take part in the movie, in full costume – for free.

GATHERING WARDROBE

Most independent productions don't have the budget to hire a team of seamstresses to custom-make each article of clothing, so the costume designer must use existing clothes and accessories.

- **Thrift shops.** Before you begin looking in department stores, check out the local thrift shop, Goodwill store, or Salvation Army. These second-hand clothes are an outstanding value, and come in a wide variety – you're sure to find what you need while staying on budget. The only downside to thrift shops is that if multiple sets of a piece of wardrobe are needed for a stunt sequence, or if the same style shirt is needed in various stages of distress, it may be hard to find multiples of the same garment.

Always keep wardrobe organized and clean so it's ready for each shooting day.

- **Outlet malls.** If it becomes necessary to purchase wardrobe new from a store, consider finding an outlet mall where designer clothes are sold for a fraction of the price. This is a good option for everyday clothes such as jeans, T-shirts, polo shirts, and dress shirts – especially if you need multiple sets. One dirty little trick is to keep the price tags on clothes you purchase, then return them once the shoot is over. In some high-production cities like Los Angeles, some local clothing designers rent or loan their clothes to the production in exchange for exposure and credit – adding credibility to their clothing line and creating a win–win situation for both the producer and the clothing designer.
- **The actor's closet.** Although the Screen Actors Guild frowns on actors using their own wardrobe, nothing fits an actor better then his own clothes. If an actor is wiling, take time to go through his closet to find appropriate pieces of clothing. Be aware that SAG requires producers to compensate actors if they bring their own wardrobe to the set.
- **Contact local seamstresses.** Often, local fabric stores know people in the community who enjoy sewing and may be able to give you references. When I shot my science-fiction movie *Clone*, I needed 30 futuristic military uniforms made. Luckily, a local seamstress was willing to donate her time and, using inexpensive materials donated by a local fabric shop, hand-sew beautiful original uniform jackets.

Jason's Notes

In searching for appropriate wardrobe for *Time and Again*, I looked under "costumes" in the phone book and found Chelsea's Costumes, a terrific costume shop with thousands of costumes in Cleveland.

I spoke with the owner about our project and explained how we were working with a limited budget. She really got excited about what we were doing and offered us a flat rate to rent all the wardrobe we needed for the film.

We borrowed Awanda's costume as well as wardrobe for dozens of extras.

Other wardrobe came from other places. Brian used his own clothes for Bobby Jones's outfit and we borrowed the sheriff uniform from a friend of mine.

I was really surprised at just how many resources were available to us for finding appropriate period attire.

Be aware that clothes must not only meet the your artistic vision, but also the technical and photographic needs of the cinematographer. Follow these simple tips when assembling the wardrobe for the shoot:

- Try to avoid white and black, as they present an exposure problem for the director of photography. Also avoid tight patterns such as tweed. Especially problematic on video formats, the patterns will create a rainbow moiré interference effect on the television screen that can be distracting to the viewers.
- Remember that you can make creative costumes out of existing clothes by layering or sewing different garments together to create different looks.
- If stunts are involved, secure multiple sets of the same wardrobe in case a piece is damaged or torn. If wardrobe is supposed to look torn and dirty, make sure that the blemishes are consistent from one article of clothing to the next.
- Remember that the wardrobe department is responsible for everything the actor wears, including jewelry, accessories, purses, shoes, hats, and gloves.
- As you locate and assemble the wardrobe, pin a tag to each garment that lists the actor it's intended for, the scenes the garment is to be used in, and which day of production it is to be used.

FIRST FITTING

Once the wardrobe has been chosen and gathered, it's important for the actors to try on each piece, and for the wardrobe department to then make any necessary alterations. Sometimes, for more elaborate costumes, the actors are shot on video or film so you can see how each appears on screen.

- Make sure that the wardrobe fits in a way that allows the actor full range of motion. If the wardrobe is too tight, or doesn't fit right, it may tear during a shot.
- Actors need to turn in every article of clothing to the wardrobe department, even if it is from their own closets. The wardrobe department is responsible for cleaning, storing, and ensuring the wardrobe is ready for each shooting day and will return the clothes at the end of production.

Label each article of clothing with the character name and scene number for which it is required.

During Production

When a movie is in production, the wardrobe department must keep each article of wardrobe organized, cleaned, maintained, catalogued, and ready for production. In addition, the wardrobe supervisor helps fit each actor into her wardrobe, ensuring continuity with previous scenes.

One way the wardrobe supervisor helps maintain continuity is by photographing each actor in the wardrobe for each scene, and adding the photograph to a continuity book, which helps the wardrobe supervisor track the look of the wardrobe from one scene to the next. This is especially important in effects scenes in which, for example, a character is in a car accident – the look of the wardrobe must match from the scene in which the accident occurs to the next scene when the character stumbles into an abandoned gas stations down the road – especially if those scenes are shot weeks apart.

- Clean and press wardrobe after every shoot and take care of every article of clothing – put it on a hanger. Don't wad clothes up and throw them in a box.
- Actors should always change out of their wardrobe before going to lunch. All too often, actors have dripped sauce on their shirt, grinding production to a halt while wardrobe scrambles to clean out the stain or find a replacement.

Once You Wrap

Wrapping a production can be just as work-intensive as preproduction. The props, wardrobe, and set dressing departments must now carefully strike, package, and in many cases return the props or furniture they borrowed. If each department kept a meticulous list of each object, its receipt, point of origin, and contact information for the owner, the return process should be fairly simple.

Before returning props, make sure props or furniture aren't needed for future shots or potential pick-ups, especially for unique specialty items.

UNIT 3
Production

i. Make-Up and Hair departments set-up and begin prepping the actors. If the hair and make-up needs are complicated, the artists and the actors may need to arrive early before the rest of the cast and crew.

i. Coffee and breakfast are set-up 30 minutes before call-time, location is unlocked and secured.

Craft Services/Catering	Cast and Crew	Make-Up/Hair	Directing

i. Cast and Crew begin arriving based at their call times and are directed to the appropriate parking areas. 1st Assistant Director walks everyone through the set before the crew begins unloading equipment in designated staging areas.

i. Meet with the entire cast and crew to review the scenes to be filmed, and runs a rehearsal with the cast in front of the crew, so everyone understands what occurs in the scene.

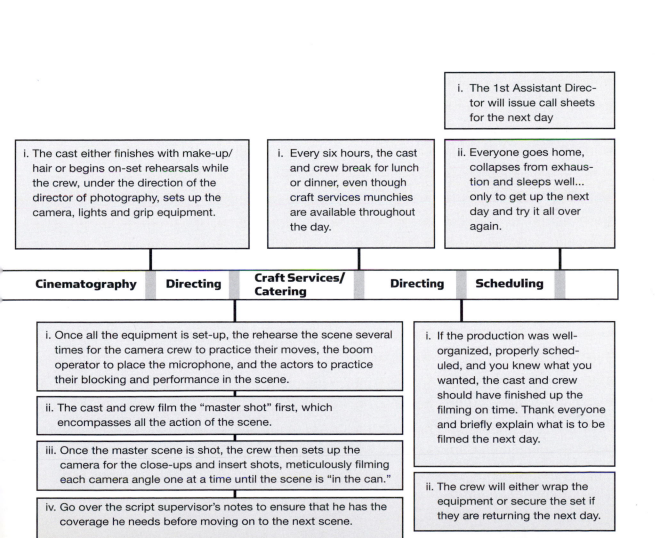

i. The 1st Assistant Director will issue call sheets for the next day

i. The cast either finishes with make-up/hair or begins on-set rehearsals while the crew, under the direction of the director of photography, sets up the camera, lights and grip equipment.

i. Every six hours, the cast and crew break for lunch or dinner, even though craft services munchies are available throughout the day.

ii. Everyone goes home, collapses from exhaustion and sleeps well... only to get up the next day and try it all over again.

Cinematography **Directing** **Craft Services/Catering** **Directing** **Scheduling**

i. Once all the equipment is set-up, the rehearse the scene several times for the camera crew to practice their moves, the boom operator to place the microphone, and the actors to practice their blocking and performance in the scene.

ii. The cast and crew film the "master shot" first, which encompasses all the action of the scene.

iii. Once the master scene is shot, the crew then sets up the camera for the close-ups and insert shots, meticulously filming each camera angle one at a time until the scene is "in the can."

iv. Go over the script supervisor's notes to ensure that he has the coverage he needs before moving on to the next scene.

i. If the production was well-organized, properly scheduled, and you knew what you wanted, the cast and crew should have finished up the filming on time. Thank everyone and briefly explain what is to be filmed the next day.

ii. The crew will either wrap the equipment or secure the set if they are returning the next day.

CHAPTER 11
Production

INTRODUCTION

Once all the preparations have been made, it's time to begin the process of physically making the movie, called *production*. Production begins once the camera rolls on set, either in the studio or on location, and continues until the final shot is in the can.

Production can be divided up into two categories:

- **Principal photography.** Principal photography is the shooting of any scenes that involve the main actors. The majority of the movie is principal photography and involves the director and the first unit crew – that is, the primary director of photography, department heads, and crew.

The 1st unit camera crew shoots the main actors in the majority of the dramatic scene, while the 2nd unit handles insert shots, visual or special effects sequences, and stunts.

- **Second unit.** Second-unit photography is a separate, smaller crew headed up by a second-unit director and second-unit DP that shoots insert shots, establishing shots, plates for visual effects, stunts, and any other sequences that do not involve the main actors. Shooting second unit allows the first unit crew

Filmmaking.
© 2011 Jason J. Tomaric. Published by Elsevier Inc. All rights reserved.

to focus on the performance and maximizes the actors' time to be working on set instead of waiting around for complicated setups to be completed.

When it's time to enter the production phase, every department should be clear on what they need to do each day, what elements and equipment are needed, and what each person's job is. Every aspect of the production should be ready to go and no creative idea left undiscussed or unplanned.

GETTING READY FOR PRODUCTION

Shooting a movie is a very demanding yet exciting culmination of months of work and preparation. When getting started in the production phase of a movie, be ready for what awaits you:

- **Long hours.** Shooting a movie often includes long, tiring hours. Be sure to eat healthy food and get enough sleep before the production begins. You'll need as much energy as you can muster, so avoid sugary junk food from the craft services table, opting instead for solid meals to help carry you through your day.
- **Stress.** Be prepared for problems and stressful situations on set – equipment will break, actors will have bad days, locations will fall through, it will rain, and you will go over schedule. The better organized you are in preproduction, the easier it will be to overcome problems as they arise. Remember Murphy's Law: If something can go wrong, it will. Assume there will be problems, keep a professional, level head and rely on your crew – everyone on set has the unified goal of producing the best movie possible.
- **Keep organized.** The secret to a smooth-running production is to be as organized as possible during the entire shoot. From organizing the equipment to keeping the office paperwork in order, always maintain a clean, safe work environment.

Sample Production Schedule

A typical production day lasts 12 hours, not including lunch. Below is a fairly typical shooting schedule.

4:00 a.m. – The location manger arrives to secure access to the location, ensure the parking is available to the cast and crew, make contact with the location owner, and prepare to direct the cast and crew to the parking and staging areas. Although the location manager has already visited the set and worked out the logistics, he now directs the grip trucks, hair and makeup trailer, portable restrooms, art trucks, and cast and crew to the appropriate staging and parking areas.

4:30 a.m. – The craft services and catering department arrives and begins setting up food and putting the coffee on so that it's ready when the crew arrived.

4:30–5:00 a.m. – The crew begins to arrive. Even though the crew's general call time is 5:00 a.m., the crew will always arrive early; remember, the call time isn't when the crew is supposed to arrive, but when they are supposed to begin to work. Arriving early gives the crew time to enjoy coffee and breakfast from craft services before working.

5:00 a.m. – This is the official call time and the crew is now ready to work. The director and cinematographer will begin talking over the first scene while the crew begins unloading the equipment and prepping the trucks. The 1st AD is busy coordinating all departments to ensure that everyone has what they need.

5:00–7:00 a.m. – The crew begins setting up the lights and camera while the art department dresses the scene for the first shot. The stand-ins have arrived to help the DP light the scene.

6:00 a.m. – The actors arrive and after checking in with the 1st AD head to hair and makeup.

7:00 a.m. – The scene is lit, the camera set up, and the actors are in makeup and wardrobe. The director rehearses the scene, and the crew should be ready to roll the first shot.

11:00 a.m. – Shooting continues until the six-hour mark, when the cast and crew break for lunch. On union shoots, the production can be penalized for shooting past the six-hour mark, paying a meal penalty to the cast and crew.

Noon – Lunch typically lasts either 30 or 60 minutes, and the 1st AD begins the clock from when the past person in line gets his food. The 1st AD will announce the ten- and five-minute warnings as the lunch period comes to a close.

Noon–4:00 p.m. – The crew continues shooting the scene.

4:00 p.m.–6:00 p.m. – The crew finishes shooting, wraps up equipment, packs the truck, restores the location to its original state and heads home. The crew has just completed a 12-hour work day, not including lunch and will have a 12-hour turnaround time between now and the next day's call time to get a good night's sleep.

6:00 p.m. – If the shooting continues, a second meal is served, as it is now six hours since the last meal. Overtime pay begins for the crew.

WHAT'S HAPPENING ON SET

Given that the proper preparations have been done – shots were planned, actors were rehearsed, the department heads had a chance to visit each location to determine the shots and lighting, locations were dressed, parking and transportation were set up, and the cast and crew are on their way – the process of shooting the movie begins.

Once the crew arrives on set, the grip and lighting trucks have been parked and the location manager has made contact with the location owner, the crew will generally make a beeline for the craft services table to grab a cup of coffee and a bagel. Professional crew members arrive early to set, well before their call time, so they can eat and be ready to begin work exactly at call time.

Begin the production day by going over the plan and logistics for that day of shooting – what scenes will be covered, where on the location shooting will take place, and how the location can be used. The 1st AD should point out the restrooms, what parts of the set are off-limits, where craft services, hair and makeup, and equipment storage is located, where the designated parking is, and all other location-specific details.

At the beginning of every shooting day, I walk the entire crew through the schedule, the scenes we're shooting, any special shots or sequences, and my overall creative thoughts on our approach to the day. Taking a few minutes to brief everyone helps the crew understand and anticipate the day's requirements.

Jason's Notes

I'll be honest with you – after working well over a thousand days on set in my career, you can always tell how well a shoot will go on day one. When I'm working as a DP, if the director knows what he wants, the crew is professional, the day is logically scheduled, and the food is good, I know it will be a good shoot. But the second the director hesitates when I ask him how he wants the next shot, I know it's going to be a very, very long day.

Then it's your turn to walk the crew through the scenes you are going to shoot. Explain what the scenes are and how they relate to the overall story, where they will be filmed, and how they fit into the production schedule. If the entire crew understands the shooting schedule, they will be much more invested in the day of shooting, feeling a part of the creative process rather than grunts moving and setting up equipment.

Once the briefing is done, you can begin work on the first scene of the day. Generally, whenever shooting a new scene, the process can be broken down into five stages: block, light, rehearse, tweak, and shoot.

Blocking

Once the production team begins a new scene, the very first step is for the 1st AD to bring all essential cast and crew members to the set so you can walk through the entire scene. During this walkthrough, block the actors, or determine their position and movement within the set. Usually, you should have spent significant time on set before the shoot to determine the blocking, although sometimes if a location is not available, you may have to block the scene the day of the shoot. Ideally, storyboards have been created to illustrate the actors' movements.

Director Steve Skrovan blocks the next scene for the cast and crew on the set of *Fred and Vinnie*.

Many novice directors, especially when under a time crunch, may elect to forgo the blocking and rehearsing phase, choosing instead to immediately shoot the scene. Choosing to shoot without the proper rehearsals means the actors may not know where their marks are, the 1st assistant cameraman will not have an opportunity to set focus marks, the dolly grip will know neither the stopping and starting points of the camera nor the speed of the dolly and the boom operator will not know where the frame line is increasing the risk of the microphone dipping into the frame. When the cast and crew is not clear on what is happening in each shot, you will have no choice but to shoot take after take, adjusting each time. This approach ultimately ends up costing more time than if you had simply blocked and rehearsed for everyone before rolling the camera.

The blocking process includes:

- **Determining the starting and stopping points for each actor.** The 2nd assistant cameraperson will use paper tape to set marks on the floor to designate the exact positions for the actors, enabling the camera crew to set focus marks, the gaffer to focus the lights on the right spots, the DP to choose the correct lens and the production designer to dress the appropriate parts of the set.
- **Determine the camera coverage.** During the blocking process, the DP will work with you to determine the placement of the camera and frame size. Usually, this is worked out in advance – for example, a simple dialog scene may consist of a master shot, close-up coverage of each actor, and any necessary inserts. Scenes with more elaborate blocking may require more intricate camera moves, so work through each camera position with the DP to ensure proper coverage of the scene.

Part of good blocking is understanding the camera angle and frame size. Always communicate this to the cast and crew.

- **Determine the lighting.** During the blocking process, the DP is discussing the lighting requirements with the gaffer and key grip – figuring out where to place the key light, accent lights, and hair lights and broadly designing the cinematic look of the scene.
- **Dressing the set.** Once the production designer understands the blocking, she will begin determining which parts of the set need to be dressed for each camera angle.

The crew sets up lights outside the windows of the location.

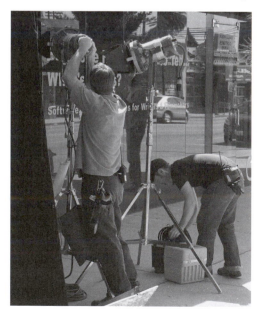

Lighting

- Once the scene is blocked, the actors are taken to the wardrobe supervisor, hair stylists, and makeup artists. The 1st AD gives the DP control of the set where the electricians and grips begin hanging lights, setting up reflectors, laying dolly track, running power to the lighting fixtures, and lighting the scene as completely as possible. Concurrently, the 1st assistant cameraman will be setting up the camera, moving the monitors at video village and prepping the appropriate lens per the DP's orders.
  - It's important for the DP to communicate clearly with the 1st Assistant Director when giving time estimates for lighting a scene. Most often, the day's production schedule has already been developed, accounting for the time needed to light each scene. Although preplanning is impor- tant, factors such as weather, unknown locations,

changes in blocking, and scheduling issues sometimes force the DP to change his lighting plan. Therefore, it is extremely important to give the 1st AD accurate estimates so she can coordinate with all the other departments.

- **Standins.** Ideally, while the DP is lighting the scene, the crew will need to see the actors in position so they can focus and tweak the camera angles and lighting. Because the actors are in hair and makeup, studying their lines and preparing for their upcoming shots, stand-ins (people who have a similar height, skin tone, hair color, and look as the main actors) are used so the DP can continue working. Low budget movies may require the actor to return to the set and stand in position. This can be both fatiguing and frustrating, as it prohibits him from doing his work. Try to avoid using your actors on set to stand in whenever possible.
- **Rehearse moves.** During this process, the DP will have the stand-ins walk through the blocking so the dolly grip and camera operators can rehearse the shot, working out any problems that may arise.

Rehearse

- Once the set is lit, the camera is in position and the actors are ready, they are brought back on set to rehearse the intricacies of the scene. Whereas the scene was roughed in during blocking, the rehearsal phase gives the director and actors a last-minute opportunity to work through emotional details of the scene. Usually, most of this emotional work has happened weeks before the shoot, but as this is the first time the actors have seen the location, they need a little time to adapt their performances to the real space of the set.

Steve rehearses the scene a few minutes before the cameras are ready to roll.

Tweak

- While the director is rehearsing with the actors, the DP is carefully watching the scene to ensure that the lighting is correct. During this time, he may make a few small last-minute adjustments to the lighting or camera position prior to shooting.

Jason's Notes

The first time I ever visited a professional set, I was shocked to see how many people were standing around. It seemed as though only a handful of people were actually working, while the rest congregated around the craft services table. What I later learned is that the people standing at crafty had already performed their jobs and were waiting for the camera crew and director to complete a series of takes so they could rush in and set up for the next take.

If correctly organized, production is an extremely methodical, calculated process, with each person understanding her job and helping the machine move forward. Every camera setup is meticulously lit, the camera is prepped, the makeup and hair are touched up, the set is tweaked, props are placed, and a myriad of other processes occur for *each and every take*.

This type of organization and on-set rhythm is how movies get finished on time and on budget.

Sound mixer John Churchman and script supervisor Dennis Marrell wait while the grip and electric departments finish lighting the set.

Shoot

- Now that the scene has been rehearsed and lit, and the cast and crew are all clear on what is happening in the shot, it is time to roll the camera. The 1st AD will call for quiet on the set and will give the commands to roll camera, roll sound, and mark the shot. After the 2nd assistant cameraman marks the shot with the clapboard, you are free to call action.
  - Be sure to let the camera run for a few moments before calling action and after calling cut – this extra footage will provide pad for the editor to work with when cutting the film.
  - During the take, watch the performances carefully on the monitor and look for authenticity, realism, and emotion from the actors. Be aware of how the actors move around the frame and how well all the technical elements play together. Does the moment feel real? Are the actors over- or underacting? Does the blocking seem real and motivated? Is the scene full of subtext, character, and driving story elements? Watch carefully and make mental notes of what to change or adjust for the next take.

The cast and crew shoot the first take from a scene in my film *Currency*.

Cut

- Once you call cut, go directly to the actors and talk to them about their performance. Be encouraging and suggest different approaches if you'd like to change a performance. While you are talking to the actors, the 1st AD should talk with the DP about the shot. Was it in focus? Was the frame clean of any stray equipment, microphone booms, and crew members or were there any other problems that necessitate another take? The 1st AD will also ask the same of the production sound mixer. Were there any problems with the audio – trucks or airplanes in the background, poor sound levels, actors turning away from the microphone?

Immediately after calling cut, I speak with actor Julian Starks about his performance, giving suggestions and feedback.

- **Briefing.** After you talk to the actors and the 1st AD talks to the crew, the AD will notify you of any problems, at which point you decide if you wants another take. If so, the crew immediately resets and gets ready to do the process all over again. You can do as many takes as needed within the time the schedule allows. After the first setup is complete and you are happy with the take, the cast and crew begin the process again for the next camera setup. Normally, shooting is slow in the morning and picks up pace as the day progresses. It is not uncommon for the production to fall behind schedule by lunchtime, which will require you to reassess the shooting schedule and possibly cut shots out of the scene to save time on set. This difficult task can be avoided by carefully preplanning the day in preproduction, rehearsing the actors, and making sure the crew knows what is expected before the day of shooting arrives.

ORDER OF ON-SET COMMANDS

Before every take on a sync–sound production, there is a series of commands that ensures that the set is quiet and every department is ready to roll. This helps keep everyone on track with what is happening.

1st AD
"Quiet on set, please!"

"Camera ready?" *

Camera operator
"Ready." *

1st AD
"Sound?" *

Audio mixer
"Ready." *

1st AD
"Actors?" *

Actors
"Ready." *

1st AD
"Roll sound."

Audio mixer
"Sound is rolling."

2nd assistant camera
"Scene 46a, Take 4."

1st AD
"Roll camera."

Camera operator
"Speed."

2nd assistant camera
"Marker."

The 2nd AC then carefully closes the clapboard before pulling it out of the shot. The camera operator may then need to reframe the shot after the clapboard is removed. Once the shot is reframed, the commands continue:

Camera operator
"Set."

Director
"Action."

These commands are rarely called on a professional set, as the crew is more than likely ready for a new take. In the event a department needs more time, simply tell the 1st AD "Standby for 10 seconds," fix the problem, then call, "Ready."

Jason's Notes

There is a definite camaraderie amongst the crew that grows stronger the longer you work together. I've worked with the same team for years, and we are like a family, going from one production to the next. The joy isn't just in seeing people you truly like each day, but knowing how each person operates – we have an almost subliminal communication whereby my crew can anticipate what I'm looking for on set and I trust them implicitly. This is how a good crew should work.

Safety

Safety is the single most important practice on set and should *never* be compromised. When shooting, minimize liability by running an organized, safety-conscious set.

- Always bring a fire extinguisher and first-aid kit on set. During the morning meeting, the 1st AD should point out where they are located and where to go in the event of an emergency.
- List the contact information for local police departments, fire stations, and hospitals on the call sheet, so in the event of an accident, everyone knows where to go.
- When working with firearms or pyrotechnics, the armorer and pyrotechnician must have a safety meeting to go over safety practices when working with firearms and explosives.
- Make sure cables are neatly coiled on the ground, are not stretched across the set, and are taped to the floor in high-traffic areas.
- Make sure C-stands, lights, and gobo arms are rigged either high or low so pointy ends aren't at eye level.

A grip properly secures a 12′×12′ overhead with rope and sandbags to prevent a wind gust from blowing it over.

- Whenever rigging overhead lights or grip equipment, always tie safety lines in case a light loosens and falls.
- Make sure all weight-bearing stands are weighted down with sandbags.
- Never overload circuits, power strips, or cube taps.
- Use dollies or hand trucks to move heavy pieces of equipment.
- When using ladders, have someone to assist, and never use a ladder that is too short for the job.

Overall, take your time, slow down, and think about what you're doing on set. The injury or death of a crew member is never worth making the production schedule.

Data Management and Workflow

It isn't uncommon to find yourself working with hundreds or possibly thousands of individual shots. Meticulously organizing your footage by naming and categorizing each clip is the key to productively editing, and this process begins on set with the script supervisor.

Script supervisor Dennis Marrell tracks what parts of the scene are covered by each camera angle.

The script supervisor maintains logs of each take, its length, any problems (both technical or performance), how much of the scene each take covers, and any other notes requested by the crew. The script supervisor then packages these notes, which serve as an index of the footage, and delivers them to the editor. The script supervisor identifies your chosen takes so the editor knows which take to use first when building the assembly cut.

- **Naming each shot.** The script supervisor is in charge of the name of every shot and works with the 2nd AC to ensure the proper naming of each shot on the slate. The 2nd AC marks each shot with a clapboard labeled with the name of the production, scene, setup, and take number.

Each shot is identified by three unique numbers or letters:

- **The scene number.** Found in the scene header in the shooting script, each scene has its own unique number. Before production begins, the script supervisor will go through the script to make sure each scene is numbered properly. Often, as scenes are added or deleted in the writing process, letters are used to identify a newly added scene. For example, a new scene added between scenes 12 and 13 would be named 12a. This can be confusing on set, because letters are used to identify the camera setup. This is why the script supervisor will renumber each scene sequentially before getting to the set.

- **The setup letter.** Every time the camera position, blocking, or shot composition changes, a new letter is used to alert the editor that the footage has new information. The script supervisor is responsible for writing down what changed in each setup, so the editor has a written guide of the contents of each setup.
- **The take number.** The take number identifies how many times the director reshoots each camera setup. Take numbers always start at 1 and progress upward. If the director decides to let the camera continue to roll and instructs the actor to continuously repeat an action until it is correct, the take number will be replaced with the word "series," alerting the editor that that take contains a series of performances before the camera cuts.

The script supervisor coordinates with the 2nd assistant cameraman and production sound mixer to make sure each shot is properly identified on both the clapboard and the sound logs.

Check out the script supervisor's notes for the film "Currency" at Filmskills.com. See page vi for details.

The scene, setup, and take number on the clapboard must always match the script supervisor's notes.

WHAT'S HAPPENING OFF SET

While the cast and crew are busy shooting the day's scenes, the production department – line producer, unit production manager, production coordinator, and production assistants – is busy making sure the crew has everything they need to shoot the scene, while organizing the next day's shoot.

- **Paperwork.** There is a lot of paperwork generated during a production – from timecards for SAG members and talent release forms to insurance

On the set of *Currency*, 1st AD Casey Slade and producer Jerry Magaña review the schedule to ensure we don't go into overtime.

certificates for locations and call sheets, and payroll and accounting requirements, the production team is seemingly buried under what seems to be an endless amount of paperwork. It's very important to keep all documents organized and up to date, because missing payment deadlines or failing to submit required union papers can result in costly fines and delays.

- **Damage control.** Regardless of how well organized a shoot is, problems always arise, making it necessary for the production department to constantly fix problems and avert potential disasters. Locations may cancel the day before the shoot, making it necessary to line up a new location, or a vendor may not be able to deliver a prop or piece of equipment. You may change your mind about a scene, making it necessary for production to get the necessary materials in order to continue shooting, a crew member may get sick (making it necessary to hire a replacement), sides (small copies of the day's scenes) need to be copied and distributed if there are changes to the script … just a few of the thousand of things that can happen on set.

- **Prepping for the next day.** The production team is always finalizing the details for the next day's shoot: from confirming locations to organizing the pick-up of set dressing, additional camera, grip or lighting equipment; renting additional transportation; and anything else needed to make sure the shoot runs smoothly.

- **Wrapping the previous day.** In addition to working on the current shoot and the next day's shoot, the production team is also busy closing out the previous day's shooting – equipment needs to be returned, rented props and set dressing returned, and vehicles moved, to name just a few tasks.

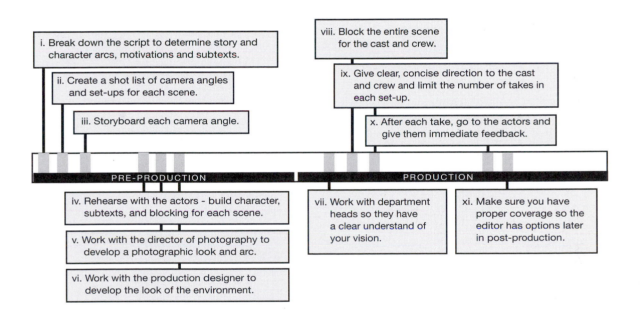

i. Break down the script to determine story and character arcs, motivations and subtexts.

ii. Create a shot list of camera angles and set-ups for each scene.

iii. Storyboard each camera angle.

viii. Block the entire scene for the cast and crew.

ix. Give clear, concise direction to the cast and crew and limit the number of takes in each set-up.

x. After each take, go to the actors and give them immediate feedback.

PRE-PRODUCTION

PRODUCTION

iv. Rehearse with the actors - build character, subtexts, and blocking for each scene.

v. Work with the director of photography to develop a photographic look and arc.

vi. Work with the production designer to develop the look of the environment.

vii. Work with department heads so they have a clear understand of your vision.

xi. Make sure you have proper coverage so the editor has options later in post-production.

INTRODUCTION

The director is the master storyteller of the movie, with two primary jobs. The first is to read the script and develop a strong mental image of how the movie will look, sound, and feel. By researching other movies, studying art, traveling, and reading, the director develops the style, pacing, and tone of the movie.

The second part of his job is to communicate to the cast and crew during pre-production, production, and postproduction, helping focus the cast and crew's artistic and technical skills towards one unified vision. The ideal director knows exactly what he wants, is able to communicate clearly and effectively, and maintains a positive, creative environment for everyone involved.

Filmmaking.
© 2011 Jason J. Tomaric. Published by Elsevier Inc. All rights reserved.

Often glamorized, a director's job is rarely simple. The degree of organization necessary to coordinate with actors, cinematographers, editors, sound designers, costume designers, hair and makeup artists, production designers, producers, and writers is incredibly essential to producing an on-time, on-budget project.

Most importantly, remember that the director is a director, not a dictator. Guide the cast and crew toward the vision and allow all participants to add their own talents to the mix.

DIRECTING DURING PREPRODUCTION

Your role during preproduction includes three main areas of focus: study the script to determine the tone, theme, and style of the movie; rehearse the actors so they can play convincing characters based on the your vision; and work with the crew as they prepare the technical and artistic elements of the movie.

Reading the Script

As a director, you will direct a script that has been written by either another writer or yourself. In both instances, it is essential to become intimately familiar with the story before moving into preproduction with the cast and crew.

Write down any notes you have about each scene – shot ideas, character directions, how a scene foreshadows a later scene – so that when you get to set, you don't have to remember everything when the pressure is on.

If you are given a script, read the script enough times that you have a complete understanding of the story arc and how every individual scene ties in with the greater story. Figure out how each scene needs to be paced, how each scene is going to start and stop, and what story elements need to be conveyed in each scene by writing notes to yourself in the margin of each page. For example, if a scene foreshadows a future plot point, one of your notes for that scene may read "scene necessary to foreshadow John's theft of the car at the end of the story by establishing his need to steal paper clips." As you read through the script, make sure every scene tightly drives the story forward and consider cutting any scenes that are superfluous.

Once the story plot points are mapped out, identify the story's deeper meaning, subtext, and overall theme so you understand how every scene and every moment supports and develops toward that theme. Most good scripts have several layers of meaning, and it's your job to identify these because they will be the foundation for the actors' performances. For example, in a story in which the theme is how family is stronger than worldly hardship, one scene may be about loss, whereas the next may be about vindication. Understanding the themes of each scene and how it ties into the overall theme is critical in directing the performances, style, and pacing of the movie.

Once you've read and identified the plot points and subtexts, begin studying the personality traits, motivations, subtexts, and histories of each of the characters and develop a clear understanding of each character's behavior. This is the foundation for beginning to work with the actors. Unless you know each character's role in the story, how can you expect to direct the actors? I do this by taking a blank sheet of paper for each character, listing each scene number along the side of the paper, and listing the motivation and subtext of the character in each scene. The description is usually only a few words, like, "Awanda's goal is to take Bobby home. All she can think about is sex," or "Bobby wants to go to Awanda's trailer so he can get washed up. He has no intention of doing anything else."

If you wrote the script yourself, you should already have a good idea about the motivations, plot, and character arcs. Be aware, however, that because you may be so familiar with the story that you may miss plot holes or confusing areas because of your deep familiarity with the subject. Try to read the script with fresh eyes as if you are an audience member seeing the movie for the first time.

Going through the script and breaking down each of these elements is important because, invariably, the cast and crew will ask you questions like:

- What is this scene about? How does it fit into the scene that came before and the scene that comes next?
- What is my character's motivation in this scene – why does she act this way?

- What is the driving subtext of this line of dialog? Why am I saying this? Is this how my character really feels? What do I really want and am I speaking the truth or masking it? How should I say this line and what is my character implying by saying this line?
- How would you like the lighting and cinematography to serve the theme?

Preparing for the Edit

Believe it or not, the editing of a movie begins well before you shoot the first frame. Filmmaking is a tedious process of shooting a scene numerous times from many angles using only one camera, and it's important to consider in preproduction how these shots will be edited together. In the editing room, the editor assembles shots so the action in the scene appears to have had occurred only once, and was covered by multiple cameras positioned around the set. This can be tricky because the quality of the edit depends heavily on how well the footage was shot on location.

When on set, always shoot for the edit by envisioning how every shot will be cut together. A great way to ensure continuity between shots is for the actors to perform the scene in its entirety and cover as much of the scene as possible from each camera setup. The more rehearsed the actors, the more consistent their performance from take to take; the more consistent the performance, the better the continuity of the footage.

Although editing is the process of assembling footage shot in the field into a meaningful, logical sequence, smart directors and cinematographers will determine how to edit the shots together before stepping foot on set. Shooting for the edit will help you better achieve your vision, control costs by eliminating extraneous setups, and streamline the editing process.

Shooting for the edit covers several aspects:

- **Planning camera angles and movements.** During preproduction, think about the relationship between each of the shots in the shot list and how they will ultimately cut together. Storyboarding the shots, or using software that allows you to animate each shot, will help you visualize the flow of each scene.
- **Plan to maximize the coverage in every camera setup.** If working on a tight budget, shooting each camera setup from a wide shot, a medium shot, and a close-up will instantly triple the options available to the editor.

Creating a Shot List

The next step is to create a shot list – or a list of camera setups and angles for each scene – by planning the actors' blocking and the camera positions on paper. Rarely at this stage does the producer have any locations locked, so although it's impossible to block specific moves, you can still determine where and when you want a long shot, a master shot, close-ups, and medium shots.

Director Steve Skrovan meets with the department heads of *Fred and Vinnie* to go over his plan for shooting each scene. Meetings like this are frequent and ensure that everyone is fully prepared when it comes time to shoot.

The goal is to arrive at the number of setups, or times the camera has to move to a different position, for each scene. This will help determine the rough shooting schedule and number of days needed to shoot the movie.

One technique I employ when planning my camera angles is to place the camera where an observer would be compelled to look during a scene. As I block the actors, I take note of where my natural human tendency is to look. If I feel the need to look at a character's face in a certain moment, odds are I will need to cover him in a close-up. If I am pulled to stand back and watch an entire action unfold, I will think about covering that part of the scene in a wide shot.

The camera is really an extension of the audience, so treat it as such. Pretend as though you were taking an audience member by the hand as the scene unfolds around you and walking her to different parts of the set to experience the action unfolding. What would be the best vantage point to see the action? Where would the audience member stand? How close or how far would she be? All these answers can translate directly into the positioning of the camera.

SETUP SCHEDULE

Title: "Clone"

Shooting Day: Sunday   **Crew Call:** 8:00am

Date: 22-Apr-10   **Call at Location:** 8:00am

Location: NASA

SET UP#	Sc. #	Ltr	Shot	DESCRIPTION	REQ. TIME set-up	shoot	ESTEM. T.O.D.	ACTUAL T.O.D.
	11	a	11a	LS EST of lobby, vidscreen	8:00am	9:00am	9:20am	
	11	b	11b	CU PADD, VFX footage alter	9:20am	9:35am	9:50am	
	11	c	11c	MS dolly of Derek, lines	9:50am	10:05am	10:30am	
	52	a	52a	Derek POV, sees Kyle and girls	10:30am	10:40am	10:50am	
	53	a	53a	MS dolly, 3-shot, Kyle talks to girls	10:50am	11:10am	11:30am	
	53	b	53b	LS dolly, Kyle approaches elevator	11:30am	11:40am	11:45am	
	53	c	53c	MS Derek as elevator doors open	11:45am	11:50am	12:00pm	
	53	d	53d	MS RA RXN Kyle, Kyle enters	12:00pm	12:05pm	12:15pm	
	53	e	53e	MS OTS Kyle, lines	12:15pm	12:20pm	12:35pm	
	53	f	53f	MS OTS Derek, lines	12:35pm	12:40pm	1:00pm	
	53	g	53g	MS EXT elevator, doors open, K leaves	1:00pm	1:05pm	1:10pm	
	53	h	53h	CU Derek RXN to scalpel, doors close	1:10pm	1:15pm	1:20pm	
	53	I	53i	MS Kyle RXN to dropped scalpel	1:20pm	1:25pm	1:35pm	
	53	j	53j	CU scalpel on ground	1:35pm	1:40pm	1:45pm	
	45	a	45a	Theresa Collins newscast	1:45pm	2:00pm	2:00pm	
				LUNCH	2:00pm		2:30pm	
	111	a	111a	MS jump cut, D storms out of office	2:30pm	2:45pm	3:00pm	
	112	a	112a	MS Spectrum approaches lab door	3:00pm	3:25pm	3:40pm	
	112	b	112b	POV from lab of Spectrum firing	3:40pm	3:50pm	4:10pm	
	114	a	114a	MS handheld, D fires at Spectrum	4:10pm	4:30pm	5:00pm	
	114	b	114b	CU RA Derek, line	5:00pm	5:10pm	5:20pm	
	84	a	84a	LS dolly, Derek learns Orin missing	5:20pm	5:45pm	6:15pm	
	86	a	86a	MS Dolly, Derek orders troops	6:15pm	6:45pm	7:05pm	
	88	a	88a	CU dolly, Derek learns Orin is POW	7:05pm	7:15pm	7:45pm	

This is an example of how your shot list will be scheduled by the 1st assistant director. Note that specific times have been assigned to each camera setup to ensure the day is completed on time.

A common approach to blocking the camera positioning of a scene is:

- **The master shot.** The master shot is a wide shot that covers the entire action of the entire scene so completely that even if you didn't shoot any other angles, the audience would be able to understand what the scene is about. The master is the universal safety shot and can always be cut to if there's a problem with any other shots or if you run out of time on set. For example, if a couple is having dinner at a restaurant, the master shot includes the two actors, the waiter, and the table in the shot for the entire scene.
- **Medium shots of each character.** Especially in a dialog scene, plan a closer single or over-the-shoulder shot of each actor. In our sample scene, there would be three medium shots: one of the man, one of the woman, and one of the waiter, each covering the entire scene.
- **Plan for any insert shots.** Inserts are shots that cover action already covered in the master shot, but are closer and draw the audience's attention to an action or detail. For example, an insert shot may be of the man pouring wine into the woman's wine glass or a close-up of the woman's hand as she temptingly caresses her wine glass.
- **Determine specialty shots.** Once you determine the basic coverage of the scene, write down any special dolly, Steadicam, handheld, or jib arm shots. In this example, we may want to shoot a dolly in from a two-shot of the actors into the waiter as he arrives, breaking up a tense moment between the dining couple.
- **Cat-in-the-window shot.** These shots are usually of unrelated people or objects in a scene that can be cut to at any time during the scene, like a cat sitting in the window, watching the action unfold. In our restaurant scene, it's a shot of a waiter waiting in the corner of the room, watching our couple dine, or a nondescript shot of another couple dining. These unconnected shots save the editor in the event there is a continuity problem or an editing issue. An editor will cut one of these shots into a scene to help bridge what could be a jarring edit, jump cut, or lapse in continuity, so always shoot a couple shots like this for each scene.

Keep the following tips in mind when planning the coverage for a scene:

- Work with an experienced line producer or first assistant director to determine how long it will take for each camera setup. Many first-time directors underestimate the amount of time it takes to setup a shot and subsequently end up running over schedule.
- If you're confident that you can shoot the basics to cover the scene, then you can consider adding specialized moves like a dolly or jib shot. Be aware that setting up dolly track and a jib arm is very time-intensive, requiring time not only to setup the equipment, but also to rehearse, set starting and stopping positions, pull focus, and coordinate with the actors and boom operator.
- When planning camera angles, think about what you want the audience to learn from each angle. There needs to be a reason the camera is positioned and framed in a certain way.

- Treat the camera as though it's an actual member of the audience that you're personally taking around the set and show them exactly what you want them to see. What would they feel inclined to look at? What do you want them to see? Where do you want them to be looking?
- Aside from the master shot, a scene is told through a number of different shots. Not every shot needs to tell the complete story. For example, in a conversation scene, dedicate one shot to focusing on one character's close-up. Then, reposition the camera to cover the other actor's close-up. In the editing room, you will then have the option of cutting to either character and can make that creative decision then.
- The best way to learn about camera coverage is not only to do it, but to follow in the footsteps of the people who are doing it right. Study the cinematography in movies to determine the placement of lights, why certain camera angles were chosen and how these choices impacted the emotional content of the story.
- The best way to learn coverage is to get in the editing room to see how well your footage cuts together. Try shooting several small sequences and then edit them to see what shots work and what shots don't.

I like to draw vertical lines through the scene with a pencil and ruler to identify how much of the scene will be covered by each camera setup. I then write the setup name in the margin next to each line.

The result will be a shot list of the scene that lists each camera setup. For example:

- Master shot of entire scene
- MS OTS (medium shot, over the shoulder) of the man
- MS OTS of the woman
- Insert of the woman's wine glass
- Dolly into waiter

Once the shot list is developed, sit down with the director of photography and 1st assistant director to build a rough shooting schedule to determine whether the budget will allow for all the proposed setups in your shot list. Be prepared to consolidate or reduce the number of setups or cut any complicated dolly, crane, or jib moves during this process.

During the location scouting process, use the shot list to determine the actors' final blocking, camera position, lighting options, and technical requirements before committing to the location. Once a location is secure, plan the final blocking and make any necessary adjustments to the shot list, so when you go into rehearsals with the actors, you already know how they will move and what the frame will be.

Keep these factors in mind when planning the coverage of each scene:

- **Frame size.** Typically, shots of varying frame sizes will cut together much smoother than intercutting shots of the same frame size. For example, cutting from a medium shot of a man pulling a wash rag out of bucket of soapy water to a medium shot of him throwing the rag onto the hood of his car to wash it, may feel jumpy. Try shooting a close-up of the bucket of water, then cutting to a medium shot of the car, then to a close-up of the man's determined face, then to a long shot of the man washing the car in the driveway. One notable exception to this guide is when shooting a dialog scene between two people, where it is perfectly acceptable to intercut between similarly composed shots.

- **Camera movement.** Plan for any dolly, jib, or Steadicam moves, pans, tilts, or zooms and make sure the movement will flow into the next shot. For example, if the camera dollies from behind a plant to reveal a long shot of a woman reading a book on the couch, the next shot may be aided by a slow dolly push-in to a close-up of her face. The kinetic movement of the camera is continued from one shot to the next through the dolly move.

- **Pacing.** What is the pace of the edit? Whether the scene is a rapidly paced montage or a slow, meandering scene, determine how the coverage will be edited in postproduction. For example, I recently shot a commercial for a new sports plane (see the commercial at www.jasontomaric.com/icon.mov). Conceptually, I wanted the audience to think the commercial was really for a high-end sports car, before revealing that the car is actually a plane. I wanted the piece to be a very quickly cut sequence of the driver stepping into the car, turning the key, pulling back the throttle, smash cutting to his face, long shot of his point of view cruising down the runway, and so on. Each of these shots ended up lasting only half a second, which required us to preplan each shot to ensure that it would cut smoothly into the next shot. The result was a testosterone-infused commercial that uses the editing style to invoke a feeling of power, fun, and elegance.

- **Necessity.** Every minute spent on set costs money. From the cost of cast and crew to equipment rentals and location fees, it can be an expensive proposition to shoot footage without knowing how it will cut together. It's worse to discover discontinuity or coverage problems in the editing room, which may require additional shooting, so proactively look at each shot, consider the music and sound effects, and determine whether each shot is truly necessary to the telling of the story.

Check out my shot list and directing notes for the film "Currency" at Filmskills.com. See page vi for details.

Storyboarding

Once you've developed a shot list for each scene, the next step is to sketch each setup and indicate specific framing, camera moves, and actor movements. These sketches are called *storyboards*.

Use storyboards to previsualize the action that occurs within each frame to convey your vision to the cast and crew. By thinking about the shots in advance, the crew is better able to prepare and plan the shooting schedule, art direction, and lighting and camera needs, and most importantly, you're better able to judge the pacing, movement, and structure of the story before getting to the set.

Quantus Pictures Inc.

Motion Picture Production Company

PRODUCTION STORYBOARDS

Production: "The Day Bobby Jones Came Home"   **Date**: June 20, 2002
Director: Jason J. Tomaric   **Producers**: Jason J. Tomaric & Adam Kadar
Director of Photography: Jason J. Tomaric   **Storyboards by**: Fredrick Allison Jr.

Scene: 16 (Bobby Jones approaches stickball game and sees his younger self)

16m - XCU of BJ's eyes. tilt up to forehead. Scar appears

16m - MS of YBJ as batter swings bat, striking YBJ in head.
YBJ goes down

© 2002. Quantus Pictures, Inc. All Rights Reserved.

Quantus Pictures Inc.

Motion Picture Production Company

PRODUCTION STORYBOARDS

Production: "The Day Bobby Jones Came Home"
Director: Jason J. Tomaric
Director of Photography: Jason J. Tomaric

Date: June 20, 2002
Producers: Jason J. Tomaric & Adam Kadar
Storyboards by: Fredrick Allison Jr.

Scene: 16 (Bobby Jones approaches stickball game and sees his younger self)

160 - LS as Bobby Jones, hits tree

16 p - Reverse/RXN of stickball players
rush to BJ -
police car pulls up
in BG.

© 2002. Quantus Pictures, Inc. All Rights Reserved.

© 2002. Quantus Pictures, Inc. All Rights Reserved.

Quantus Pictures Inc.

Motion Picture Production Company

PRODUCTION STORYBOARDS

Production: "The Day Bobby Jones Came Home"
Director: Jason J. Tomaric
Director of Photography: Jason J. Tomaric

Date: June 20, 2002
Producers: Jason J. Tomaric & Adam Kadar
Storyboards by: Fredrick Allison Jr.

Scene: 16 (Bobby Jones approaches stickball game and sees his younger self)

16 v- sheriff approaches BJ. BJ walks to camera, (see scer)
looking at Young BJ.
16v (con't) sheriff arrests BJ.

© 2002. Quantus Pictures, Inc. All Rights Reserved.

Remember that revising shots on paper is a lot cheaper than revising shots on set or in the editing bay. The alternative to previsualizing the movie with storyboards is arriving on set with no one on the cast or crew knowing what you want or how a scene is to be framed, lit, or dressed. Time will be wasted and you may not get the desired coverage, as you'll be too worried about how to cover the scene with the camera rather than focusing on perfecting the performances.

Do not, however, be so heavily reliant on the storyboards that you can't deviate from them if elements out of your control affect the shoot. Often productions run over schedule due to technical problems, scheduling oversights, or weather-related issues, forcing you to cut shots and even entire sequences at the last minute. Flexibility in adapting the storyboarded shots makes it easier to adjust to the continuously changing demands of the shoot.

Although storyboards are used to help work out shot angles and camera positions, you can also use them to determine how the shots will be edited together. One outstanding technique is to cut the storyboards together in the editing room and record the scripted dialog to create a storyboard movie, even adding music and sound effects. Watching the edit from one storyboard to the next will give you a sense of pacing and shot flow. Virtually all major movie studios use these techniques to work out the pacing and flow of shots well before going into production, saving both time and money.

Once a tool utilized only for special effects sequences, previsualization software can used to create an *animatic*, or animation, of each scene, allowing you to play with the camera coverage, editing style, and frame composition before stepping foot on set. Remember, it's better to spend the time in preproduction and guarantee usable results than shoot blindly in the field and discover problems later in the edit bay.

STORYBOARD TIPS

- Draw framelines and characters accurately to properly convey actor blocking and camera positions.
- Establish the shot size and framing of subjects is within the frame. The reader should be able to determine if the shot is a long shot, medium shot, or close-up.
- Include important set, set dressing, prop, and wardrobe information in each frame.
- Convey movement of subjects and objects in the frame with single, bold arrows.
- Convey camera movement with 3D arrows.
- Label each storyboard frame with a brief description of what is happening in the shot, and even lines of dialog. A well-done storyboard should incorporate all elements of the script so that it reads like a comic book. Pictures representing the visuals, sound, and dialog are written below each frame.
- When representing different characters, draw a simple characteristic to differentiate one character from another, such as a hat and necktie for the lead male character and a bow and dress for the lead female character. Storyboards don't have to be great works of art – just tools to convey the framing of the object or subject within the scene.

- Try drawing the scene first on blank paper, then draw the frame box around the action you want. Sometimes, it's easier to storyboard this way than to draw the shot within predrawn frames.
- Spend extra time storyboarding any shots that incorporate digital effects. Consider working with the digital effects artist to develop any digital effects shots so that they are properly shot and framed for their post needs.

Example of how a close-up is drawn.

Example of how a medium shot is drawn.

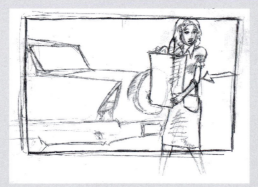

Example of how a long shot is drawn.

Once complete, storyboards should be copied and distributed among the department heads. I also find it valuable to post a spread of the storyboards on an empty wall of the production office and on set so everyone can readily access and see them.

Although many filmmakers create storyboards by hand, there are a number of 2D and 3D programs that make rendering storyboards easy. For creating 2D storyboards, check out a program called Storyboard Artist, and for 3D boards, try Poser and DAZ Studio.

- Take your favorite movie scene and storyboard it, shot by shot. Study *why* the filmmaker made certain choices about camera placement, lighting, and timing. Reverse-engineering a scene is a great way to understand coverage and the choices of the filmmaker. Even though a shot may last only a fraction of a second on screen, the director spent dozens of hours planning, shooting, and editing that moment for a very specific reason.

REHEARSING ACTORS
The Actor's Responsibility

The actor bears the responsibility of creating his character under your guidance. By better understanding the actor's process, you can more effectively work with him to create a multidimensional character.

- **Backstory.** The actor is responsible for creating her character's backstory. What was her life like and what events in her life lead to the events of the movie? Although you play a role in helping the actor craft her backstory, she is solely responsible for doing the work.

The cast of *Time and Again* did a lot of research into the 1950s so that their characters were accurately portrayed.

Jason's Notes

Remember that good actors prepare for the role on their own. A good director is there to guide them, not do the   work for them.

- **Research.** It is the actor's responsibility to do the research necessary to render an accurate on-screen performance. If the actor is playing a policeman, then he may consider working with a local police department to learn the life of a cop on the street. If she's playing a British queen, she must understand the life, customs, time period, and behavior of a British queen. Each role requires a different amount and type of research, the responsibility of which falls on the actor.
- **Delivery, dialect, and behavior.** If you're shooting a period film, or a movie that involves a language other than the actor's native language, consider hiring a consultant or acting coach to train the actor in the proper dialect or accent. It is the actor's responsibility to learn the proper dialect of his character. In addition to the spoken word, the actor must also learn how to carry himself. Whether its learning the mannerisms of a real-life person for a biopic, or understanding the social mores of the 1890s, the actor has been hired to convincingly play the role and is expected to fully understand the person he is playing.
- **Memorize lines.** This, although it should go without saying, is a the true mark of a professional. In the same way that professional crew members arrive on set with the tools they need to do their job, so too must actors arrive on set with their lines memorized and with a firm understanding of the scenes they are performing. Actors who don't memorize their lines cost the production time and money as the crew must shoot take after take, all because of the actor's lack of preparedness.

Your primary job on set is to work with the actors to get the best performance for the story, and this process begins long before the cameras roll, during rehearsal. Once the actors are cast, work with the actors to craft their character's history, motivations, and subtexts so they can play their characters realistically during the time of their lives in which the movie takes place. This is when the homework you did by defining the subtexts, themes, and motivations of each scene in your script is helpful.

When working with actors, I use a three-rehearsal process to get everyone on board and in line with my vision of the movie.

Rehearsal 1: The Table Read

The first rehearsal, a table read, is the actors' (and probably your) first time hearing the script read out loud. This is the first time the actors are meeting each other, so providing snacks and drinks to create a relaxed atmosphere is a great way to break the ice and allow the actors to get to know each other. Once you feel comfortable, assemble everyone and pass out a copy of the most current draft of the script. Begin the rehearsal by thanking everyone and introducing them to your vision.

Before beginning the table read, it's important to paint a broad picture of your vision for the movie:

- What inspired the idea for the movie and why have you chosen to make it? What is your intended objective for the movie once its finished?
- How do you envision the style, pacing, and feel of the story? Reference other films of similar tone and style.
- What is the theme, or moral of the story? What feeling or thoughts do you want the audience to walk away from the film with?
- How do you envision the overall feel of the performances?

Once you establish the overview of the story, introduce each actor to his or her character with a brief introduction and description of how you envision the character.

Jason's Notes

Some directors don't say anything during the table read, allowing the actors to find their creative footing and bring their ideas to the role first.

During the table read, the actors read their own characters. Choose an actor with a small part in the script to read the narrative directions. Listen carefully to how the dialog sounds and take note of the pacing of the story, noting where the story lags, where dialog sounds unnatural, and any other problems that surface. Do not interrupt, but listen to the entire read-through from the beginning to the end. If actors have questions about specific scenes, ask them to write down the question and ask it once the read–through is complete. Table reads can take several hours, so it's important to get through the read-through uninterrupted.

The goal is to establish the story, characters, and plot points in broad brush strokes. This is not the time to delve too deeply into each character, but give the actors a launching point so they can begin doing their homework on their own time.

Once the read-through is complete, ask the actors what they thought, answer any questions they may have, and discuss any perceived weak spots in the script. Listening to the actors' feedback on the first read-through is an outstanding opportunity to gauge how well the story unfolds, especially considering the actors are reading the material for the first time, are unbiased, and have significant interest in making sure the movie is done as well as it can be done.

At the conclusion of the table read, ask:

- Does each actor understand his character's arc? Are there any moments of the story that are unclear?
- Does each actor understand the importance of each scene? Is the subtext and overall theme clear?
- Did the dialog sound natural? Are there any lines that can better reflect the character (and actor's) personality? Did the character arcs work?
- Which actors immediately understood their character and which will need more help?
- Does each actor seem committed to and invested in the project?
- Are there any strengths the actors have that can bring a unique depth to their characters?

After the table read, take the time to discuss your vision for the character with each actor, listening to each actor's ideas. Because they are playing the role and have a fresh perspective on the story, they usually bring unique ideas you may not have thought of. Have an open mind and create an environment conducive to creative thinking.

This is an interesting transition point where you have to start relinquishing control of the characters to the actors. Up to this point, the characters have existed in your mind; you wrote their actions and their dialog and envisioned how they look and behave. It's time to pass that creative torch to the actors so they can own the role and develop it in their own way. As a good director, you should be there to help the actor as she develops her character into a living, breathing person.

Rehearsal 2: Developing the Characters

Professional actors will develop the backstory of their characters on their own, but inexperienced actors may need some help, which is where the second rehearsal can be a valuable tool.

Whereas the first rehearsal introduces the actors to the basic story, theme, and style of the movie, the second rehearsal helps the actors delve deeper into their characters by crafting the backstory and subtext of their characters with you.

A truly exceptional exercise for helping create each character's backstory involves seating the cast in a circle around two chairs. One chair is for the actor, who must always remain in character, and the other is for you, who will

Angela Nicholas mentally prepares on set for her portrayal of a woman whose husband was just brutally abducted, in my movie *Currency*. Angela and I put in most of our time developing her character well before we got on set.

play the role of a psychologist. Take each actor through his character's life by asking questions that help shape memories of past events, like, "Tell me about your first day of school" or "Tell me about the moment in life you were the most afraid." Each question should be tailored to develop events in the character's life that motivate his actions in one of the scenes of the movie. For example, in a scene in which a character watches a man get run over by a car, consider creating an event in the character's life that explores how he coped with death – say, the death of his father. Even though the father's death isn't mentioned in the script, you can reference this backstory on set when directing the actor. During this exercise, ask questions like:

- Let's talk about the day you learned that your father died. What were you doing when you found out? How did you feel as soon as you heard the news?
- Do you remember the day of the funeral? What were you thinking about as you sat in the back of the car on your way to the cemetery? How did you react when you saw the casket for the first time?
- What was the first time your father's death really hit you? What were you doing? How did his death change you?

Although this is primarily an improvisational exercise for the actor, you must steer the "session" to guide each actor through the development of his character with the type of questions you pose. Performing this exercise in front of all the actors allows everyone to build their characters' backstory into the other characters' backstories.

The objective of this exercise is twofold: the actors understand their characters' personalities, history, and motivations, and are now able to develop the characters on their own. The second benefit is that you can reference these prebuilt memories on the set when directing a moment. For example in the scene in which the character sees a man getting hit by a car, you can mention, "Go back to the day you learned that your father died. Feel the numbness you felt at that moment for this scene," to give the actor a real, tangible moment that is true to the character.

Jason's Notes

Psychology has always been a hobby of mine, and as an avid student of personality temperaments, I find that understanding how different personalities interface with the world helps me as a director understand the inner workings of a character and effectively communicate with the actor responsible for realizing that character. Knowing whether a person is more introverted or extraverted, whether she takes information in through facts or intuition, whether she processes this information analytically or emotionally, and how she acts on these conclusions is the basis for understanding fundamental principles that drive our everyday behavior. The more you recognize these patterns in real life, the more effectively you can turn a character from a page in the script into a living breathing person with a soul on screen.

DIRECTING THE SUBTEXT

Directing actors is all about understanding what happened in the character's life up to the point the story takes place. One common mistake of first-time directors is that they tend to direct a moment without any regard to the history, circumstances, and personal trials and challenges in the character's life that may affect his behavior in that moment. For example, when I am teaching a class, to the casual observer who doesn't know me, I am simply a teacher, but my behavior in the moment is shaped by many other influences in my life. Earlier that day, I got in a fight with my significant other, my car broke down, and I'm concerned about how much it will cost to fix; I'm also worried about whether my friend will show up to drive me home from work, and I'm hungry.

All these short-term factors influence my behavior as I stand in front of the class and give the day's lecture. The subtle nuances of my behavior will automatically come out because they are motivated by these other thoughts, not because I was directed to "act like I have something on my mind." In this case, I actually do.

When directing actors, describe for them other outside factors that may be influencing their behavior in the scene. The more layers, and the more a character feels these undercurrents of thought and emotion, the more realistic and subtle a performance will be. Remember, it's all about directing what lies beneath the words – not the words themselves.

This can be called the *subtext* of the scene. Although the character is doing one thing, his actions are motivated by another. For example, if you were in the grocery store and you ran into a guy you haven't seen in years who bullied you in high school, you may exchange pleasantries, talk about your career and life after high school, and maybe even throw out an offer to have lunch to get caught up on old times. Although this seems like a civil conversation on the surface, the undercurrent may be one of hatred, as old memories are conjured up of when the bully shoved you into the lockers and beat you up. You may be secretly happy he's been unemployed and twice divorced and you're intent on having lunch is to see how miserable his life is. This subtext drives the actor's performance, and it is important to understand this when directing.

Always know what the character wants in each scene. Although they might not say it through the dialog, the actors should have a clear objective of their characters' goals – what they want to achieve by the end of the scene. A well-written scene will always introduce an obstruction that prevents them from achieving the results they want. This conflict is what makes for good drama.

AFTER THE SECOND REHEARSAL

Now that the actors have an understanding of their characters with your blessing, they are free to research their roles, study the script, and apply what they learned on their own time. Feel free to meet individually with each actor to craft any finer points of the character or discuss specific moments, working out the subtext and motivation for specific scenes.

In much the same way you broke down the story so that you're clear about the driving motivation of each scene, so too must the actors:

- **Intent.** An actor must be clear on what his character wants in every scene. Whether the character achieves this objective is defined by the script. For example, in one scene, Tommy is asking Bob for relationship advice, and during the conversation, Tommy asks Bob who he is dating. Although this scene may appear simplistic on paper, Tommy's underlying motivation is to find out if Bob has been sleeping with his best friend's wife, and everything Tommy says is designed to find the answer to that question. Good actors will have a firm understanding of their character's intentions in each and every scene.
- **Subtext.** A corollary to intent is subtext. What is the character really saying? In well-written scripts, there is a difference between what the character says versus what she means.
- **Where in the story.** Actors must be clear about their character's arc throughout the story, so that when scenes are filmed out of order, they can jump into the character's mindset.
- **How does the character appear to the world.** Actors must be consciously aware not only of what their characters say and what they really mean underneath the words, but how they want others to view them. Does the scrawny teenager want to be perceived as a strong decision maker? Does the frustrated wife want others to perceive her marriage as perfect? Understanding these three key components will help an actor create a multidimensional character full of inner conflict.

Although this is the actor's job, it is important for you to assist the actor to ensure he is taking his character in the proper direction. The stronger the communication between you and the actor in this preproduction phase, the better the actor's on-set performance will be.

Rehearsal 3: Scene Specifics

The third rehearsal involves *blocking* the actors' movements for each scene. Plan movements, discuss camera angles, and work out natural blocking until each scene feels kinetic and fluid. Because this rehearsal rarely occurs on set, explain and translate the blocking in a way that can be easily adapted to the actual set. Begin rehearsing major scenes and work through to the medium scenes so the actors understand how minor scenes connect the main story beats.

Jason's Notes

Early blocking is a wonderfully kinetic exercise that gives the actors the freedom to move around the set without the technical constraints of lighting, sound and camera. It's okay to let the blocking unfold naturally – see where the actors move and why. If this rehearsal occurs early enough in the preproduction process, you can revise the shot list and storyboards to accommodate the resulting blocking.

Some questions to tackle with the actors:

- Discuss each character's intent and goal for each scene. What is her objective? Does the character obtain her objective, or does she fail?
- Even though the actors are playing the words written in the script, work out what each character is really trying to say. Define this subtext for each character in each scene.
- Discuss any themes or subplots in any given scene so the actor understands how the scene fits into the greater story.

This rehearsal is a great time to discuss each character's emotional state in the moments before the scene and where they are headed in the scene following. Avoid working on the emotional context too heavily, as the actors should remain fresh for the day of shooting.

By the end of this rehearsal, each actor should feel comfortable with how to play each scene. This blocking combined with the research each actor has done on his character will greatly help the actors feel extremely comfortable when they arrive on set. By this time, each actor should know the following for each scene:

- What is my character's objective in the scene?
- What is my character really feeling, regardless of whether I say it?
- Where is my character coming from in the moments before the scene begins?
- Where is my character going in the moments after this scene?

Over-Rehearsing

Every director has a different style of rehearsing actors. Some directors prefer light rehearsals so that the first time actors truly perform is on set in front of the camera. Other directors prefer to rehearse every emotion and every moment beforehand. The decision on how to rehearse should be based on the nature of the story, the experience of the actors, and your experience.

In Hollywood productions, actors rarely rehearse – they prepare for the role on their own time, arrive on set, act, make adjustments based on the director's feedback, and go home. For less experienced actors, more rehearsal time may help boost their confidence on set. But avoid over-rehearsing – scenes can be so heavily practiced and discussed that when it comes time to shoot, the scene becomes about mechanical execution rather than a natural performance discovered in the moment.

Exercises During Rehearsals

There are a number of exercises you can use to help an inexperienced actor develop the subtext and motivation of his role. Use these exercises sparingly and only in an instance in which the actor is having difficulty finding his character's motivations:

- **No words.** During rehearsal, the actors should convey their objective and subtext by playing the scene only through their actions. For example, if a wife has learned that her husband has cheated on her during a scene in which she's making breakfast, she may be unsuccessfully try to hide her betrayal. Even though the words on the page are about how she should prepare the eggs, her actions speak differently. Use this exercise to craft this physical subtext by removing the dialog.
- **Act the subtext.** Set the script aside and talk to the actor about the subtext of the scene and what the character is really trying to say. Ask the actor perform the scene by improvising dialog that reflects how the character feels instead of what he's saying. Once you feel as though he has a good grasp of the subtext, have him play the written scene while incorporating the subtext. Overplaying the subtext for the sake of exercise is a great way to help the actor get in touch with what the character's intent is behind the words.
- **Jibberish.** Another powerful rehearsal tool to helping the actor get in touch with the subtext is to have her speak in jibberish. Perform the scene with an emphasis on inflection and intonation, not words. Ask the actor to communicate what she means through action rather than words.

If you've properly rehearsed, worked with the actor to develop the backstory, identified the subtext of each scene, discussed the character's motivations, and setup where the character is coming from emotionally in the previous scene and what his objectives are, then let go and let the actors do what they do best. Remember that good actors are artists who simply need to be directed in the right direction so they can play a convincing role, not dictated to and handheld through every bit of minutiae.

WORKING WITH THE CREW DURING PREPRODUCTION

In addition to working with the actors, you'll also be asked to make important decisions about production design, cinematography styles, and locations. Your vision and ability to focus a creative team are essential in keeping the production on time and within budget, and ensuring a pleasurable experience for everyone.

The daily demands of preproduction can be intense, with dozens of people from different departments asking you hundreds of questions a day, often requiring immediate answers. It can be very overwhelming unless you have done your homework in advance and can be clear about what you want. You should be able to give concise, decisive answers and direct each department in the right direction. Waffling or changing your mind will just cost time and money, make your crew frustrated, and maybe even make them lose their confidence in your abilities.

Conversely, don't be too dictatorial. Moviemaking is a collaborative effort and everyone involved is an artist with a unique talent or specialty. Recognize these talents, give a direction for the crew to go in, and then step back and let them do their job. These artists will infuse their own experiences and skills into their work and feel a greater sense of pride than if you hold their hands through every step.

Jason's Notes

Making quick decisions is critical to good directing, and you can do this best if you've spent the time breaking down the script in advance. Remember all those notes I told you to write in your script earlier in this chapter? This is when they become really helpful in providing unified direction to the crew – you already answered many of the questions the crew is now asking. You just did it on your own time in a less-stressful environment.

The director's duties during preproduction include:

- Studying the script
  - Determine story plot points, theme, and story arc.
  - Plan the visual and storytelling style of the movie.
  - Build the shot list and storyboards.
- Rehearsing with actors
  - Discuss the theme of the movie with the actors.
  - Help actors build their character's backstory, motivations, and personality.
  - Rehearse blocking and pacing.
- Working with the crew
  - Scout locations and determine blocking.
  - Work with the director of photography to determine the visual look and feel of the lighting and shooting style.
  - Work with the production designer on set dressing, wardrobe, and props.
  - Help develop the shooting schedule.
  - Coordinate with department heads.

DIRECTING DURING PRODUCTION

Your primary responsibility on set is to the actors: coaching, guiding, and supporting their efforts. In addition to this main responsibility, you must wear several other hats, all of which involve coordinating the efforts of all departments.

Before You Shoot a Scene

When you're on set and ready to begin shooting a new scene, the cast and crew have spent weeks preparing: you determined the camera angles and blocking; the director of photography has designed the lighting; the production designer built and dressed the set and locations based on your shot list; and the actors know their blocking. Although the cast and crew have spent a lot of time discussing the scene in preproduction, they have yet to see it all come together, which is why whenever you begin a new scene, it's best to run a rehearsal in its entirety for everyone to see before breaking it up and shooting it in segments.

Blocking

Blocking is the process of determining the actors' positions and movements around the set, affording the camera the most interesting angle, finding the most aesthetically pleasing part of the set to shoot, and factoring in lighting and sound requirements. As a result, the more experienced you are in how the technical aspects of production work, the more effective you will be at blocking a scene so that it meets every department's requirements.

Odds are this is the first time your cast and crew are seeing the set, and may have some ideas on how and when the actors and camera should move during the scene. Listen to their suggestions and feel free to make small changes in blocking, but keep in mind that major changes in blocking may require additional time to light and can put you behind schedule.

Aside from minor adjustments on set, most of this work should have been done during preproduction. When the cast and crew arrive on set, the day should be about carrying out the details of the plan, not figuring things out for the first time. The more time you spend preparing in preproduction, the more smoothly the shoot will go:

- Consider how you will block a scene when scouting a location, even using your accompanying crew members as stand-ins. Before you commit to a location, it's important to ensure it works for the actors' movements, the camera and lighting placement, and all other technical and aesthetic needs of the scene. Although there are small refinements on the day of the shoot, the rough blocking should have been determined early in the preproduction phase.
- Good blocking feels natural and motivated. Think about why an actor should begin walking, or why she should sit down on a particular line. The movements should feel natural to both you and the actor.
- Give the actors blocking cues. For example, "Stand up when you say 'I thought you already took care of that.' Your cue to stand is on the word 'care.'" Work with the script supervisor to ensure that the actors maintain continuity with their blocking and dialog.

- Assist the actors in finding their marks by using gaffer's tape to set T-marks on the floor to identify specific starting and stopping points for actors.
- Set marks on the floor to determine where the camera should stop and start if a dolly or crane is being used. This helps the camera operator correctly frame the shot consistently in each take, the 1st AC consistently pull focus to keep the actors sharp, and the dolly grip time out the speed and stopping position of the dolly with ease.
- Help the actors block out and ignore the camera, crew, lighting, and boom microphone so they can delve deeply into their roles and not perform for the crew. You can do this by giving the actor techniques to deal with the equipment. For example, if there is a bright light shining in through the window, advise the actor to use the light as though it were the sun, basking in its warmth. This visual cue may help inexperienced actors adapt to the technical challenges of acting.

Ultimately, good blocking feels kinetic and real – while addressing the technical needs of the production. Work closely with the actors, the director of photography, and the 1st assistant director to find a balance between performance and the technicalities of shooting the performance within the allotted timeframe.

Working with Actors Before You Roll

After you run through the entire scene, the crew will burst into action, setting the camera, rigging lights, dressing the set, and preparing to shoot. During this time, work with the actors to help them achieve the right mindset for the moment they are about to perform.

I always tell the actor three things before we roll the camera: where you character is coming from, what your character wants in this moment, and the true subtext of what your character is saying.

There are three main points to review with each actor before they are ready to shoot:

- **Before and after.** Walk the actor through what her character is doing, feeling, and thinking in the moments that lead up to the scene you're shooting. It can also be helpful to rehearse these moments to help the actor get in the proper frame of mind. Describe what the character is doing in the moments after the scene is finished. This will give the actor a context for the scene and help her lead into the performance.

- **Motivation.** Every character has a purpose or objective they wish to fulfill in every scene. Although you and the actor have worked this out in the rehearsal stage, it's important to reiterate what the character wants in this scene. This objective is the guiding through-line for the scene. Let's say the scene is about a mother asking her little boy how his school day was. Although he's telling her about his math test, he's secretly trying to sneak cookies from the cookie jar behind her back. This objective makes the scene not about math tests, but about the little boy talking about math tests to keep his mother from seeing him steal cookies.

- **Subtext.** How does the character really feel beneath the lines? Although he may be saying one thing, what is he really thinking and feeling? Directing the subtext is the most powerful way to achieve a realistic performance.

If you and the actors have done your homework during the rehearsal process, this should be all you need to say. The actors will then go to their trailers or their rooms and mentally prepare for the scene.

- Most first-time directors will direct the actors with a surface direction such as "Act happier" or "Scratch your head when you say 'I don't know.'" These directions don't give the actors anything to work from but instead limit their ability to craft a real performance. Instead, give the actor a subtext to work from, such as "You are really attracted to this girl and every time she looks at you, you're afraid she notices the rash on your forehead. Because you're so afraid of rejection, try to subtly cover your forehead up. In reality, you're drawing even more attention to the rash, making the moment even more uncomfortable for the two of you."

- Remember that actors are artists and enjoy practicing their art. Give the actors a general direction and let them craft a performance. Treat the actor/director relationship as though you were both on opposite ends of a football field and you run to meet each other at the 50-yard line. It's a creative collaboration, with each side respecting the other.

- Be open to feedback from your cast and crew. Remember that filmmaking is a collaborative process that involves many artistic people, all of whom are probably very passionate about their work. Listen to them, but when it comes time to make a decision, stand firm.

- Never demonstrate what to say or how to do something. Asking an actor to mimic the way you say something kills the art of acting and will turn the actor off to you.

- Give actors something to do during a scene. Most people never stand and stare at the person they're talking to. Most conversations are held while one

I used the process of signing the check in the restaurant scene from *Currency* to help break the character's eye contact – all of which subtly helps the audience understand their relationship.

person or both people are busy doing something: washing dishes, changing a flat tire, or looking through papers. Directing this type of business will help make a performance more real.

- Inexperienced actors are more likely to overact than underact. The result is a showy, theatrical, and ultimately unconvincing performance. If this is a problem, talk to the actors in simple terms and help them internalize the moment by acting the subtext rather than the dialog itself. Allowing actors to improvise the dialog in the scene can also help.
- If an actor is having a difficult time with a particular moment, help him remember a similar moment in his own life he can draw upon for reference.
- If you're shooting an emotionally intense scene, it's perfectly acceptable to call for a closed set, which means that the 1st assistant director requests any unnecessary crew members to leave the set. This will help create a more intimate setting for the actor to perform.
- Try to minimize the number of takes in emotional scenes to avoid overtaxing the actors. The more takes you do, the more you risk stale, over-rehearsed performances that will lack spontaneity and real emotion.

Watch a video on how to work with actors on set at Filmskills.com. See page vi for details.

Balancing Performance with Sound and Picture

When the audience watches a movie, they experience a complete soundtrack, sound effects, visual effects, color correction, and editing style – all of which support the actors' performances. Unfortunately, actors and crew members on set do not have the luxury of seeing or hearing all these elements when the scene is being filmed. It is therefore your responsibility to paint as complete a picture of what the audience will see and hear so the actors can give a performance that works in conjunction with all the other creative aspects of the movie.

For example, in the opening title sequence of *Time and Again*, I asked actor Brian Barron to balance the crushing exhaustion of the prison break with the overwhelming sense of freedom of having had recently escaped. His objective was to play the scene with two motivating factors: fatigue and his basking in his newfound freedom. Cinematically, I chose to shoot the scene with wide, sweeping vistas and used warm, soft lighting to convey to the audience that this field is safe – Bobby Jones is safe and free.

I'm explaining to Julian Starks what the camera is going to do during one of the scenes from *Currency*. Understanding the frame size and camera movement helps Julian know how his performance will read on screen.

The audience, however, got a very different feeling from the scene, once I added the sound design and music. Although the look of the scene was warm and comforting, I chose a music score that added a foreboding overtone by using discordant, cold instrumentation. I was able to instill an emotional response in the audience using techniques other than the acting. The final result is a scene that although Bobby is tired and content in the field, the audience senses something wrong, and that unbeknownst to Bobby Jones, something is about to happen.

Jason's Notes

You, the director, are the only person who can see the final movie in your head, and it is your responsibility to describe this vision to the actors so they know how their performance will be complimented with the music, sound effects, and special effects.

Sound effects, cinematography, music, and visual effects can all create these overtones, with each aspect adding to the drama of the scene. Acting is only one part of this dramatic "pie," and by walking onto set with a firm understanding of how all these elements work together and explaining this balance to the cast and crew, you can fine-tune the performances to the proper level and intensity.

Getting Enough Coverage

Although a wise director will step on set with a clear vision of how to cover the action in each scene, she will further cover herself by shooting as many options as possible of each setup, then decide in the editing room how to piece the scene together.

The process of making a movie actually involves making three movies: the first is made when the script is written. Virtually limitless in its look and scope, the movie exists as an interpretation of the script in the minds of the cast and crew, each envisioning a different look and feel.

The second variation is created when the movie is shot on set: the actors give a face and a personality to the characters, the production designer creates the environment, and the director of photography sets the tone with the lighting. All these creative contributions result in a movie that may or may not be close to your original vision.

The third version of the movie takes shape in the editing room when the script is thrown aside in favor of assembling the footage that was shot. Moving scenes, reordering shots, and cutting entire sequences can drastically change the story as it was originally conceived both in the script and on set. Thus, the third version of the film is born.

Knowing the story may be revised and changed in the editing room, it's wise to prepare for these changes in advance. Shoot as much coverage of each scene as possible so the editor can try different versions in the editing room. This is especially important if the edited version of the movie deviates from the original script. The shots you thought were scraps or outtakes suddenly become critical in stitching together the revised story.

This isn't a license to point and roll the camera in every direction, but rather to thoughtfully cover the action in ways to protect the edit.

Here are some tips to cost-effectively increasing the amount of coverage on set:

- Shooting as much coverage as possible doesn't necessarily mean adding additional setups, but rather shooting variations of the frame size in each setup. Once you have a take you like, shoot a close-up of the same take, then shoot a long shot of that take. You may want to cut lines out of a scene, and if that cut can't be covered with a reaction shot, it's possible to jump cut from a medium to a close-up of the actor. If continuity is consistent, the edit should be virtually invisible to the audience.

- Always shoot clean reaction shots. Especially when shooting over the shoulder shots, back the foreground actor out of the frame and shoot the main actor's reaction shot cleanly. It's difficult to perform the same action twice, especially in a lengthy scene such as a dinner scene. When did he pick up the wine glass? When did she take a bite of the bread? Intercutting between shots with inconsistent continuity is jarring and distracting. By shooting clean reactions, the editor can always use this shot to bridge an edit of two shots of the other character.

Shooting a Dialog Scene

Dialog scenes make up a significant portion of a movie, and when they're done right, they draw an audience in to the moment between the characters. These moments can be subtly crafted not only on set, but through the use of editing. Your choices of when to cut, how long to hold a shot, and when to cut to a reaction shot all help shape the way a dialog scene unfolds. It's really important to realize just how much power the editor has over a scene in the editing room, and giving the editor these options depends on how the scene is shot on set.

PART 1: PADDING

During the master shot, direct the actors to perform the scene as they normally would, overlapping lines, cutting each other off, or interjecting as written. Because both actors appear in the master shot, the editor has no options to edit, so shoot the scene as you would like the audience to see it.

Shooting the close-up coverage requires a completely different approach. Shoot each actor's lines cleanly, making sure the actors do not step on each other's lines. Even if the scene calls for the characters to cut each other off in say, an argument scene, make sure each actor's lines are recorded separately in each of their close-ups. You can overlap the dialog as much as you want later in the editing room.

Jason's Notes

Be liberal when rolling the camera – don't be afraid to let the camera roll a bit before calling "action" and after calling "cut." There are usually priceless moments that occur when the actor isn't acting.

There are a number of benefits to this approach:

- **Emotional control.** This technique provides a lot of emotional control in the editing room – the editor can increase the tension of an argument by increasing the overlap of the dialog, so it appears the characters are talking over each other, or he can decrease the tension by separating the lines allowing a beat in the conversation for a character to think about what was said. He can add pauses and cut insert shots, essentially changing the nature of the scene in the editing room.

■ **Sound control.** When shooting close-up coverage of a dialog scene, the audio recording engineer on set is recording the audio of only the actor on camera. Any audio recorded of the other actor will sound distant and hollow, as it is recorded on the on-camera actor's microphone. By allowing padding between each line, the editor can easily cut out the off-screen dialog and replace it with the other actor's on-screen audio. It may seem that setting up microphones for both actors would alleviate these problems, but the off-camera actor's dialog is useless anyway, as there is no corresponding picture. The off-screen actor is doing nothing more than feeding the lines to the on-screen actor.

There are also challenges in using this technique:

■ **The actors need to alter their on-set performance.** In order for this technique to be effective, the actors need to focus on not overlapping their lines with the other actors. This can be distracting to some actors and can affect the natural emotional flow of the scene. It's important to sit with the actors to explain why this variation in performance is necessary.

■ **Overlapping dialog makes it nearly impossible for the editor to assemble the scene, forcing him to cut around the dialog instead of cutting for the emotion of the scene.** Even though a performance feels real on set, it may not work technically and will severely affect the quality of the scene.

Production sound mixer John Churchman listens to the ambience on set to make sure it is within acceptable levels.

PART 2: AMBIENCE

The second technique in recording on-set dialog is to remove as much of the ambient sound as possible. Ambient sound is the sound of a location – the waves at the beach or the cars and passersby on a busy city street. Although these sounds add realism to the scene, these ambient sounds are always added later in the editing room, giving the editor control over what type of ambience to use, as well as the volume and tone of the sound. Were you to record the ambience naturally on set, you wouldn't be able to remove or change it once it was recorded.

Recording the ambience on set poses another problem. It changes. Say you have two actors talking to each other. When you shoot one actor's lines, the microphone placement will not only record his dialog, but also the ambient sound. When you switch the camera to shoot her lines, the *tone* of the ambience changes because you changed the microphone position. When edited together, the shift in ambience draws attention to the edit. Although you can use noise reduction filters and EQ settings to reduce the affect of the ambience, you can never fully eliminate it.

So when you're shooting a dialog scene on set, reduce as much of the ambience as possible so that you record only the actor's dialog and movement.

After You Call "Cut"

Director Steve Skrovan gives feedback to Bill Rutkoski and Scott Chernoff on the set of *Fred and Vinnie.*

Once the scene is finished and you call "cut," your primary responsibility is to go directly to the actor to give him feedback while the 1st assistant director confers with the director of photography and the production sound mixer to determine the technical quality of the take. If the performance was what you were looking for, simply say, "Good Job. Let's try it again." If you'd like to go see a different performance, always be positive and *suggest* a different approach. Actors can be sensitive and sometimes vulnerable when they open up in front of the camera and rely on positive support from the director.

Be simple and clear in your direction, such as "That was great, but let's try it a little smaller," or "Give it a little more energy," or "I like how fidgety you were in the last take, but this time, make your movements a little more subdued." Generally, this is the extent to which you will need to adjust the performance.

- **Always be positive and supportive.** The secret to suggesting change is to "try" a different approach. Never tell the actor she played the scene wrong or made a mistake. Understand that playing a moment is subjective and isn't necessarily right or wrong.
- **Once you decide to shoot another take, quickly reset and roll again, while the actor is still in the proper frame of mind.** The more time passes between takes, the more difficult it will be for the actor to get back into the proper mind set. Some directors like to roll multiple takes without stopping the camera.

Directing Extras

Extras are nonspeaking actors who work in the background to bring life, movement, and a sense of realism to a scene. Extras are the patrons in a restaurant behind the main characters, they are the passersby on the street and the people sitting around our characters in the movie theater. Extras add production value, scope, and size to a movie. In Hollywood movies, the job of directing the extras usually falls on the 1st assistant director, but in independent movies, that job will probably fall on your shoulders.

Working with kids requires special patience and very simple, clear direction.

Although Hollywood productions rely on the casting services of professional agencies such as Central Casting, finding extras for a low-budget movie can be as easy as tapping into local resources:

- Contact local theatres, schools, and university theatre programs. Many aspiring actors are willing to work for free simply to get the chance to be in a movie.
- Avoid shooting in high-production towns like Los Angeles or New York. These cities attract people who are looking to make a living as actors and it is more difficult to find people who are willing to work for free than in nonproduction towns.
- Always research the setting and time period of your story so you can both costume and direct the extras so they convincingly portray the environment.
- Providing food on set is a great way to help attract extras.

Working with extras is similar to working with the principal cast:

- Be as concise as possible as to what each extra needs to wear and bring to the set. On larger budget movies, the production provides hair, makeup, and wardrobe for the extras, although this may be cost-prohibitive on lower-budget projects.
- Be sure to provide an area on set to hold the extras between takes. This area needs to be off the set and out of the way of the crew.
- Make sure you have appropriate restroom facilities to accommodate the number of extras working on set.
- When directing extras, explain to them the nature of the scene and what type of atmosphere they need to create in the background.

The extras outside the theatre in my film *Time and Again* were all actors from the Geauga Lyric Theatre Guild. Organized by Stacy Burris, they not only added life to the scene, but graciously did so for free.

- Extras are rarely experienced actors, so they need extra attention and positive feedback. Be clear in your direction and quick in your praise.
- If necessary, give groups of extras specific direction, especially if their action is happening directly behind the principal actors.
- Beware of extras who try to draw attention to themselves. Move them to the back, out of sight of the camera. Good extras are invisible to the audience.
- Extras should never talk during a take, even if they appear to be making noise or speaking on camera; they should always mime the action so sound editors can put the sound of the background in later.
- Always be supportive. Many extras have never had any experience shooting a movie and are probably volunteering their time. Always thank them and let them know when they do a good job.
- Make sure each extra signs a release form before stepping on set.
- Keep a mailing list of the extras so when the movie is finished, you can notify each person of how to see the film.

Directing the Crew

Directors come in two varieties: the kind that is technically gifted, but has a hard time working with actors, and the type that is great with actors, but feels out of place with technical process of moviemaking. Although your primary responsibility is to the actors, the more you know about the role of the crew and the technical aspects of filmmaking, the better you will be able to translate your vision to the screen.

Working with the crew is much like working with actors – they are artists in their respective crafts and need direction on how their contributions fit into the overall production.

- *Know what you want!* Do not show up on set without being clear as to what you want. Tell the cast and crew what you are looking for in a scene and do not second-guess yourself or rely on the crew to tell you what to do. This is the single biggest complaint from crew members about first-time directors. You are the *only* person who knows how to tell the story.

- Communicate clearly. You may feel like you are oversimplifying a concept, but in reality, walking through every detail is critical in helping the crew understand what you want.
- Encourage communication between department heads.
- Don't try to do everything yourself. Surround yourself with people who know their jobs and do them well, and let them do it. Directors who try to wear too many hats are taken away from what should be their primary focus – the actors.
- Listen to the advice you receive from the crew, especially if they are more experienced than you.
- If you are in doubt, always hire a good, experienced cinematographer who can guide you through the process, help you with setting up shots, and even give you guidance with the actors.
- Balance the attention you give to both the cast and the crew. Remember that your first obligation is to the actors. The 1st assistant director will manage the crew, but you still need to know what you want from them.
- Hire a good crew and let them do their jobs. You shouldn't have to worry about the sound levels or if there's enough light in the scene. Trust that your crew will do the best they can so you can focus on the job of directing.
- Always run through the scene with the actors once for the crew so they can see how the scene plays. Doing this before each new scene will help the crew understand what each setup covers in the overall scene.
- Stay calm and positive. Your attitude will determine how the entire set will run. If you're stressed, the cast and crew will feel it!

Script Supervisor

The script supervisor's primary responsibility on set is to maintain the internal continuity of the production by watching the script, logging any deviations in performance by the actors, recording the setups and how each one covers the scene, and logging each and every shot made on set – essentially creating an index of shots for the editor. The script supervisor's duties on set include:

- **Continuity.** The script supervisor is responsible for watching and tracking continuity from shot to shot including screen direction, deviation from scripted lines, and actor blocking. Because scenes are filmed out of order, the script supervisor notes the positioning of props, like the level of water in a glass, or the position of an actor's arm on the back of the couch, so these details remain the same from take to take and setup to setup.
- **Shot coverage.** The script supervisor is also responsible for marking how much of each scene is covered in each camera setup. This allows you to instantly look at these notes to determine whether you have the coverage you need for the scene.
- **Changes in dialog.** The script supervisor is responsible for noting any changes the actors make in the dialog. Improvised lines are noted in the script so the editor knows what takes have variations of the dialog.

Scene	TK	Sound	Print	Time	CR	
						Facing Pg 69
94	1	SYNC		·56	52	THREE SHOT - FRED - VIN - MGR. (ENTER
	2			1 04		B.G. L-RT: MGR, FRED, VIN), MGR. 'OPEN'
	3			58		BED, VIN - FRED X L-RT F.G.
	(4)		✓	1 01		
94A	1	SYNC		54	52	OTLS - FRED - VIN, MGR EXITS RT DOWN,
	2			58		FRED - VIN LOOK O-S.L. DN. (TO MGR)
	(3)		✓	1 00		MGR RISES, FRED - VIN EXIT L, MGR EXIT RT
94B	(1)	SYNC	✓	52	52	CU - FRED, LOOKS O.S. RT (TO MGR),
						O.S. RRT (TO VIN)
94C	1	SYNC		58	52	OTRS - MGR, ENTERS CAM L, Xs TO
	2			F S	PROPS	SOFA (L BG), 'OPENS' SOFA, RISES, LOOKS O.S. L
	(3)		✓	1 00		TO VIN - FRED, VIN - FRED X FG L-RT, MGR
						BENDS O.S. RT
94D	1	SYNC		1 00		CU - MGR, LOOKS O.S.L. (TO VIN - FRED)
	(2)		✓	1 01		
94E	1	SYNC		56		THREE SHOT - FRED - VIN - MGR, FRED - VIN
	2			1 02		X HEAD ON TO F.G.
	3			1 00		
	4			1 02		
	(5)		✓	1 01		
94G	1	SYNC		58		TWO SHOT - VIN - FRED, ENTER CAM RT,
	(2)		✓	56		LOOK O.S.F.G. RT. (TO MGR) EXIT RT
	3			53		O S NOISE [GOOD FOR FRED'S TURN TO MGR - SOUND?]

The script supervisor's notes track continuity, scene coverage, and the director's preferred takes. The notes are given to the editor as an index of the footage.

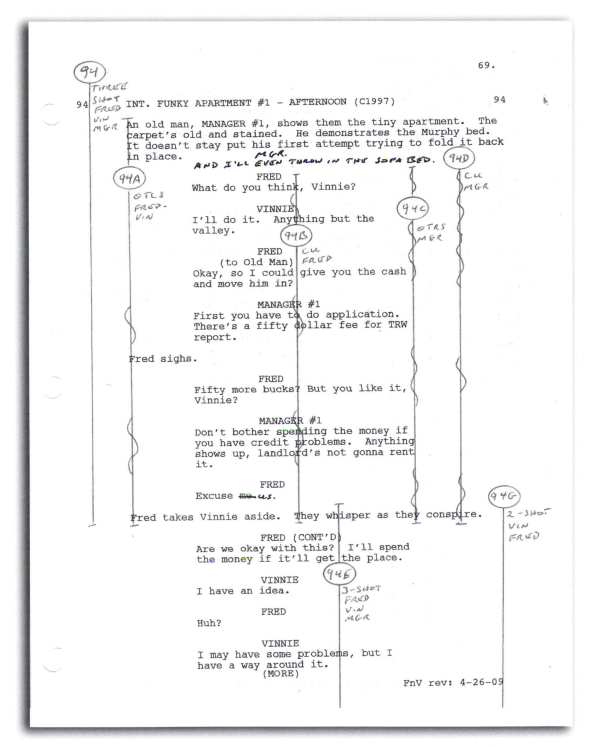

94 THREE SHOT FRED VIN MGR

94 INT. FUNKY APARTMENT #1 – AFTERNOON (C1997) 94

69.

An old man, MANAGER #1, shows them the tiny apartment. The carpet's old and stained. He demonstrates the Murphy bed. It doesn't stay put his first attempt trying to fold it back in place.

AND I'LL EVEN THROW IN THE SOFA BED. MGR.

94A OTLS FRED- VIN

94D CU MGR

> FRED
> What do you think, Vinnie?

> VINNIE
> I'll do it. Anything but the valley.

94B CU FRED

94C OTRS MGR

> FRED
> (to Old Man)
> Okay, so I could give you the cash and move him in?

> MANAGER #1
> First you have to do application. There's a fifty dollar fee for TRW report.

Fred sighs.

> FRED
> Fifty more bucks? But you like it, Vinnie?

> MANAGER #1
> Don't bother spending the money if you have credit problems. Anything shows up, landlord's not gonna rent it.

> FRED
> Excuse ~~me~~ us.

Fred takes Vinnie aside. They whisper as they conspire.

94G 2-SHOT VIN FRED

> FRED (CONT'D)
> Are we okay with this? I'll spend the money if it'll get the place.

> VINNIE
> I have an idea.

94E 3-SHOT FRED VIN MGR

> FRED
> Huh?

> VINNIE
> I may have some problems, but I have a way around it.
> (MORE)

FnV rev: 4-26-09

The script supervisor's notes track continuity, scene coverage, and the director's preferred takes. The notes are given to the editor as an index of the footage.

- **Technical notes.** The script supervisor notes any technical issues such as out-of-focus takes or background noise that interferes with the audio so the editor knows if a take has a problem. Anyone on the crew can ask the script supervisor to make a note for the editor.
- **Keeps the script current.** The script supervisor ensures that everyone on the cast and crew has a current version of the script.
- **Logs shooting days.** The script supervisor creates daily production reports that include the continuity logs; the time the production started and stopped; the times of the first shot, last shot, and meal breaks; a breakdown of the pages, scenes, and minutes that were shot that day; and the numbers of takes and retakes.

Jason's Notes

The script supervisor creates the index of shots for the editor, so when the footage arrives in the editing room, the editor knows exactly what was shot, where the problems lie, and which takes the director prefers.

Directing Problems

There are a number of problems that plague a first-time director, often as a result of poor preplanning or the lack of a concise vision:

- **Overshooting.** Directors who aren't confident in their plan tend to over-shoot a scene from too many angles, wasting time and falling behind schedule. Take the time in preproduction to walk through the coverage of each scene so that when you arrive on set, you are confident in the number of camera angles you need to cover the action properly.
- **Indecisive direction.** The director who constantly looks to the crew for help in directing a scene is a director who doesn't know what he wants. This is the most dangerous situation to be in because you end up in a boat with no captain. As a director, take the time to sit down and map out what you want, not only for each scene, but for the entire story. The cast and crew appreciate a director who knows what he wants to do, even if he is wrong sometimes.
- **Lack of communication.** Many directors may have their vision in their head, but have a difficult time effectively communicating it to the cast and crew. Often, directors fear that they will sound stupid and simplistic when they explain what they see, but an effective director will communicate as clearly as possible what she wants to have happen. Remember that the cast and crew have no idea what the director is looking for and need everything spelled out in as much detail as necessary for them to do their jobs.

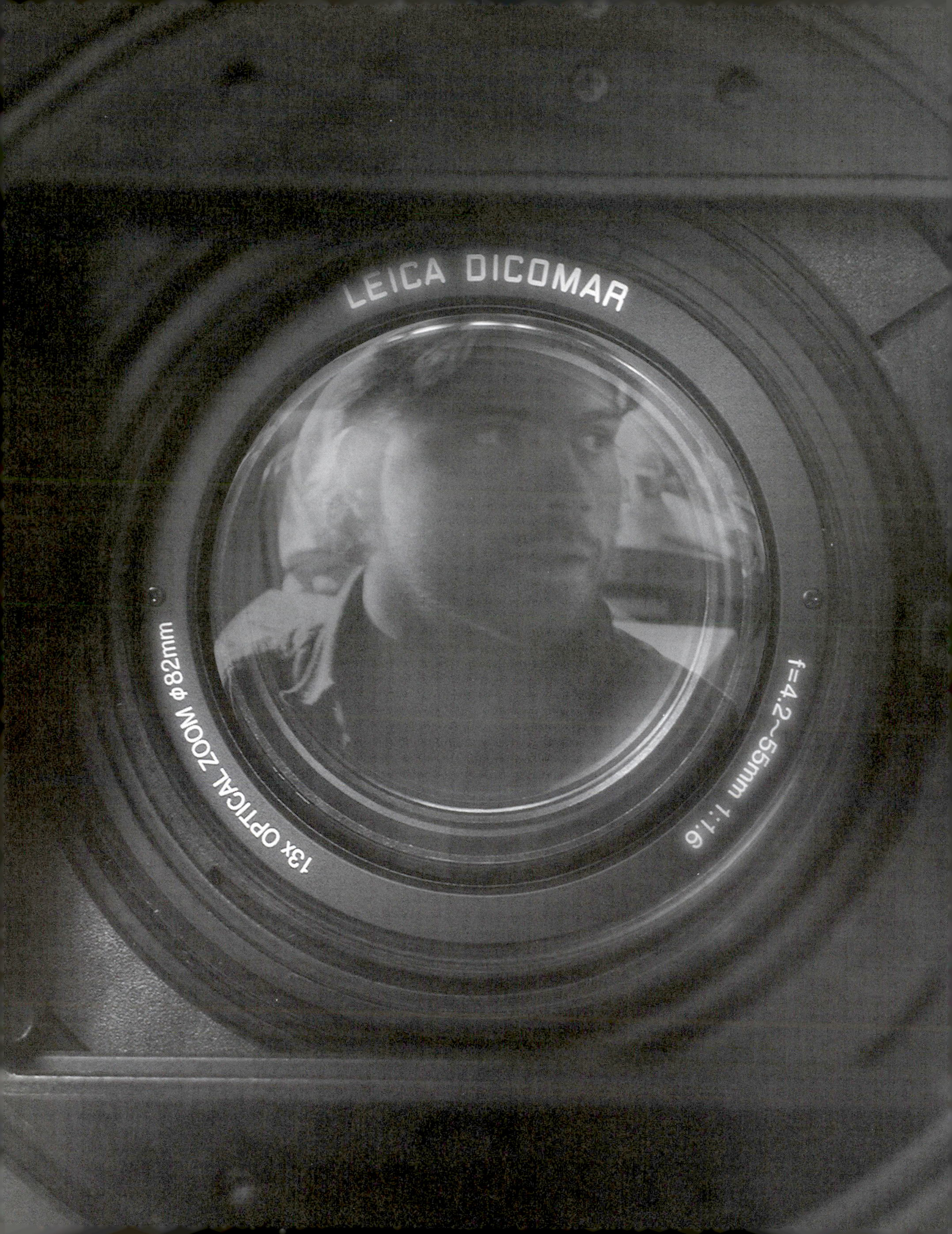
LEICA DICOMAR
13x OPTICAL ZOOM φ82mm
f=4.2~55mm 1:1.6

CHAPTER 13
Cinematography

293

INTRODUCTION

Cinematography is the art of lighting and photographing a scene. Much like photography, which involves taking single photographic images, cinematography refers to cinema or a series of moving images over time.

Cinematography can be broken down into two different, but very related categories: lighting and the camera. One job aspect of the director of photography

Soundstages like this one at Panavision in Los Angeles provide the power and resources necessary for the director of photography to create the right look for the movie.

Filmmaking.

© 2011 Jason J. Tomaric. Published by Elsevier Inc. All rights reserved.

(also known as the DP or cinematographer) is to create the look of the movie through the lighting. By coordinating with the grip and electrical department, headed by the key grip and the gaffer, the DP lights each set not only to meet the photographic requirements of the medium he's shooting on, but also to create a mood that complements the story.

The second element of the DP's job is to understand the camera, how it operates, where to place it, how it should move, which lens to use, and how to frame the action for the best emotional and logical impact.

THE DIRECTOR OF PHOTOGRAPHY

The director of photography is one of the most important people on set and your most valuable asset. As the liaison between you and the crew, the DP's job is to help you translate your ideas for a scene into camera blocking, lighting, angles and lens choices that not only fulfill the emotional requirements of the scene, but also provide the editor with enough coverage to properly assemble the scene in post.

Director Steve Skrovan and I discuss a shot on the set of *Fred and Vinnie*.

The director/DP relationship is powerful and unique. Your responsibility lies with the actors and crafting the story; the DP is responsible for crafting the look, emotion, and movement of the story through lighting and the lens, so communication and mutual understanding are important between you and the DP. Often the most experienced person on set, a good DP seeks to balance your skill set, even offering advice on blocking the actors and camera, scene coverage and the overall production process, if you choose.

Jason's Notes

I have the unusual benefit of working as both a director and a director of photography, so I certainly understand each person's perspective. As a director, I've always viewed the DP as most experienced person on set, whose knowledge of the entire filmmaking process, from paper to the editing bay is invaluable in helping me craft a quality product. I've learned very quickly to hire the best DP I can find and trust his insight. As a DP, I love working with directors who let me help them craft their vision the best way possible with the time and resources at hand. It all comes down to collaboration and partnership.

DIRECTOR OF PHOTOGRAPHY OR CINEMATOGRAPHER?

The term *cinematographer* has been a point of contention for some time now; some professionals insist that it applies only when the director of photography and camera operator are the same person, although this is far from being uniformly the case. Others think the term *cinematographer* should apply only when shooting on film; still others feel that a cinematographer's job reaches far beyond the photographic look of the movie, and hence that the term *director of photography* is too limiting, given the scope of duties and responsibilities. Ultimately, it is a choice of personal preference.

The director of photography, although overseeing the entire crew, officially coordinates the photographic operations of the movie with three department heads: the camera operator, who heads the camera department; the gaffer, who heads the lighting and electric department; and the key grip, who heads the grip department. Each manages a crew in their department and relays orders from the DP to these crew members.

To learn more about the camera, grip, and electric crews, check out Chapter 8.

Watch a video detailing the relationship between the director and cinematographer at Filmskills. com. See page vi for details.

Hiring the Director of Photography

When choosing a DP for a project, avoid hiring a film school graduate; instead, look for an experienced DP who has worked her way up through the ranks. In the Hollywood system, many film school graduates begin their careers by working in a camera rental facility sweeping floors, driving trucks, and trying to make connections with cinematographers as they come in to rent cameras for real productions. If they are successful in making a good contact, they may get a job as a second AC on a feature. The 2nd AC is in charge of loading the film, maintaining camera logs, and marking each shot with the clapboard. After

working on a few dozen features as a 2nd AC, he will be able to move his way up to a 1st AC. Responsible for pulling focus, setting up, maintaining, and moving the camera, the 1st AC will work in this capacity for several dozen films until he graduates to the camera operator position. The camera operator operates the camera and will work in this capacity for several movies until she is asked to DP a film. This is the standard path most people take to working as a director of photography.

Today, with the affordability of high-quality digital camera systems, many aspiring DPs purchase their own gear and begin a career as a DP, bypassing the traditional Hollywood system. Although these young DPs may know how to produce a quality image, their lack of experience in the production process can be detrimental to you and the movie. Remember that a good DP needs two basic skills: a keen photographic eye and the experience to successfully guide the production.

I work very closely with my gaffer David Sheetz and key grip Tom Hunt, especially on this commercial, which required us to light over a mile of race track at night.

Steve and I had a fantastic working relationship on set. We complimented each other's skill sets, which made working together not only fun, but ultimately beneficial for the movie.

When it comes time to hire the DP, consider the following tips to help you find the best, most qualified person:

- Contact local film commissions, post an ad on craigslist.org or any crew web site, and ask for online links to web sites or DVD demo reels. When you begin looking at DP reels, look at the following issues:
  - Are the shots well framed and motivated by the story?
  - Is there a strong visual continuity from shot to shot? Even though this responsibility ultimately lies with the director, if the shots don't work, then ask why the DP didn't help the director improve the quality of coverage.
  - Does the lighting have a style that positively contributes to the story? Does the picture look professional? Are there any shots that are over- or underexposed?
  - How does the camera move? Are camera movements necessary and do they contribute to the story, or are they frivolous?
  - Does the cinematography pull you into the story?
- Meet with prospective DPs to see if your styles are compatible. Look at her demo reel and talk to her about her approach to lighting a scene. Discuss your story and see if it resonates with her. Much like auditioning an actor, your quest to find a cinematographer lies not only in your comfort level with her craft, attitude, and professionalism, but also in her ability to work with you to fulfill your vision.
- Once you choose your DP, sit down with him and show him scenes from movies that you like the look of. Gather various examples of styles, camera movements, and lighting that you'd like to see in your movie and listen as the DP explains how to approach these styles. You both should be on the same page as to the style and look of the movie, enabling the DP to determine the equipment needed for the production. Discuss:
  - **Camera movement.** Are you looking for static setups? Tableau shots? Handheld, documentary-style shots? Dolly or crane moves? Steadicam? Long takes? Short takes? How are you looking for the camera to interact with the environment and the set?
  - **Lighting.** Are you looking for flat (1960s Technicolor), colorful (*Amélie*), black and white (*Schindler's List*), monochromatic (*Minority Report*), or tinted lighting (*The Matrix*)?
  - **Style.** Do you want a documentary (*Babel, Traffic*), poetic (*Amélie*), or dramatic (*Titanic*) style?
  - **Editing.** How will the movie be cut together? Are you using long shots? Quick, rapid MTV-style cuts?
- While discussing these elements, an experienced DP will be able to help you balance your vision with the realities of production, scheduling, and equipment availability. Listen to her: she will be your greatest asset on set.

The key to a successful collaboration with the DP is open communication of ideas, thoughts, and technical methods. Never hesitate to ask questions and always understand the complexities of achieving your vision – always tell the DP *what* you want and trust him to figure *how* to do it. Most neophyte directors could benefit by partnering with an experienced DP who can help with the blocking, framing, and pacing of the movie.

CINEMATOGRAPHY: CAMERA

The Camera

The DP's primary tool is the camera, and it is the window to the audience. Regardless of whether the movie is being shot on film or digital video, a firm understanding of how the camera works and how to frame is the key to achieving Hollywood-quality results.

The art of cinematography is about crafting the frame and every detail, and professional cameras give the DP control over virtually every setting.

- Avoid using automatic camera functions like auto-focus, auto–white balance, or auto-iris. You're an artist! Don't let your tools tell you how your shot will look; instead, control your equipment to get the look you want.
- Try using a tripod or other camera stabilizing system unless the story requires otherwise. Shooting handheld may be quicker, but the results will always be amateurish. You never want your audience to be pulled out of the story by a shaky camera.

Operation of the camera can be broken down into two categories: the way the camera and its settings function, and choosing where to place the camera and how to approach the framing of a subject. First, let's review how the camera functions by introducing the most powerful part of the camera: the lens.

Jason's Notes

I'm going to stop for a moment, because I have a feeling you're looking at this chapter, wondering why I'm spending so much time explaining the technicalities of cinematography in a directing book. The reality is that if the script is the outline of the picture you want to paint, then the camera, the lens, and the lighting are your paintbrushes. Even though you have a DP who knows this stuff, the more you understand what the tools can do – and even more importantly, what they can't – the more likely the images on screen will resemble the images in your head. Learn these tools, what they do, and how to use them, and most importantly, learn how to speak the language of cinematography.

Choosing the Lens

The lens is the single most powerful tool in your arsenal. Although there are lots of film-look software programs available, a mastery of the lens is the best way to create a motion-picture-quality look. What's really exciting about the lens is that it works the same in every camera, whether it's a disposal camera from the drugstore or an expensive Panavision 35 mm film camera. The principles we're going to identify are all a matter of optics and the way that light interacts with the lens.

Before we start, you need to understand that there are two types of lenses: prime lenses and zoom lenses.

PRIME LENSES

A prime lens has a fixed focal length, or angle of view. The lower the number, such as 12 mm, the wider the angle, and the higher the number, such as 120 mm, the narrower the view and the closer the lens brings us to the subject. Typically, prime lenses come in a set from which the director of photography will choose the ideal lens for the desired field of view and depth of field for the shot.

Prime lenses typically come in sets that include 25 mm, 35 mm, 50 mm, 85 mm, and 100 mm. You can always choose which focal lengths you want when custom-building your lens set.

Prime lenses have fewer pieces of glass for light to pass through than zoom lenses, which results in a sharper, crisper image, making them the first choice among directors of photography, especially when shooting a movie that will be projected or shot under low light conditions. Although primes are more expensive to rent than zoom lenses and require more time on set to change, the results are well worth the cost and effort.

Many professional camcorders accept either 35 mm or 2/3-inch bayonet-mounted interchangeable lenses, giving the director of photography the opportunity to use primes. For cameras that have built-in lenses, 35 mm adapters can be attached to the front of the camera and accept 35 mm lenses. Despite the advantage of obtaining a look closer to that of film, the amount of light lost through the adapter requires up to four times more light on set to obtain the same exposure than if the scene were photographed without the adapter.

ZOOM LENSES

Zoom lenses feature variable focal lengths because of additional pieces of glass added to the lens. The majority of video cameras feature noninterchangeable zoom lenses and offer greater flexibility and ease of use. Although they are faster to work with when setting up a shot, zoom lenses aren't ideal for high-quality motion picture usage because the added glass elements required to zoom reduces the amount of light that reaches the imaging plane.

Jason's Notes

The biggest secret to making Hollywood-quality movies lies in the lens you choose and how you use it. Many filmmakers spend thousands of dollars on high-format cameras, quality lighting equipment, and camera support equipment, never realizing that if they use a cheap lens, the potential clarity and sharpness of the recording format will never be fully utilized. The quality of the optics, especially in high-resolution formats like HD or 35mm film, make a substantial difference in the quality of the image. Rent the highest-quality lens you can find, even at the expense of being able to afford the best recording format.

The Five Rings of the Lens

Every lens has five basic controls that the director of photography can manipulate to obtain the best technical and artistic image. Professional cameras with better optics afford a wider range of control than consumer or prosumer camcorders, and having a firm understanding of these five controls will help improve the image of even the cheapest camera.

The five rings of the camera lens.

Ring 1: Focus

The first control of the lens is the focus ring, which adjusts a piece of glass in the front of the lens barrel to focus light entering the camera from a measured distance onto the film or CCD. You may have noticed the 1st assistant cameraman in behind-the-scenes videos of Hollywood movies measuring the distance from the lens to the actor with a tape measure. He marks these measurements on the camera so he knows the precise distance and focus setting for each of the actor's blocking marks.

If focusing using a zoom lens, the camera operator will zoom all the way in on the actor's eye, set the focus, then zoom back to the proper focal length. This ensures that the actor is in the sharpest focus and eliminates the need to measure the distance from the actor to the lens.

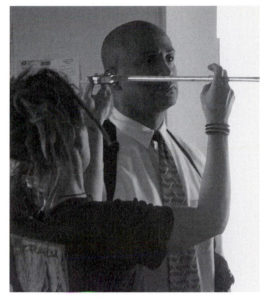

1st assistant camera Vanessa Joy Smith measures the distance from the camera to actor Julian Starks for focus.

PULLING FOCUS

Setting the focus once at the beginning of a setup works, provided neither the actor nor camera moves. In situations in which one or both move, the 1st assistant cameraman must "pull," or adjust the focus, during the shot to ensure that the actor remains in sharp focus throughout the shot.

Pulling focus is a very important skill that takes years to master. The trick lies in the fact that a lens measures distances logarithmically, not linearly. If an actor stands 50 feet away from the lens and walks 2 feet toward the lens, the 1st AC needs to rotate the lens barrel a little bit. If, however, an actor is only 10 feet from the lens and walks 2 feet toward the lens, the first AC must rotate the barrel almost one-fifth of the way around. This may seem easy, but when the DP chooses a long focal length, the first AC may have a depth of field that is only an inch deep, making it challenging to keep the actor in focus.

Jason's Notes

This is one of many reasons why it's important for you to block each scene for the crew before the cameras roll. By finalizing each actor's positions on set, the 1st AC can measure and set focus marks while you rehearse with the actors. Some directors choose to shoot without a camera rehearsal, making it difficult and sometimes impossible for the 1st AC to focus on the fly.

Follow focus units are designed to help the 1st assistant cameraman pull focus. The two marks on the white ring identify the focus marks measured from the actor's starting and stopping points on set.

If it's necessary to pull focus on a shot, use these simple steps to maintain focus throughout the shot:

- Once you're happy with the actor's blocking, the 2nd AC will use colored gaffer's tape on the floor to mark the actor's starting and stopping positions.
- If the shot requires a dolly move, the dolly grip will mark the starting and stopping points of both the camera and the dolly.
- The camera and the actor go to their first position so the 1st AC can measure the distance from the actor to the imaging plane. The 1st AC will draw a thin line on the follow focus to indicate the first focus mark. They will then move to the second position, set the focus, and mark that as the second mark on the lens. This continues for any position at which the 1st AC requires a focus mark.
- Rehearse the action to ensure that the actor, dolly grip, and 1st AC are all in sync with each other.
- Shoot the scene and keep a sharp eye on the monitor to make sure the entire shot is in focus.

WATCH A RACK FOCUS

The following four stills are taken from` the opening sequence of *Time and Again*. In this shot, neither the camera position nor the focal length changed. Rather, I racked focus from the wheat in the foreground to Brian, who was about 250 feet away. The lens was set at 175 mm at an *f*1.8.

Pulling focus is a challenging art, especially when shooting with a shallow depth of field (you'll learn more about this in "Ring 2: Focal Length"), but also requires careful preplanning and execution on set.

- Remember that the longer the focal length, the shallower the depth of field and the more difficult it is to keep the subject in focus.
- The larger the imaging sensor (for example, on 35 mm CMOS cameras like the RED or DSLR cameras), the shallower the depth of field. Give the 1st AC time to set marks – these are tough formats in which to keep the image sharp, especially when working with a long focal length.
- Combining camera moves with moving actors will require additional time to block the action, set focus, and properly pull the focus for the shot.
- Using 35 mm lens adapters on HD cameras allows the use of 35 mm prime lenses and the desired shallower depth of field that emulates the look of film cameras; however, because of the way the optics work, the distance markings on the 35 mm lenses may be inaccurate, making focus pulls even more difficult.

HYPERFOCAL DISTANCE

Every lens has a special focus point that when set, gives the largest possible depth of field. In other words, when you set a lens at its hyperfocal distance, the deepest possible area will be in focus.

The hyperfocal distance is half the focus setting to infinity. So if the hyperfocal distance of a particular lens is 20 feet, then everything from 10 feet to infinity is in focus. If the hyperfocal distance is 8 feet, then everything from 4 feet to infinity is in focus.

There are instances in the story where you may want to convey a sense of expanse and depth in the shot, or maybe you want to stack the actors in the frame so they are both sharp – the best way to achieve these looks is setting the lens to its hyperfocal distance.

If the hyperfocal distance at a particular focal length is 50 feet, then everything from 25 feet to infinity will be in focus.

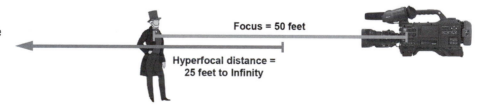

Focus = 50 feet

Hyperfocal distance = 25 feet to Infinity

Ring 2: Focal Length

The *focal length* is the measurement (in millimeters) from the optical center of the lens to the imaging plane (the film itself or, if you're using a video camera, the CCD). Zooming is the process of changing the focal length, wherein zooming out shortens the focal length and zooming in lengthens the focal length. Remember that prime lenses have fixed focal lengths.

Most people equate zooming with getting closer or farther from the subject. Although this is one function of changing the focal length, there are a number of other qualities of the image that change, each of which are powerful tools in drawing your audience's attention to what you want them to look at.

What Happens When You Change The Focal Length?	
Shorter Focal Length (Zoomed Out)	**Longer Focal Length (Zoomed In)**
Farther from subject	Closer to subject
Deeper depth of field	Shallower depth of field
More, exaggerated depth	Flatter image
Perception of faster time	Perception of slower time

- **Shot size.** Changing the focal length has a significant impact on the look of your image. The most obvious is the difference in shot size. Longer focal lengths bring the audience closer to the subject, whereas shorter focal lengths give us a very wide angle. Believe it or not, the change in shot size isn't the primary reason most DPs change the focal length of the lens.

Left Image: A short focal length exaggerates the depth in the shot while keeping everything in focus.
Right Image: A short focal length compresses the subjects in the shot, even though they are sitting the same distance apart. Also notice how the depth of field is much shorter, focusing your attention to the woman in the foreground.

- **Depth of field.** The depth of field is the range in front of the lens in which objects are in focus. If a woman is standing in the depth of field, she's in focus. If she's standing outside the depth of field, she's out of focus – and the farther outside the depth of field she stands, the more out of focus she is. Changing the focal length, the iris and the distance of the subject from the lens affect the depth of field.

- **Creating a shallow depth of field.** Lengthening the focal length (zooming in), opening the iris, and moving the subjects close to the camera lens are three ways to create a shallow, or small, depth of field.
- **Creating a deep depth of field.** Shortening the focal length (zooming out), closing the iris, and moving the subjects away from the camera lens are all ways to create a deep depth of field.
- **Shifting the Depth of field.** Whereas the focal length determines how big the depth of field is, the focus determines where the depth of field is. Moving the depth of field from one subject in the foreground to a subject in the background is called racking or pulling focus. The farther apart the subjects are and the shallower the depth of field, the more effective the technique.

A shallow depth of field is created with an open iris and/or a long focal length.

A deep depth of field is created with a closed iris and/or a short focal length.

You can move the depth of field closer to or farther from the lens by racking focus.

Jason's Notes

As a director, understanding how the lens functions and how it can affect the emotional feel of a shot is a very powerful ability. When you're directing actors, it's important to understand the subtext of what's really happening in the scene and sometimes the best way to convey these emotions isn't through the performances, but through the lens. Do you want to use a long lens to compress the distance between actors in an over-the-shoulder dialog scene to convey closeness? Or do you want to use a short lens to convey the sense of depth as a character is overwhelmed by the vastness of her surroundings? Perhaps you want to use a shallow depth of field and use focus to draw the audience's attention to a particular object in the frame. The more you understand the principles and functions of the lens, the easier it will be to communicate with the cinematographer and tell an engaging story.

- **Depth.** The third change in the image when shortening or lengthening the focal length is depth perception. A short lens (short focal length) will exaggerate the distance between objects in the foreground and background. A longer focal length will flatten the image and the viewer won't be able to determine how far apart the foreground subject is from the background image.
- **Time.** One effect of using a long lens to flatten out a shot is the illusion of slowing time. If an actor were to start walking toward the camera from a distance of 200 feet, and you were to shoot him with a long lens, the resulting image would be so flat that it would appear as if the actor weren't moving forward at all. This creates the illusion of time slowing down, because the character doesn't seem to be making any forward progress. Fight scenes, on the other hand, are usually shot with short lenses, because the increase in depth adds to the intensity and exaggerates the motion of the actors.

Jason's Notes

As the director of photography on the feature film *Fred and Vinnie*, directed by the executive producer of *Everybody Loves Raymond*, Steve Skrovan, I chose a very distinct cinematic arc for the story through the use of my focal length. In the story, Fred is a lonely, middle-aged loser whose only real friend is an overweight shut-in from the East Coast, Vinnie. When Vinnie decides to visit Fred, life seems wonderful. The two spend time together, share tales of their mundane lives and form a friendship like neither had ever had. As the story progresses, Vinnie's stay begins to wear on Fred . . . his snoring, inability to get a job, and very presence drives Fred to the brink of insanity. Finally, before he can't take it anymore, Vinnie moves out, giving Fred his desperately needed space.

I wanted to develop a cinematic language to help support Fred's emotional journey with Vinnie without drawing too much attention to the cinematography, so I chose to use the focal length to do so. In the movie, there are three movements. In the first movement, I used medium focal lengths (20–50 mm) to convey Fred's boring life. The image had a flatness that, when combined with monochromatic lighting and desaturated colors on set, helped convey the monotony of Fred's day to day schedule. When Vinnie arrived, I used shorter focal lengths (7.7–20 mm) to open up the frame, create a deeper shot and convey the sense that Fred's world has expanded. As the story progresses and Vinnie's presence wears on Fred, I gradually use longer and longer focal lengths to flatten the image and reduce the field of view. This gives the feeling of claustrophobia – Fred's apartment feels smaller, Vinnie always seems to be in Fred's space, and the scenes feel very uncomfortable between the two – all because a long focal length reduces the field of view and compresses the distance between the people in it. Finally, at the end of the movie, when Vinnie leaves, I used a very short 5.5 mm lens to really open up the apartment, making it appear very deep and spacious – Vinnie's overbearing presence is finally gone and Fred can breathe again. So in much the same way Fred and Vinnie have their own character arc throughout the story, so to does the cinematic look, through the use of lighting and lens choice.

Ring 3: The Iris – Exposure

Any optical instrument, whether it's a camera or an eyeball, has a certain limit to the amount of light it is capable of seeing. In order to regulate the light to within this optimum range, lenses have an iris, or aperture, that opens and closes. In a camera lens, the size of the iris is measured in *f*-stops.

Mathematically, an *f*-stop is the focal length of the lens divided by the diameter of the aperture opening.

$$f\text{-stop} = \text{focal length/lens opening}$$

When a lens iris is set at *f*4, the diameter of the lens opening must be multiplied by 4 to arrive at the lens focal length; when it is set at *f*2.0, the diameter of the iris opening must be multiplied by 2 to arrive at the focal length.

This ratio results in the oddity that the smaller the *f*-stop number, the more *open* the iris is, and the larger the *f*-stop number, the more *closed* the iris is.

The *f*-stop scale on every camera lens is:

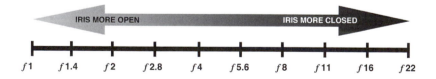

IRIS MORE OPEN ← → IRIS MORE CLOSED

*f*1　　*f*1.4　　*f*2　　*f*2.8　　*f*4　　*f*5.6　　*f*8　　*f*11　　*f*16　　*f*22

Practically, opening the iris by one *f*-stop *doubles* the amount of light let into the lens. Closing the iris by one *f*-stop *halves* the amount of light let into the lens. The engineers who designed early optics wanted each *f*-stop to represent either a doubling or a halving of light, so the resulting *f*-stop numbers happened to be fractions instead of whole numbers. For example, if a camera were set to *f*5.6 and we open the iris to *f*2, we would be increasing the amount of light by 8×. Why? Opening the iris from *f*5.6 to *f*4 doubles the light being allowed through the lens, then *f*4 to *f*2.8 doubles the light again (to 4 ×), and then *f*2.8 to *f*2 doubles it again (from 4 × to 8 ×).

As is the case with the focal length, changing the iris has a variety of other effects. Not only is the amount of light let into the lens affected, so is the depth of field. The *more open* the iris, the *shallower* the depth of field. The *more closed* the iris, the *deeper* the depth of field. Many cinematographers will choose their exposure setting first, based on the resulting depth of field, and will light the scene for that particular exposure.

Jason's Notes

Remember that not all objects or flesh tones have to be perfectly exposed. Especially when shooting film, which has a much greater latitude, you can vary the exposure of the actors to complement the emotional tone of the story. It's okay to slightly underexpose an actor's face in a devious moment, or to overexpose an actress's face in moment of clarity as she walks into the sunlight for the first time after being bedridden for the past year. Choose your exposure based not only on the technical requirements of the medium on which you're shooting, but also on the dramatic needs of the shot.

Exposing Digital Video

Although you can still expose the image by using a light meter to determine the proper f-stop setting on a digital camera's lens, most prosumer and professional camcorders display diagonal lines called zebra stripes in the viewfinder over any overexposed area of the frame. Zebra stripes are only a visual indicator in the viewfinder and are not recorded over the final image. Using the menu settings in the camera, you can set at which brightness level zebra stripes appear, the most common being 75% (ideal for exposing flesh tones) and 100% (the threshold for overexposure.) It is always important to have at least one part of your frame be at or near the 100 percent exposure to fill out the contrast range.

Zebra stripes, which indicate areas of the frame that are overexposed, are not recorded – they are simply a guide to help you set the proper exposure.

Zone X
100% reflectivity

Zone IX
70% reflectivity

Zone VIII
50% reflectivity

Zone VII
35% reflectivity

Zone VI
25% reflectivity

Zone V
18% reflectivity

Zone IV
12.5% reflectivity

Zone III
9% reflectivity

Zone II
6% reflectivity

Zone I
4.5 reflectivity

Zone 0
3.5% reflectivity

The Zone System

One of the easiest ways to understand exposure is to look at the *zone system*, created by famed photographer Ansel Adams. The zone system provides a visual reference for the brightness values of objects shot on film or video by creating eleven zones from black to white. Zone 0 is black, and zone XI is white. Each zone in between is twice the brightness of the next darker zone, or half the brightness of the next brighter zone, depending on which way you choose to look at the scale. Because opening the iris of a camera by one *f*-stop doubles the amount of light being let into the lens, we can say that the difference from one zone to the next is one *f*-stop.

Zone V is middle gray and the brightness value to which all light meters are calibrated. That means that anytime you take a light meter reading of an object and set the iris to that reading, the object will appear as zone V, middle gray.

The zone system does not represent specific exposures, but provides a visual reference for how the brightness of an object should appear, based on an average light meter reading of zone V. For example, if a spot meter gives you a reading of *f*2.8 and you set the iris at *f*2.8, then the object you metered will appear zone V, middle gray. If your light meter reads *f*8 and you set the iris to an *f*8, then the object you metered will appear zone V, middle gray. Setting the iris to the light meter reading, regardless of the reading, will always make the metered object zone V, middle gray.

You may not want the objects to appear at middle gray, especially if the object is brighter, like a T-shirt or a white car, or darker like a leather couch or piano. For example, let's say we're shooting a glass of milk and our light meter reading gives us an *f*5.6. Because light meters are calibrated so that the reading corresponds to middle gray, the milk will appear as bright on screen as zone V, middle gray, if we set the iris to *f*5.6. The problem is that the milk will look gray, not white, so it will be necessary to adjust our exposure. Taking the zone system into consideration, we may want the milk to appear more like zone VII, so because zone VII is two *f*-stops brighter than zone V, we'll need to open the iris two *f*-stops from 5.6, which is *f*2.8. Now the milk will have a zone VII brightness.

Conversely, if we are shooting a glass of red wine and our light meter is giving us an exposure of *f*4, then by setting the iris to *f*4, the wine will have a brightness value of zone V. As the wine is actually much darker and is much closer to zone II, the difference between zone V and zone II is three *f*-stops. So we will close our iris three *f*-stops from an *f*4 to *f*11 to properly capture the true brightness of the wine.

Jason's Notes

Whenever I begin a new feature film, I meet with the actors to take a light meter reading of each person to gauge how far their flesh tones vary from zone V. The way I do this is by setting up a very flat, even light and spot metering an 18% gray card to give me the base exposure. From there, I will use a spot meter to take a reading of each actor's forehead, recording the value. So if my 18% gray card reads *f*8, and my leading lady's face reads an *f*11, then I know that each time I take a light meter reading of her face on set, I need to open the iris up one *f*-stop to properly expose her flesh tones. Once finished, I have a handy guide I can reference to help me compensate the exposure for each actor on set.

Ring 4: Macro Focus

Lenses are designed to focus incoming light onto a CCD or film, but there's a limit to how close an object can be to the lens and still remain in focus without compromising the exposure. Most lenses are designed maintain exposure by restricting focus to within a couple feet of the lens, making extreme close-ups impossible. Manufacturers present a solution by introducing another piece of glass in the lens that gives the operator the ability to focus on objects within a couple feet of the lens, called *macro focus*. The macro focus function is virtually invisible on consumer cameras because the camera automatically switches from standard focus to macro focus whenever an object gets too close to the lens. Professional cameras, however, have a separate ring on the lens that allows the operator to set the macro focus manually.

The beauty of macro focus is that it exhibits the same changes in depth of field and perceived depth as standard focus. Using this technique and convincing miniatures, you can rescale objects to appear large by working close to the lens.

LENS CARE

The lens is the audience's window to the action on set, so make sure the lens is always maintained in good working order.

One of the primary responsibilities of the 1st assistant camera is to take care of the lens by keeping it free of dust and scratches with a can of compressed air to blow away dust or debris. If the compressed air isn't enough, the 1st AC will use a camelhair brush, available at local photography shops, to lightly brush away the dust. As a last result, a lens tissue can be used to lightly wipe debris off the lens, taking special care to not to scratch the lens coating.

Making sure the lens is clean is one reason you'll often see the 1st AC checking the lens with a flashlight at the beginning of each setup.

Ring 5: Back Focus

Lenses are either permanently built into the camera body or interchangeable. The problem with swapping interchangeable lenses between camera bodies is that each lens needs to be calibrated so that the image is properly focused onto the CCD. Because each camera is built differently and the CCD is set either closer or farther to the lens, each lens has a *back-focus* adjustment used to focus the image squarely on the CCD.

The back focus should be set each time a new lens is mounted on the camera. Although a qualified engineer should calibrate the lens, it's possible to set the back focus using a back-focus chart.

CAMERA FUNCTIONS

Once light passes through the lens, it enters the camera body, where it can be altered both before and after it hits the imaging plane. Besides a multitude of in-camera color grading options that can finesse the picture, such as the black level, gamma curve, color balance, and knee controls, you should be familiar with a few basics that can heavily alter the look of your footage.

Shutter Speed

In film cameras, the shutter is a rotating disc with a pie-shaped opening that allows light to pass through it to expose each frame. The wider the opening, the longer each frame is exposed, resulting in greater motion blur. Narrower shutter angles create a sharp, jittery look, like the opening scene in *Saving Private Ryan*, when the Allied forces attack the beaches of Normandy.

In video cameras, changing the shutter speed has the same effect, but the "shutter" is a digital function that controls how long the CCD registers light for each frame.

The shutter speed is usually set to an angle of 180, or half the exposure time of a frame. For a more film-like look when shooting video, consider shooting with a slightly faster shutter speed.

- Maintaining the same exposure when changing the shutter speed requires compensating by either opening or closing the iris. For example, if you change the shutter speed from 1/30 second to 1/60 second, the light hitting the CCD is being cut in half. You must either double the amount of light on set or open the iris one *f*-stop to compensate.
- Think carefully about working with a faster shutter. You may need to add more light to expose each shot adequately, and additional lighting fixtures will add to the equipment budget.

Changing the shutter speed gives you a wide rage of looks – on one extreme, the sharp, staccato look of a fast shutter speed can help add a kinetic furry to a scene. Movies like *The Bourne Identity* and the opening battle in *Saving Private Ryan* used a fast shutter speed in the action sequence. Conversely, slow shutter speeds add motion blur, creating a dream-like feel. I recommend avoiding slow shutter speeds, because if you decide you don't like the look, it can't be removed in the editing room. Alternatively, there are several software plug-ins that can replicate the effect and ultimately give you more control over the image.

Gain

Gain is to video what film speed is to film cameras. *Gain* is a setting that electronically boosts the sensitivity of the imager, making it more sensitive in low-light situations. The downside, as with faster film, is that the resulting image is grainier and noisier.

Gain is used primarily in documentaries and newsgathering situations in which it's impossible to light, but the reduction in image quality is acceptable to the viewing audience. If you're shooting a narrative film, avoid using gain at all cost, because the image degradation is irreversible. If you want a grainy, contrasty image, filters and plug-ins in the editing room allow you more flexibility and control over the look.

White Balance

Different light sources have different colors and, although difficult to see with the naked eye, are painfully evident to the camera. For example, tungsten light has a warm orange hue, fluorescent light has a green hue, and sunlight at noon on a cloudless summer day has a blue hue. As a result, objects lit by these light sources are tinted, resulting in the need to correct for the tint.

This process, called *white balancing*, involves holding up a white card under the light source illuminating the set, zooming in on it so that the card fills the frame, and then pushing the camera's manual white balance button. Doing so tells the camera that the light falling on (and reflecting off) the white card should be rendered as white. The camera will then adjust the colors in the shot accordingly. For example, if you are shooting a living room scene lit by table lamps and you white balance to tungsten, the lamps will not cast an orange light, but a white light. Similarly, if you white balance under the blue hue of sunlight, the camera will render the sunlight as white light.

Avoid using both the camera's auto–white balance feature and the preset white balance settings. These automatic settings are calculated in the factory for specific color temperatures and rarely match the actual color of the light you're shooting under.

There are also ways to cheat the white balance to tint the overall look of the shot. Instead of white balancing to a white card, as is standard, place a lightly

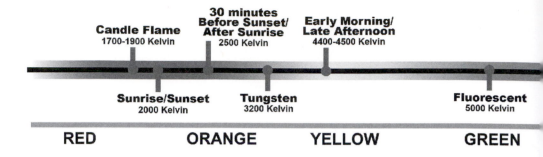

colored gel over the lens and then white balance to a white card. This forces the camera to remove the color of the gel to make the white card appear white. When you remove the gel from the front of the lens, the shot will be tinted the opposite color.

Do not use a deep-colored gel and overtint your shot, because once the color information is gone, it cannot be replaced. Unless you're confident in using this trick, it is always better to tint your image during the editing process, when you can always change or undo the effect.

COLOR TEMPERATURES

Why is the tint of light called "color temperature" when it has nothing to do with the heat of the light source? In the late 1800s, British physicist William Kelvin theorized that a block of carbon (called a *black body*) would glow as it was heated. It first produced a dim red light, increasing to a brighter yellow as the temperature rose, and eventually produced a bright blue-white glow at the highest temperatures.

The temperature of the carbon black body corresponded directly to the wavelength of light it emitted, hence the term "color temperature." As a result, the color temperature scale is used as a quantifiable measurement of the color of light. For example, the color of light emitted by a tungsten filament is equal to the color of light emitted from the carbon when it is heated up to 3200 Kelvin. Hence, the color temperature of tungsten is 3200 K. It's important to note that this has nothing to do with the heat temperature at which the tungsten filament burns.

Instead of using the Celsius scale, Lord Kelvin devised a new scale for temperature called the Kelvin scale. The Kelvin scale establishes 0 at absolute zero – the temperature at which all atomic movement freezes, which, in case you were wondering, is −273.15 degrees Celsius.

Here are the color temperatures of some common light sources.

High Noon
5600 Kelvin

Cloudy Sky
8000-9000 Kelvin

HMI
5400 Kelvin

Overcast Sky
5800 Kelvin

Summer Blue Sky
12,000-28,000 Kelvin

BLUE   **VIOLET**

Color Temperature Chart

Summer sky	9600–12,000 K
Partially cloudy	8100–9500 K
Summer shade	8000 K
Light summer shade	7100 K
Average daylight	6500 K
Overcast	6000 K
Midsummer	5800 K
HMI	5500 K
Average noon	5400 K
Fluorescent	5000 K
Late afternoon	4500 K
Early morning	4400 K
Hour after sunrise	3500 K
Tungsten	3200 K
Half-hour after sunrise	2500 K
Sunrise/sunset	2000 K
Candle flame	1900 K
Match flame	1700 K

WORKING WITH A PRODUCTION MONITOR

One of the most critical tools on set is a properly calibrated production monitor. Although expensive (a good field monitor can cost anywhere from $500–$5,000), professional monitors offer calibration tools so that you know the image displayed on the monitor is exactly what is being recorded. This is especially important when shooting in digital formats, in which novice directors and DPs tend to gauge lighting and exposure based on how the image looks on the monitor.

The process for properly calibrating a monitor, which is the responsibility of the 2nd AC, is as follows:

1. Connect the monitor to the camera and, through the camera's settings, activate the color bars. Color bars are used to ensure that all the video devices through the production chain are properly calibrated. Always view the monitor in a dark room or in a low-light environment to ensure proper calibration.

2. To set the luminance, or brightness, of the monitor, look for the three vertical gray bars in the lower-right portion of the color bar chart. You'll notice that the left bar is black, the middle bar is dark gray, and the right bar is light gray. Adjust the brightness on the monitor until the two bars on the left appear black and the rightmost bar is barely visible.

3. The next step is to adjust the contrast. Look at the white square in the lower-left corner of the color bar chart and turn up the contrast until the white begins to bloom into the surrounding boxes. The contrast is properly set when the edges of the white box are sharp and defined.

4. Professional monitors have a "blue-only" mode that turns off the red and green cathode ray tubes or pixels, displaying only blue. If your monitor doesn't have a blue mode, try placing a Wratten 47b blue gel over the monitor

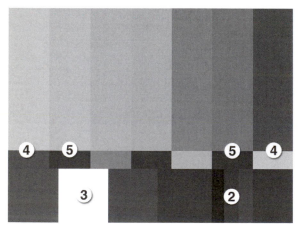

so it filters out all colors except blue. Adjust the chroma (color) setting until the two outside bars match the same brightness as the bars below them. When properly calibrated, the two bars should appear as one.

5. To adjust the hue (phase or tint), adjust the setting until the two inner bars match in brightness to the bars directly beneath them. It may be necessary to readjust the chroma and hue together, as one will influence the other.

6. The monitor will be properly calibrated once top and middle bars match each other in the first, second, sixth, and seventh columns.

7. Turn off blue mode – the image you're seeing is true and accurate.

CINEMATOGRAPHY: LIGHTING

Lighting is as important to crafting the emotional tone of the scene as the actors' performance T. One of the most common mistakes made by independent filmmakers is either neglecting the craft of lighting altogether or, even worse, using light simply as a way of illuminating the subject enough to expose the shot.

As you read about the concepts of lighting in this next section, think about the application of these techniques to the story – the use of color, contrast, and the specularity of a light source all contribute to the way a character appears on screen and are subconsciously judged by the audience. Although lighting is the DP's responsibility, the more you understand these techniques, the better you can balance the art of the actors' performance with cinematic technique to achieve your ultimate vision.

The Qualities of Light

It's important to understand not only what light can do and how it affects the audience's emotional reaction to a shot, but how to effectively communicate your vision to the director of photography. Instead of asking to "make that light more intense and a little more focused," learn the proper terminology, such as "increase the brightness by one stop but make it less specular."

There are a number of basic attributes of light that are key to understanding how to light a set:

BRIGHTNESS

The brightness is the amount or intensity of light emitted from a light fixture. The light output of a fixture is measured in *foot candles* – the amount of illumination made by one candle from one foot away. Fixtures themselves are referred to by the wattage of the lamp inside. Wattage is not the exclusive factor in determining the light output of a fixture, as the type of bulb plays a major role. For example, to create the same intensity as a 1,200-watt HMI, you would need a 5,000-watt tungsten light, simply because the gas globes of an HMI burn significantly brighter than their tungsten counterparts. When you factor in color correction, the light loss incurred by a full blue gel would necessitate the use of a 10,000-watt tungsten fixture to match the light output of a 1,200-watt HMI. Brightness is also dependent on the distance of the fixture from the subject. Although this seems elementary, light wattage and placement becomes especially critical in scenes where the actors need to move long distances towards or away from the light. One trick to lighting a large area is to use a larger-watt fixture placed a farther distance from the actors. This will give a longer, more even spread than a closer, lower-wattage fixture.

FALLOFF

Falloff is the decrease in the intensity of light as it spreads out from the source. Different fixtures have different degrees of falloff, each of which are appropriate for different cinematic applications. For example, Kino-Flos are fluorescent lights with a very fast falloff, making them ideal for lighting close quarters where you may not want a lot of light spilling onto the set walls. On the other hand, HMI PARs without a lens are extremely focused lights and have a very long falloff, capable of illuminating objects hundreds of feet away.

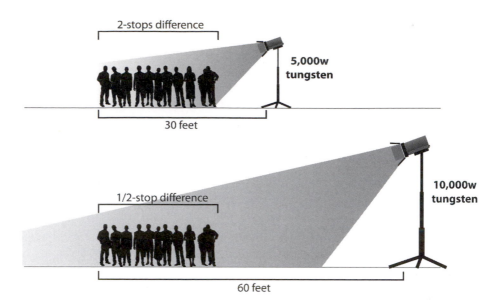

COLOR

Although the emotional impact of color can be discussed at length, the technicalities behind the color of light are just as critical. Choosing which color temperature light source is dependent on the type of film stock you're shooting, or how you set your white balance.

- **Know your medium.** The first deciding factor of the color of light is based on the film stock on which you're shooting. Daylight balanced film uses 5600 K (blue daylight) as the white base, whereas tungsten film stock has a white base of 3200 K. If shooting digitally, you'll have more flexibility through the use of white balancing to correct the color temperature. Often times, the director of photography will want to balance all the light sources together using gels, whereas other times, gels can be used to slightly tint a light off the baseline. For example, if you're shooting with tungsten film at night and working with tungsten lights, all the light will read as white when the film is later exposed and processed. For a warmer look to bring out the actors' flesh tones, use a quarter orange gel to lightly tint the key light.
- **Emotional tone.** Psychological studies have long proven the emotional reactions elicited by various colors. Whereas red tends to increase anxiety, green is calming. So too can the color use in a film have a significant subconscious impact on the audience's emotional reaction to the story. Throughout the preproduction process, work with the director of photography to decide on a color palette for the movie. *Minority Report* and *Dark City* used a very monochromatic look with heavy blue hues to create a menacing, shadowy feel; the remarkable French film *Amélie* used a wide range of colors to paint the vivid imagination of the title character on the screen.

SPECULARITY

Specularity is the size and brightness of the reflection of a light source on a subject. Light sources that have a high specularity can be clearly seen on a subject.

USING A LIGHT METER

Light meters measure either the amount of light falling on the light meter (called an *incident light meter*) or the amount of light reflected from a subject (called a *spot meter*). Both types of light meters are used in specific situations:

I'm using an incident light meter to measure the amount of fill light falling on Casey Slade's face.

- **Incident light meter.** If you want to determine the overall brightness of light in a particular area, such as sunshine outside or a wash of light from a light source, hold the incident light meter under the light and the resulting reading will give you an *f*-stop that will properly expose middle 18% gray.

- **Spot meter.** The problem with incident meters is that they do not compensate for the reflectivity of your subject. For example, if you have a fair-skinned actor standing next to a dark-skinned actor, the amount of light reflected off each of their faces can differ by several stops, even though the amount of light falling on each of them is the same. Spot meters feature a viewfinder that enables you to focus on a specific part of your subject to measure the brightness of reflected light. Although a more accurate instrument when determining exposure, a spot meter requires a little more skill when translating the reading to the proper exposure:

  - **Always meter in line with the camera lens.** Because a spot meter is reading reflected light, it's important to take readings from the camera's perspective.

  - **Setting your exposure to a given reading will result in that subject appearing at 18% gray.** Translating the results of a spot meter reading requires a degree of skill. Understanding that if you take a meter reading of an actor's forehead and get a result of *f*5.6, by setting the camera iris to a 5.6, the actor's forehead will appear at 18% gray. But what happens if you're working with actors of differing skin tones? An actor with pale skin tones will appear too dark, as her skin may be brighter than 18% gray. It is up to the cinematographer to interpret the light meter reading and choose to open the iris one *f*-stop to an *f*4 so the actress' skin tones are accurately portrayed. Conversely, actors with flesh tones darker than 18% gray may appear too bright, requiring the camera iris to be closed to compensate.

I'm taking a spot meter reading to determine how much light is being reflected off my subject.

All light meters have two basic settings that need to be set to allow for an accurate exposure:

- **ASA.** Determine the speed of the film, CCD, or CMOS chip of your camera.
- **Frame rate.** Enter the number of frames per second the camera is set to capture.

DIRECTION

The angle of the light focused on the subject plays a critical role in the look of the lighting. There are virtually limitless options in the placement and direction of a light, options that should be selected based on the following details:

- **Motivation.** Is there a window or a table lamp that should logically dictate the direction of the lighting? Are there any other practical light sources that will give the director of photography an idea as to where lights should be placed? Look for motivating light sources during the location scout and use them to help you when designing the lighting.
- **Technicalities.** A good director of photography will place lights so they require minimal adjustments during the course of the shooting of a scene, carefully designing the lighting plan so the lighting mostly works for all the camera setups. Although there will always be changes from setup to setup, the key light, ambience, and even the rim light should be somewhat consistent in direction from shot to shot.
- **Style.** The lighting style of the movie will also dictate the direction of the lighting. Romantic comedies and sitcoms use heavily diffused frontal key light with a low contrast ratio; some dramas seek a heavy key light placed opposite the camera side of the actor's face. Determine how the placement and direction of the lights will affect the dramatic tone of the movie.

WRAPAROUND

The *wraparound* is the severity of the transition from the bright to dark sides of an actor's face, not to be confused with the contrast ratio (the ratio of dark to light). Harsh wraparound can be created with a smaller light source focused directly on the actor with little diffusion. Soft wraparound can be created with either heavy diffusion, or a large light source such as a soft box. You can see examples of soft wraparound in early cinema when the women were lit with

Soft wraparound. By using a large diffused light source, we can create a soft wraparound, softening the transition from the bright to the dark sides of the face.

Hard wraparound. Notice the distinct line that separates the bright and dark sides of Don Argonsky's face. This is hard wraparound.

very soft, diffused lighting that fills in shadows caused by wrinkles and imperfection of the skin. Combine soft wraparound with a light diffusion filter on the camera to create exquisite beauty lighting.

SPREAD

The spread determines that area of coverage of the light. Open face and Fresnel lights have the ability to be flooded or spotted, enabling the director of photography to either focus the light onto a small area, or expand the coverage to cover a wider area. The spread also has an impact on the brightness: a light set to spot is brighter than a light set to flood. Although the spread can be roughly set at the light head, barn doors, snoots, scrims, and flags can all be used to further shape the light.

Spot comparison. The light fixture on the left is an open-faced tungsten light set to spot. The light fixture on the right is a Fresnel set to spot. Notice how much cleaner the Fresnel light appears, all due to the glass lens that focuses the light.

Three-Point Lighting

One of the most common lighting techniques and the foundation of most lighting setups is called *three-point lighting*, which utilizes three different types of lights:

- **Key light.** The key light is the main source of illumination on the subject and is generally placed about 45 degrees off the camera line. Off-setting the key creates shadows on the face and brings out depth and dimension. The harsher the key light, the more pronounced the shadows. The more diffused the light, the softer the shadows.
- **Fill light.** The key light will create shadows, and the "fill" is used to fill in some of those shadows without adding so much light that the shadows are completely lost. Fill lights can either be the ambient light on set or be added with something as simple as a bounce board. Remember that the fill light is never as strong as the key. Often times, if you're working on location with plenty of ambient light, the DP will use only a couple light fixtures to augment the key light and bump up the contrast ratio on the actor's face, using the existing ambience as the fill.

■ **Rim/back light.** Positioned so that it is almost facing the key light, the back light is a very subtle accent that brings out the actor's shoulders and back of head, separating him from the background. There are many ways to separate an actor from the background, but using a rim light is still one of the most popular.

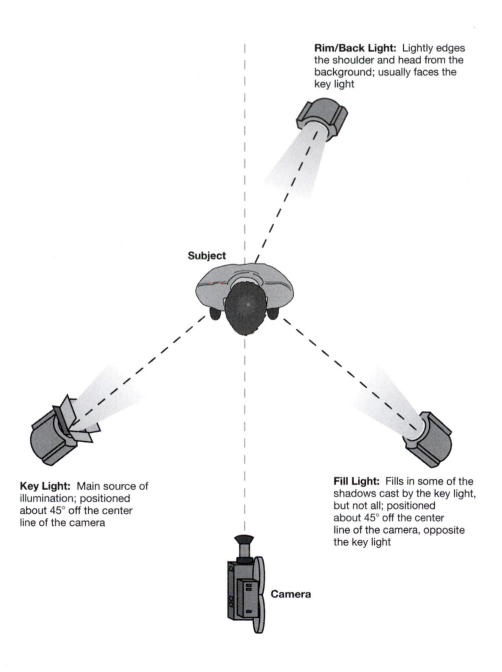

Rim/Back Light: Lightly edges the shoulder and head from the background; usually faces the key light

Subject

Key Light: Main source of illumination; positioned about 45° off the center line of the camera

Fill Light: Fills in some of the shadows cast by the key light, but not all; positioned about 45° off the center line of the camera, opposite the key light

Camera

Key light: We used a 1,200-watt HMI (which is equal to a 5,000-watt tungsten light) through a 4'x4' silk diffusion.

Back Light: We used a 300-watt tungsten light to accent Awanda's hair.

Fill light: We used a 4'x4' white bounce card to fill in some of the shadows created by the key light.

Although the three-point lighting technique is a classic approach to lighting, there are many variations that can be used to help create a high-quality look, even on a low budget. The next time you watch a movie or television show, take note of how often these techniques are used:

- **Place the camera and the key light on opposite sides of the actor's eye line.** In the traditional three-point lighting demonstration, the

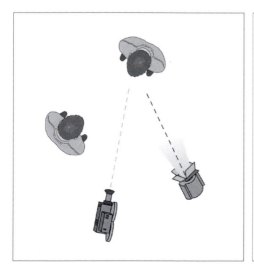

(left) Placing the key light and the camera on the same side of the actor's face is both flat and unflattering. (right) Try shooting against the key to draw the audience's attention to the actor's eyes.

Although this setup requires more room on set, anytime diffused or bounced light is used, it creates a much more pleasing look for the actor.

actor almost always faces the camera. Realistically, actors rarely look directly into the camera, but rather off to the side of the lens, usually at another actor. The trick to placing the key light is to determine the actor's eye line, or the direction of his gaze. If the camera is on one side of the eye line, then place the key light on the other side, focused on the far side of the actor's face. This technique brings out the depth and details of his face while allowing the fleshy part of his cheek to fall slightly into shadow, helping frame his eyes, nose, and mouth and creating a sparkle in his eye.

- **Light the actor brighter than the background.** Try lighting the actor at least one *f*-stop brighter than the background to help her pop out of her surroundings. One common problem in low budget films occurs when the actors and set are so evenly lit that there is no sense of depth within the frame. Lighting the actor and blocking any spill off the background is a great way to guide the audience's eye to what you want them to see – the performance.
- **Use reflected light.** Focusing a light directly on the actors though effective, isn't the most flattering light. Try bouncing the light off a reflector, a piece of white foam core or bead board to soften the light – soft light sources fill in imperfections of the skin and help make an actor look great on screen.

Working with Shadows

It makes sense that lighting a subject involves directing a light at the subject and turning the light on. But although this approach works some of the time, it results in harsh shadows and makes it obvious to the audience the subject is lit.

In real life, we are able to determine depth and distance because we have two eyes that work together, each one seeing an object from a slightly different angle. The process of our brain piecing these two angles together, called *triangulation*, helps us determine depth. Incidentally, the closer an object is to our eyes, the more depth-sensitive we are. The farther away it is, the more difficult it is to determine depth. For example, if you hold a baseball at arm's length and move it 12 inches toward your face, your brain will detect that change in distance much more than if a friend, standing 100 feet away, moves the ball 12 inches closer to you. It's the same reason you can't judge the distance between stars – the angle from the stars to our left eye and the stars to our right eye is so narrow that we can't tell how far away they are from us, or from one another.

Unfortunately, a camera doesn't have depth perception, because it only has one "eye" – the lens. In order to create depth, you have to create shadows through the use of lighting. New 3D cameras now feature a second lens, which mimics the way we see the world. Regardless of whether you're shooting a monoscopic or stereoscopic image, shadows are critical in shaping and creating depth.

INTERNAL VERSUS EXTERNAL SHADOWS

Shadows can be divided into two categories: shadows an object casts onto other objects and shadows an object casts onto itself.

- **External shadows** are created when a light casts a shadow of the subject onto another object, which can draw the audience's attention to the presence of the light. Although you generally don't want to see an actor's shadow cast on the back wall, you may want to create an external shadow of tree branches, a venetian blind, or simply a hard edge to break up a bland background. One of the key grip's primary responsibilities is to shape light by creating pleasing external shadows.

A cucaloris, or "cookie" for short, is a grip tool used to break up light into random patterns on a surface. Although you can use the standard wood or metal varieties, anything can be used to cast patterns – tree branches, vases, or any other light-refracting or -blocking objects.

Jason's Notes

Professional cinematographers light actors so their external shadows fall outside the frame. Shooting against the key light is one of the primary methods of eliminating what is often viewed as an amateur mistake. Ultimately, the correct type of shadows are desirable in creating a sense of depth and dimension.

- **Internal shadows** are cast by the subject onto itself, resulting in contrast. For example, by off-setting an actor's key light, the actor's facial features cast a shadow onto his own face, giving the illusion that his nose, brow, and lips protrude from the sphere that is his head. If you were to place the key light directly in line with the camera, there would be no internal shadows visible and the result would be a contrast-free flat image.

Shadows are important in helping define the shape of objects on the flat screen. For example, notice the how the key light on the frame left size of Don Argonsky's face causes a soft shadow on the frame right side of his face. This adds shape and dimension to his facial features.

LIGHTING A SCENE

When the director of photography first steps onto a set or scout a location, it can be an overwhelming experience trying to figure out how to light the scene. Where does he start? Where does he put the key light? How does he work with the ambience? Here are the steps he takes, so you have a better understanding of the process of lighting a set.

1. Look at the Existing Ambient Light

In the ideal situation, the DP would be working on a pitch-black sound-stage and have complete control over all the lighting and reflective surfaces. Unfortunately, on location, you will be forced to contend with windows, sunlight, overhead lights, and reflected sources, so planning the lighting to work *with* these ambient sources will greatly improve the look of the film. The worst ambient light sources are nondirectional, even light. Although there may be plenty of light, if it is evenly spread or diffused on the set, the result is a low-contrast, flat look. Use locations that have a directional ambience, such as windows on one side of the room or focusable spot lights in the ceiling. The more directional the ambience, the easier it will be to control.

Remember that you can always add a key light to increase the contrast ratio of your subject, even with a flat ambience. Or, you can use 4'×4' floppies to reduce the light, creating a negative fill. Try to work with the ambience instead of fighting it.

LIGHTING TERMS

- **Baby**—a 1,000-watt light
- **Blonde**—an open face 2,000-watt light
- **Brute**—a 225-amp, DC-powered arc light
- **Deuce**—a 2,000-watt light
- **Junior**—a 2,000-watt light
- **Mickey**—an open-face 1,000-watt light
- **Midget**—a 500-watt light
- **Redhead**—a 1,000-watt light
- **Senior**—a 5,000-watt light

2. Determine the Direction of the Light

The next step is to determine the position of the key light. The DP will watch the blocking rehearsal, determine the camera's position for each setup, then begin placing lights. Once he knows where the camera will be placed for each setup throughout the scene, he will attempt to place the key light so that it works for each angle. Be careful: if you change the blocking after the set has been lit, the DP may need more time to reposition the lights, costing valuable time on set.

TIPS ON LIGHTING A LARGE AREA

If the crew has to light a large area, the DP may choose to use either a directional light source or an ambient light source. An example of a directional source would be an 18 k (18,000-watt) HMI rigged on a crane or cherry picker to illuminate a dark street. The light would be positioned deep into the set to serve as a blue backlight, casting sharp shadows and high contrast to mimic moonlight. If you're shooting on city streets, crews will often wet down the street to create reflections of city lights instead of dark pools of underexposed concrete.

Alternatively, using balloon lighting over an exterior set can create a soft ambience that brings up the overall illumination of the set without sharp shadows.

Inside soundstages, there are several ways to create a soft ambience, including overhead soft boxes, arrays of Kino-Flos, large broad lights called space lights designed to light interior studio sets, and massive helium-filled balloons designed to fly large light fixtures to provide a large, broad overhead light when shooting exterior night scenes, and for low-budget productions, 12"–30" paper spheres with a tungsten light bulb inside called china balls.

To create a soft ambient light on the set of *Fred and Vinnie,* we installed 12'×12' silks with duvatyne (a light-absorbing black fabric) skirts above every room of the set.

3. Determine the Amount of Fill Light Needed to Balance Out the Key Light

Once the key light has been placed, the DP will assess the amount of fill light needed to increase or decrease the contrast ratio. Remember, the less fill you have, the more contrasty and dramatic the shot will look; the more fill you add, the lower the contrast ratio and the flatter the lighting will be on the subject. Adding a fill light source could be as simple as reflecting a light onto a white bounce card or using a soft box.

4. Add Rim Light if Necessary

Determine whether a rim light is needed to help separate the actor from the background. Make sure the rim light is motivated by a light source that the audience can see in the shot, either a window or a lamp in the background, and for realistic lighting designs, try to keep the rim light very subtle and not overly harsh.

Once the actors are lit, the DP will look at the scene to determine whether any accent lights are necessary. Does the background need any splashes of light? Or perhaps the wine glasses on the table might benefit from a kicker to help them sparkle. While adding accents like this, don't forget to also include shadows, because good lighting stems from both light and shadows.

Gaffer David Sheets uses a walkie-talkie to help the electricians properly focus the key light for the shot.

LIGHTING OUTSIDE

Many times, especially when working outdoors, you have only one light source: the sun. Although this may seem like a limitation, the sun is the most powerful light source available and can be easily reflected, bounced, and diffused to move, shape, and craft the light to serve the needs of your shot.

When working with the sun, treat it in the same way you'd treat the key or rim light. The only difference is that you need to move the subject and camera to position the sun in the ideal location. Many times, locations are selected because of their east–west orientation, enabling the DP and 1st assistant director to schedule specific shots based on the sun's position.

Working with sunlight begins by choosing the position of the subject relative to the position of the sun. There are two ways to approach shooting using the sun as the primary light source:

- **Use the sun as the key light.** Position the actor so the sun is illuminating the far side of the actor's face, opposite the actor's eye line. This is much easier to do before 11:00 a.m. and after 2:00 p.m., when the sun hangs lower in the sky. Avoid shooting around noon, because the sun tends to cast shadows on the actors' brows, creating deep, cavernous shadows over the actors' eyes. Use a bounce board to fill in some of the shadows, especially if the sun is too direct.
- **Use the sun as a rim light.** Position the actor so the sun is positioned behind her, then use a bounce board or reflector to bounce the sunlight as the key light. I recommend using a silver reflector, which is available at most camera stores.

During the location scout, many DPs will either recommend or decline a particular location because of its east–west orientation. Even if the exterior location is visually perfect, there are several factors to consider before locking a location:

- **How much workable daylight is there?** The 1st assistant director will look at the script and estimate the amount of time needed to shoot a particular scene, or to shoot all the scenes at one given location. He will then determine whether there is enough workable sunlight to be able to complete your shot list.
- **How much time will it take to chase the sun?** *Chasing the sun* is a term that refers to the constant adjustments to the grip equipment needed to compensate for the sun's movement. Reflectors, diffusion, and overheads

The crew set up a 20′×20′ silk over the shooting area to soften the harsh Los Angeles sun.

all need to be moved, which takes time and manpower. The schedule will determine whether the day will permit extensive rigging changes.

■ **Are there geological or architectural features that will cut into the sunlight?** Sunlight calculators provide sunset and sunrise times based on the moment the sun crests the horizon to the time the sun dips below the horizon. The actual time may vary if the sun travels behind a building or a mountain range. Often, location scouts will perform a light survey, during which they sit at a location all day and note the exact times of direct sunlight. These times are important to know when determining the daily shooting schedule.

■ **Plan for lighting changes.** A good director of photography will be able not only to plan camera angles to allow a consistent look of the lighting throughout the day, but determine a way to shape the changing sunlight so the look of the final footage is consistent in the scene. Often this involves flying a large 20′×20′ silk over the set so direct sunlight is diffused, then focusing the direction of the sunlight with shiny boards.

■ **Be prepared for weather changes.** Even the best-laid plans are subject to a cloudy day, where overcast conditions make it much more difficult to reflect light. Instead of bouncing light to increase the illumination levels on one side of your subject, DPs will use solids to reduce the light, creating negative fill on the opposite side of the actor. Whether you add light to one side or subtract light from the other, the goal is to create a consistent contrast ratio from shot to shot.

■ **Make sure you have room to rig.** Reflectors and overheads can take up a lot of space, so when scouting a location, make sure there is ample room to rig the necessary fixtures. Sometimes, it becomes necessary to place reflectors on nearby building rooftops, or rig overhead silks to a neighboring structure. Be sure to discuss these requirements with the location manager so she can secure all necessary permissions and permits from surrounding property owners.

Overheads and Reflectors

Lighting an exterior set with overheads and reflectors can be easy, provided the grip department has the resources to safely and effectively build the rig. In most instances, the sun will either be too harsh, or too spotty from cloudy conditions. In either situation, they will build a 20′×20′ silk and rig it 8 to 10 feet above the actors by supporting it with stands, or rigging the frame to a building, trees, poles, or any other secure structure. Always make sure the overhead is tied down in both directions, so changing winds do not blow over the overhead, causing a danger to the cast and crew. Once the overhead is in place, the resulting light should be much more consistent, even as the sun moves during the course of the day.

We use a 20′×20′ reflective material called Ultrabounce to create a soft reflection onto the actors as they walk through a field.

The next step is to use reflectors placed outside the coverage area of the over-head to direct the key and rim lights onto the actors. The DP's choice as to whether to use a large-area reflector like a 12′×12′ silver lamé or Ultrabounce or whether to use a smaller shiny board should be determined by the blocking of the scene. The more the actors move around, the larger the reflector needed to ensure that the actors remain in the light. If the actors are stationary for the entire scene, a smaller reflector such as a shiny board can be used.

The grips will place the reflector in the same place as a key light, then sculpt the light with flags, nets, and silks. Remember, the entire rig is based around the moving sun, forcing the crew to constantly readjust the equipment to maintain a consistent look, so plan your shots accordingly and don't be too ambitious with your exterior shot list.

Maintaining the Proper Contrast

Lighting actors outside is no different than lighting them inside. Minding the attributes of light such as the contrast ratio, wraparound, and color still apply, but on a much larger, rougher scale. If the look of the scene requires a 3:1 contrast ratio, the DP can achieve this with the proper choice and placement of reflectors, silks, and solids. For example, placing a larger and softer reflective source like a 12'×12' Ultrabounce within 10 feet of your lead actress will create a very soft wraparound, whereas using the hard side of a shiny board on a sunny day from 15 feet away, squarely focused on the lead actor, will create a higher contrast, harsher wraparound. In much the same way a cinematographer will choose to use a softbox over a raw open-face light, so too can he create the quality of light through your choice of reflectors.

Grips await blocking decisions so they can properly focus shiny boards.

Using the sun as a rim light, a 4'x4' sheet of bead board can be used to reflect the sun, serving as a key light.

Low-Budget Options

There are a number of low-budget approaches to working effectively in sunlight:

- Obtain foam core or bead board from your local craft store to reflect sunlight and create a softer light on the subject.

- Use mirrors to reflect direct sunlight onto the subject. The more mirrors you use, the brighter the light.
- If you need to soften the sunlight directly, consider renting a silk stretched across an 8-, 12-, or 20-foot frame that is rigged over the actors. Because these professional tools can be expensive to rent or purchase, consider building a frame out of 1.5-inch PVC pipe and then, using a white bedsheet or shower curtain to serve as diffusion, softening harsh sunlight on your subject.

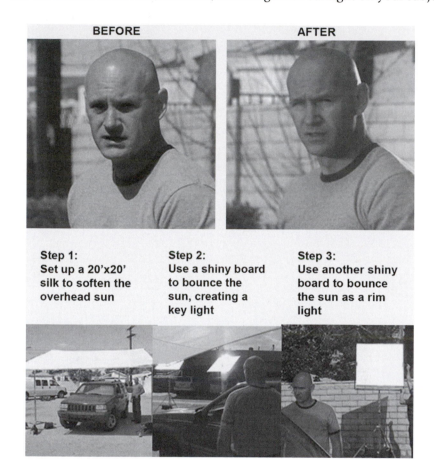

BEFORE | AFTER

Step 1:
Set up a 20'x20' silk to soften the overhead sun

Step 2:
Use a shiny board to bounce the sun, creating a key light

Step 3:
Use another shiny board to bounce the sun as a rim light

CINEMATOGRAPHY: FRAMING AND COMPOSITION

One of the biggest cinematic differences between amateur and professionally produced movies is how shots are framed. With an almost limitless number of possibilities as to where to place the camera and how to frame up a shot, a careful eye and some forethought will greatly improve the quality of the frame.

Although this sounds simplistic, the audience sees only what you point the camera at. Especially in the low-budget realm, creative camera angles and careful framing can help sell limited locations, basic production design, and even simple lighting.

Aspect Ratios

The first step in understanding how to best compose a shot is the shape of the frame itself, called the *aspect ratio*, or the ratio of the width of the frame to the height of the frame. Referred to as a dimension such as 16:9 and 4:3, the aspect ratio refers to the shape of the frame, not the size.

INTENDED ASPECT RATIO	SIZE	DESCRIPTION
16 × 9	.3775 × .2123	Digital CCD Area
16 × 9 (2.40:1)	.3775 × .1579	Digital CCD Extended Area for Anamorphic
1.37:1	.404 × .295	Regular 16mm Camera Aperture
Various	.486 × .295	Super 16mm Camera Aperture
Various	.980 × .735	35mm Full Camera Aperture
2.40:1	.825 × .690	Anamorphic Projection Aperture
1.85:1	.825 × .446	35mm 1.85:1 Projection Aperture
2.40:1	.945 × .394	Super Panavision 35mm Extracted Area for Anamorphic Projection
1.33:1	.792 × .594	35mm TV Transmitted Area (SMPTE recommended practice)
	.713 × .535	35mm TV Safe Action
1.78:1	.945 × .531 (16 × 9)	4-Perf Transmitted Area
Various	.980 × .546	Panavision 3-Perf 35mm Camera Aperture
1.78:1	.910 × .511 (16 × 9)	3-Perf Transmitted Area
2.29:1	2.072 × .906	65mm Camera Aperture
2.20:1	1.912 × .870	70mm Projection Aperture (Panavision Super 70mm)
2.40:1	1.912 × .797	Extracted for 2× Projection

Film and video formats have many different aspect ratios and the decision as to which is best is based on both creative and technical reasons. Most film-makers will agree that shooting with a wider aspect ratio more closely mimics the human eye's area of view and is more aesthetically pleasing. However, distributors, like TV stations, may frown on broadcasting wide-screen, letterboxed movies.

Converting from one format to another can create problems because the aspect ratios may not match. There are number of techniques used to resolve these issues.

NTSC 4:3 frame.

35mm 1.85:1 frame.

A letterbox preserves the 35 mm aspect ratio when converted to NTSC.

Letterbox

Converting one film or video format to another can be challenging, especially when the aspect ratio of the two media is different. In this instance, a 1.85:1, 35 mm film frame is wider than an NTSC 4:3 television frame, so one possible option is to reduce the 35 mm frame in size so it fits inside the NTSC frame. The top and bottom areas are then left black. Although it may seem as though the top and bottom of the frame are cut off, the letterbox format allows the viewer to see the entire 35 mm frame. Today, letterboxed images are increasingly used and are widely accepted by audiences.

Pan-and-Scan

In past years, many distributors and broadcasters would not accept letterboxed movies, preferring the pan-and-scan technique instead. This process involves blowing up the 35 mm frame so that it fills the NTSC frame. Because the 35 mm frame is wider than the NTSC frame, the sides of the picture are cut off, losing up to 40% of the image. Critical elements in the movie may be lost outside the NTSC frame; therefore, the 35 mm frame can be constantly shifted left and right to "reframe" in order for critical objects to appear.

Rules of Composition

There are a number of guidelines that help the camera operator best utilize the area of the frame. Although these guidelines can easily be compromised, they provide the most aesthetically pleasing look and should be heavily considered. From classic paintings to modern motion pictures, you'll begin to notice these conventions used again and again.

Unlike letterboxing an image, cropping cuts off almost 40% of the 35 mm film frame.

The 35 mm frame must be shifted to the left and right within the NTSC frame to ensure important subjects and objects aren't cut off. This move, called "pan and scan," can be jerky and disorienting.

RULE OF THIRDS

The Rule of Thirds is designed to help the camera operator determine where to place important objects in the frame. Instead of centering a subject, place the subject a third from either side of the frame or a third from the top or bottom. Here's how it works: Place an imaginary tic-tac-toe board over the frame and place the subject on one of the lines. For example, frame an actor's eyes one-third from the top of the frame, or when shooting a sunset, place the horizon one-third from the bottom of the screen. These examples demonstrate framing of horizontal elements, but the same concept applies to the placement of vertical elements. If there is a single tree silhouetted against the setting sun, the tree should be placed either a third from the left or a third from the right of the frame. As is the case with every rule, there are always exceptions. Symmetry in the frame can be a powerful storytelling device when employed properly. As you develop your shots, think about why you may want to either follow or break framing convention.

LEAD ROOM

An operator should frame not only for an object or subject, but also for the action of the subject. If an actor were to look directly into the camera lens,

Camera: Master shot of
Bobby and Awanda – In
this frame, Awanda is
STILL looking FRAME LEFT
at Bobby while Bobby
looks FRAME RIGHT.

Line of action

Camera: CU on
Awanda – In this frame, Awanda is
looking FRAME LEFT at Bobby who is
looking FRAME RIGHT.

By crossing the line of
action, this shot of Bobby
WILL NOT edit correctly
with the shot of Awanda.
Both Bobby and Awanda
are looking FRAME LEFT.
Editing them together will
make it appear as though
they are facing the same
direction.

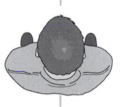

Camera: CU on Bobby –
In this frame, Bobby is STILL
looking FRAME RIGHT.

he should be centered in the frame with his eyes a third from the top of the screen. If the actor were to turn his head frame right, pan right to allow room for him to look into. The more drastic to the side the action is, the more lead room must be provided.

THE RULE OF 180

If you and I were standing on set, we would be able to see every object in the room, know the geography of the room, and have a sense of spatiality. The audience, however, sees only what the camera sees, and when the camera shoots a series of close-up shots, the geography of the room and the objects in it are never fully revealed to the audience. Take, for example, two people facing each other, talking over a restaurant table. If you're standing on the set, you know they're facing each other. But if the only camera coverage is two single close-ups, it is possible to misplace the camera so that it looks as though the two people are looking in the same direction, incorrect as it may be.

The Rule of 180 prevents this geographic confusion from taking place. In order to apply this rule, draw a line, called the *line of action*, between the two subjects, as though you were connecting the dots, except that this line extends infinitely in both directions. The rule specifies that the camera must remain on one side of the line of action. You can choose any camera angle, any distance from the actors, any lens type, and any camera height, provided the camera always remains on the same side of the line.

There are three exceptions when the camera is allowed to cross the line:

- In the first exception, the camera must first cut to a shot on the line before it cuts to a shot over the line. In the instance of a car chase, a shot on the line could be a point of view of a driver, or a car could drive over the camera, or, if placed on a bridge, the camera could shoot directly down onto the cars driving underneath. Once we establish a shot on the line, the camera is free to either return to its original side of the line or cross to the other side for the duration of the scene.
- In the second exception, the camera crosses the line during a dolly, Steadicam, or handheld shot during the take. If the camera moves across the line of action, the audience is watching as the camera crosses, preserving the geographic layout of the set. If the camera crosses, the next shot must occur on the same side the camera ends up on.
- In the third exception, the line of action crosses the camera. For example, if two actors are seated at a table and one of the actors stands and walks across the frame, then the line has effectively moved across the camera. The next shot must be taken from the new position unless one of the above-stated exceptions is applied.

Remember that the Rule of 180 is a guide you can use to determine where to put the camera for the next shot. Regardless of whether you followed the rule or used an exception, the next shot must always take place from the correct side of the line to avoid confusing the audience.

EYE LINE

When shooting a dialog scene between two actors, place the camera close to the line of action so the actors are facing the camera as much as possible, with their eye line just off the side of the lens. A common mistake committed by many new filmmakers is to place the camera too far away from the line of action, framing a profile shot instead of a full-facial shot. The more an actor faces the camera lens, the greater the audience will emotionally connect with him.

HEADROOM

Headroom is the distance from the top of the actor's head to the top of the frame. If you follow the Rule of Thirds and always place the actor's eyes a third from the top of the frame, the headroom should automatically fall into place.

BACKGROUND

Make sure the background is free and clear of any distracting elements like plants or phone poles that, if improperly framed, appear to grow from the actor's head. Using tools to throw the background out of focus will draw the audience's attention toward the subject of the shot. Think and preplan the background of every shot from an art direction, set dressing, and color standpoint to ensure that the background serves the story.

FOREGROUND

Add depth to shots by shooting through foreground elements. Fences, objects on a table, plants, and even shooting through car windows all add several layers of depth to a shot and can help frame a subject. Always think in terms of what the background, midground, and foreground elements are in the frame. If you have access to a dolly, consider opening a scene by dollying from behind an object or slowly dollying in front of, or through, a foreground element. These subtle techniques help add production value and make for interesting shots.

BALANCE

Always make sure that elements in the frame feel balanced, so the rough shape, color, and brightness of the primary objects complement each other.

Jason's Notes

Don't be afraid to cheat! In many instances, I would frame up a shot and decide that it needed a little more spice to make it interesting. Provided it didn't interfere with the continuity of previous shots, I would add elements in front of the camera lens to provide an interesting foreground to shoot through, or we would move and finesse the set dressing in the background, always taking time to scrutinize the frame before rolling off a take.

Sometimes small changes like moving a plant into the frame or removing artwork from the wall that competes for the viewer's attention can make a big difference in the balance and feel of the shot.

Don't be afraid to experiment and, provided you have the time, make each shot a masterpiece that you could print, frame, and hang on the wall.

Shot Types

Communication with the director of photography starts by understanding the size of the frame and how the actors will look in the frame. In the film industry, there are specific terms that relate to each frame size. Following are the most common frame types and examples of what they look like:

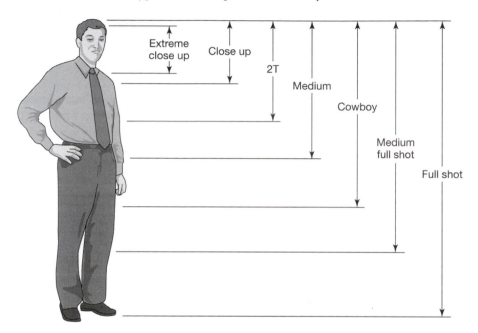

- ■ **Establishing shots** are wide shots, intended to show the audience where the following scene is taking place. These shots serve to set up, or establish, the location.

- A **master shot** is a wide shot that covers all the action of a scene from the beginning to the end. Usually a simple shot, master shots sometimes incorporate a dolly move to keep them from being stagnant. Master shots always include everything the audience needs to see to understand the scene.

- A **full shot** is a full head-to-toe body shot of the actor.
- In a ¾ **or Hollywood shot** the frame cuts the actor off at the knees. This shot is not used often in modern cinema because cutting off a subject at the joints is considered bad composition and looks awkward.
- A **medium shot** is the most common shot and frames the actor from mid-torso to his head.

- A **two shot** includes two actors, usually standing next to each other. A two shot has two actors in the frame, a three shot has three actors in the frame and so on.

- A **walking two shot** is a two shot, except that the actors are walking during the shot. They can either stop or start or be walking when the camera rolls.

- A **standing two shot** is a lock-down shot in which neither the camera nor the actors move.
- A **reversal** is a shot in which two actors are facing each other, such as across a dinner table, and the camera cuts from a medium shot of one actor to a medium shot of the other actor, hence "reversing" the shot.

- An **over-the-shoulder shot** (OTS) is a medium shot of an actor over the shoulder of another actor. An OTS shot frames one side of the shot with the back of the actor's head and shoulder. As a general rule, the audience should see only one ear of the actor facing away from the camera.

- A **close-up** is a tight shot framing an actor's head and shoulders. The close-up focuses the audience's attention on an actor's facial expression and is a very powerful frame, but should be mixed in with a variety of other shots to keep the sequence from feeling claustrophobic.

- A **deep focus** shot has all elements in frame are in focus. Also called a "deep depth of field," this can be achieved by using a short focal length (zooming out) and closing the iris.

- In a **shallow focus** shot, only certain objects in the frame are in focus. You can achieve a shallow depth of field by lengthening the focal length (zooming in) and opening the camera's iris.

- A **Dutch angle** shot has the camera intentionally tilted out of horizontal. This adds power and emphasis to the shot.
- **Panning** is horizontal movement of the camera on its axis, usually while on a tripod.
- **Tilting** is vertical movement of the camera on its axis, usually while on a tripod.
- A **pedestal** is vertically raising or lowering the camera. This term is used in television production. On a film set, the term is "boom up" or "boom down," when using a pneumatically controlled dolly.
- A **tracking shot** involves moving the camera laterally, side to side.
- In a **high shot**, the camera is positioned above the subject and is shooting down, making the subject look inferior.

- **MOS** is short for "mit out sound" (German), which identifies a shot recorded without sound.
- A **montage** is a series of shots interwoven with transitions to show the passage of time.

CINEMATOGRAPHY: TECHNIQUE

Cinematography is both a right-brain and a left-brain exercise – a balance between art and technique. We've spent time talking about some of the tools you and the director of photography can use to craft the look and emotional subtext of the movie, and in this section we're going to look at a few ways you can use these tools.

Here are a few pointers to keep in mind when you're directing on set:

- Always block the master shot first, covering the entire action of the scene from beginning to end. Then move in for close-ups and coverage. This gives the director of photography the opportunity to plan the lighting for the entire scene, then tweak it for the close-ups.
- Always rehearse each setup to ensure the crew understands the blocking, giving them an opportunity to perform the tasks for which you hired them – setting focus, practicing dolly moves, establishing boundaries for the microphone boom, and so on. Skipping the blocking and rehearsal stage means the crew is shooting blindly.
- Before you're ready to shoot a take, look over the shot in the viewfinder or on a monitor to double-check framing, blocking, focus, and set. Always carefully check the frame before you start shooting for stray production equipment, soda cans, garbage, or even crew members. Also, make sure there are no bizarre objects such as light poles or trees positioned behind your actors in a way that makes it look as though they were sticking out of the actor's head.

- Let the camera roll for several seconds before calling "action" and after yelling "cut." This padding can always be trimmed in the editing room, but may prove invaluable for transitions or fade-outs.
- Always keep good logs of the shots taken on set. Camera logs are forms on which you record the shot number and description, the focal length and exposure settings of the lens, and any comments. These logs are invaluable when editing, saving a tremendous amount of time when searching through the rough footage.
- Be precise with every camera angle and shoot each shot with the intention of covering a particular action. Remember that each scene is a combination of camera shots and not every shot has to cover the entire scene in its entirety. Be sure the director of photography is clear as to the reason for every single camera setup.
- Think of creative angles that accentuate the performances. Unique shots are fine, provided that they support the story and the characters. The cinematography should *never* draw attention away from the performances.
- When covering a scene, shoot a variety of long shots, medium shots, and close-ups. Remember that the more variety an editor has to choose from, the more dynamic the scene will feel on the screen.
- Never set the camera up and have the actors perform in front of it. Involve the camera; move it around the set and treat it like an audience member. What does the audience want to see? What is happening in the scene that would motivate the audience to look in a certain direction? Think about this if you're ever in doubt as to where to place the camera on set.

Getting the Film Look

Film has such a rich, organic look that many filmmakers work hard to mimic when shooting video. Here are some tricks to creating a film look for your video:

- **Shoot in 24p.** Film cameras capture in 24 frames per second. For a long time, video cameras were locked into capturing 60 fields per second because of technical restrictions of the NTSC format. With the advent of high-definition video, camcorders are able to capture true 24 progressive frames per second, mimicking the look of film.
- **Use a shallow depth of field.** The second major component in achieving a film look is to shoot on cameras with the largest CCD or CMOS chip. The bigger the imaging plane, the shallower the depth of field and the more film-like the image will look. Most movies are shot on 35 mm film, which, because of the large frame size, yields a very shallow depth of field. Even in wide shots, the background can be in soft focus. Because video cameras use smaller 1/3", 1/2", and 2/3" CCDs, the depth of field is not as shallow – a limitation the director of photography can somewhat overcome by shooting with a longer focal length, opening up the iris, and slowing down the shutter speed. To more closely mimic the depth of field of 35 mm film, try shooting on a 35 mm CMOS-chip based camera, like a DSLR or the RED camera.

- **Fill out the contrast range of the camera.** Film has a greater latitude than video, which equates to much richer blacks and more details in highlights; it's important to light the scene with as much contrast between the bright and the dark areas as the format will allow. Always make sure there is a perfect black element and a perfect white element in each frame.
- **Shift the gamma curve.** The gamma curve (brightness of the midrange values) for video-acquired images is much more linear than that of film. In postproduction, shift the curve to more closely reflect the gamma response of film.
- **Move the camera.** Controlled camera movements are typical of high-budget Hollywood productions, so the more you can move the camera with dollies, jibs, and cranes, the higher the production value.
- **Filters.** Consider using a Tiffin 1/4- or 1/8-grade Pro-Mist filter to soften highlights. Film tends to bleed overexposed elements into surrounding objects, whereas highlights in video are often sharp and crisp. Using softening filters will help soften the effects of overexposure in the frame.

Keeping Organized

Each day of shooting will yield dozens of shots, takes, and setups. It is critical to organize and track each shot carefully so that each shot can be easily located in postproduction.

USING A CLAPBOARD

The first step in organizing shots is to mark each take with a *clapboard* (also known as a *slate*), for two reasons. The first is to identify the name of the production, the shooting date, the director and director of photography, which roll of film or video tape you are shooting, the scene, the setup and take, any filters used, and whether the take has recorded audio so the editor knows where in the movie this take must go.

The second purpose of the clapboard is to assist the editor in syncing the audio to the visuals if the audio has been recorded on a separate unit. You cannot record sound directly to film, because film is designed only to react to light. As a result, a separate audio recording device is required, usually a Nagra (reel-to-reel analog recorder), DAT (digital audio tape) recorder, or digital hard drive recorder. Technology has progressed to the point where audio engineers record the sound from the set directly to a laptop computer.

Although technology is progressing, it is still necessary to sync, or line up, the audio with the visuals: hence the clapboard, which provides a visual sync indicator to the editor. For each take, once the sound recording device and the film camera are rolling, the second assistant cameraman verbally speaks the film title, scene, setup, and take. It sounds like this, *"Time and Again,* Scene 45 apple, Take 3 . . . marker."* Then he claps the clapper. This action provides a visual cue for the editor so he can line up the sound of the clap with the visuals of the clap. Once synced up, the rest of the take should line up and remain in sync.

■ **Recording audio into the camera.** It is not necessary to clap the clapboard when the audio is being fed directly into a video camera, because the audio is already synced to the visuals. When marking this type of shot, the second 2nd assistant cameraman just holds the clapboard from the top, with her hand covering the clapper.

■ **Recording sync sound.** When recording audio into an external recording device, it's critical to clearly mark each shot by clapping the arm on the clapboard. The 2nd AC should always place the clapboard in frame with the arm open and ensure that the camera has a clean view of the slate. Carefully close the arm with precision to avoid motion blur. If it's dark or the clapboard is not properly lit, he should use a flashlight to illuminate the information on the slate and the closing action of the arm.

■ **Recording MOS (mit out sound).** If recording with no audio, the 2nd AC should place her hand between the clapper and the clapboard. This indicates to the editor that there is no audio associated with that take.

■ **Tail slate.** There may be instances when it's easier to mark a shot at the end of a take rather than the beginning. To indicate a tail slate, the 2nd AC holds the clapboard upside down and marks the shot and then quickly turns the clapboard right side up so the editor can read the information.

Jason's Notes

The clapboard is a tool, not a toy. One of my biggest pet peeves on set is when a person plays with the clapboard or messes around with what's written on them. Clapboards are expensive tools, and treating them like toys is a rookie mistake and a great way to get fired.

Smart Slates versus Dumb Slates

So far, we've talked about dumb slates – that is, a clapboard that has no connection to or communication with any other equipment on set. Smart slates feature an LED time code display that matches the time code being recorded by the audio device. Wirelessly transmitted from the production sound mixer, the time code runs in real time when the arm is open on the slate. Closing the arm freezes the time code at the moment of closure, giving the editor a precise reference for syncing the audio to the picture.

Camera Logs

The 2nd assistant cameraman will maintain camera logs to track the scene and shot numbers, description of the shot, camera settings, and a rating for each take. Camera logs help the editor quickly and easily find the best takes from each tape, provide a reference for the director of photography should a scene or take ever need to be reshot, and help the DP match the camera settings for any pickups that need to be shot sometimes months later.

The Media Manager

Many popular cameras record to P2 cards, flash cards, or other types of solid-state media. Because of size limitations, cards need to be downloaded to hard drives and then reformatted so the crew can resume shooting. As a result, a new position of media manager has been created on set. This person is responsible for transferring data from the cards to a hard drive, then importing the data into the editing software. Because there is a lot of time spent waiting on set, the media manager can sometimes assume the responsibilities of an assistant editor by naming and organizing the footage for the editor.

The responsibilities of the media manager include:

■ **Transferring data from solid-state media.** When a card has been completely filled, the 2nd assistant cameraman will hand deliver the card to the media manager. Most cards will have tab that, when toggled, will prevent erasure. The 2nd AC will always pop this tab to indicate that the card has footage on it that has not yet been transferred. The media manager will then copy the raw contents of the card to a hard drive.

Camera Log

Production: Date: Page:
Studio: Logs by:
Director: Location:
Director of Photography: Scene:

☐ Day   ☐ Night   Filters:
☐ Dusk   ☐ Dawn   Effects:
Weather: Notes:

SHOT #	DESCRIPTION	F-STOP	FOCAL	RATING

Dana Strom not only uploaded and organized the footage we shot on set, but also roughly assembled the footage so we had a strong edit to watch at the end of each shooting day.

- **Organizing the footage.** Each production will have different requirements for the organization of the rough footage. Generally, the contents of each card will be placed in its own folder, labeled "Card 1," "Card 2," "Card 3," and so on. The card number is also written on the clapboard so that each shot is linked to its corresponding card. For multicamera shots, it's helpful to add a camera letter to each card. For example, Card "1a" is the first card shot on A-camera; "3b" is the third card shot on B-camera; and "2c" is the second card shot on C-camera.

Panasonic's P2 card is part of a solid state tapeless recording system for their HD camera line.

- **Backing up data.** Once the footage has been transferred to a hard drive and the card reformatted, the hard drive becomes the master. Should anything happen to the hard drive – someone dumps coffee on the table, or a hard drive falls, gets rattled in transit, or crashes – the footage could be lost. It's imperative to have a second backup drive on set so that once the footage has been copied to the first drive, a redundant backup can be made. For larger productions, it's wise to invest in a third hard drive that is kept off-site. At the end of each shooting day, back up that day's footage to the third drive in case something happens to the first two on set.

During postproduction, use the first drive as the main editing drive, and the second drive as a backup. Often, if you have access to an editing suite, you can keep the second drive, so that the editor need only to send the project file to you. You can then easily relink the clips to view the editor's progress. The third drive should be locked away and never touched; use it as a backup if something happens to the first two.

- **Renaming clips.** Many formats, like Panasonic's P2 format, will give each clip a random name, which creates a challenge in the editing room. One of the responsibilities of the media manager is to take a copy of the script supervisor's notes and rename each clip on set, replacing the cryptic native filename with the scene, setup, take, and shot description. For example:

  12a-2 master shot
  12b-4 LS, Henry enters room
  12c-8 MS, Henry enters room
  12d-4 MS, Lucy sits
  12e-6 CU Lucy's hands

- **Highlighting the selects.** Once all the clips are renamed, the media manager should highlight your preferred takes, called *selects*, at both the desktop and editing software level. This information can be garnered from the script supervisor's notes.

By organizing the footage on set, the editor will be able to immediately begin editing the project, saving both time and money by not having to perform the work of an assistant editor.

For longer projects like a feature film, consider hiring a media manager who knows how to edit. In addition to importing, renaming, and organizing the media, the media manager can build an assembly cut of the movie so at the end of each shooting day, you can watch a rough cut of the scene. This allows you to see problems in performance, lapses of coverage, or any technical issues so you can immediately reshoot a shot. It's cheaper and easier to add a shot while shooting than it is to schedule a pickup day of shooting once the production is wrapped and the project is deep in postproduction.

SHOOTING GREEN/BLUE SCREEN

Green screen is a process by which a single color is selected in the frame and digitally replaced with another image or video source. This process is called *keying* and an image can be keyed any number of ways, including keying out a specific luminance (brightness) level, or in this case, keying out a particular color (chromakey). The green screen process is a popular method for extracting actors or objects and compositing them into another environment.

Green Screen versus Blue Screen

Although any color can technically be keyed, blue and green are the primary choices of directors of photography. First, green and blue are both the color opposites of flesh tones, minimizing the chance of keying out part of an actor's face. In general, the choice of whether to use blue or green depends largely on the actor's wardrobe or the color of the objects in the shot. If the actor is wearing blue jeans, consider using a green screen. If the actors is wearing a green shirt, consider using blue screen. Nothing in the foreground should have the same color as the background screen – if it does, you will end up keying through your subject.

- Green screens are more reflective than blue screens and require less light to illuminate. Choose a green screen when working with limited lighting resources, or when a lot of light is required for high-speed cinematography. Often, green screens are chosen when shooting indoors reducing the amount of light needed for exposure, and blue screens are used outdoors in direct sunlight.
- Before computer-generated imagery (CGI) was adopted as the primary visual effects tool in the industry, models were shot against a red or orange screen illuminated with infrared light, which greatly reduced the risk of bounceback from the background onto the model.
- When traveling, neon-green poster board purchased from an office supply store is a great inexpensive solution. It's cheap and can be taped together to make a screen of virtually any size, and its highly reflective color is easily lit and picked up by digital cameras.

Digital versus Film

There are two types of blue screens and two types of green screens. The first set of blue and green screens, called *chromakey blue* and *chromakey green*, are designed for use when shooting film and aren't as saturated in color as their digital counterparts. Film has a much wider tolerance for color and brightness, making it better suited for these muted colors.

When shooting digitally, a special type of green and blue screen was created called *digital blue* and *digital green*. The colors are much brighter and feature much stronger, saturated color, making them easier for CCDs to capture.

Compression

Once light enters the lens, digital cameras separate it into the red, green, and blue components before they are compressed and saved either to tape or to solid state media. Unlike the red and blue channels, which are heavily compressed, the uncompressed green channel retains much of the original data. Using a digital green screen thus makes for a much easier key in postproduction because of the amount of data in the green channel. The edges around the subject are sharper and more defined, enabling the software to isolate and cleanly remove the green screen. The overall quality of the key is much better than if a blue background were used.

Shooting green screen also depends heavily on the type of digital format used:

- **Number of chips.** When shooting green screen plates, choose a 3-CCD or a CMOS camera. Single-CCD or single-chip cameras use one CCD to convert all the light into the recorded electrical signal, whereas a 3-CCD camera will break the incoming light into red, green, and blue channels. Of these three channels, the green channel contains the color information for the green screen, so by keeping it separate from the red and blue channels, the resulting image is sharper with no color bleeding. The final key will be clean, and edges around the keyed subject will be sharp.

- **Format.** Once the camera converts light into an electrical signal, it is then compressed for storage on either a tape or onto another digital medium like DVD or a solid-state card. Different formats will compress the footage differently, mostly by throwing away color information, information that is critical to creating a clean chromakey. When shooting green screen, avoid formats like consumer analog formats, MiniDV, and HDV, because in these the compression is so severe that attempting to pull a key will result in stair-stepping along the edges of the subject. Choose a professional broadcast format like DVCProHD, Digital BetaCam, HDCAM, or any uncompressed formats for the optimal key. Although it may be more expensive to shoot, the resulting images will yield a clean, flawless key.

Lighting a Chromakey Screen

Lighting a green or blue screen can be tricky, and the final quality of the key is dependent on your ability to properly shoot the screen on set. Follow these tips for shooting a good green or blue screen. For ease of discussion, I'll refer to the background screen as a green screen, although this information applies to any color you may choose.

- **Choose the appropriate color for your background.** Make sure the color of the background is unique and isn't present in the actors' wardrobe or in the subject. When shooting digitally, consider using a digital green screen.
- **Light the screen evenly.** Even lighting is the single most important aspect of obtaining a good key, as the compositor will be able to select a narrower range of green for a cleaner key. As a general rule, a well-lit green screen should not vary in brightness by more than half a stop at most. There are several ways to evenly light a green screen:

  - **Cyc lights.** Most green screen plates are shot at professional studios against a smooth, curved wall called a *cyc*. The cyc is painted green, and broad overhead lights are rigged from the grid in the ceiling to create an even light, especially when lightly diffused. Cyc lights are inexpensive, easy to hang, and are ideally suited for lighting large areas and are commonly used on standard 18-foot-high lighting grids.
  - **Space lights.** Space lights are large, soft lights hung from a studio grid. Unlike cyc lights, which can be focused onto the green screen with minimal spill onto the subject, space lights are placed in the center of the stage, and flood the area with light. Although the green screen is evenly lit, the subject is also flooded with light, making it extremely difficult to control.
  - **Kino-Flos.** Kino-Flos are an outstanding lighting option for smaller green screens. When lighting interview subjects, products, or other small contained objects, 4'×4' bank Kino-Flos are the perfect choice. Studios with smaller cycs can benefit from 4'×8' bank Kino-Flos, called Image 80s. Because Kino-Flos can be outfitted with different color bulbs, the best choice for lighting green screen is either the 5000k green bulb, or

the 5600k daylight globe. Although tungsten bulbs will work, the blue hue of the daylight bulb brings out the green color frequency, making the green screen more saturated on screen.

We used Kino-Flo Image 80s to create a soft, even light on the green screen cyc for a commercial.

■ **Reflected light.** If you don't have access to a lighting grid but still need to light a large green screen, buy four 4'×8' sheets of foam core, black on one side and white on the other. Tape two of them together along the long edge and open them up like a book sitting on the short edge with the white side on the inside. Build two of these and place each one just off both the left and right sides of the frame. Inside these reflectors, place a 1.2k or 4k HMI focused into the foam core. You have just made a large 8'×8' soft source that illuminates the green screen. Position the foam core so it blocks any spill off your actors.

■ **Always light the green screen first.** Lighting a subject in front of a green screen can be tricky, because the DP needs to light both the green screen and the subject without the light from one affecting the other. When lighting the green screen, avoid any unnecessary light spill and try to keep the subject in darkness. The DP will then create a separate lighting setup specifically for the subject.

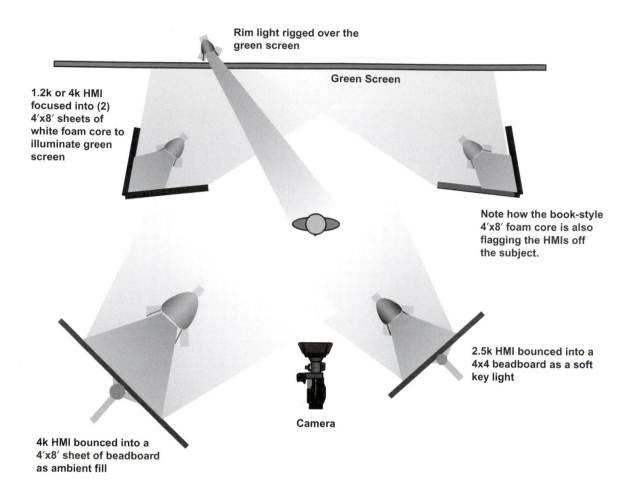

Rim light rigged over the green screen

Green Screen

1.2k or 4k HMI focused into (2) 4'x8' sheets of white foam core to illuminate green screen

Note how the book-style 4'x8' foam core is also flagging the HMIs off the subject.

2.5k HMI bounced into a 4x4 beadboard as a soft key light

Camera

4k HMI bounced into a 4'x8' sheet of beadboard as ambient fill

- **Properly expose the green screen.** A good rule of thumb is to expose the green screen roughly one f- stop below the brightness of the subject's key light. If you're using a waveform monitor, the luminance of the green screen should be around 60 IRE, or 60% brightness value.
- **Avoid spill.** If the actors are positioned too close to the green screen, green light will be reflected back onto the actors, making it extremely difficult to key them out later. Avoid green spill by placing the actors at least 8 or 10 feet away from the background. When working on a green screen floor, place a furniture pad or duvatyne on the floor whenever it's not in the shot to eliminate upspill.
- **Ensure good separation of the subject.** Make sure your subject is properly lit so there is a distinct difference between the subject and green screen. When shooting actors with dark hair, add a rim light to increase separation. When shooting blond actors, reduce the rim light and consider rigging a flag to reduce the light on the subject's head.

Using a backlight is a great way to separate your subject from the background. In this photo, the backlight is very strong, so as to simulate the sun, which would be digitally composited in later.

- **Avoid reflections.** Be extremely careful when shooting reflective objects to ensure that they do not reflect the green screen. Reflective surfaces like marble, granite, glasses, and jewelry can cause compositing problems.
- **Avoid spill.** Make sure your subject is far enough away from the green screen to avoid any green spill on your subject. It's nearly impossible to cleanly key a subject that has too much green spill. If you're shooting against a green cyc with a green floor, consider laying down furniture pads on the ground to avoid green reflection bouncing off the floor.
- **Know what the background will be.** In narrative projects in which the subject is being keyed into a real environment, make sure to light the subject properly so that the key light is the same as the background plate in color, intensity and texture. It's a good idea to have the background images available on set as reference.

Shooting Full Body

I've shot over a thousand green screen shots in my career, and one issue that arises every time is whether to frame the actor's feet. The setup required to properly shoot an actor head-to-toe is significantly more expensive and time-consuming than framing a loose medium shot in which the bottom frame line falls midthigh.

- **You will need a full green cyc with floor.** Because it's a full-body shot, a smooth, even transition is needed in the green screen, curving from the wall behind the actor to the floor underneath them. It may be necessary to rent a professional studio with the proper facilities, costing upwards of a thousand dollars a day. If you shoot a medium shot, the DP can set up a flat green screen behind the actor in practically any location.

■ **Lighting is more complicated.** It's time-consuming, and requires additional lighting equipment and more crew members to evenly light the cyc from wall to floor without any variation in the brightness. This can take several hours, whereas lighting a flat greenscreen behind the actor can take less than half an hour and a couple Kino-Flos.

■ **The lens settings and placement of the camera when shooting the green screen subject must match the lens setting and placement of the camera shooting the background plate.** It is very difficult to get the perspectives, lighting angles, and optics correct to seamlessly key an actor from head to toe into an environment. Pushing into to a tighter medium shot provides much more leeway when compositing the background image.

It's much easier to light and shoot a medium shot of an actor against a partial green screen (left) than a full-body frame (right).

CHAPTER 14
Audio Recording

ii. Choose a recording format: sync sound or directly to the camera.

iv. Rent necessary sound recording equipment and purchase tape stock.

vi. After each take, the production sound mixer relays any sound problems to the 1st assistant director.

PRE-PRODUCTION

PRODUCTION

i. Hire a production sound mixer and boom operator.

iii. Scout each location – determine how to minimize ambient sound.

v. When on set, the boom operator works with the camera operator to find the optimal position for the microphone.

vii. Sound logs are turned into the 1st assistant director at the end of each shooting day.

INTRODUCTION

Audio is 50% of the movie-going experience, and unfortunately one of the last technical considerations made by the production team. Imagine *Star Wars* without the epic sound of the X-wing fighters passing by, or the intimate, crystal-clear dialog of *Titanic*. Sound plays an ironic role in movies – it has as much, if not more, of an impact than the visuals, yet remains virtually invisible to the audience. Good audio rarely draws attention to itself, and the art and technique of making an impactful yet invisible audio track requires skill and an excellent ear.

Sound is nothing more than changes in air pressure that originate from a vibrating source; the stronger the waves, the louder the sound. These waves are measured in increments called *decibels*, "db" for short, which measure the smallest amount of change in a sound wave that our ears are capable of detecting. In much the same way that film has a range of sensitivity to the brightness of light, sound recording devices have a range of the volume of sound they are capable of recording. For analog recording devices, this range is around 70 db. For digital recording devices, the range is greater, at 100 db, from the quietest sound capable of being detected to the loudest sound.

Filmmaking.
© 2011 Jason J. Tomaric. Published by Elsevier Inc. All rights reserved.

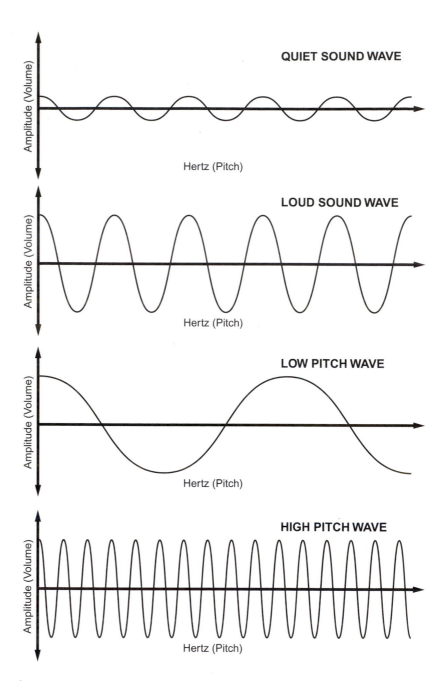

QUIET SOUND WAVE

LOUD SOUND WAVE

LOW PITCH WAVE

HIGH PITCH WAVE

Sound waves.

The amplitude of the wave determines the volume of the sound; the frequency determines the pitch. Measured in *hertz*, or Hz, the lower the frequency, the lower the pitch of the sound, and the higher the frequency, the higher the pitch. Human hearing can detect sounds as low as 20 Hz and as high as 20,000 Hz, although this ceiling is reduced as you get older.

The goal in recording a strong signal-to-noise ratio is to use as much of that dynamic range as possible, without exceeding it.

Jason's Notes

Every time I'm hired to shoot a project, my first call is to John Churchman, Production Sound Mixer Extraordinaire. His ability to consistently record clean dialog on set saves the production time and money in the editing room by allowing us to use almost all the on-set audio instead of having to ADR the dialog, record the Foley, and recreate the sounds effects track. If there's one thing I've learned on set, it's that if John asks for an extra minute to adjust a microphone, I give it to him.

ANALOG VERSUS DIGITAL

Sound travels in sinusoidal waves that move the pickup device in a microphone. The microphone then converts these waves into an electronic signal, which is then recorded onto the recording device. In early days of recording, the sound waves were recorded in a way that preserved the true curve and all the nuances of the sound waves. This type of recording, called *analog recording*, results in rich, textured audio. Tape cassettes, records, and reel-to-reel recorders are all analog formats.

The analog signal is recorded by capturing the signal and using magnetic heads in the recording device to position magnetic particles on the tape into a pattern. Playback heads read the position of the particles and reconstruct the signal. Because particles can be oriented in any one of an infinite number of ways, the analog signal can be recorded with great detail and warmth. Despite the richness of the sound, analog recording's major setback is the loss of quality each time a copy is made. This is called *generational loss*, which occurs each time a copy of a copy is made. Each time a copy is made, the recorder copies the position of each particle to a new tape, although a certain amount of unavoidable error is introduced and the particle's position is close to the original, but not identical. The result is degraded signal that further randomizes each generation.

Digital recorders sample the audio wave thousands of times per second and convert the resulting signal to a binary code, so that instead of recording particles in one of an infinite array of patterns, they record them in one of two: 1 or 0. The higher the number of samples, or the sample rate, the higher the audio quality. The result is a sound signal that can be broadcast and copied without loss because any error added can be easily detected and corrected. The major downfall of digital recording is that recording devices do not capture the true

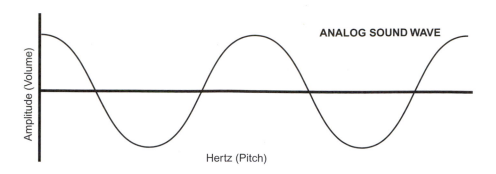

ANALOG SOUND WAVE

Amplitude (Volume)

Hertz (Pitch)

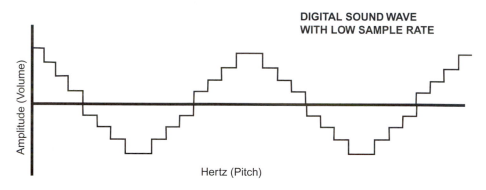

DIGITAL SOUND WAVE
WITH LOW SAMPLE RATE

Amplitude (Volume)

Hertz (Pitch)

sinusoidal wave, but break it down into a number of samples, resulting in what many audio experts describe as a loss of warmth and presence.

Whereas the sample rate is the number of samples per second, the bit depth is the amount of data recorded in each sample. A bit is the smallest, most basic amount of data, which in binary is a 1 or a 0. An 8-bit data stream will have 8 bits, or 10010101. A 16-bit stream, which is the most common bit depth for digital video recorders, has a data stream with 16 bits, or 1010010100110101.

Common sample rates and bit depths in the recording industry are:

> **Telephone:** 8 kHz (8000 samples per second)
> **MPEG/PCM compressed audio:** 11.025 and 22.050 kHz
> **CD:** 44.1 kHz (44,100 samples per second) at 16 bits per sample
> **MPEG-1 audio** (VCD, SVCD, MP3): 44.1 kHz
> **DV:** four tracks of 32 kHz (32,000 samples per second) at 12 bits or two tracks of 48 kHz (48,000 samples per second) at 16 bits
> **Digital TV, DVD, DAT:** 48 kHz
> **DVD audio, Blu-ray, HD-DVD:** 96 or 192 kHz

Advances in increased sample rates have made digital sound recording comparable to the quality of analog recording and an industry standard.

MICROPHONE TYPES

There are a variety of microphone types; each one is designed for a specific purpose.

Omnidirectional

Omnidirectional microphones have a pickup pattern that captures sound in all directions, making them ideal for recording ambient sound. Omnidirectional mikes should not be used to record dialog because they record too much of the surrounding ambience, making it difficult to hear the actors' lines clearly. Omnidirectional mikes are usually inexpensive and can be found at your local electronics or video supply store.

Cardioid

Cardioid microphones have a heart-shaped pickup pattern that is more sensitive to sounds in front of the microphone than to the sides. Cardioid mikes are usually used for singers, public speakers, and reporters when the mike can be placed 3 to 6 inches away from the mouth. Any farther and the vocals begin to lose their presence. Because of this limited proximity, cardioids are not the best choice for recording dialog.

Shotgun

Shotgun microphones have a narrow pickup pattern of 5–25 degrees and are designed to record sound from an optimal range of 1 to 4 feet. Shotgun microphones are ideal for recording on-set dialog because the narrow pickup pattern somewhat reduces ambience on the set, helping the spoken word stand out in the recording.

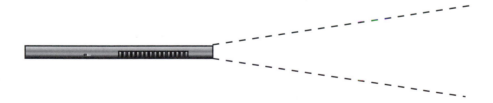

Lavalier

Lavalier mikes are clip-on mikes with a very tight cardioid pattern used for on-camera interviews in which it is acceptable to see the microphone in the shot. Usually clipped to a necktie or lapel, the mike should ideally be placed over the subject's sternum so that it picks up not only the voice, but also the low-end resonance from the chest cavity. Lavalier microphones work best when they are within 1 foot of the subject's mouth.

PREPPING AUDIO

The location scout is the time when the director and the key department heads look at a potential location to determine whether it will work creatively in the story and technically for the production.

Part of determining the feasibility of a location is to listen for any sound problems that may exist and figure out how, if possible, to reduce or eliminate them. Sound sources that may cause problems when recording audio include:

- **Air conditioners or air handling units.** The blowers, although they may be quiet, emit a broad-spectral sound that is nearly impossible to remove in postproduction. Take the time during the location scout to figure out how to turn off all air handling systems.
- **Refrigerators and appliances.** Often the bane of location sound mixers, appliances cause intermittent hums in the background that change tone and intensity when the microphone is repositioned during setups. Figure out how to turn the fridge and freezer off, and as a tip, leave your car keys inside. Then no one will leave until you remember to turn the fridge back on.

Jason's Notes

I remember when we were shooting at the Chester Diner for *Time and Again*. There was a long row of coolers for deli trays and various pastries that would have wreaked havoc on our sound, especially considering that we only had two days to shoot the coverage we needed. Knowing in advance that these coolers would cause problems in any shots for which we needed to record sound, we contacted a local grocery store manager who let us move all the food out of the diner's coolers into theirs. We were then able to turn every appliance and cooler off, put fake food inside the coolers, and save the audio for the scene. This only goes to show that a little preproduction can save you major headaches in postproduction.

- **Sirens.** Note the locations of hospitals, fire stations, and police stations and whether they are active around your location. Sirens and alarms not only ruin your audio, but also cause major time setbacks as you wait for ambulances, police cars, and fire engines to get far enough away so you can resume shooting.
- **Schools.** Check to see if there is a school nearby and determine whether the children and school buses passing by in the morning and afternoon will disrupt your audio.
- **Airports.** Is there a nearby airport and, even more importantly, is your location within the arrival or departing flight path? If so, calculate the time between flights and schedule your shots accordingly. The script supervisor will keep you aware of how much time you have before the next flyover.
- **Freeways.** Listen for highly directional ambient sources like freeways. Although it may sound quiet on location, pointing the microphone in different directions will change the volume and tone of the ambience and make it very difficult to match from one shot to the next in the editing room. If you have a choice, shoot away from freeways, intersections, and roads.

- **Beaches.** Although the beach has a romantic allure for filmmakers, it almost always signals immediate death for the audio track. The directional crashing of waves is nearly impossible to filter out of the recording mix, and changes in the microphone position will make the change in the sound of the ambience abrupt and disruptive to the audience.
- **Camera noise.** The camera itself can be a source of noise. From the sound of the magazines to lens motors, the operations of the camera are loud enough to be picked up by a microphone. Use a barney or a thick padded blanket draped over the camera to muffle some of the camera noise.

Jason's Notes

Consider this: you, as a director, are scouting houses for your next film and you find the perfect location. It matches your vision, the colors and layout are perfect, and you can practically see your characters moving through each room. The big problem is that it's next to the freeway. No matter where you are in the house, you can hear the cars. If you choose to shoot in this house, you may later learn in postproduction that the audio you recorded on set is unusable because of the changing volume and tone of the freeway ambience. The sound engineer tells you that the only option is to ADR, or rerecord the actor's dialog. So, at a rate of around $100/hour, you spend dozens of hours with the actors recreating the performance, timing, and emotion of each and every line of dialog, racking up a bill into the thousands.

At this point, the dialog sounds great, but you then learn that you need to recreate the Foley (the sounds the actors make while interacting on set). So the sound engineer spends countless more hours rerecording footsteps, movement of props, and clothing rubbing together to rebuild what you should have recorded originally.

So dozens, possibly hundreds, of hours later and thousand of dollars in the hole, it suddenly seems like that exquisite house, although artistically perfect, wasn't a good technical choice to shoot in. Perhaps it would have been better to have chosen a house that might not have been as artistically perfect, but that was at least away from the freeway.

ROLE OF THE SOUND TEAM ON SET BEFORE ACTION

When working on an independent film, a lot of attention is spent rehearsing the actors, setting up the lights, tediously blocking the camera, and making sure that makeup and hair look good. Unfortunately, sound doesn't seem to get the same attention and time the rest of the departments receive. Although the audio is half the movie-going experience, the boom operator always seems to be the last person to rush in as the director is about to call action, struggling to find a position that doesn't cast shadows while he's being prodded by the first AD to hurry up. The result is unspectacular sound that eventually comes back to haunt the filmmaker later in postproduction.

The proper way to achieve high-quality sound on set is for the boom operator and production sound mixer to be in constant communication with the rest

Production sound mixer John Churchman always ensures that the recorded audio is of the highest quality by being in constant communication with the director and director of photography.

of the crew to determine the best possible position from which to record sound.

- While you are rehearsing the scene for the cast and crew, the boom operator should be watching the blocking, taking note of the positions of the lights and camera in order to determine the most optimal position to place the microphone in the set. Ideally, the shotgun microphone should be 1 to 4 feet away from the actors, always pointed at the chest of the person speaking, and positioned about 45 degrees above their heads. The microphone should move with the actors so that the actors are always facing it. Because the shotgun microphone has such a tight pickup pattern, it's easy for the actors to move in and out of the microphone's range, so the boom operator must constantly adjust the position of the boom for optimum recording.

- Once the boom operator has located the ideal microphone position, she asks the camera operator what the frame is in order to determine the amount of headroom in the frame. She then places the microphone above the actors and slowly lowers it until it appears in the shot so she knows how close the microphone can be to the actors before it breaches the frame.

- The boom operator then determines how he will move relative to the actors' blocking so that his microphone remains at a consistent distance and always points at the actors' chests. He must always be aware of the positions of lights so as not to block any light or cast shadows on the actors or the set.

- Once in place, the boom operator will wait until you are ready for a camera rehearsal. During this rehearsal, the production sound mixer will set the levels for the recording based on the actors' delivery and any final blocking alterations are made.

- The sound department is ready and awaits the first AD's call for a take.

- After you call cut, the boom operator confers with the first AD and notes any problems with the audio and then waits for you and the first AD to decide whether to pursue another take.

XLR AUDIO INPUTS

RECORDING TO THE CAMERA

There are two ways to record audio when shooting with a digital camera. The first is to plug the shotgun microphone directly into the camera, and the second is to record the audio to a separate recording device.

If you are recording the audio directly into the camera, you will need:

- Shotgun microphone
- Boom pole

- XLR cable
- XLR splitter

If you want the production sound mixer to have more control over the audio, plug the microphone into a sound mixer and plug the sound mixer into the camera. This will free the camera operator from the pressure of having to monitor the audio levels while watching the frame during a take. Usually, with this configuration, the audio mixer should be able to generate a 0-db tone that is used to set the camera's input levels to 20 db. After the camera input level is set, put a piece of tape over the gain levels so no one accidentally changes the levels. From that point, the production sound mixer will monitor and adjust the levels of the incoming sound source from his mixer.

SYNC SOUND

Sync sound means the audio is recorded to a device other than the camera. When recording sync sound, the microphone is plugged into an audio mixer that is then run into an external recording device. The recording device's independence from the camera gives the boom operator the freedom and flexibility to move around the set, untethered from the camera.

Used in film production because audio can't be recorded onto film, and used more often on high-definition productions, recording sync sound offers a variety of benefits and drawbacks for the filmmaker:

- Sync-sound recording allows the sound recording device to be placed anywhere on set, giving the boom operator and production sound mixer greater flexibility and range of motion around the set.
- Recording sync sound shifts the burden of monitoring the audio levels from the camera operator to the production sound mixer. This allows the camera operator to focus on the frame.
- Running the microphone into the camera yields very few choices as to the recording format of the incoming audio. For DV and HD cameras, audio is recorded at 48 kHz, 16 bits. Sync-sound recording devices offer a wide variety of sample rates and bit depths, allowing the filmmakers to record very high quality sound.
- Many new flash media–based recording devices allow instantaneous recording, playback, and transfer of sound files by shifting from tape-based recording to recording onto digital media.
- Several sync-sound recording devices record multitracks that allow the use of multiple microphones on set, each with its own channel. This allows the editor to choose between separate microphones to build the best audio track. Using multiple microphones while recording into the camera requires that the multiple feeds be mixed down to two channels, making it impossible to separate later.
- One drawback of sync-sound recording is the cost of the recording device. Some common recording devices are:

- **Nagra.** Nagra is an older, reel-to-reel analog recorder that was popular for its high sound quality and durability. Nagras were the primary recording tool used on set prior to the advent of digital recording technologies.
- **MiniDisc.** This format is a small recordable disc housed in a plastic casing. Developed for the consumer market, the MiniDisc never caught on in professional applications because the sound was overcompressed. This compression makes it a poor choice for location-based audio recording.
- **DAT.** Short for "digital audio tape," this format is a standard in professional audio recording and is still used on set today. Recording to inexpensive tapes, DAT recorders are inexpensive and durable, although adverse weather conditions may affect the contact point between the tape and the recording heads and cause audio dropouts.
- **Digital.** Digital recorders record directly to a hard drive and record reliable, high-quality audio. Digital recorders allow the user to play, seek, transfer, and delete individual clips instantly and offer a wider range of compression and audio formats.

- Recording sync sound requires the editor to line up the audio and visuals manually in the editing room. Although this process is not difficult, it is time-consuming.

BOOM HANDLING TECHNIQUES

The boom pole is used to suspend a microphone over the actors on set. Although using a boom pole seems easy, there are a number of techniques that are used to reduce boom-handling noise and improve the quality of the recorded audio.

- After the microphone is placed in the shock mount, tape the XLR cable to the end of the microphone end of the boom pole, alleviating any pressure or stress on the microphone. Be sure to allow enough slack so the microphone can be tilted up or down depending on the angle of the boom pole.

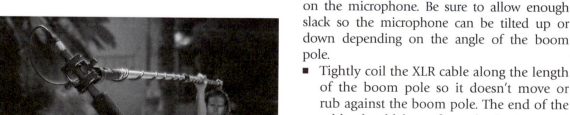

  - Tightly coil the XLR cable along the length of the boom pole so it doesn't move or rub against the boom pole. The end of the cable should hang from the back end of the boom pole.
  - When holding the boom, lock your hands in position as if your hands were glued to the boom. Do not move, twist, or rub your hands against the boom during a take because the microphone will pick up handling sounds.

- When holding the boom during a take, extend your arms straight above your head, as though you were hanging from a tree limb. This relieves muscle fatigue and helps keep the boom parallel to the top frame line, minimizing the risk of clipping the corners of the frame.
- Always point the microphone at the actor's chest and hold at a 45-degree angle in front of the actor, moving with the actor so the actor never falls outside the pickup pattern of the microphone.
- Never put the microphone in anyone's face.
- If you ever need to change the boom's position during a setup, notify the production sound mixer in the event that he needs to recheck the sound levels.
- When recording a scene in which the actors are walking, or there is complicated blocking, consider taking off your shoes to minimize the sound of your footsteps.
- When not in use, place the boom in the corner. Do not lay it on the floor or against a wall as it can fall, or be stepped on, damaging the microphone.
- Always wear headphones when operating the boom to ensure optimal placement of the microphone and to listen for any noise that could disrupt a take.
- Remember that changing the distance from the microphone to the subject is a much bigger problem than changing the distance from the subject to a light source. Maintain an equal and consistent distance between the microphone and the subject for optimum sound quality.

RECORDING WITH A SHOTGUN MICROPHONE

Most dialog on set is recorded using a *shotgun microphone*, a highly directional microphone that is usually suspended over the actors using a boom pole. Shotgun mikes are the best for isolating dialog spoken by the actors and their movements while reducing the ambient sound.

Shotgun microphones can be purchased for $500– $2,500 from Audio-Technica, Sennehiser, and Neumann or rented from an equipment rental company. In addition to the shotgun microphone, you will also need a shock mount, which suspends the microphone in a series of rubber bands to minimize boom-handling noise; a zeppelin or wind sock to place over the microphone to reduce wind noise; and a boom pole. Boom poles can be made inexpensively, or they can be rented. Be sure to have plenty of XLR cables on set, not only to ensure enough distance between the camera and microphone, but also 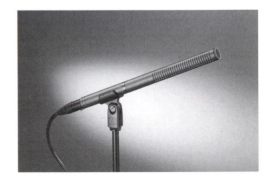 for backup in case one of the cables goes bad. Run the shotgun directly into the camera or external recording device and be sure to monitor the audio with headphones from the recording source. If you're recording the audio to the camera, plug the headphones into the camera. If you're recording to an external recording device, listen to the audio from the device.

Build an Inexpensive Boom Pole

Professional boom poles can cost up to $1,000, but why spend that money if you can build one for less than $100? A terrific, low-budget boom pole can be constructed from a telescopic paint roller extender available at a hardware store. Purchase a paint roller handle that will screw onto the end of the pole. Unscrew the roller from the handle and screw a shock mount (you can pick one up from a music/audio store) to the handle. Now you have a homemade boom pole.

USING LAVALIERS

Lavalier microphones are outstanding for recording interviews for documentaries or news, actors for corporate and industrial videos, and actors on stage. Although they can be used in film production, lavalier microphones are not the best choice for recording on-set dialog because the need to conceal them in an actor's wardrobe increases the chances the fabric will rub against the microphone and ruin the audio. However, by hiring a qualified production sound mixer who can place the lavalier microphone on the actor before each camera set-up, monitor the sound quality throughout each take and make mike placement adjustments as needed, lavaliers can provide near perfect recordings due to proximity and focused pickup pattern.

Lavaliers are best used in the following situations:

- Lavaliers allow localized recording of actor's lines by being placed within a foot of the actor's mouth. Provided the wardrobe allows for easy concealment of the microphone, cable and transmitter pack, lavs can be the best choice for dialog recording.
- Lavaliers can be placed closer to the actor's mouth in high-ambience locations, helping to improve the sound quality by increasing the signal-to-noise ratio.
- Use them when interviewing a subject or shooting a corporate video in which it is acceptable for the microphone to be seen.
- Use them in closed, cramped quarters such as in a car, when positioning a shotgun microphone is impractical. A common trick for recording sound in cars is to mount a lavalier mike above the sun visor of each actor and run the mike cable into a separate DV camcorder on the floor. Although separate from the main camera, which can be placed anywhere in or out of the car, this sync-sound rig produces surprisingly good results with minimal syncing efforts in the editing room.
- Where ambience is too loud, such as on a beach, using a lavalier microphone will help reduce ambience that a shotgun will more than likely pick up. A conversation between characters on the beach can be recorded using a little bit of audio trickery and careful art direction. Try running a lavalier mike up the pole of a beach umbrella and drilling a tiny hole on the side of the pole to stick the mike through. Place the umbrella close to the actors so they fall within the one-foot pickup pattern. The mike will pick up the dialog while reducing the ambience, which will be added in later.
- Lavaliers are sometimes used when actors are far away from the camera and positioning a shotgun microphone is impossible. Be aware that intermixing audio recorded by a shotgun and a lavalier will yield very different sounds and could prove challenging to edit.
- Although lavalier microphones record strong dialog, they will not pick up ambience and an actor's interactions with her environment as well as a shotgun mike. Often, using a lavalier requires additional Foley work in postproduction to fill in the sounds that weren't recorded on set.
- One challenge of using lavaliers is that they are fixed in one position on an actor's body, so when the actor turns her head, her voice may trail off as she talks away from the microphone.

WIRELESS MICROPHONE SYSTEMS

Wireless systems use a transmitter connected to the end of a microphone to send the audio signal to a receiver mounted on either the camera or a sync-sound recorder. Wireless systems free the boom operator from the confines of being tethered to the recording device by XLR cables and allow microphones to be mounted on actors or sets without unsightly cables. Although beneficial, wireless systems are prone to a number of problems.

Some of the benefits of working with wireless systems:

- The number of cables running to and from the boom microphone, camera, or sync-sound recorder is reduced.
- They allow wireless lavalier mikes to be inconspicuously placed on the set or on actors.
- The production sound mixer can be located anywhere on or off set, as long as he is within the range of the transmitter.
- The boom operator has the freedom to move and place the microphone anywhere without worrying about tripping on cables.
- They save setup time by reducing the need to rewire and restring XLR cables from the microphones to the production sound mixer.

Some of the drawbacks of wireless systems:

- All wireless devices are prone to picking up transmissions from other devices, especially radio stations and other wireless transmitters on similar frequencies. Purchasing high-quality UHF systems gives users the flexibility to change frequencies for cleaner audio.
- The wireless signal can be disrupted by large metal objects like fences, trucks, buildings, and power lines, which may introduce interference. This interference can be minimized by using fresh batteries in the unit and minimizing the distance between the transmitter and the receiver.
- Wireless lavalier transmitters may be difficult to hide on actors, but can be attached to their belt, thigh, or ankle using straps or gaffer's tape.
- The range of wireless systems can affect the quality of the audio. The greater the distance between the transmitter and the receiver, the weaker the signal.
- Wireless transmitters and receivers require a lot of battery power. Be sure to have plenty of extra batteries on set.

One of the most common types of wireless microphone is a wireless lavalier, which consists of a small fingernail-sized microphone attached to a transmitter via wire that the actor usually wears on his belt. The transmitter is a battery-powered unit about the size of a pack of cigarettes. The receiver is connected to the camera, usually with XLR inputs. With a range of about 50–1,000 feet, depending on the quality of the mike, wireless microphones are mostly used for "walk and talk" scenes that would be difficult to record with a boom pole.

Always use headphones on set and listen for interference as the scene is being recorded.

AMBIENT SOUND

Ambient sound is the background noise of a location. For example, waves, seagulls, and wind are the ambient sounds of a beach, and traffic, horns, and people talking are the ambient sounds of a city street. Although ambient sounds are important in helping establish the location, they must be reduced as much as possible so that on set, the only sounds recorded are the actors' dialog and their movements. Ambient sounds are then added to the entire scene in postproduction, helping add consistency to a scene. There are several techniques to help minimize the ambience. Most importantly, listen on set during the location scout to determine what sounds are present. Most often, the ambient sounds will be air conditioning units and refrigerators. Talk to the location owner about turning these off on the day on the shoot.

Interior locations are easier to control because the walls absorb much of the sound from the outside. Shooting outdoors makes controlling ambient sounds more difficult. If you're in a noisy location, bring several packing blankets (available from your local mover) and hang them on C-stands to create movable "sound walls" that can be positioned between the actors and the source of the sound. Place the sound blankets behind lights and the camera after all the equipment has been set up. If you're recording in a church or a large room with a lot of echo, try placing the packing blankets on the floor under the actors to absorb the sound. It is important to minimize the ambience as much as possible to save time and money in postproduction. If there is too much ambient noise, you may need to ADR the actors' dialog and then recreate the Foley and ambience. This is a time-consuming and expensive process that can be avoided by using these techniques on set.

WORKING WITH EXTRAS

There may be scenes that involve background actors or extras, such as a restaurant, bus station, auditorium, or any other public place. Although in real life you can hear the ambience of people talking, laughing, chatting on cell phones, arguing, and otherwise interacting with their environment, when you film that moment in a movie, filmmakers instruct the extras to *act* as if they are talking but to *say nothing*. The only sound that should be heard on set when the cameras roll is the sound of the principal actors delivering their lines and their interaction with the environment. The rest of the ambience is recorded later and mixed in during the editing process, giving the filmmakers control over the balance between background sounds and dialog.

Jason's Notes

A few years ago, I shot a short film called *The Overcoat* that featured a scene in a grocery store. In order to control the environment, we closed down the store on a Sunday night; populated it with extras; turned off the overhead music, coolers, and appliances; oiled the shopping cart wheels; and asked the extras not to make any sounds when the camera rolled. Although it seemed bizarre to see people miming their actions, it allowed us to record the actors' dialog cleanly and without competition from background noise.

Later, in the editing room, we added the sounds of people talking, squeaky shopping carts, tacky elevator music, beeping price scanners, bag boys loading up groceries, and a baby crying, among other sounds that added to the realism of the moment back into the scene. As a result, we were able to control the volume of each individual sound so nothing competed with the dialog. The result was a scene that appeared to be recorded in a busy, bustling grocery store.

SOUND LOGS

The production sound mixer should maintain complete and comprehensive sound logs, which list the audio take, the scene and setup, the timecode of each take, and any notes regarding the quality of each take. These sound logs will help the editor determine which take is best to use and aid in finding a particular take.

TIPS FOR RECORDING GOOD ON-SET AUDIO

- Choose locations that are as quiet as possible, away from freeways, airports, hospitals, police stations, and fire stations.
- When in the location, disable anything that makes noise, including refrigerators and air conditioners.
- Use a shotgun microphone to isolate and record *only* the dialog from the actors and *never* use the built-in microphone in the camera.
- Position the microphone on a boom pole above the actors at a 45-degree angle and aim the microphone at the actor's chest.
- The camera operator and boom operator should be listening to the audio over headphones to ensure maximum sound quality.
- Make sure that the audio levels average between ~3 and ~6 db on the audio meters and *never* hit or exceed 0 db.
- Record with XLR (or balanced) cables only from the mike to the camera. Using unbalanced cables creates an antenna that picks up unwanted signals like radio stations.
- If there is a lot of ambient noise such as traffic, waves on a beach, or wind, try setting up several stands and hanging furniture pads or other thick material around the set to absorb some of the sound before it hits the microphone.
- At the end of the shoot, in each location, always record 30–60 seconds of the ambient sound of the location. Ensure the cast and crew stand perfectly still so the room tone is as pure as possible. This will come into play during the editing process, in which the room tone will be used under shots with no audio, or to fix problems with the ambience track.

PRODUCTION
SOUND
REPORT

Date _____

Scenes _____

Roll _____

Production _____   Frame Rate _____

Client _____   Sample Rate _____

Director _____   Bit Depth _____

Sound Mixer _____

Sync ☐

To Camera ☐

Transfer Circled
Takes Only ☐

NOTES _____

_____

_____

_____

Scene	Take	Timecode @ Slate	Comments
		: :	
		: :	
		: :	
		: :	
		: :	
		: :	
		: :	
		: :	
		: :	
		: :	
		: :	
		: :	
		: :	
		: :	
		: :	
		: :	
		: :	
		: :	
		: :	
		: :	
		: :	
		: :	
		: :	
		: :	
		: :	
		: :	

CHAPTER 15
Hair and Makeup

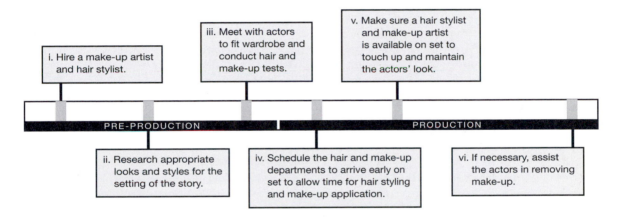

i. Hire a make-up artist and hair stylist.

ii. Research appropriate looks and styles for the setting of the story.

iii. Meet with actors to fit wardrobe and conduct hair and make-up tests.

iv. Schedule the hair and make-up departments to arrive early on set to allow time for hair styling and make-up application.

v. Make sure a hair stylist and make-up artist is available on set to touch up and maintain the actors' look.

vi. If necessary, assist the actors in removing make-up.

PRE-PRODUCTION

PRODUCTION

INTRODUCTION

Makeup and hairstyling are an essential part of making a movie, for both practical and technical reasons. Whereas the creative aspects are obvious, it is important for a hair and makeup artist to monitor the continuity of the actors' look as well as to ensure that the actors aren't shiny or sweaty or have hair that will draw attention away from their performance.

STRAIGHT MAKEUP

Straight makeup (or *beauty makeup*) is noneffects makeup designed to maintain the actor's flesh tones, minimize oil and shine that show up under production lights, and help facial features stand out on camera. Both male and female actors wear makeup that is usually applied by an experienced makeup artist at the beginning of each production day and touched up before every take, ensuring that the actor's look remains consistent during the course of the scene.

Most makeup is applied so that the actor looks natural. Although we often think of plaster-faced news anchors or highly made-up fashion models, most movie actors wear makeup applied to look like they're not wearing makeup. The ability to create

Filmmaking.
© 2011 Jason J. Tomaric. Published by Elsevier Inc. All rights reserved.

Makeup artist Jason Blaszczak touches up Brian Ireland.

a natural look is difficult and often requires skills beyond traditional daily makeup application.

Even elements like sweat and dirt must be carefully maintained by makeup artists to ensure consistency from take to take.

- Determine the work load during preproduction, the number of actors to be made up, the amount of makeup, and the complexity of the makeup, and then figure out how many makeup artists are needed.
- Discuss how much time is needed at the beginning of each day to apply makeup on the main actors and schedule call times for actors and makeup artists accordingly.
- Remember to factor the cost of makeup materials into the budget. Even though makeup artists may be willing to work for free, many will expect to be, and should be, compensated for the cost of their materials.
- Makeup artists should discuss the look of the lighting with the director of photography. The color of the lighting, harshness, and wraparound and whether the light is a bluish outdoor light or warmer tungsten light that will affect the look of the actors. Make sure the makeup complements the lighting.
- Test the makeup on the actors before getting to set to save time and alleviate problems with colors chosen or the application process.
- Make sure there are adequate facilities and power for makeup artists and hairstylists to do their jobs on set. Although you may be shooting in a remote location, it is important that the artists have the resources they need.
- Once the actors' hair and makeup is done in the morning, it is important to touch it up for each and every take, requiring that a hairstylist and makeup artist be on set and ready to tweak the actor's look before the camera rolls.
- When producing a period film, hairstylists and makeup artists can help create a convincing and believable look for each character, but keep in mind that time needs to be factored into the schedule for them to do their jobs.
- Take Polaroid or digital photos of the actors to maintain a continuous look throughout the production of the movie.

Makeup in Preproduction

In much the same way a cinematographer changes the lighting throughout the movie to reflect the emotional subtext of each scene, the key makeup artist and key hair stylist break down the script and develop a change of the character's look based on the emotional content of each scene. The intensity or subtlety of the look is determined from numerous meetings with you in preproduction.

Test Shoots

For characters that require elaborate makeup, shoot a test scene with the actor in full hair, makeup, and even wardrobe to see how the character looks on screen. After viewing the results, subtle changes can be made – perhaps the flesh tones are too pale or too ruddy, the hairstyle might conceal the actor's eyes too much, or the look just isn't quite right. It's always better to work out the details of the hairstyling and makeup before production actually begins.

During Production

Once an actor arrives on set, she is taken to the makeup artist and hairstylist. On low-budget movies, this may be the same person, but if a lot of actors need to go through the makeup chair, or the hair styling is elaborate, additional artists should be hired. In general, male straight makeup and hairstyling is much easier and faster than a woman's hair and makeup and should be scheduled accordingly.

Once on set, a hair stylist and makeup artist should always be present, checking the actor before each and every take. Before asking the cameras to roll, the 1st assistant director will often call for "last looks," which gives the stylist an opportunity to apply a coat of powder, touch up the lipstick, or adjust a stray hair.

Continuity

When a character undergoes an emotional transformation during the story, makeup and wardrobe are used as tools to help support this character arc. Because scenes and even shots are filmed out of order, makeup departments carefully document and track the look of each character's makeup and hair from one scene to the next so it can be easily reproduced and is ultimately continuous throughout the story.

Once the makeup is complete for a scene, the makeup artist and hair stylist photograph the actor in a frontal and profile shot. These photos are labeled and added to a reference book, helping ensure the overall continuity of each character's look.

MAKEUP TERMS

- **Straight makeup**: The standard, noneffects beauty makeup applied to male and female actors.
- **Special effects makeup**: Prosthetics, foam latex appliances, gashes, cuts, and bruises all fall under this category. Special effects makeup artists require special training to perform these types of effects competently.
- **Key makeup**: The lead makeup artist to whom all other makeup artists answer.

Jason's Notes

Developing the look of the female characters was extremely important in creating a realistic 1950s film, so key hairstylist Deb Lilly and key makeup artist Jason Blaszczak did a lot of research before *Time and Again* went into production. We studied 1958 hairstyles and makeup trends and performed several tests on the actors to make sure that the look of our characters was accurate.

The two most striking changes were in Jennie Allen, who played Awanda, and Paula Williams, who played Bobby Jones's mother, Martha.

The platinum-blond hairstyle (that nearly ruined Jennie's hair) completely transformed Jennie by giving her the Marilyn Monroe look I had always envisioned for the story. We worked to make sure that Awanda's hair would work with the pink waitress outfit, coordinating her look with the hair, makeup, and wardrobe departments.

Paula's transformation was even more incredible. Jason's makeup job and Deb's hairstyle were so different from Paula's normal look that Paula's own sister didn't recognize her. Unbelievably, Paula is not wearing a wig in the film!

These looks, while drastic in real life, appear as normal on screen and accepted as what these women would have looked like in July 1958.

Jennie without makeup.

Jennie with makeup.

Paula without makeup.

Paula with makeup.

BUILDING A MAKEUP KIT

If the production is so small that the budget doesn't allow for a makeup artist, consider building a small makeup kit to use on set. A basic makeup kit can include:

- **Pancake.** Pancake is a powder that is tinted to match the skin tones and is used to reduce shine. There are numerous shades, so be sure to perform tests on the actors before arriving on set to ensure a color match. Pancake is applied over the entire face as a finishing makeup.

- **Greasepaint.** Extremely thick makeup used for theatrical applications that helps facial features stand out.
- **Concealer.** Covers imperfections of the skin, blemishes, acne, and circles under the eyes. After applying concealer to problem areas of the skin, apply pancake to cover and blend the makeup.
- **Powder.** Lighter than pancake and usually translucent, powder is used all over the face to reduce shine. Be sure to keep plenty of powder on set to keep sweaty actors looking dry.
- **Highlights.** Highlights are used to accentuate parts of the face by drawing attention to or away from facial features like the nose, cheekbones, or chin by creating fake "shadows." Use highlights to make a large nose appear smaller or to reduce the appearance of a double chin.
- **Blush.** Adds a touch of color to an actress's cheekbones.
- **Lip color.** Adds color to an actor's lips.
- **Lip gloss.** Adds a sheen to an actor's lips.
- **Eye liner.** Applied around the actor's eyes to bring out the shape and details of the eyes.
- **Mascara.** Applied to bring out the eyelashes.
- **Application tools.** Latex sponges, lip brush, powder puff, fluffy powder puff, cotton swabs.
- **Cold cream.** Used to remove heavy makeup while protecting and moisturizing the skin. Cold cream helps reduce damage to the skin caused by makeup.
- **Removers.** Makeup remover.
- **Miscellaneous.** Aprons, drop cloths, facial tissues, cotton balls, cotton swabs.

PROSTHETICS

Makeup prosthetics are foam latex appliances that are glued to an actor's body to create everything from simple special effects like burns, scars, and cuts to major makeup effects like turning an actor into a monster or alien. These appliances are created from a mold that is taken of the actor's face to ensure that the appliance fits correctly. Then, using the mold as a reference, the makeup artist is able to sculpt a foam latex appliance that will be painted and glued to the skin.

Foam latex is an effective material for appliances because it mimics the look and movement of human skin and muscle, is lightweight, and is able to "breathe."

It is advisable to hire an experienced makeup prosthetics artist if appliances are needed for the story. These makeup effects look terrific when they're done properly.

- When using makeup prosthetics, be sure to schedule enough time on set to allow the application of the makeup appliance.
- Talk to the makeup artist in advance to determine the cost of materials needed to produce the desired effect.
- In productions with a heavy effects work load, it may be necessary to bring numerous makeup artists to the set.

SPECIAL EFFECTS MAKEUP

Special effects makeup includes everything from blood to scars. These basic effects can be easily and inexpensively accomplished with common ingredients available from the grocery store.

Jason's Notes

Time and Again ends with the camera dollying out from Bobby Jones, who is kneeling in the prison yard about to die from a shotgun wound. Because of the length of the shoot and how long the audience would be staring at the wound, Jason Blaszczak created a wound that could be applied within an hour while the crew reset the shot.

The prison gave us only one night to shoot the entire prison break as well as the final shot, so we were racing against the sun to finish the scenes. Because of the time crunch, we couldn't wait for Jason to apply a complete makeup prosthetic, so he jury-rigged a shotgun blast makeup effect that worked well.

Thanks to tight scheduling, Jason's smart thinking, creative lighting, and Brian's terrific performance, we were able to convince the audience that Bobby was shot in the chest, making the end of *Time and Again* as powerful as I envisioned.

- **Fake blood.** Go to the grocery store and purchase corn syrup. Similar to maple syrup, corn syrup is clear to yellowish in color and has the consistency of blood. Mix it with a few drops of red food coloring and a dash of blue to make a deep-red blood-like color.
- **Scars.** Go to the grocery store and purchase unflavored gelatin. Mix one tablespoon of gelatin into a tablespoon of near-boiling water so it completely dissolves. Be sure to avoid any bubbles. Wait for the mixture to cool, and then apply it to the skin, building and molding it as needed. Be careful because the gelatin will cool and harden quickly. Once dry, apply regular makeup to match skin tones.
- **Sweat.** Try using baby oil in a spray bottle. The oil won't evaporate as quickly as water and provides a great sheen for the camera.

HAIRSTYLING

Working with a professional hairstylist can add an artistic touch when creating the look of a character, establish a time period, and ensure hair continuity from one scene to the next. Be mindful of extras as well as principal characters. With a movie like *Time and Again*, each extra needed to have hair styled by our makeup team before every shooting day. This made the 1950s era the story was set in look realistic.

When working with hairstylists, provide the necessary resources on set for them to work, including access to power, a trailer, tent, tables, makeup chairs, and mirrors. For *Time and Again*, hairstylist Deb Lilly worked everywhere from bathrooms in nearby homes for the dirt road scenes to under tents in Chardon to process the nearly 100 extras for Bobby Jones's run through the town.

- When talking with a hairstylist, find out if the actor needs to go through any hair treatments prior to each shooting day. Jennie, who played Awanda, needed extensive sessions to dye her hair the platinum blond color that turned her into Awanda.
- When casting, notify the actors during the audition process if there are extensive hairstyle requirements, such as if a man needs a buzz cut for a military role.

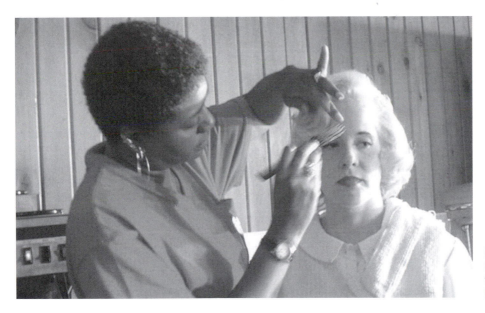

Key hair stylist Deb Lilly puts the finishing touches on Jennie Allen's hair.

CHAPTER 16
Craft Services and Catering

i. Circulate requests for special food needs (vegetarian, allergies).	iii. Purchase perishable food the night before or the morning of each shooting day.	iv. Have craft services (especially coffee) available 30 minutes before call time.	vi. Provide a meal every six hours.

PRE-PRODUCTION **PRODUCTION**

ii. Purchase bulk non-perishable snacks and food within a week before the shoot.	v. Replenish craft services throughout the day.	vii. Always remove trash at the end of the day.

INTRODUCTION

The cast and crew of any movie will tell you that second to being paid, the availability of good food on set is the most important aspect of a movie production. Especially if the project is a low-budget project and the cast and crew are volunteering their time, providing craft services and catering is essential not only to keep everyone's energy up, but also to maintain positive morale on set.

It's standard industry practice to provide a meal every six hours. Although larger-budget movies hire a caterer to prepare a hot breakfast and several lunch or dinner options, meals on low-budget productions can be as simple as sub sandwiches, pizza, or pasta and salad. Always keep meals healthy and varied, and you will have a happy, productive cast and crew for a whole day of shooting.

In producing an independent movie, craft services and catering will most likely be the most expensive line item on the budget. Do not cut back on the food for the set – it is often said that if the cast and crew are well fed, they will follow the director anywhere.

The food on set can be divided into two different categories: craft services and catering.

Filmmaking.
© 2011 Jason J. Tomaric. Published by Elsevier Inc. All rights reserved.

A well-stocked craft services table on set is without a doubt, hands-down, unquestionably the most important thing on set. Good crafty = happy crew.

CRAFT SERVICES

Craft services are buffet-style snacks and drinks served continuously throughout the shooting day. Featuring an assortment of hot and cold drinks, fresh fruit, vegetables, deli meats, candy, and snacks, craft services helps keep everyone going during long production days.

Usually a freelancer who specializes in preparing and managing the craft services table is hired to purchase the food, bring the tables, and prepare and maintain the food during the course of the day, although on low-budget projects a production assistant can be assigned these duties.

When planning craft services, be aware of the shooting location and the weather conditions and plan the food selection accordingly. In general, most craft services items must be easy for the crew to grab and eat on the run.

BREAKFAST

Craft services usually arrives and is set up 30 minutes before call time, so any crew members wishing to eat breakfast can arrive early on set.

A typical breakfast spread includes:

- An assortment of bagels.
- Cream cheese, butter, and jelly in individual packs. Avoid purchasing jars as it can get messy.
- An assortment of donuts.
- An assortment of muffins.
- Fresh fruit: apples, bananas, pears, and peaches. Cut them into small, easy-to-grab pieces.
- Hot coffee with cream, sugar, nondairy creamer, coffee stirrers, and coffee cups. Consider bringing a coffee maker to the set, as coffee is the primary drink of choice throughout the day.
- An assortment of juices, especially orange juice and apple juice.
- Bottled water (lots of it).
- An assortment of cereal travel packs with milk. The crew can eat out of the box.
- An assortment of yogurt.

THROUGHOUT THE DAY

After breakfast, the craft services table is updated with new selections throughout the day. Common items include:

- Mixed nuts
- Trail mix

A typical craft services table on set.

- Peanut butter and jelly
- Bread for sandwiches
- Potato chips and pretzels
- Raisins
- Fresh fruit
- A deli tray
- Raw vegetables
- Granola bars
- Chocolates and candies
- Chewing gum and breath mints

Also include a variety of hot and cold beverages throughout the day:

- Coffee . . . all the time
- Hot water and a variety of teas
- Bottled water (try buying half-size bottles of water, as less will go to waste)
- Caffeinated and caffeine-free soda
- Juice

If you're working on a tight budget, approach local grocery stores and ask them to donate craft service items. Also be sure to check out large wholesale stores where you can buy bulk items inexpensively. Send a production assistant on a craft services run several days before the shoot for nonperishable items and have him pick up fresh food items the morning of each shooting day.

Most film sets serve hot meals buffet-style, with two or three entrée choices, a vegetarian entrée, vegetables, beverages and a dessert.

Here are some tips for setting up a craft services table on set:

- Craft services food should be easily accessible and easy to grab during the day. Avoid food that needs to be overly prepped.
- Set up the craft services table near the set, but not so close that it is in the way.
- Be aware of bugs, wind, or animals that may disrupt the food, so pick a location where the food will be safe for the entire day of shooting.
- Have fresh coffee ready three hours after call time and three hours after lunch, when the crew starts to slow down. Also have abundant coffee ready after dinner, especially if the shooting goes into the night.
- During the location scout, determine where power can be drawn for the coffee pot and toaster. Make sure the location owner has given permission to serve food on set and approves the designated location.

CATERING

Catering includes the full meals served for lunch and dinner. Typically provided by a catering company or restaurant, catered meals consist of boxed meals or a buffet-style layout. Full meals should be served six hours after call time and every six hours afterward, based on standard industry guidelines. In fully paid union situations, cast and crew members are paid extra money if the meals are served late because shooting runs overtime.

Catered meals usually include a choice of two different entrees, one of which is pasta or rice; a salad; several sides; and a dessert. Larger-budget productions can increase the selection of food, and sometimes a chef is hired on set to prepare custom meals for the cast and crew. Be sure to include vegetarian and vegan entrées.

When I produced low-budget films, I would negotiate with local restaurants to prepare the food, bring the food to the set, set up the tables, serve the food, and clean up afterward, allowing the crew to focus on the production. For *Time and Again*, for which the budget was limited, I was able to convince several restaurants to donate food, free of charge. I also approached grocery stores that donated beverages, condiments, plates, napkins, and utensils, and even some sides like potato salad and cole slaw. If we weren't able to negotiate these deals, the producers and I would make big containers of pasta to bring to set, which is cheap and easy to prepare and provides a hearty meal.

Choose food that is healthy and energy-inducing. Remember that shooting a movie is long, tedious work, so having good food on set will help maintain everyone's energy level and make for a much more pleasant demeanor on set.

When choosing catered meals, here are some suggestions that are both nutritious and inexpensive:

- Sub sandwiches (meat, tuna, and vegetarian)
- Pasta, either hot or cold; pasta salads
- Pizza (although not for every meal, please)
- Chicken (always good for protein)
- Fresh salads

TIPS FOR ON SET

- If the location you're working on has a refrigerator, ask them if you can use it. Don't assume you can. Always clean it out at the end of each shooting day.
- *Never, ever* serve alcohol on set, even if the actors are "drinking" in the scene. Every alcoholic beverage can be faked using diluted soda, juice, or food-colored water.
- Provide vegetarian options or any other special dietary requirements of the cast and crew. Send out an email before production asking cast and crew members if they have any special requirements.
- When ordering food from a restaurant, contact the manager a week in advance to make all necessary preparations, including the number of people being served, types of food, delivery and pickup information, time the food is needed, and cost.
- Be sure to bring plenty of garbage bags so you can dispose of your own trash yourself. Never use public trash cans or private dumpsters, unless you have permission to do so.
- Assign a production assistant the duty of picking up and maintaining the craft services table if you cannot afford a dedicated craft services company.

UNIT 4
Postproduction

i. Comb through the rough footage and decide the best takes to use.

ii. The editor begins assembling the rough footage into scenes, making editorial decisions based on the director's vision.

iii. Once the rough movie is assembled, the begin altering and adjusting the order, length and timing of the movie to improve the quality of the storytelling, understandability and pacing.

iv. The movie is screened before a test audience to see how they react, which parts of the movie are slow or difficult to understand, and how they feel about the film when it's over. The audience reaction is heavily considered when making changes to the movie during post-production.

Editing **Visual Effects** **Editing**

i. The visual effects team will begin taking the rough footage and adding digital effects, color correcting and enhancing various shots, then give them to the editor to put back into the final movie.

i. The opening and closing credits are created and edited into the movie.

ii. Additional editorial changes are made as the director and editor continue to refine the edit.

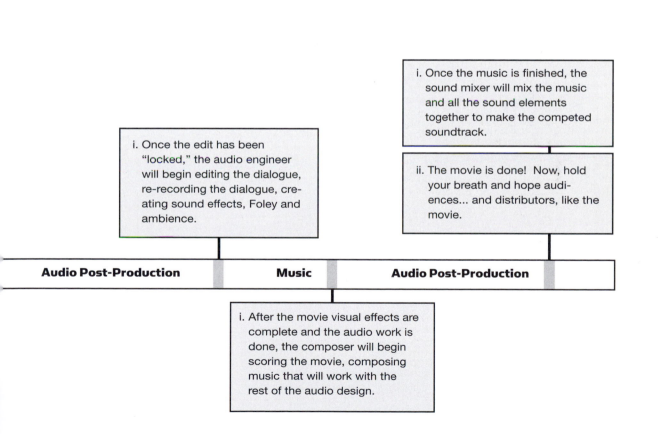

i. Once the edit has been "locked," the audio engineer will begin editing the dialogue, re-recording the dialogue, creating sound effects, Foley and ambience.

i. Once the music is finished, the sound mixer will mix the music and all the sound elements together to make the competed soundtrack.

ii. The movie is done! Now, hold your breath and hope audiences... and distributors, like the movie.

Audio Post-Production

Music

Audio Post-Production

i. After the movie visual effects are complete and the audio work is done, the composer will begin scoring the movie, composing music that will work with the rest of the audio design.

CHAPTER 17
Editing

i. The assistant editor digitizes or imports rough footage into a non-linear editing system.

iii. Discuss the style of the film with the editor and choose the best takes for each scene.

vi. Refine the primary story, subplots, character arcs, pacing and emotion of the movie.

vii. The editor adds rough or complete digital effects to the rough cut for timing.

xii. Final credits are added and the movie is rendered and exported.

POST-PRODUCTION

v. Give the editor feedback and rework the overall story and order of scenes.

xi. Individual shots and entire scenes are color corrected.

iv. The editor builds an assembly cut, editing the footage to the script.

viii. Rough sound effects are layed in to help tell the story.

ii. Organize footage by labeling each shot with a scene, set-up and take number both at the desktop and editing software level.

ix. Screen the rough cut for a test audience to determine problems in pacing, characterization and comprehensibility.

x. The editor tweaks and polishes the edit, adding transitions and perfecting every cut.

INTRODUCTION

It is in the editing room that the most important part of the movie-making process occurs. Lit solely by the dim glow of production monitors, the editor meticulously pieces together the potentially thousands of individual shots to create a sweeping sense of emotion and pacing, and ultimately a story that will move hearts and minds. Running alongside the understanding of the hardware and software is a river of emotions and feelings that may not actually exist in the rough footage, but can be created by how the shots are assembled.

Filmmaking.
© 2011 Jason J. Tomaric. Published by Elsevier Inc. All rights reserved.

Editing a movie is the process of trying and retrying, assembling and disassembling, shuffling and shifting each shot so the whole movie becomes greater than the sum of its parts. In this chapter, we will look at the editing process from a creative standpoint – not which button to push or how to add transitions, but rather the basic core of editing: when to cut from one shot to the next, how to create emotion, and why one edit works and another doesn't.

WORKING WITH THE EDITOR

The editor holds a very special position in the filmmaking process. An artist in his own right, the editor is tasked with assembling the rough footage in a way that fulfills your vision. However, whereas you have been involved with the film for months, possibly years, the editor has an objective point of view and can spot problems in story and pacing you may never see. For this reason, you must trust the editor and give him breathing room to build the story.

Watch a video detailing the relationship between the director and editor at Filmskills. com. See page vi for details.

Jason's Notes

My editor, Brad Schwartz, is my best friend – I trust him implicitly, know the story is in his best interests, and am confident that he will argue with me to fight for what he believes is the right editorial decision. I not only enjoy but want that creative banter, because by the end of the day, regardless of which of us wins the argument, the story ultimately triumphs.

Objectivity

The biggest disservice you can do for the film is to sit over the editor's shoulder and direct each edit. This common mistake not only takes away the editor's creativity as an artist, but also your ability to make objective decisions as to how the film will cut together. Let's face it: you have spent months, possibly years, working on the movie and you know every detail of the story. Subsequently, plot holes may be invisible to you as you mentally fill in gaps with your knowledge and familiarity with the story. That's why working with an editor is so important – editors come onboard later in the process and aren't exposed to the creative process during production. When they receive the footage, they can objectively build the story with the available shots.

Be smart and give the editor guidance that allows her to build the assembly cut alone. Once the assembly cut is finished, you can come in fresh, watch the film, and give the editor notes as to what changes need to be made.

Jason's Notes

Low-budget productions that cannot afford a postproduction supervisor rely heavily on the editor to coordinate with the sound editors, the composer, colorist, and all other postproduction people, essentially serving as the hub of the digital wheel.

When to Hire the Editor

The decision as to when to hire the editor is dependent on the budget. Ideally, the editor will be brought on board in preproduction, so he is involved early in the creative decision-making process. Once the film enters production, the editor receives the footage daily, assembling the film as it is shot, allowing the editor to spot problems in the edit and notify you if you need to reshoot an out-of-focus shot or get an insert that would help the flow of the story. By the time the film is shot, the editor will have the assembly cut completed, greatly expediting the postproduction process.

The less-ideal option is to hire the editor after the footage has been shot. Although this saves money up front, it may cost more money to budget reshoots and pickup days if a scene doesn't work.

One viable option is to hire a media manager on set who can also work as an assistant editor. Because this individual is already on payroll and has hours of time between transfers of shot media to hard drives, adding the duty of assembling each scene saves both time and money in post production.

What to Look for when Hiring an Editor

Unlike hiring a cinematographer or production designer whose demo reel work is easy to critique, it's difficult to assess the quality of an editor's work. A scene that appears simple on screen may have been an editing feat of assembling discontinuous shots, poor performances, or fixing technical issues. On the contrary, scenes of spectacularly fast edits could have been easily edited because of an overzealous director's desire to overshoot coverage of every scene.

Jason's Notes

Finding an editor who knows how to use the software is easy. It's the skill of crafting emotion from the rough footage, pacing the story to engage the audience, and building a rhythm that separates the real editors from the button pushers.

If you're hiring an editor for a narrative film, look beyond stylistic editing of montages, music videos, or commercials, as these artistic projects don't provide good insight into an editor's ability to craft a story. When interviewing an editor, ask to watch one of her dramatic projects. Ask about specific scenes, what motivated certain edits, or challenges she faced when cutting the scene. Determine how the editor approached the story and what motivated her edits.

Once you feel confident about the editor's storytelling abilities, show her the rough footage from one of your scenes and ask her how she would approach the edit. Why would she cut from one shot to the next? Why would she use cuts instead of dissolves in the montage sequences, and how would she build the arc for the story through the edit?

The most important factor is trust: do you trust the editor to best represent the story and commit to making it as good as it can be? If the answer is yes, then consider bringing the editor on to cut a few sample scenes before hiring her.

Some tips and tricks to keep in mind when working with an editor:

- **Concentrate and focus.** The editor is the keeper and manipulator of the footage, builder of the story, and the objective eyes of the director. Tasked with building the best possible story out of potentially thousands of shots, sound effects, lines of dialog and music cues, it's important to be completely immersed in the story and footage. Part of being able to concentrate is setting up a quiet area where he can work uninterrupted. Make sure the editor can aside specific time to work on the film, turning off the phone or television so that he can fully immerse himself in the world you are creating. Although it takes hundreds of people to produce the footage, it really rests on the shoulders of the one editor to put it together.
- **A good editor spends more time thinking than editing.** The actual physical process of cutting a film is fairly quick and easy, but the majority of the editor's time is spent discussing the ordering of scenes, what shots work and which don't, options and alternate ways of telling the story, how to improve the performances, and how to correct pacing issues and address the flow of the story with you. The editing process involves a little bit of cutting, but a lot of thought, discussion, and analyzing to determine whether the edit has improved the movie. Welcome and be open to this dialog, for it is in these conversations that the real art of editing happens.
- **If you're directing the movie, bring on an experienced, objective editor.** No matter how good of an editor you think you are, *never* cut your own film. You know it too well and will mentally fill in plot holes because you know the story so well. You need the objectivity of a third party.

EDITING SYSTEMS
Building an Editing System

A decade ago, footage was edited by linking two VCRs, one that played the rough footage and a second that recorded selected clips onto a blank tape. A

Linear editors forced editors to cut the story from the beginning to the end, and although this limits the editor's creativity, it also really forced the editor to think about each edit and why it was important.

movie was cut linearly, from the beginning to the end, limiting the editor's ability to make changes earlier in the program.

Nonlinear editing frees the editor from this restriction by allowing the editor to edit any part of the movie at any time while preserving the integrity of the original footage. Sophisticated software brings a myriad of editing, titling, transition, and effects tools right to the desktop of your home computer.

Nonlinear editors work on the principle that rough footage is digitized, or converted into the binary language of ones and zeros, and stored on a hard drive. An editing program like Apple Final Cut Pro, Avid, or Adobe Premiere is then used to assemble the clips into a logical sequence, add titles and transitions, color correct, and even composite clips together. The software isn't altering the original files on the hard drive at all, but is rather creating a playlist, in much the same way a CD player can be programmed to play music tracks in a certain order. Just as the CD player does not affect the actual media on the CD, nonlinear editing systems reference but don't affect the clips on the hard drive.

As you edit a sequence, the editing program plays the marked sections of each movie file from the hard drive fast enough to appear continuous and seamless. If the editor changes a movie clip by changing the color, brightness, adding any filters, titles or transitions, the computer must calculate the changes and render new frames. Many of these effects can be rendered in real time, although

Nonlinear editing systems give you, the director, the opportunity to change any part of the movie at any time. This flexibility, though certainly improving the story, can make it difficult to know when to put the proverbial paintbrush down.

complicated effects may require additional rendering time for the computer to play them. If this happens, the computer saves the newly rendered shot on the hard drive and plays it at the appropriate time in the sequence. For example, if a shot dissolves into another shot, the computer will play the original first clip up to the dissolve, then it will play the new clip it made of the dissolve, then it will jump back the play the original latter half of the second clip. To the viewer, this process is seamless.

Because it is a nondestructive process, editors can undo, change, and alter previous edits at any time, in any part of the movie.

Some of the most common editing programs include:

- Apple Final Cut Pro
- Apple iMovie
- Avid Media Composer
- Media 100
- Avid Xpress Pro
- Avid FreeDV
- Adobe Premiere Pro
- Pinnacle Studio
- Window's Movie Maker
- Sony Vegas

Monitors

Many editors and colorists base the look of a production on how it appears on the monitor, so it's important to have a properly calibrated production monitor. Unlike consumer monitors, production monitors have a higher resolution, greater dynamic range, and finer calibration controls. Although professional production monitors cost thousands of dollars, you can be certain the image you see on screen is what you're actually getting.

Speakers

Good speakers are to sound what a good monitor is to the picture. Using professional, flat speakers ensures you hear the entire sound spectrum, from extremely low end to high end. Unlike consumer speakers, which are capable of playing only the mid-range sound, professional speakers allow editors to hear the low rumble of ambient sound, high-pitched ringing from fluorescent lights, and other extremes that may be heard only on high-end sound systems.

Backups

With nonlinear editing being the predominant form of editing a movie and the entire movie existing entirely on a hard drive, it's important to continuously and religiously back up your data. Traditionally, a project has three redundant hard drives. One drive is the working hard drive used to edit the footage; the second hard drive is a perfect copy of the working drive, backed up on a daily basis; and the third hard dive is generally updated weekly and kept off site in the event of a fire or other catastrophe.

Jason's Notes

Your hard drive is like the camera negative. It *is* the movie, the footage, the sound design – an entire financial investment. Always play it safe by backing up your data as often as possible, because the one day you get lazy and decide not to back up is the day your hard drive will crash. 'Tis the Law of Murphy.

Hard drives can overheat, the platters can crash if dropped, or the drive mechanism can simply fail. Any of these instances can cause an immediate crash of the drive wherein the data is lost. Data recovery specialists can pull data off failed hard drives, but at cost of sometimes thousands of dollars.

FTP Accounts

It's often necessary to share movie files, transfer sound effects, voice-over recordings, music scores, and a host of other file types during the editing process. Because most email servers have a 10 MB limit for file attachments, consider setting up an FTP account so that other members of the postproduction team can easily upload and download large files. If you have a web site, you should be able to contact your hosting company to set up an FTP site. If not, there are a number of low-cost online FTP services available.

FTP sites are incredibly valuable to share rough cuts of the movie – the editor can upload a cut for you to watch, providing instant feedback wherever in the world you may be.

Stock Libraries

A fantastic addition to every editing suite is a collection of stock music, animations, and graphics. When you purchase a stock library, you are allowed to use the content in any of your productions, even if they are for profit. The purchase price of a stock library includes the license to use the materials in any way except to resell the content in its original form.

There are a number of stock resources available:

- **Stock music.** Typically organized into themes such as jazz, suspense, wedding, or corporate, each CD comes with 10–30 compositions, each with a 10-second, 15-second, 30-second, 60-second, and 3- to 4-minute version. Use shorter lengths for TV commercials and longer lengths for long form projects like movies or industrial videos. Generally, cheaper music libraries are all MIDI-based electronic scores, whereas some higher-priced stock music features a real orchestra for a richer, fuller sound.
- **Stock animation.** Stock animation libraries feature 10–40 full-screen animations for documentary green-screen interview backgrounds, title sequences, transitions, or text on-screen segments. Featuring everything from smooth slow-moving patterns to eye-popping designs, stock animation can add interest and production value to any production.
- **Stock footage.** If you need a shot of the Eiffel Tower, the Siberian tundra, or a field of fig trees, extensive stock footage libraries will lease you the shot you need – for a price. Available in practically every format, simply choose the shot, the length, format, and resolution. Stock footage can cost anywhere from hundreds to thousands of dollars per second, so be sure you know what you need before purchasing.

ORGANIZING THE FOOTAGE

Once the editor receives the footage, he must organize the clips at the desktop level, which entails creating folders for each scene, then placing each clip in its respective place. Although the specific structure of organizing files may differ from project to project, the basic framework applies.

- Create a master folder for the entire project, so when transferring the project from one editor to another, or backing it up, you can be confident all the files are included within the project folder.

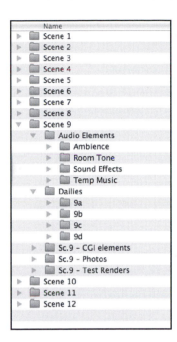

Always begin by organizing the footage at the desktop level.

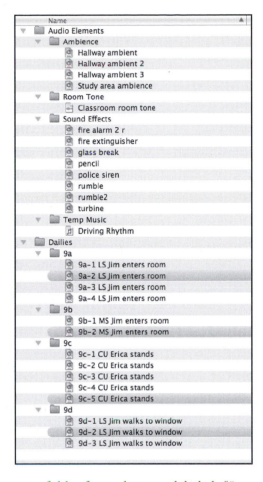

This is how we organized the footage for scene 9 at the desktop level. Notice how easy it is to find various shots, sound clips, and visuals.

- Within the master folder, create a folder for each scene, labeled, "Scene 1," "Scene 2," "Scene 3," and so on. In each scene folder, create separate folders for rough footage, ambient sounds, sound effects, music cues, test renders, graphics, animations, notes, and any other folder you may need.

- Make sure each file has its own descriptive name. Be sure to label each shot with the scene number, setup letter and take, along with a brief description. This will help you find a shot when you're in the thick of editing the movie.

In addition to organizing the shots at the desktop level, shots and sequences should have a similar organizational structure in the editing software in which you're working. It is now the responsibility of the assistant editor to import and organize the footage inside the editing software. Even though each editor will have her own preference as to how the footage is organized, here are some common ways to prepare the project for editing:

- Create a folder for each scene, labeled by the scene number, location, and whether the scene was an interior or exterior. Within each scene folder, create subfolders for: rough footage, sounds effect, ambience, temp music,

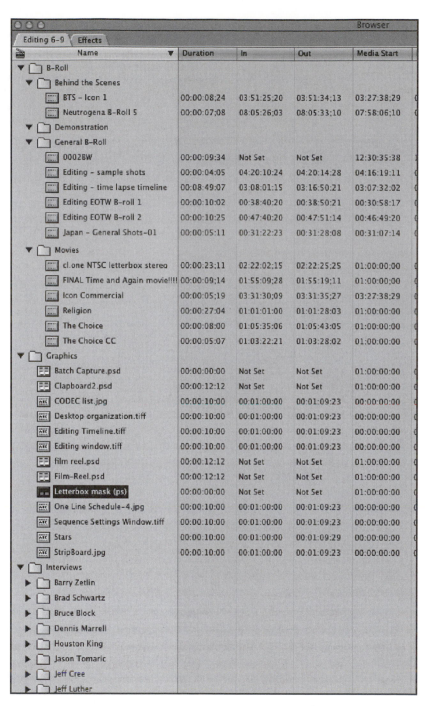

Just as you would at the desktop level, keep all your media assets organized in the editing software.

voiceovers, audio, graphics, animations, still photos, or any other media assets you may be working with. This method essentially groups all the scene-specific media in one place.

- A second method involves creating master folders for rough footage, sound effects, music, animation, graphics, temp music, and so on, then creating subfolders for each scene.
- Regardless of how the media is organized, it should be easy to navigate, should another editor work on the project. There's no greater hindrance to the editing process than having to stop to search for a file.
- Use the color-labeling option within the editing software to mark each shot for easy identification. For example:

  - Director's selects/best takes: green
  - Insert Shots: blue
  - No good takes: red
  - Establishing shots: yellow

Before you begin editing, always familiarize yourself with the rough footage by watching all the source material and making any notes about outstanding takes.

Jason's Notes

Even though the process of organizing the footage first is tedious and time-consuming, it will ultimately speed up the editing process, allowing the editor focus on the pacing and the flow of the story rather than looking for the third take of the second setup of scene 87.

THE ASSEMBLY CUT

The first stage of editing a movie is called the *assembly cut*. Once the footage has been organized, categorized, and labeled, the editor begins methodically assembling each scene using the selects, or your choice of the best takes from each setup. The editor's objective is to assemble a rough version of the movie, focusing on the broad brushstrokes of building the story. The editor usually follows the script during the assembly phase, so you can see the movie as originally envisioned, regardless of any problems.

The editor is not overly concerned with the details of continuity, pacing, titles, transitions, or color correction. The purpose of the assembly cut is to rough in all the footage into a story that can be watched from beginning to end. The time to work on problem areas, readjust scenes, manipulate subplots, fix character flaws, and any other story issues is during the rough cut phase.

It's common for shots to be missing. Visual effects shots, second unit shots, and establishing shots may still be in production. An editor will usually place a black title card with a brief description of the missing shot so the viewer has a clear understanding of what will eventually be there.

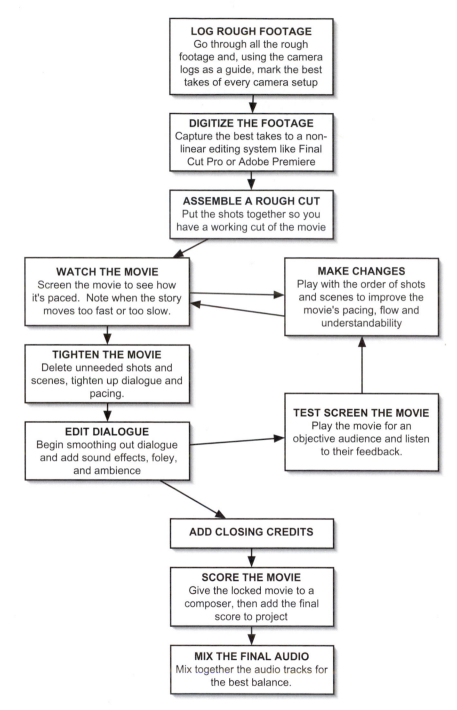

LOG ROUGH FOOTAGE
Go through all the rough footage and, using the camera logs as a guide, mark the best takes of every camera setup

DIGITIZE THE FOOTAGE
Capture the best takes to a non-linear editing system like Final Cut Pro or Adobe Premiere

ASSEMBLE A ROUGH CUT
Put the shots together so you have a working cut of the movie

WATCH THE MOVIE
Screen the movie to see how it's paced. Note when the story moves too fast or too slow.

MAKE CHANGES
Play with the order of shots and scenes to improve the movie's pacing, flow and understandability

TIGHTEN THE MOVIE
Delete unneeded shots and scenes, tighten up dialogue and pacing.

TEST SCREEN THE MOVIE
Play the movie for an objective audience and listen to their feedback.

EDIT DIALOGUE
Begin smoothing out dialogue and add sound effects, foley, and ambience

ADD CLOSING CREDITS

SCORE THE MOVIE
Give the locked movie to a composer, then add the final score to project

MIX THE FINAL AUDIO
Mix together the audio tracks for the best balance.

Editing Guidelines.

Jason's Notes

I have a love/hate relationship with the assembly cut. As much as I love seeing all my scenes come together, it's often heart-wrenching because the edit never seems to be as good as I envisioned in my head. If there's anything I've learned, it's to not judge the film too harshly at this stage – a lot can be done still, and from music to

sound effects, a lot still needs to be added. The assembly cut is really about the broad brushstrokes of building the story. Focus on the overall structure and don't get caught up in the details – there will be plenty of time to meddle with each scene.

- The assembly cut is to the editing process what the first draft is to the writing process. As the movie is being assembled, look for pacing problems, character and plot arcs, and comprehensibility, but keep working broadly.
- It's common for the assembly cut to feel choppy, like a series of disconnected scenes strung end to end. Don't get too concerned at this stage, as creative editing techniques during the rough cut phase can be used to help restructure parts of the story to fix these problems.
- If there are voiceovers or narration, the editor will usually record these lines himself, placing these temporary tracks for pacing and story comprehensibility. The placement of temporary voiceovers like narration or the other end of a phone call help the editor determine the timing of a sequence. If there are changes to a scene throughout the editing process, it's easy for the editor to rerecord the temp tracks until it's time to bring in the real voice actors.

The Role of the Director

Before beginning the editing process, you should discuss the story, pacing, and editorial style with the editor before he begins assembling the footage. Watch other movies for reference to provide an idea of the style of the edit. Wise directors will then step aside, leaving the editor to build the story alone. Neophyte directors who don't yet trust their editors, or feel the need to micromanage the process, are doing both the film and themselves a severe disservice.

Jason's Notes

If you're smart, you will go home and sleep or take a vacation. Recover from the stressful shooting process and allow the editor to assemble the footage so you can come back fresh and with renewed objectivity.

Remember, nothing in the edit is set in stone and anything can be changed. Being able watch the movie from beginning to end with fresh eyes will be in the best interest of the movie.

Let's be honest: you've been living closely to the story and are intimately familiar with the footage, performances, and the evolution of the story throughout the entire production process. You know which shots were painful to get and which are your favorites. As a result, you have all but lost your objectivity as to whether shots work. It is therefore advisable to let the editor, who has not been overly exposed to the footage or the story, to bring a fresh perspective to the footage. She will assemble the story based the footage that exists, not the footage you think exists. The editor's objectivity can help identify plot holes, confusing movements, and problems in character and plot arcs.

The best movies come out of a collaborative relationship between you and the editor. Always be open to new ideas; try different approaches and editing sequences in ways you may not have thought of before. Remember, there are a million different ways to assemble the footage to tell the story . . . you and the editor need to be willing to experiment until you find the one best one.

Be sure to save multiple versions of the edit project in case you need to go back to an earlier version. Before making a big editing change, save the film in a new project in case it doesn't work out.

The assembly cut is usually the longest version of the movie, with all filmed scenes being edited into the movie. It is not uncommon for the rough cut phase to last months, especially on low-budget productions. The Director's Guild of America rules give directors a minimum of ten weeks after the completion of principal photography to build the first cut of a movie before the studio and producers are allowed to have input.

Tips for Editing the Assembly Cut

- **Make sure there is a clear reason for cutting from one shot to another.** For example, a woman entering the room motivates and justifies the cut to her medium shot, or a man reacts to his friend explaining how someone hit his car the night before. The timing of the cut can imply guilt, empathy, or indifference. Be very conscious when editing, asking yourself *why* you're cutting to the next shot.
- **Don't give too much.** When a scene peaks, or reaches its climax, cut out of it. Try to cut out of a scene a beat before the audience expects. This will keep them wanting more and uphold the pacing of the movie.
- **Make sure each shot gives the audience new information.** When cutting to a new shot, always test the shot by asking what new information is being given to the audience: a wide shot may reveal the setting of the scene; cutting to the hand of a woman spinning a wine glass during a date can convey her sense of boredom, although she says she's interested; cutting to a man looking past the person he's talking to lets us know he's secretly watching something and is using his conversation as a cover. Every shot should reveal a piece of information that furthers the story. For example, in a dialog scene, the audience is already listening to the words spoken by the characters, so unless the character who is speaking is doing something different than what's being

said, try cutting to a reaction shot of the other person. His expression supplements the audio: how is he reacting to what's being said? Does he question it? Does he support it? The nonverbal cues given by the listening character can add a lot of depth and information to the scene. When given the option, cut to a shot that gives more information: a reaction shot, an insert shot, or use the audio to bridge the audience to the next scene.

■ In action scenes, intercut shots of bystanders reacting to a passing foot chase or shots of the surroundings into a car chase. These techniques help add color and depth to the scene and improve the pacing.

It's amazing how you can change the entire intent of a scene simply by reordering a couple shots. The more coverage you have, the more options you have.

■ **Avoid cutting to the same shot more than once.** Repetition is boring, so when possible, cut to a different angle. One outstanding way of providing this option to the editor is to shoot each setup on set in a long shot, a medium shot, and a close-up. This allows the editor to cut to a slightly different shot, although the camera angle may be the same.

■ The one exception to this guideline is in static dialog scenes where intercutting between matching medium shots of the speaking characters is acceptable to the audience. However, in this same dialog scene, if you used a wide establishing shot to open the scene, try to avoid using the same shot later. Look for a shot from another angle that provides new information, gives a new view of the setting, and gives the audience something new to look at.

■ **Ensure that the edits smooth out the motion within the scene,** giving the illusion that the scene occurred in real time and was covered by multiple cameras. The best editing is often invisible, allowing the action to perfectly bridge each edit. The editor's ability to create this seamless feel is often dictated by the quality of the footage shot, the script supervisor's attention to continuity, and your preplanning. One technique to create a seamless edit is to cut on motion, allowing the action of the character to bridge two shots.

■ **Make sure that every shot you cut to is important to the story.** Remember that the audience is going to be looking for importance in any person or object you show on screen.

- **Focus on the subplots.** A movie isn't made up of just the one plot arc, but of four to five subplots that, although contributing to the A story, are ultimately their own self-contained stories. When editing a movie, try removing the scenes that make up each subplot and edit each one as its own stand-alone movie, making sure the setup, conflict, and resolution feel complete. Once the subplot works, place the edited scenes back into the movie and focus on integrating the subplots into the A plot.
- **Don't be afraid of the varying the pacing of scenes.** Movies edited in a consistent tone and tempo quickly become boring. Whether it's a dialog-heavy drama or an in-your-face action movie, pacing that is too consistent can become tedious and visually fatiguing. Intercut fast scenes with slower scenes, allowing the quiet moments to play out. Varying the dramatic intensity like a roller coaster will not only engage the audience, but also give them time to absorb the story and characters.
- **Begin and end each scene with continuing action to avoid a jerky "start–stop" sense while watching the movie.** By cutting on motion, the flow from one scene to the next will feel smoother, and the pacing quicker.
- **When faced with a continuity error, choose to edit for proper emotional continuity than physical continuity.** Let the edits be driven by the content first, then technique.
- **Keep establishing shots quick.** Dwelling on them will only serve to slow down the story. Although establishing shots may be important to telling the story, they can also slow down the pacing, so consider bridging the audio of the scene over the establishing shot so the character begins to speak immediately. This will both serve to help the pacing as well as set the scene. Most locations only need to be established once in the movie, putting the majority of establishing shot in the first act. Remember the first act is about setting up the who, what, why, when, and where of the story, making establishing shots critical in setting up the world in which the story takes place. As the story progresses and the audience already has a clear understanding of the world, establishing shots become less and less important, dragging down the story more than supporting it.
- **If a scene doesn't serve to push the story forward or is unimportant, then cut it out of the movie.** Avoid falling in love with a shot so much that you're unwilling to cut it.
- **Let the movie become greater than the sum of its parts.** Don't be too quick to judge a problematic scene until you can see the scene in context with the rest of the movie. Surrounding scenes give new meaning to the scene in question.

Once the Assembly Cut Is Complete

Once the assembly cut is complete, burn a DVD copy and watch it outside the editing room, taking notes and immersing yourself in the movie. Look at what's working and where the problem areas are, talking specific notes so you can later sit with the editor to work on problematic areas. When producing this

DVD, setup the editing software to display the movie timecode on screen so you have a point of reference when talking about problem areas.

- If you're going to hate the movie and feel depressed that your vision didn't quite make it to the screen, this is when that will happen. The assembly cut can be difficult to watch because the film quite simply might not work. The pacing is off, performances may feel rocky, none of the sound or music is in; you are literally watching the movie in its most raw, naked state. Remember, you have a lot of work to do, and chances are that the final edit of the film will look very different that the assembly cut.
- Look at the order of the scenes. Although the movie may have been cut according to the script, is it possible to reorder scenes, subplots, or even lines of dialog to improve the story? A movie screens much differently than a script reads, so don't be afraid to deviate from the script to make the film stand on its own.

Remember the assembly cut is all about the big picture and is intended to look at the large dramatic movements of the film.

THE ROUGH CUT

If we were to compare the editing process to the writing process, the assembly cut would be comparable to writing the rough draft and editing the rough cut would be similar to the rewriting process. Much like a sculptor throws a block of clay onto the potter's wheel and begins to refine the shape of the bowl, so the editor refines the story, character arcs, pacing, and plot in the rough cut.

Jason's Notes

The secret to addressing a problematic scene is to take the best available shots and work primarily with them, allowing the scene to form organically with the footage you have. You can always pull reaction and insert shots from other takes, tweak audio, and use L-cuts to cover a problem, but don't start with a solution already in mind – let the scene form itself.

The assembly cut includes all the scenes shot on set and is edited to the script, but the story may or may not work as well on screen as it does on paper. The story may lag in certain places, or may feel too rushed. The second act may drag, or secondary characters may not feel fully developed. The actors may have delivered a performance too strongly in one scene, yet in another critical scene the actors may have underperformed. The opening of the film may not establish the main character as well as it should, or the end might not bring sufficient closure to the A plot or subplots. Perhaps parts of the story are confusing; the characters' motivations may be unclear, the story may jump around or feel too choppy. Often, scenes may work well on their own, but when edited with the other scenes, the movie lacks cohesion, feeling more like a string of scenes than a unified story.

The beauty of nonlinear editing programs is that you can always change an edit. Don't get frustrated if part of the movie isn't working – you can always go back and experiment to find a solution.

It is natural for these problems to exist at this stage of the editing process and they should not be a cause for concern. Rather, the you and the editor need to discard the script and look at how to sculpt the movie based on the existing footage. How do you take what you have and make it work? The solution may involve changing the order of scenes, cutting, moving, or altering subplots, using transitions, montages or intercutting scenes to create an emotion that did not previously exist. Entire subplots may be removed, and even characters may be cut.

One valuable technique is to review all the takes, to see if your original selects were the best choice. Now that you can watch the movie as a whole, the editor may find that a different take of an actor's performance may work better, thus improving the overall quality of the scene.

Remember that the rough cut is still rough, so don't be afraid to try different ways of editing the footage. Even the craziest ideas may work in the most unexpected way. Your goal should be to find the best possible way to assemble the footage.

- **Act breaks.** Look to see if the end of each act falls at the proper place in the story. For example, in a 100-minute movie, Act I should end and the conflict be introduced at the 25-minute mark. Act II should run from 25–75 minutes, with the turning point occurring at around 50 minutes. Act III should begin at the 75-minute mark. Shifting scenes so these plot points fall at the appropriate act break can greatly improve pacing.

- **A plot.** Make sure each and every scene in the A plot supports and helps the story move along. As an exercise, try temporarily removing each subplot and focus only on the primary plot. Does it make sense? Are there any gaps in logic or continuity? Does every shot and scene help drive the story forward, and if not, can they be cut?
- **Subplots.** Look at each subplot and make sure it works on its own. Does it have a beginning, middle, and end? Does it help support the A story? If the movie is running too long and needs to be shortened, can a subplot be removed without affecting the A story?
- **Characters.** Are the character's actions and emotion believable? If an actor's performance doesn't work, are there other takes that may work better? Can it be covered with a reaction shot? Can scenes be rearranged to make the character's journey more interesting?

Working on the rough cut means looking at how the flow of the entire movie works from beginning to end, while also looking at the inner workings of every scene. Sometimes these two techniques go hand in hand, when large structural changes to the story may require refining and tweaking individual scenes. Be aware of how ideas and changes affect both.

- **Sound effects.** The rough cut is an outstanding place to begin dropping sound effects into the movie. Because the editor is trying to assess the pacing and ensure the story makes sense, sounds design can often pull a scene together. Whether it's the ambient sound of the location, a phone ringing, or a radio playing in the background, these rough sound elements can really pull a scene together. In low-budget projects, it's not uncommon for the editor to be responsible for the sound mix once the picture has been locked. Carefully selecting the proper sound effects during the rough cut process can lighten the work load later in the sound edit.
- **Music.** Nothing pulls a scene together like a musical score. If you have a clear idea as to the type of music you want, consider laying a temp track or preexisting piece of music against the scene to serve as a musical guide. Though the benefits of a temp track are obvious, try to avoid falling in love with it as it will severely limit the composer's creative ability to write a truly unique custom score for the film. Also avoid editing scenes too closely to the temp track. Invariably, the composer's work will be slightly different requiring a reedit for timing.

Tips for Editing the Rough Cut

- When you finish editing your movie, put it away for a week or so and come back to it with a fresh eye before you make final tweaks.
- Once you have a strong rough cut, try watching the rough footage one more time to see if any unused takes may work better.

Test Screenings

It's during the rough cut that both you and the editor will get burnt out, losing the ability to know whether the changes you are making are really working. It's valuable to get input from objective audience members to determine whether the story makes sense, characters are engaging, and the pacing feels right.

Planning small, intimate screenings of 8–12 people will give you an opportunity to talk to the audience members about their thoughts and feelings about the movie:

- Did you care for the characters? What did you like or dislike about them?
- Did any parts of the story seem to drag? At any point did you find yourself feeling fidgety or bored?
- Were the first ten minutes engaging, and if you were to see this movie on television, would you feel compelled to continue watching it or would you change channels?
- Was the end enough of a payoff? Did you feel satisfied with the way the film ended?

Listen intently to their comments and pay close attention to any problems they have with confusing parts of the story, areas where the pacing lags, sequences that feel too long or too short, and character actions that don't seem motivated. Consider these comments and begin to tweak the edit to solve some of these problems.

Jason's Notes

Everyone is a critic – or so they think. Believe it or not, the ability to give valuable constructive criticism is very much a rare skill that most people do not possess. It's not until you enter a test screening that you see just how many people are incapable of providing insight you can actually use in the editing room.

Test screenings can provide as much confusion as insight. Be very careful when listening to audience feedback, as audience members will often tell you about the movie *they* would have made instead of providing critical feedback about the movie *you* made. Often, the best indicator of where problem areas exist is simply watching the audience's body language while the movie is playing. If people are shifting in their seats or getting fidgety, it's a good sign that there's a problem. Always sit in the back of the room and take careful note of this behavior, as it will tell you much more than the question and answer period after the screening.

- Show the movie to an objective test audience and avoid being defensive. Rather, listen intently to their feedback and carefully weigh the validity of their suggestions.

- Remember that you can't make everyone in the audience happy. Every person in the audience will have comments and feedback about your movie. It's important to differentiate between the story the audience "wishes" to see, versus the comments that critique the story that "exists."
- Don't take the advice of your friends and family too seriously. They have a very slanted bias towards your movie and will not give you objective advice.

THE FINE CUT

By this phase of the editing process, the best takes from each camera setup have been selected, the character and plot arcs make sense, and the story is well-paced. Once you have approved the overall movie, agreeing that it is as good as it is going to get, the overall changes are finished and the movie moves into the fine cut phase.

The *fine cut* refers to the process of technically polishing every frame of the movie to ensure that every transition is correct, continuity from shot to shot is correct, establishing shots are properly timed, inserts and cutaway shots are tight, and dialog scenes are as tight as possible. The editor meticulously combs through every single edit to make sure it is flawless.

The fine cut can be looked at more as technical quality control, as most of the artistic decisions have already been made and approved in the rough cut process.

Locking the Picture

Once the edit is 100% complete, the producers will *lock the picture*, to ensure that no more visual edits will be made that affect the length of the movie. Although final CGI shots will replace placeholders and the movie will be color-timed, the timing of the edits or the length of the movie will not change. The movie has been locked and the editing is complete.

The importance of locking the picture is critical, as the movie will now be given to the composer, sound editors, colorists, Foley artists, and ADR editors for the next editorial phase. Changes to the timing of the film will greatly affect these departments, costing time and money.

Sound mixers, composers, and color timers will all reference the locked picture's *timecode*, a numerical numbering system that gives each frame its own distinct number. For example, every person will be working with the same frame at 01:24:12:04, or one hour, twenty-four minutes, twelve seconds, and four frames. Working with a common timecode allows the editor to easily assemble the various elements, from music to sound effects, without the need to finesse each clip to find sync.

Sometimes the timecode is displayed on screen, running at the bottom of the frame, providing a visual reference for everyone working on the movie.

Approvals

In the independent world, the director usually has the final say over the final cut, or final creative control over the edit of the movie – a position greatly envied by many studio directors. Studios are contractually obligated by the Director's Guild of America to allow the director to submit his version of the film to them, at which point they have the power to re-edit the film for purposes of marketing and distribution. There are several factors that dictate the studio's reasoning. Films for broadcast must be cut to a specific time to fit into a specified time slot, the studio may add or remove scenes so they better appeal to the targeted demographic, and scenes may be cut because the violence level may change the rating, such as from a PG-13 to an R, either opening up or restricting audience access. These changes can be difficult for the director, whose sole motivation is maintaining the integrity of the story, which can be very different from the studio's motivation to produce the most marketable product possible.

During the rough cut and fine cut phases, the film will be critiqued and analyzed by everyone from producers, executives, financiers, marketing and publicity specialists, sales reps, and distributors, all of whom will weigh in on the edit, offering suggestions that may not necessarily improve the artistic merit of the film.

Studios often have extensive test screenings that can sometimes result in entire scenes being reshot. Test screenings can either take place in a standard movie theater where written questionnaires are distributed to the audience, or in special screening rooms in which audience members continuously record whether they like or dislike the movie in real time with a handheld, computer-monitored dial. The results are tracked and organized by demographic, so producers can tell who has problems at various points throughout the film. This information is then taken back to the editing room where an editor can address these issues.

Directors working independently often have the final control over the film, although some investors may want to influence the film to ensure the film's marketability. Although this creative freedom is ideal for the story, some guidance in improving the marketability of the film is critical to appease distributors in the global marketplace.

Jason's Notes

This is the phase of the editing process in which the studio director is jealous of the independent film director. With executives, distributors, and producers all contributing their opinion, the film can quickly become diluted with the influx of ideas. Although this may seem like a challenge, it can help bring valuable insight toward making the film marketable – and ultimately profitable.

There are times where the director so vehemently disagrees with studio changes that he removes his name from the film, opting instead for the credit "Directed by Alan Smithee," a pseudonym used by disenchanted directors.

CONCEPTS OF EDITING

Relationship Between Shots

The process of visual storytelling, whether the medium is a comic strip, cartoon, or motion picture, involves juxtaposing images that have no real meaning by themselves, but take on a greater meaning when placed in a series with other images.

Take for example the following shot: a young man runs down the sidewalk in busy New York City. This shot, by itself, means nothing. We cannot tell to what or from what he is running or even why he is running.

If we take a completely unrelated shot and edit it either before or after the shot of the young man running, it will give added meaning to the shot. For example, let's edit a shot of a dog running before the shot of the man running. Even though the dog and the man do not appear in the same frame, the audience will automatically associate the two shots together and assume that the dog is chasing the man. Or we could replace the dog with a shot of the sky, filling with storm clouds. The audience now thinks that the man is running to avoid the storm. Or we could place the shot of a young woman waiting, looking at her watch. Now we're implying that the man is late for a meeting. No matter what shot we place before or after the man running, the shot is, after all, simply of a man running. It means nothing by itself, but stands to gain a greater meaning from whatever precedes or follows it.

This is the basic principle of filmmaking: assembling a series of seemingly unrelated shots to tell a story. Shots edited together make a scene, and scenes edited together make a film. Don't try to pack every story element into one shot, but rather let the collective power of multiple shots tell the audience what you want them to know.

Editing Techniques

Famed editor Walter Murch said it best when he described, in order of importance, the criteria used to determine an edit point. When making an edit, make sure the edit is done for one of these reasons, in order of importance:

- **Emotion.** How does the edit make the audience feel in the moment? When cutting to the next shot, ask whether that edit contributes to the emotion of the scene; does it increase the tension, the sorrow, the happiness? Above all else, edit for emotion.

Jason's Notes

If I had to summarize the techniques of editing into one list, this would be it. First and foremost, always edit for emotion. Does the edit help add to the emotional feeling of a scene?

- **Story.** Does the edit drive the story forward? Does the story make sense? Does each edit push the plot forward or is it simply filling time? Does each shot add information to the story or to the characters? What is the audience learning about the story in each shot?
- **Rhythm.** When two people talk to each other, there is a rhythm, or a cadence of their conversation. When editing, do the cuts preserve or enhance this natural rhythm? Do the movements of the characters feel smooth from one shot to the next? In addition to the rhythm of the dialog and blocking, does the rhythm of the shots feel right? Are establishing shots too sort or too long? Are master shots too slow? What is the overall rhythm of the shot length and shot choice in the edit?
- **Eye-trace.** Does the edit follow the audience's focus from one shot to another? Does the audience's attention flow naturally from one shot to the next?
- **Two-dimensional placement.** Does the edit respect and adhere to the Rule of 180? Are screen direction and each actor's eye lines correct?
- **Three-dimensional space of action.** Does the edit respect the physical/special relationship between objects and characters in the scene? Is the location and setting of the story honored?

Cutting on Motion

Imagine for a moment that you're filming a basketball game with ten cameras positioned around the arena. Sitting behind a switching console, you are able to instantly switch to the camera with the best view of the action. Because the game happens in real time and occurs only once, your coverage of the game and choices of camera angles will be made in the moment, without much preplanning. The result is a kinetic, live feel that would be difficult to replicate, even with extensive rehearsals.

One of the reasons why the action feels so real is that the edit point, the place where you would cut from one camera angle to another, usually falls in the middle of some action, a lay-up, a rebound or free throw. Even though you're cutting between ten cameras, the editing isn't noticeable, because the action of the game ties all the camera angles together. For example, you may have a long shot of a player running up to the hoop, and as he jumps up for a slam dunk, you cut to a close-up of him in midair from under the net. His action of slam dunking the ball bridges the two camera angles, making the cut almost invisible.

Unlike a basketball game, movies are shot with one camera. The point of editing is to cut together these multiple single-camera angles to create the same flow that you would have by shooting the scene with multiple cameras and switching live between them. This is the principal of cutting on motion; when editing two shots together, let the action in the scene bridge the edit point of the two shots. For example, if a character is sitting down in a chair and you want to cut from a medium shot to a close-up, cut from one shot to the next *as* the character is in the process of sitting down, *not* before he starts to sit down or after he already sat down. Cut on his motion of sitting. By cutting on motion, the flow of cutting from one camera angle to another will be much smoother.

Continuity

We have all seen movies where two people are sitting on a couch talking to each other and in one shot, the guy's arm is on the back of the couch, and in the other shot, his arm is across his lap. These errors, called *continuity errors*, occur because scenes in a movie are shot out of order and are assembled later. For example, in a scene where a man and a woman are having dinner, the first shot is a long master shot where we see both the man and the woman and all the action of the scene. The cast and crew will shoot the scene from the beginning to the end, multiple times, from this one camera angle until the director is happy with the shot. When they are finished, the actors leave the set and the crew repositions the camera for the man's close-up. The gaffer changes the lights, the set decorator redresses the part of the set that is visible in the new camera angle, and the production sound mixer repositions the microphone, to name just a few of the activities that occur between camera setups. Once the camera, lighting, audio, and set are ready, the actors return to the set and the director films the entire scene again, framing only the man in a close-up. After shooting several takes and making minor adjustments to the performance, the crew again moves the equipment, this time preparing for the woman's close-up. And the process begins again.

Jason's Notes

If the script supervisor did her job properly on set, the editor shouldn't have any major issues with continuity in the editing room. The worst problems happen when there is no script supervisor. This forces the editor to edit around continuity rather than for the emotion of the scene.

The editor must then take these three different camera angles and edit them together so that it appears as though they occurred once and that the moment was covered by multiple cameras. Continuity errors occur when the actors change their performance, either intentionally or by accident, or if a crew member accidentally moves a prop or a set piece.

Avoiding continuity errors is the responsibility of the script supervisor, who notes the position of people and objects, changes in dialog, camera coverage, or anything else that may not be continuous from one shot to the next. Even though the script supervisor is watching, there may still be a continuity error that she misses.

Editing a Dialog Scene

Editing dialog can be tricky, especially if the scene was shot at a location with a directional ambience that changes tone and volume from one shot to the next. Although removing distracting ambience like traffic, wind, or waves is nearly impossible, there are techniques to reduce the sudden impact of changing ambience from one shot to another.

Let's say we have two characters, Dave and Jessica, talking at a restaurant together. Although the restaurant was relatively quiet, the microphone still picked up the ambience of outside traffic on the busy city street. Because of the blocking and microphone position, the ambience is louder behind Dave's shots than Jessica's.

- Find the best take of Dave's close-up performance and drag it to track 1 on the timeline. Using the razor blade tool, slice out Jessica's lines as close to the beginning of her first word and as close to the end of her last word as you can, keeping as much of the ambience in the middle as possible. Delete Jessica's segments from the track, leaving an open space.
- Mute track 1 and drag Jessica's close-up take to track 2. Use the same technique to carve out Dave's performance, leaving as much ambience at the head and tail of each of Jessica's lines.
- Keeping Dave's clips on track 1 and Jessica's on track 2, slide the clips together so the conversation sounds natural, even slightly overlapping the lines. Remember that people tend to talk over each other instead of waiting for the other person to finish speaking before responding. Mimic this pattern as you edit the dialog.
- Create a crossfade at the beginning and end of every clip. The crossfade should start at the beginning of the clip and end just before the character begins speaking, covering only the ambience and at the end of the clip, begin at the very end of the last word to the end of the clip. The more of a pause the actors added between lines, the longer the crossfade can be and the smoother the transition from one clip to another. As a note, make sure that crossfades don't overlap each other, or you will hear a dip in the audio. Crossfades should exist only under another clip.

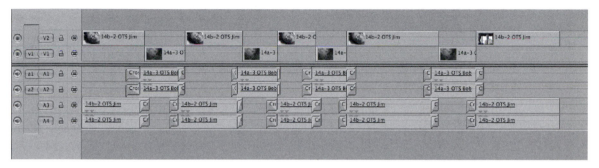

Jason's Notes

As a director, why do you have to know this? Doesn't the editor worry about these things? In short, yes – until it affects the story and you can't cut a scene the way you want because it wasn't shot properly. By understanding the process an editor goes through, you will be better prepared in the field and know how to better direct the cast and crew to get the most usable footage.

- By this point, the dialog in the scene should sound natural and the ambience should smoothly fade in and out while the other character is speaking.
- Once the dialog has been edited and sounds natural, unlink the audio from its connected video clip. This enables you to change the in point and out point of the video without altering the audio so that you can change when the camera "cuts" from one character to the other.
- Once finished, the base close-ups have been edited and the scene flows well from one character to another. Now, add any insert shots or master shots to the third video track. Placing each character, master shots, and insert shots on different tracks makes it much easier to change the scene in the future than if all the footage were cut on a single track.

Tips for Editing a Dialog Scene

Although a dialog scene may seem pretty simple to edit, there are a number of ways to psychologically influence the audience's perception of the characters and the story all in how a scene is edited.

Holding on a reaction shot of one character while the other character is telling a story draws you into what the first character is thinking and how he is reacting to the story. For example, Jerry and Anthony went to high school together and haven't seen each other in years. In this scene, the two are sitting alone in a 24-hour diner at 2:00 a.m., telling stories of their lives over the past ten years since graduation. Jerry is telling Anthony how he was married, but his wife accidentally sliced her hand while cooking. She couldn't stop the bleeding and collapsed on the floor. Jerry happened to come home minutes later, but could not save her. She had lost too much blood and died in his arms. As a director, you have three camera setups: the master shot, Jerry's clean close-up, and Anthony's clean close-up. Although it may seem easy to determine when to edit from Jerry to Anthony, consider the psychology of the following options:

Option 1: While Jerry is telling the story, hold the shot on Jerry for the entire story. This has the effect of drawing the audience into his tale, reliving the incident with him and feeling his emotions. Cutting away to Anthony's reaction may detract from the mesmerizing effect of holding the shot.

Option 2: Hold on Anthony's reaction for the entire story. By drawing so much attention to Anthony's reaction, the audience begins to think that Anthony had a much greater involvement. This could foreshadow his involvement in Jerry's wife's death, or imply that Anthony has an equally horrific story. If this is the direction the script takes, this editing choice may add depth to Anthony's character.

Option 3: Intercut between the Jerry and Anthony. This gives the audience time to absorb and see how each men are dealing with the story. Although this provides an omniscient viewpoint, it may detract from the power of the story.

When sitting in the editing room, think about where and to whom you want the audience's attention to be drawn. Your choices as to when and to what to cut to play a tremendous impact on the emotion of the scene.

- In life, when you are talking in a group of three or more people, take note of who you're looking at and why you felt motivated to look at a certain person at a particular time. If this moment were a scene, every time you looked should be an edit point from one shot to another. Fluid editing should move the audience's attention from one shot to the next in the same way we would feel motivated to look at another person in a real life conversation.

Jason's Notes

A great example of holding on a shot occurs in *Jaws*, when the fisherman tells the tale of how his boat sank and the men were picked off one at a time by the shark. One reason the scene was so effective is that Spielberg never cuts away from the fisherman during his tale, drawing the audience into the moment.

- Make sure edits are tight within a scene. Don't put pauses between lines of dialog. Try overlapping lines of dialog.

Montages

Montages are video collages that use a variety of shots edited together with transitions to convey the passage of long periods of time by only showing the key moments of an event. For example, in a montage of Eric, a high school athlete preparing for a game, the montage may consist of the following shots:

- Eric trains in the weight room and lifts only a little weight
- Eric runs through tires on the football field and collapses in fatigue
- Eric tries to catch a pass and misses
- Eric drinks a protein shake with friends
- Eric crashes at home on the couch after practice
- Eric gets yelled at by the coach
- Eric bench presses 185 pounds quickly
- Eric tries to catch a pass and misses
- Eric practices alone on the field at night
- Eric does push-ups at home before bed
- Eric runs on the field
- Eric tries to catch a pass and catches it

This montage, although consisting of only 12 shots, conveys Eric's progression in his attempt to win the big game. Montages can be powerful when the right images are used.

Jason's Notes

Montages, although a powerful technique, have become almost cliché in their usage. When using a montage, try to find a creative way to demonstrate the passage of time to give the audiences something they haven't seen before.

Using a *motif*, or a reoccurring style throughout the montage, can help draw the audience's attention to key moments in a sequence, highlighting the character's progress in an artistic, noncliché manner. For example, in a montage of a boy building a model car, we can shoot a series of over-the-shoulder shots of the boy holding a photograph of the car he aspires to build. He can lower the photograph to reveal the actual model-in-progress sitting on a table, allowing the audience to see his vision of the final car, and the progress he is making. Intercut with shots of the boy gluing pieces together, painting each part, and using tools to delicately assemble the model, we use the photograph two or three more times in the montage as a benchmark for his progress until, in the final moment of the montage, the boy lowers the photograph to reveal the completed model.

Instead of using traditional dissolves from one shot to the next, creative shooting can make a montage even more visually engaging. For example, in a montage where a woman is preparing a banquet dinner, the camera may always dolly left to right, starting behind a foreground object like a stack of cookbooks, revealing her scouring through the cookbooks searching for a recipe, then ending behind another foreground object like flower pot sitting on the counter. The second shot may begin behind a product display at a grocery store and dolly right to reveal our hero filling a shopping cart with ingredients, before dollying behind another product display, again blacking out the frame. You might use the same technique of beginning and ending each dolly shot from behind an object for each shot in the montage. With each foreground object completely blacking out the frame, the editor can conceal the edit point so the camera appears to move, uninterrupted through both time and space. Techniques such as this not only make the montage visually engaging, but provides a unifying technique to make the montage feel cohesive.

The narrative techniques for editing a montage are just as important as the techniques for editing a standard scene:

- **Make sure every shot progresses the sequence.** Because a montage is a time-compressed version of an ordinarily lengthy process, it's critical that each shot anchors the character's progress. Look at each shot and question how it's adding to the story. Does the shot need to show more or less progress? Does the audience understand that the character is or is not progressing? Does every shot in the montage contribute to the character's goal?
- **Remember the emotion.** It's easy to shoot a montage that shows the audience what a character is doing, but it's equally important for the audience to know how the character is feeling. For example, in our montage of Eric's preparation for the big game, we may intercut shots of him walking past the fence where college students are playing. He may take a moment to watch, inspired and further driven by the motivation of playing college ball. We may then later cut to a shot of him jogging through his neighborhood when a little boy throwing a football with his dad in the front yard pauses to watch Eric run by. Seeing Eric's journey from the perspective of the college athlete (the person Eric aspires to be) and a little boy (a person who aspires to be like Eric) helps us tie the emotional journey of preparation in with the physical preparation for the game.
- **Use music and sound design.** Creating a successful montage also lies in the use of sound to help denote the passage of time and progression of the character. Though a music bed helps tie shots together into a cohesive piece, sound design can play an equally important role.

Edit Types

There are a number of editing tricks used by professional editors to help stitch together unrelated shots into a smooth scene.

B-ROLL

A term typically used in documentary or news-style production, *B-roll* is the alternate footage shot used to accentuate the story told by the primary footage of a program. For example, if the primary footage is an interview of a woman who runs a cookie company, the B-roll includes the shots of the baking process, shots of the dough being prepared, dough being put in the oven, and the cookies coming out of the oven. These shots are usually of a similar style to the primary footage.

There are several tips to consider when shooting and editing B-roll:

- **When shooting B-roll, make sure each shot has plenty of pad on either end of the shot.** For example, when panning across the front of a building, let the stationary camera roll for several seconds before panning, then once the pan is complete, let the camera continue to roll for several more seconds. It's better to have the extra footage and not need it than to need it and not have it. Shooting plenty of pad on the head and tail of each shot gives the editor the option to add long dissolves in and out of the shot.
- **Hold static shots for at least ten seconds.** Shots always feel longer when you're shooting than they actually are. Watch the timecode counter in the viewfinder to make sure you have at least ten seconds. Some editors require 20–30 seconds of each shot. Remember, it's easier to cut a shot if you don't need it all than to need it and not have it.
- **When shooting B-roll, try to shoot a long shot, medium shot, and a close-up of each setup.** Doing this will triple the amount of usable footage. These changes don't require moving the camera, but simply zooming in and reframing.
- **Think in terms of sequences.** B-roll is designed to tell a story, so try to shoot sequences of four to six shots that can be intercut and assembled into a continuous story.

L-CUT

Also called a *split edit*, an *L-cut* is when the audio and visual cut of two juxtaposed shots occur at different times. Used to help conceal the edit and improve the flow of a scene, L-cuts are primarily used in editing dialog.

JUMP CUT

A *jump cut* occurs when two shots of continuing action are edited together, but there is a discontinuity between the two shots. A jump cut is a jarring edit that draws attention to the discontinuity. Some jump cuts are intentionally used to add confusion to the scene.

AXIAL CUT

An *axial cut* occurs when the editor cuts from one shot to either a tighter or wider shot from the same camera axis. Axial cuts can occur if the camera

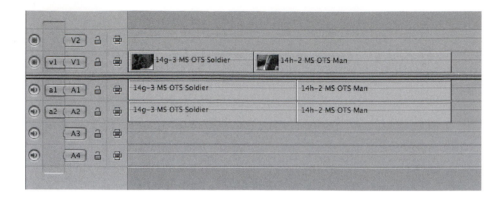

Example of an L-Cut.

shoots a scene once from a long lens, then without moving the camera, again from a short lens. The camera can also physically move toward or away from the subject without moving side to side. Axial cuts are used to draw emphasis to an action by cutting to a closer shot of the subject on a key line or action.

TRANSITIONS

Transitions are editing techniques used to segue from one shot to another. There are three basic types of transitions:

- **Cut.** The cut is the most common and simple transition where in the last shot ends and on the next frame, the next clip begins.

- **Dissolve.** A dissolve occurs when one clip fades out while the other clip simultaneously fades in. Dissolves imply a passage of time, especially when dissolving to an establishing shot or when used in a montage.

- **Wipe.** A wipe uses a shape pattern that moves across the screen to transition from one clip to another. One side of the wipe pattern is the first clip, and the other side is the second clip. Whereas wipes are fun and catchy to watch, they can be distracting to the viewer, drawing attention to the editing and away from the action on the screen. Wipes are commonly found in industrial videos, promotional and advertising spots, and wedding videos to transition from one picture to the next. Avoid using wipes in a narrative film.

CROSS-CUTTING

Cross-cutting involves editing back and forth between two scenes for the sake of emphasizing the similarities or differences between the scenes. For example, cross-cutting a scene of an athlete practicing for a race with a scene of his friend sitting at home watching television establishes the differences between the two characters' work ethic. Conversely, cross-cutting between similar scenes can add emphasis or dramatic tension to each scene. For example, in *Fred and Vinnie*, we intercut a scene of Fred – a middle-aged, shy character – in a session with his therapist discussing his reclusive tendencies with a scene of him on an awkward first date at a pizza shop. Intercutting these two scenes helped make the entire sequence funny in its irony.

CUTAWAY

A *cutaway* is a reaction shot that breaks away from the continuous action of a scene to show another person. Typically used to conceal an edit, the cutaway is a vital tool in covering continuity errors, improving pacing, and helping actors' performances.

SOFT CUT

Whereas a hard cut places two shots back to back with no transition, a *soft cut* involves placing two shots together with a one- or two-frame dissolve.

Color Timing

Now that the movie is locked, it moves into the next phase of postproduction, when the footage is color-timed, titles and graphics are added, the sound is mixed, dialog is rerecorded, music is written, and any remaining visual effects are added.

The first of these steps is *color timing*, in which the brightness, contrast, and color of each shot are adjusted. Sometimes shots are color-timed because they simply do not match. In an exterior park scene, the angle on one character may have been shot in broad daylight, yet the reverse angle of the other actor may have been shot with light cloud cover. The cloudy shots will appear bluer and less contrasty, so that intercutting between the two angles will be jarring. When faced with a scene like this, a colorist will often warm up the cloudy shots and increase the contrast, attempting to match the first angle. Although it's nearly impossible to create a perfect match, the colorist can get the shots to match enough to not be distracting.

Scenes with mismatched brightness values can also be corrected. Slightly underexposed shots can be brightened, shots where flesh tones were exposed too brightly can be reduced, and shots of varying brightness values can be balanced out to provide a consistent look across the scene.

The colorist's ability to correct the brightness values of a shot is limited if any of the following two factors occur:

- **The shot was overexposed.** Film is more forgiving in overexposed images, softly letting images fall to white, whereas digital video will cross the overexposure threshold more abruptly. In either case, if an image is overexposed, it will appear as white on screen. In HD formats, white is recorded with no possibility of restoring the overexposed image later in post. It's critical for the director of photography to properly expose each shot on set, as a colorist can do nothing with overexposed elements.
- **The shot was underexposed.** Similar to the problems encountered with overexposing, underexposing a shot means that underexposed elements will fall to black, losing all detail. In a way, underexposed footage is much less forgiving, because even if a dark object is within the latitude of the medium, the majority of compression in video occurs in dark values. Brightening up an underexposed element will increase the grain and compression artifacts typically hidden in the shadows.

Footage shot with high gain or at the low end of an HD format's latitude are especially prone to grain and artifacts. There are special software solutions that reduce the graininess of a shot, but at the expense of the sharpness of the rest of the image. Many cinematographers will properly expose a nighttime or dark scene so even it looks "too bright" on set, to give the colorist plenty of data to work with. Remember, it's always easier to throw away picture information and create a clean look than start with little picture information and need more.

It used to be that cinematographers took great pains to shoot footage as close to the director's vision as possible on set. Elements were creatively and intentionally over and underexposed and colors were chosen and deliberately used on set so the resulting footage was as close to the final look as possible. Because today's color timing tools are so sophisticated and offer filmmakers such a wide array of options, the cinematographer's duty is just the opposite – shoot footage as neutrally as possible on set, so the director can play with the color palette in postproduction. This generally means avoiding over- or underexposing elements, avoiding heavily colorizing a shot, avoiding excessive contrast, and shooting the footage with as much color and brightness information as possible. Using color timing tools in the postproduction process, a colorist can give shots more contrast, tint shots, or even portions of a shot, and add grain and even camera shake. By creating the look in the colorist's room, you can try different looks and, most importantly, can undo something you don't like – an option previously unavailable a decade ago.

Color Timing for Creative Reasons

Color timing isn't just about ensuring footage meets technical requirements, but is instead about creating a unique look. For example, the desaturated, green hue of *The Matrix* was created in the color timing process, and in my independent film, *Time and Again*, the warm look of the 1950s was also created in postproduction.

Music videos are an example of using color timing to create an extreme color effect. Colorists don't color the footage for any reason other than artistic choice.

The Coloring Process

- Sit with the director of photography and the colorist and look at reference movies to determine the look of the final footage. Sometimes, a DP will prefer to color-time the movie herself, allowing her to fulfill her original creative vision.
- The colorist will look at each scene and determine which shot is the "matching shot" against which all the other shots will be timed.
- The colorist will go through each shot one at a time and, using a waveform monitor to quantify the brightness values and a vectorscope to quantify color values, will systematically adjust the brightness, contrast, and color values of each shot so they match each other. Colorists need to be careful that white values do not exceed 100% and black values are appropriate to the video format. HD and PAL formats base black at 0%, whereas the old NTSC format used in North America places black at 7.5%. Understanding the base black value for the format ensures the movie doesn't come out too dark or too washed out.
- Once all the shots match each other in a scene, the colorist can apply an overall look to the entire. Whether it's a tint, bleach bypass, cross-processing, increased contrast, or any one of a number of "looks," these effects are laid over the entire scene.

Titles

Title sequences, captions, and subtitles are all important elements of a movie, and although creating titles is very much an art, there are a number of technical requirements to which the editor must adhere to ensure the titles appear as intended.

- **Safe action zone.** Most CRT television sets and monitors display only 90% of the frame, with the other 10% projected off the edge of the screen. When framing a shot, be sure to keep all action within the 90% boundary of the frame.
- **Safe title zone.** Because 10% of the image is projected off the edge of the screen, any graphics and images are at risk of running into or off the screen edge. It's for this reason that we use a second boundary marking 80% of the frame in which all graphics and text must be placed.

The outer box represents the 90% safe action zone, and the inner, 80% box represents the safe title zone. Always place all images, text, and graphics inside the safe title zone.

- **Lines thicker than three pixels.** In standard definition formats, horizontal lines thinner than three pixels will flicker on screen. Make sure all horizontal lines are at least three pixels thick.
- **Choose sans serif fonts.** In standard definition formats, serif fonts either flicker or lose their detail because of resolution limitations of the NTSC signal. When choosing fonts, select thicker sans serif fonts.
- **Color safe.** NTSC colors can bleed if they are oversaturated, especially reds and blues. Oversaturation is not a problem in high definition formats.
- **Alpha channel.** When importing graphics to layer or composite into another video image, be sure to create the graphic with an alpha channel. This will make the background transparent so that only the graphic appears.

Credits

Credits appear at the beginning and end of a movie and list all the people who worked on or contributed to the film. A cast or crew member's credit is the most important form of acknowledgement you can give and is often more important than receiving a paycheck.

The opening credits are reserved for the key cast, department heads, and production companies responsible for the film financing. The closing credits list the rest of the cast and crew, vendors, and those people the producers wish to thank.

- Make sure you include everyone in the credits. One good way of ensuring this is by going through the release forms. Extras are generally not listed in the credits unless they have been featured in some way on screen.

- Double-check the spelling of each person's name.
- Have fun with the look and design of the opening credits of the movie and use font, size, animation, and color to set the tone for the story.
- I use Helvetica 8–10-pt. font for the closing credits. I find this to be the optimum size for reading and speed.
- When I make the credits for one of my movies, I lay out the credits in a page layout program like QuarkXpress or Adobe InDesign, which allows me to set them in a dual-column format. I then export the text as a PostScript file and import it into Adobe After Effects. I can control the credits like a graphic and set them to move across the screen in the speed I want. The result are professional and easy to read.

Compression

Imagine that you have just moved to a new town, but you don't have a car yet. One day, you get a taste for orange juice, so you take your bicycle to the local grocery store and pick up a gallon of delicious, freshly squeezed, pulpy juice. As you stand in the checkout line, you realize that you have no way of transporting a gallon of juice home – your bicycle basket isn't big enough. So you return the gallon of OJ in favor of a small can of orange juice concentrate. This juice was filtered and processed at a factory so that it could be compressed into a small container, where it also lost its flavor and vitamin-rich pulp. You pay, stick the concentrate in your jacket pocket, and head home, where you add water to restore the concentrate back to a gallon. Although you still end up with a gallon of orange juice, the concentrate has been filtered and reduced in quality to make it more transportable.

Digital video works the same way. In its raw form, video is beautiful and full of detail with bright, vivid colors. Unfortunately, uncompressed standard definition video is around 30 MB/sec, and high definition is closer to 300 MB/sec. The cost of managing such a high data rate would drive up the cost of camcorders, computers would need to be faster with better data throughput, and drive space requirements would increase significantly. Because of the impracticality of transporting raw video, engineers developed a way of compressing the video and reducing the file size by averaging some of the detail and color information. This is done by special algorithms called *codecs*, which stands for "compressor/decompressor."

Much like the process the factory used to compress orange juice, codecs serve to compress digital audio and video for any number of applications, and there are several of them. A few examples of codecs include the following:

- MPEG-2 is the standard codec used in DVD players. Designed for high-quality NTSC and PAL video, this compressor is vastly superior to preceding analog VHS formats.
- Sorenson, H-264, and Flash are all different codecs used for compressing video for the Internet. Specially designed to maintain high quality and low file sizes, these codecs are ideal for downloadable and streaming videos.

Animation
BMP
Cinepak
Component Video
DV – PAL
DV/DVCPRO – NTSC
DVCPRO – PAL
DVCPRO HD 1080i50
DVCPRO HD 1080i60
DVCPRO HD 1080p25
DVCPRO HD 1080p30
DVCPRO HD 720p50
DVCPRO HD 720p60
DVCPRO50 – NTSC
DVCPRO50 – PAL
Uncompressed 10–bit 4:2:2
Uncompressed 8–bit 4:2:2
Graphics
H.261
HDV 1080i50
HDV 1080i60
HDV 1080p24
HDV 1080p25
HDV 1080p30
HDV 720p24
HDV 720p25
HDV 720p30
HDV 720p50
HDV 720p60
Apple Intermediate Codec
Motion JPEG A
Motion JPEG B
MPEG IMX 525/60 (30 Mb/s)
MPEG IMX 525/60 (40 Mb/s)
MPEG IMX 525/60 (50 Mb/s)
MPEG IMX 625/50 (30 Mb/s)
MPEG IMX 625/50 (40 Mb/s)
MPEG IMX 625/50 (50 Mb/s)
MPEG–4 Video
None
Photo – JPEG
Apple Pixlet Video
Planar RGB
PNG
Apple ProRes 422 (HQ)
Apple ProRes 422
TGA
TIFF
VC H.263
Video
XDCAM EX 1080i50 (35 Mb/s VBR)
XDCAM EX 1080i60 (35 Mb/s VBR)
XDCAM EX 1080p24 (35 Mb/s VBR)
XDCAM EX 1080p25 (35 Mb/s VBR)
XDCAM EX 1080p30 (35 Mb/s VBR)
XDCAM EX 720p24 (35 Mb/s VBR)
XDCAM EX 720p25 (35 Mb/s VBR)
XDCAM EX 720p30 (35 Mb/s VBR)
XDCAM EX 720p50 (35 Mb/s VBR)
XDCAM EX 720p60 (35 Mb/s VBR)
XDCAM HD 1080i50 (35 Mb/s VBR)
XDCAM HD 1080i60 (35 Mb/s VBR)
XDCAM HD 1080p24 (35 Mb/s VBR)
XDCAM HD 1080p25 (35 Mb/s VBR)
XDCAM HD 1080p30 (35 Mb/s VBR)
XDCAM HD422 1080i50 (50 Mb/s)
XDCAM HD422 1080i60 (50 Mb/s)
XDCAM HD422 1080p24 (50 Mb/s)
XDCAM HD422 1080p25 (50 Mb/s)
XDCAM HD422 1080p30 (50 Mb/s)
XDCAM HD422 720p50 (50 Mb/s)
XDCAM HD422 720p60 (50 Mb/s)
H.263
H.264
JPEG 2000
Sorenson Video 3
Sorenson Video
Xiph Theora

Here are just a few of the many codes in which you can compress your project.

- DV-NTSC and DV-PAL is the revolutionary standard definition, digital video codec used in popular standard definition consumer and prosumer DV formats.
- HDV is an ultracompressed high definition consumer format. Recorded to tape, this codec used extremely high compression, resulting in motion artifacts and degradation in dark regions of the frame.
- HDCAM and DVCPRO are both professional, high-quality high definition codecs.

When choosing the right codec for your project, be sure to thoroughly research the pros and cons of each codec.

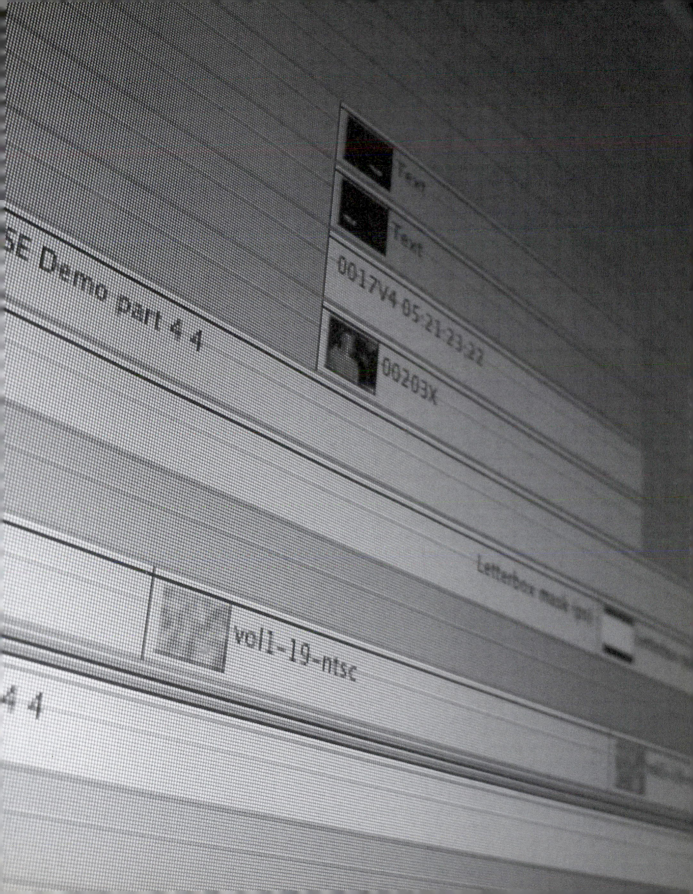

SE Demo Part 4 4

Text

Text

0017V4 05:21:23:22

00203X

Letterbox mask on

vol1-19-ntsc

4 4

CHAPTER 18
Visual Effects

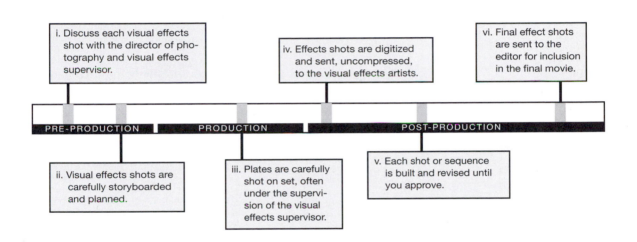

i. Discuss each visual effects shot with the director of photography and visual effects supervisor.

iv. Effects shots are digitized and sent, uncompressed, to the visual effects artists.

vi. Final effect shots are sent to the editor for inclusion in the final movie.

PRE-PRODUCTION PRODUCTION POST-PRODUCTION

ii. Visual effects shots are carefully storyboarded and planned.

iii. Plates are carefully shot on set, often under the supervision of the visual effects supervisor.

v. Each shot or sequence is built and revised until you approve.

INTRODUCTION

Whereas special effects are physical effects that occur on set, such as pyrotechnics, weather effects, miniatures, and forced-perspective sets, visual effects are created solely within the realm of the computer. Footage is either digitized and manipulated using sophisticated programs or created from scratch with every element being built within the modeling and animation software.

Visual effects can be organized into two basic categories: 2D compositing and 3D animation. Two-dimensional compositing is the process of using flat, or two-dimensional images, photographs, animation, film, or video clips, and layering them into existing footage. Although the content of these images has depth, the images themselves are flat. Three-dimensional animation involves modeling, applying textures, lighting, and animating a three-dimensional object in the computer so that it can be viewed from any angle creating, in most instances, a life-like, photorealistic image.

Incorporating visual effects into your movie can yield spectacular results if the process is well organized. However, hasty shooting and adopting a

Filmmaking.
© 2011 Jason J. Tomaric. Published by Elsevier Inc. All rights reserved.

To create the illusion of clouds flying by, we shot our actor, Adam Marcinowski against a green screen so we could easily isolate the foreground from the background.

"fix-it-in-post" attitude will cost both time and money, with the final results rarely appearing perfect.

Visual effects, when done well, can be convincing and impressive, but if they are not executed properly or realistically, they will cheapen the quality of the movie, drawing the audience's attention away from the story and to the bad effects work. Make sure the story is strong enough to stand on its own and is not dependent on visual effects to carry it.

There are a variety of ways visual effects can be integrated into your movie:

- **Complete CGI.** Some sequences may be completely computer-generated, such as a spaceship in orbit around a planet or a demon arising from the fiery depths of hell. These shots require animators to create not only the subject, but the entire environment, including lighting, atmosphere, and the physics behind the interaction of objects. Much like building and dressing a set, animators must create every object that exists within the frame. CGI shots can be extremely expensive and time-consuming to produce and are often difficult to make to look realistic.

- **Augmented shots.** Augmented shots include already-photographed shots that are later altered, added to, or subtracted from. Examples include:
  - **Green/blue screen.** Green/blue screen, as mentioned earlier, is the process of digitally replacing a specific color with another visual element – footage, animation, or a photograph. Green and blue screens are most commonly used to provide the greatest separation from the foreground subject. For more information on how to properly shoot green screen footage, see Chapter 13.
  - **Rotoscoping.** Whereas shooting an object or subject against a monochromatic background like a green screen or blue screen makes it easy to isolate the subject, it sometimes becomes necessary to cut out a subject or object from a non–green screen frame. This technique requires a compositor to meticulously and systematically cut the subject out frame

by frame. Although rotoscoping an object with straight lines, such as a car, is easy, objects with less-well-defined edges like hair can be challenging and time-consuming. Rotoscoping is usually a last resort and can be avoided by choosing to properly shoot green screen.

- **Digital extensions.** This technique is used to add to existing set pieces or environments to either expand the environment or to conceal the real environment photographed on the set. For example, if budget allows for only a single wall to be constructed, compositors can digitally build a sweeping cityscape around the wall, replacing whatever part of the frame currently exists, with a photograph, 3D element, or other video footage. Digital set extensions have replaced the traditional technique of photographing a matte painting.
- **Compositing.** Compositing involves the layering of multiple elements on top of the existing footage. Whether the elements are footage, photographs, or any other element, added elements are intended to either add to or cover specific areas of the frame. For example, if a television appears in a shot, it's common to shoot the blank screen, then use software in postproduction to track the motion of the camera, digitally

Raw green screen footage   **Final Composite**

Plates of actors shot against a green screen, and the final frame into which the background elements have been composited.

adding the image that appears on the screen. This technique is useful when the footage appearing on the TV screen hasn't been shot yet.

- **Image warping.** Warping is a technique in which images are reshaped, altered, or adjusted within the frame without additional compositing. For example, a visual effects artist may reduce the waistline of a female model in a TV camera, or increase the size of a strawberry falling into a bowl of cereal.
- **Color isolation.** Although most color alteration occurs in the editing bay, advanced color techniques in which a full-color object appears in a black-and-white world, or specific colors pop out from the desaturated background, all require the technical finesse and resources of a visual effects artist.

COMPOSITING (2D)

Compositing is the process of digitally layering multiple flat images or video clips together to create the final shot. This technique can be used to replace the sky, add an image to a blank TV screen, place a map behind a weatherman, or add any layer or source over another. Compositing programs such as Adobe After Effects, Apple Motion, and Autodesk Flame are powerful, professional-grade applications that provide a tremendous array of compositing tools for the animator. Although the learning curve on these programs is steep, there are a number of training classes in major cities across the country. Even if you are working with a visual effects artist, understanding the basics of how the software works will help you better prepare for the integration of visual effects in your movie.

DEFINITIONS

Visual effects are created when animation, matte shots, composited elements, and computer-generated elements are added to live-action footage.

Physical effects are effects that are built and exist in reality, as opposed to computer-generated effects. Examples include models and miniatures, special makeup prosthetics, creatures and monsters, specialty vehicles (like the Batmobile), on-set tricks and gags, and special props.

Mechanical effects include weather-related effects like rain, snow, wind, and hail, as well as pyrotechnics such as explosions, bullet hits, and car crashes.

Digital effects include effects created within the realm of the computer such as computer-generated monsters, environments, vehicles, and spaceships.

In *Time and Again*, the majority of the visual effects were composites. As an example, in the opening of the diner scene, the script described Awanda cooking and setting her food on fire. Because it wasn't practical or safe to use real fire on set, we shot Jennie's performance behind the stove first without fire. Called a background plate, this shot was used as the foundation for the composite.

Anatomy of a Visual Effects Shot
A look at how we created a sprawling European rotunda using a small green screen soundstage and some smart compositing techniques. You can see the final commercial at www.jasontomaric.com/sunscreen.mov.

Marble Rotunda
Made by layering still images of various objects to create the illusion of depth, the entire rotunda was created digitally, then animated in After Effects.

Sky Background
We added timelapse footage of clouds behind all the layers in the composition to imply rapid passage of time.

Floor
The floor was made from photographs of a piece of marble tile and a decorative marble compass. Composited and textured to look like one piece, the floor draws the audience's attention to the woman in the center.

Woman
The woman in the center was shot against a green screen. The only real element in the entire commercial is her, the dress and the bed on which she sits. All the lighting was designed to move around her to simulate the rising and setting sun.

Foreground Columns
The columns in the foreground were actual models shot on a turntable to give the illusion of depth as our virtual camera pushes into the room.

Visual Effects montage.

To create the fire, I found some stock footage of a torch flame against a black background. Using Adobe After Effects, I was able to cut the torch flame out from the black background digitally and lay it over the background plate of Awanda in the kitchen. I then created a mask to crop off the top and bottom of the flame so it looked like it was behind the counter. The result is a realistic shot that tells the story and was safe to produce.

THREE-DIMENSIONAL ANIMATION

Three-dimensional (3D) animation is the art of creating objects, setting lights, and moving a camera – all within the virtual world created within the computer. Keep in mind that 3D animation is completely different from 3D or stereoscopic techniques for which audience members need to wear special polarized glasses to see the depth of the shot. Programs like Maya, LightWave, and 3D Studio Max afford animators the ability to create digital models of people, objects, and settings; stretch digitally created skins over the wireframe models; add texture and interactivity with light; calculate the physics of how the objects move and interact within the environment; place lights; add cameras with real interactive lens functions; and render the final image into a flat, realistic 2D image.

Most Hollywood films use computer-generated imagery (CGI) in place of traditional hand-built models or old school tricks like matte paintings, forced-perspective models, and physical and mechanical effects. CGI is often cheaper and offers filmmakers limitless options for creating and manipulating the environment of the story, even after the footage has been shot.

Jason's Notes

Just because the camera in a 3D world *can* perform any imaginable move doesn't mean it *should*. It's easy to get overexcited about the limitless cinematic possibilities, but understand that the crazier the camera moves, the more it may draw attention to the effect, pulling the audience out of the story. As a general rule, always think of each visual effects shot within the context of the story, not as its own standalone shot.

In the low-budget arena, inexpensive software and a well-equipped computer can provide a myriad of options never before available to filmmakers. If the tools are available, high-quality effects can be produced inexpensively, although it still requires a lot of time to finesse and complete each effect until they appear real and can be smoothly integrated into the rest of the movie.

3D animation, such as the shuttlecraft from my feature film *Clone*, is impressive, but very costly and time-consuming to produce.

There are a number of steps to create a realistic 3D object.

- **Wireframe model.** The first step of creating a 3D object is to model it. Modeling is the process of taking a rudimentary primary shape and molding it into a 3D mesh, or wireframe skeleton, of the object. The more detailed the model, the more realistic it will appear on screen – the lighting, shading, and interactivity with its environment will bring out the details of the model. There are a number of companies that sell existing 3D models of practically anything, saving animators the time and research of building objects from scratch. Vehicles, people, animals, structures, and everyday objects are all available from vast model libraries.

A train engine in wireframe.

- **Texturing.** Once the model is complete, the next step is to skin, or wrap the wireframe mesh with its surface. Surfaces can be photographs or digitally created images. Surfaces are given a set of photographic traits:

A train engine wireframe with a no-detail, flat shading applied.

  - **Color.** What is the color of the surface? Most surfaces are painted to lifelike realism to include aging, cracks, distress – general imperfections that help make an otherwise perfect object appear more organic.
  - **Reflectivity.** How much light is reflected off the surface of the object. A black couch may only reflect 20% of the light to the camera, whereas a silver sphere will reflect 100%.

■ **Specularity.** How visible and sharp the reflections of light sources in an object are. A pinpoint light source has high specularity in a chrome sphere, but low specularity in a wood sphere.

■ **Transparency.** Can you see through the object? Metal has 0% transparency, and glass may have 95% transparency. Objects such as plastics and glass can all have varying degrees of transparency.

■ **Texture.** Is the object's surface flat or is there a 3D surface, like the dimples of a golf ball? These features are generally considered in both modelling and surface maps to ensure that light properly interacts with the object.

A texture map has been wrapped around the wireframe.

■ **Lighting.** In much the same way that a cinematographer lights a subject and an environment in real life, animators also design and implement lighting into the virtual world. Direction, intensity, color, and softness are all contributing factors to realistic lighting.

The train engine has been digitally lit to reflect the lighting of the environment.

■ **Animation.** Once all the models in the shot have been completed, the animator will animate the movement of the models, lights, and camera within the scene. By adding keyframes to a timeline, the animator can create keyframes, or the stopping and starting points of each object, with the computer calculating the move from one keyframe to the next. There are a number of ways to vary the change from one keyframe to the next, the physics of which are tailored to the particular movement of each object.

- **Render.** Once the scene has been animated, the computer must now go through a process of calculating, or rendering, each frame based on the parameters the animator specified. Lighting, reflections, and complex movement can add to the rendering time significantly. Once the shot is rendered, if there are any changes to be made, the animator must rework the animation and rerender. Generally, low-resolution renders are created for preview purposes that drastically reduce the processing time, especially if the render is still a work in progress.

PREPARING VISUAL EFFECTS IN PREPRODUCTION

Visual effects work can run a wide range of costs, all of which should be accounted for during the preproduction process. When budgeting effects work, consider both the physical costs of generating all the necessary elements on set as well as the post work itself.

- **Hire a visual effects supervisor.** Visual effects can be a very complicated and expensive process, so it's best to hire an expert to guide you through the process. To find a visual effects artist, contact your local film commission, local production and postproduction facilities, or even college and university art programs, many of which have a visual media department with computer animation classes. Students interested in breaking into the animation industry may be willing to create free effects for your film as a way of expanding their demo reels. Trust and rely on the experience and technical expertise of a visual effects supervisor.
- **Determine the number and type of effects.** The first step is to break down the script to determine how many and what types of visual effects are required. An experienced visual effects supervisor should help you create this list – there are effects that may seem complicated but are really easy to create and other effects that although they appear simple to create, are extremely difficult.
  - **Creatures and animals.** In a horror film, can a creature be created practically or does it require a range of movements that require a digital version? Are there any animals such as a flock of birds performing a specific action or a nonexistent creature like dinosaurs? Animating organic, living creatures, from designing the creature, to mapping the surfaces, designing the kinematics, or movement, of the creature, and finally rendering the creature, is a time-consuming and expensive process. Contact a make-up prosthetics artist to calculate the cost of making a creature costume, then determine based on the script whether it's more effective to create the creature practically or digitally.

SET-UP SCHEDULE

Title: Neutrogena

Shooting Day: 1 of 1   **Crew Call:** 8:00am

Date: 21-Sep-08   **Call at Location:** 8:00am

Location ProHD Studios

SET UP#	Sc. #	Ltr	Shot	DESCRIPTION	Set-Up Time set-up	shoot	ESTEM. Finish	ACTUAL T.O.D.
				Crew Call	8:00am	10:00am		
1	3		1	L.S. Dolly past column		10:00a	10:30a	
2	1		2	E.C.U. Dolly into Laura	10:30a	11:15a	11:30a	
3	7		3	C.U. Laura looks up, sees Scott	11:30a	11:45p	noon	
4	5		4	L.S. to M.S. into Laura's back	noon	12:30p	1:00p	
5	4		5	M.S. Dolly around Laura	1:00p	1:30p	2:00p	
				LUNCH		2:00p	2:30p	
6	2		6	Bird's Eye view of Laura	2:30p	3:15	3:30p	
7	6		7	Scott walks from behind column	3:30p	4:00p	4:15p	
8	8		8	M.S. Scott looks up	4:15p	4:15p	4:30p	
9	9		9	M.S. Scott and Laura join hands	4:30p	5:00p	5:15p	
10	10		10	Scott and Laura walk into sun	5:15p	5:30p	5:45p	
11	11		11	Scott and Laura kiss	5:45p	5:50p	6:00p	
12			12	Fabric Shots	6:00p	6:30p	7:30p	
				Crew Wrap		7:30p	8:00p	

Every shot of the sunscreen commercial was carefully planned on set – well in advance.

- **Vehicles.** Are there vehicles such as spaceships, planes, or cars that need to be created? Creating simple solid surfaces such as metal, wood, plastic, stone, and glass is relatively easy and can be inexpensive to create, although be aware of the challenges of creating realistic reflections in CGI models. Are there any special plates or reference photos needed from the set to create reflections or lighting references? Be sure to budget the time and resources needed to acquire all the necessary elements to complete the animation.

- **Locations.** Are there any establishing shots of a specific time period that cannot be practically shot? Does the script call for a panning shot of a Western town in the 1850s? Can a portion of the set be constructed on location, then digitally extended to create a larger town? Creating digital extensions can be fairly inexpensive, especially if the original plate was shot with a static camera – as a general rule of thumb, adding digital effects to a moving shot are always more time consuming than working with a static camera.

- **Screens and views.** Are there any television screens, window views, reflections, or views outside a moving vehicle that need to be created? In some instances, such as a television screen, the image needs to be motion-tracked and composited into the existing footage, and possibly rotoscoped, if a foreground subject passes in front of the composite. In other instances, where a scene is shot of actors inside a "moving" car, the car may be stationary in a soundstage with a green screen placed far outside the windows. The view outside the car can then be composited in during the postproduction process.

- **Weapons and pyrotechnics.** Are there any scenes that include weapons, lasers, or explosions that cannot be shot with live pyrotechnics? Although these effects can be added to a shot, part of compositing a light-generating object like an explosion or laser beam means also adding the effects of the luminescent object onto all other objects in the shot. An explosion will illuminate all surfaces facing the fireball – all of which should either be shot live on set using lighting effects or digitally added to create a realistic and believable effect.

- **Removals.** Visual effects artists are often hired to remove the wires that support stuntmen or on-set special effects rigs. These removals can be relatively simple in cases where an actor is shot against green screen and the wires do not cross any other object in the shot. But if the wires happen to cross over faces, bodies, or parts of the set, one shot can take weeks to correct. Do everything possible on set to minimize the intrusion of wires across actors.

- **Weather effects.** Rain and snow can be added into any establishing shot. Sophisticated software plug-ins can create depth to these effects so that rain appears to taper off the deeper into the shot you look, but to complete the technique, compositors should cut out objects in the frame so the rain or snow appears to fall behind them.

- **Storyboarding.** Once the script has been broken down and a list of visual effects has been created, work with the visual effects supervisor and

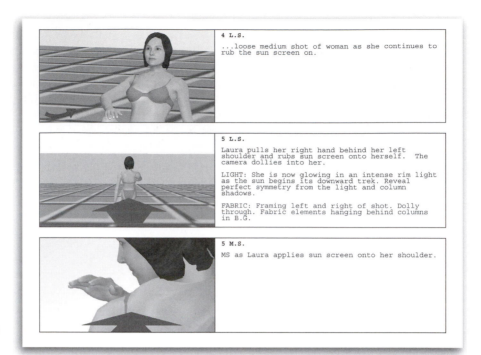

4 L.S.
...loose medium shot of woman as she continues to rub the sun screen on.

5 L.S.
Laura pulls her right hand behind her left shoulder and rubs sun screen onto herself. The camera dollies into her.

LIGHT: She is now glowing in an intense rim light as the sun begins its downward trek. Reveal perfect symmetry from the light and column shadows.

FABRIC: Framing left and right of shot. Dolly through. Fabric elements hanging behind columns in B.G.

5 M.S.
MS as Laura applies sun screen onto her shoulder.

We developed storyboards with Frame Forge before going on set to shoot the elaborate effects plates for the sunscreen commercial.

storyboard artist to draw every frame of every sequence. The goal is to figure out the composition of each frame, movement of objects and subjects within the frame, and specific camera movements. In some instances, rough animation, called *animatics*, are created to work through sophisticated camera movements and character actions. Both storyboards and animatics give you a visual representation for each shot, enabling the visual effects supervisor to design the steps needed to execute each shot, and the line producer to determine a cost for each shot. In complicated sequences, edit animatics together with a loose dialog, sound effects, and music track to help judge pacing and timing. It's easier and cheaper to change a shot in this early phase than when the full-resolution version is created.

- **Budgeting.** The next phase is to assign a cost to each visual effects shot. Factors such as the number of visual effects artists needed to model, texture map, light, and animate the elements within the frame, software costs, rendering time, and costs of outputting the frames are all scalable. More often than not, the cost of effects shots exceeds the allotted budget, making it necessary to either cut back on the number of effects shots or reduce the complexity. There are a number of ways to simplify effects to save money while retaining the creative intent:
  - **Choose 2D over 3D.** Overlaying images over the frame are almost always cheaper than modeling, lighting, and compositing 3D images. This does not mean that a 3D look cannot be achieved with 2D means.

Jason's Notes

I recently directed a TV commercial featuring a woman applying moisturizer in a spectacular marble European rotunda. Shooting in a location like this would have been both impractical and expensive, so I decided to shoot the entire commercial in a green screen soundstage, with the only real elements being the woman, her dress, and the couch she was sitting on. To create the background, we photographed and assembled real-life objects for each of several layers – the background wall, the midground columns, and the rings of the ceiling. By choosing camera moves mostly on the Z-axis, we created a 3D space with only 2D images, creating the effect on a limited budget. You can see the final commercial at www.jasontomaric.com/sunscreen.mov.

- **Don't move the camera.** Compositing 2D or 3D images over a static camera frame is exponentially easier than over a moving shot. Look at each visual effects shot and determine which shots can be accomplished with a static frame. Remember, your compositor can digitally pan, tilt, and zoom into any frame to create an organic feel to any frame. Try to limit the extent of each of these each moves as increasing the size of the frame to accomplish the effect degrades the overall resolution. In general, you can safely increase the frame by 10% without any noticeable effect.

- **Take photos instead of building CGI environments.** Whenever possible, using existing photographs to create an environment is much cheaper and easier than creating objects within the realm of the computer. Even when effects are needed in sci-fi movies, extreme macro close-ups of surfaces can create a myriad of interesting shapes and patterns. For example, for a bird's eye view of a rocky planet, shoot a close-up of a chocolate cookie, with the chocolate chips removed to create "craters."

- **Remove organic elements.** Whereas solid objects such as an apple, a chair, or a car can be easy to animate and render, organic elements such as fire, water, smoke, fabric, fur, and hair require massive amounts of rendering time to calculate the complexities of each element and how the light and physics of the environment affect the movement and appearance of the element. Correctly animating organic elements requires a certain degree of trial and error, which means rendering a shot to see how the element looks, changing the parameters to improve the look or movement, and then rerendering. Reducing the number of organic elements help save time and money. One option is to shoot organic elements practically whenever possible. For example, in my sci-fi feature *Clone*, we augmented dozens of exterior train shots by shooting moving backlit smoke against a black background, then compositing it into the shot of the CGI train. This not only saved time, but by adding a realistic organic element, helped create a more realistic shot.

Jason's Notes

As a director, it's really important to understand the basics of how visual effects are created. When you conceptualize an idea, knowing how the tools work and, even more importantly, how much they cost is a great way to help you shape your vision within the constraints of the schedule and budget. If you know how to create a spectacular image with simplified techniques, both your audience and clients will be happy.

DURING PRODUCTION

Each shot intended to be used as part of a visual effect is called a *plate*. For example, in a green screen shoot, the footage of a man in front of the green screen is called the foreground plate, whereas the footage that will replace the green screen is called the background plate. Properly shot plates are key to simplifying the job of a visual effects artist. Whenever you're shooting visual effects plates on set, I'd recommend inviting the visual effects supervisor on set to ensure the plates are properly photographed. One small change to the lighting or positioning of an object on set can save or cost a visual effects artist dozens of hours in post. For example:

- **Edges and transparency.** When shooting green screen footage, be keenly aware of any object with soft lines that may appear in front of the green screen. Objects with poorly defined edges, transparency, or translucence, such as plants, a wine glass, and lace curtains will all create immense challenges when trying to key out the green background, especially if shooting with a digital format. Look carefully at the frame before shooting to ensure that all lines encroaching the green screen are as sharp and defined as possible.
- **Reflections.** When shooting a set with a green screen, be aware of green surface reflections. For example, on a dining room set with a green screen outside the window into which a sprawling cityscape will be composited, if the dining room table reflects the green color, then it will be keyed out and appear transparent. To correct this problem, the visual effects artist will need to rotoscope, or cut out, the table, digitally remove the green color, and create an accurate reflection – all time-consuming techniques. The proper way to shoot this plate is to choose a table with a less reflective surface, select a camera frame in which the green reflection is nonexistent, or dress the table with a tablecloth to cover the reflection. A little time on set can save a lot of time in the compositing room.
- **Always write down camera settings.** Much like shooting in the real world, the 3D camera abides by the same physics as its physical counterpart such as distances, focal length, depth of field, and lighting contrast ratios. When shooting on set, carefully measure the camera's distance from key subjects and objects on set, the lens settings – focal length, focus, and iris – and the placement, brightness, and softness of each light. Providing this data allows the effects artist to recreate these conditions in the digital world, ensuring a more realistic integration of CGI elements into the frame.

- **Think in 3D.** When adding CGI elements to a frame, remember that certain objects have a degree of reflectivity, meaning that in the surface of a car, you'll be able to see a reflection of the world that exists behind the camera. Always take photographs 360 degrees around the set so an effects artist can add realistic reflections in objects.
- **Shoot background plates.** Always shoot versions of a shot without the foreground subject or object in the frame. Let's say we have a shot in which a man walks up to a futuristic shuttlecraft sitting in a store parking lot. Knowing the shuttlecraft will be completely computer-generated, the shot is filmed with the man walking up to an empty parking lot. However, it's also important to shoot the same shot without the man to give the animator a clean background. This background can be used for a number of purposes – from creating reflections in the shuttlecraft windows to digitally extending the set so the camera can "pan" across the final effects shot.
- **Avoid using filters.** Shoot each shot as cleanly as possible – without any softening or enhancing filters in front of the lens. Adding CGI elements to a frame shot through a Pro-Mist softening filter makes the animator's job much more difficult. Remember, many of these filters and looks can be created in the editing room and applied over the finished shot.

Jason's Notes

I created several visual effects in *Time and Again* to help cut production costs, by creating landscapes and set dressing and even by adding digital 1950s cars in the background. All the effects were free because I was able to use my limited experience in Adobe After Effects to create them on the Mac system at home.

- **Fire in the diner kitchen.** I added the flame burning behind the counter in the diner digitally because using real pyrotechnics on set was too dangerous and would have cost too much money. In creating the digital fire, I masked off stock footage of a torch flame, so it appeared to be behind the counter, and

This frame is what we originally shot on set. This layer, called the background plate, will serve as the foundation for the composite. We will have to add the fire into this shot.

This frame is a stock video of a torch flame that will be added to the background plate. Compositing software like Adobe After Effects or Shake allows you to remove the background, especially if there's a large difference in color or brightness between the object and the background. In this case, the black background was easy to knock out.

This is the final composite of the two elements. Notice how the top and bottom of the flame have been cut off to give the illusion that the flame is behind the counter. We also cut out, or rotoscoped, the waitress so she appears to walk in front of the flame.

even masked the waitress who walked in front of the flame, so it appears to be behind her. This effect took only a few hours to create.

- **Digital mailbox.** As Bobby Jones rides his bike home, he passes a mailbox with his parents' names on it. Because we didn't have enough money to buy a real mailbox and create a sign, I decided to add it digitally. When it came time to create the mailbox, I simply walked up and down my street until I found a mailbox I liked. I took a few pictures with my digital camera, imported the pictures, and digitally cut the mailbox out from the background using Photoshop. I then created the sign with his parents' names and imported the final still image into After Effects. I then needed to add the image to a moving dolly shot, so I hand-tracked the image to match the camera movement. Finally, I added a digital focus pull and color-corrected the shot.

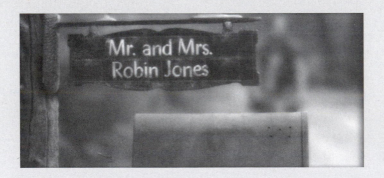

■ **The town square.** I really wanted a vast, sweeping shot of the 1950s town as Bobby left the diner, realizing his whereabouts for the first time. Because it wasn't possible to secure enough cars and shut down the town square for one shot, I created the entire shot digitally. I took my DV camcorder to the top of one of the buildings in town and rolled off a few minutes of footage. Then, using After Effects and Photoshop, I digitally painted masks to cover all the cars, while still retaining the movement of trees and flags. I then scoured the Internet for pictures of 1950s vehicles that matched the same lighting and angle as in my shot. After cutting them out from their background, I used After Effects to place them on the now-empty street and animated them moving down the road. After a final pass of color correction and softening of the entire image, it seamlessly matched the surrounding shots and convincingly showed off the town.

■ **Digital picture frame.** When Bobby Jones sneaks into his bedroom, he sees a picture frame sitting on the shelf. The photo was digitally added. The photo we needed to have in the frame wasn't ready at the time of the shoot, so I used After Effects to track the camera movement and insert the photo into the frame, complete with a reflection in the glass.

CHAPTER 19
Postproduction Audio

453

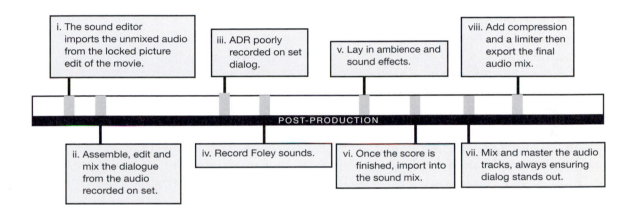

i. The sound editor imports the unmixed audio from the locked picture edit of the movie.

iii. ADR poorly recorded on set dialog.

v. Lay in ambience and sound effects.

viii. Add compression and a limiter then export the final audio mix.

POST-PRODUCTION

ii. Assemble, edit and mix the dialogue from the audio recorded on set.

iv. Record Foley sounds.

vi. Once the score is finished, import into the sound mix.

vii. Mix and master the audio tracks, always ensuring dialog stands out.

INTRODUCTION

Once the visuals of a movie are edited and the picture locked, it's time to focus on editing the audio. Audio postproduction work includes rerecording dialog, mixing in music and sound effects, balancing the levels of each sound element, and making sure the audio is within the proper technical parameters for exhibition.

Considered even more important to the audience in making an emotional impact than the visuals, people can detect far more sound cues than visual images, making the sound design a very important, but often overlooked, aspect of the moviemaking process. Sound design, ambience, and music bring together the continuity of the movie by turning a series of choppy cuts into a fluid narrative. Creating the sound is a very creative job and good sound designers can raise the quality of a movie to extraordinary new levels.

Before beginning work on the audio, be sure that you are completely finished editing the picture. Timing between shots should be locked, digital effects added, titles and transitions added, and the entire visual aspect of the movie finished. Locking the picture is important so that the audio engineers know what sounds need to be created and mixed into the soundtrack. Reediting the visuals of a movie will throw all the audio files out of sync and require additional work to realign large portions of the movie.

Filmmaking.
© 2011 Jason J. Tomaric. Published by Elsevier Inc. All rights reserved.

THE FIVE AUDIO TRACKS

Audio in a movie can be broken up into five different categories: the dialog, Foley, ambience, sound effects, and music.

Mike Farona works on the audio of *Time and Again* at Neon Cactus Studios.

Track 1: The Dialog Track

When recording audio on set, record the dialog with as little ambient sound as possible. This is especially important when producing a film that will be distributed internationally because the dialog track is often laid onto the master tape separately from the music and sound effects. This allows distributors in each foreign country to remove the English dialog track and record a new, translated track in the native language of the audience. The cleaner the dialog track, the easier it is to work with.

Jason's Notes

I find that the most time-consuming part of audio post is dialog editing. It's in this stage that you either love or hate your production sound mixer – his choice to hold the roll to turn off the refrigerator is now saving you hours of work in the studio. The cleaner the sound recording on set, the easier this process can be.

Mixing the Audio for *Fred and Vinnie*

When I mixed the audio for the feature *Fred and Vinnie,* I ran the dialog tracks through a five-step process designed to equalize the tone and volume of all the dialog tracks.

- **Crossfade each clip.** Add as long a crossfade as possible from one dialog clip to the next without cutting into the dialog to smooth the transition between each line. The audience will notice abrupt changes in the background ambience and crossfading can minimize this shift.

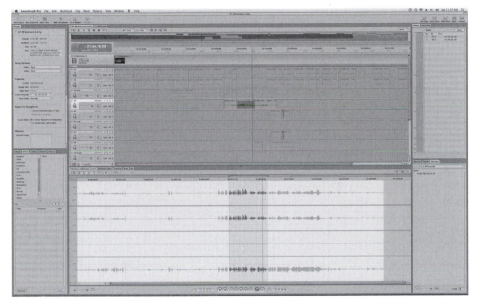

I used Soundtrack Pro to mix the audio for *Fred and Vinnie.* As a director, it's important to understand the audio process so that you know the power of audio, what sounds you need to record on set, and most importantly how the actor's performance can be influenced by the sound.

- **Apply noise reduction.** If a lot of background ambience was recorded with the dialog, I try to use noise reduction software to sample and remove as much of the background noise without affecting the tonality of the dialog. In situations where there is more ambience behind one character's lines, I will place one character's dialog on one audio track and the other character's on another audio track to apply separate noise reduction filters. Be careful when using noise-reducing plug-ins; if you remove too much, the dialog will begin to sound tinny and full of artifacts.

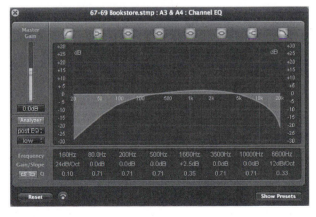

EQ plug-in for Soundtrack.

- **Apply EQ.** I always apply a parametric EQ to all dialog tracks and roll off, or reduce, the low 20–75 Hz, a frequency range at the lower end of human

Compressor plug-in for
Soundtrack.

Limiter plug-in for
Soundtrack.

We used a sound-
dampened booth to
record clean ADR and
voice-overs for both *Clone*
and *Time and Again*.

hearing that will rattle speakers and make the dialog muddy. Removing these frequencies keeps dialog crisp and sharp, leaving the low frequencies available for sounds effects and ambience. I also roll off the high frequencies from 10,000–20,000 Hz. Buzzing lights, ringing from digital compression, and vocal tones in this range tend to be overly shrill, so by rolling them off, I am narrowing the vocal frequencies to the sweet spot of between 200 and 5,000 Hz.

■ **Apply a compressor.** Compressors equalize the overall volume of the dialog by bringing up the quiet lines and bringing the loud lines down. It's important for the dialog throughout the movie to be consistent, so the audience doesn't have to constantly adjust the volume from one scene to the next. Be careful to not overly compress the dialog, as it can easily sound bad on high-end sound systems.

■ **Apply a limiter.** Limiters prevent the sound from reaching a specified volume, eliminating distortion. Used in conjunction with a compressor, limiters will cap the volume so the dialog is at the same level throughout the movie.

ADR

If the dialog is poorly recorded on set, it is possible to use a technique called ADR (automated dialog replacement) to rerecord an actor's dialog in a studio setting. To ADR a scene, an actor enters a sound booth, watches a monitor with the final cut of the movie rolling, and listens to the original recording from the set on a pair of headphones. The audio engineer will then cue up and repeatedly play each line that needs to be rerecorded one sentence at a time. The actor then recites the dialog to match the timing and emotional delivery of the original. Once the first line is recorded, is in sync, and is properly performed, the actor can then move on to the next line until the problematic dialog has been replaced. Once this process is finished, the audio engineer must EQ (equalize), or change the tone of the recording and add reverb to match the tone of the room in which the scene takes place. This process yields excellent audio quality, but is very time-consuming and expensive and sometimes still doesn't match the original audio recorded on location.

- If you need to ADR problematic lines, be sure to ADR the entire scene. It is very difficult, even with the best software, to match the tone of dialog recorded in the studio with location audio.
- ADR is a very expensive and time-consuming process. For low-budget projects, it's smarter to choose locations where the sound can be controlled to avoid the ADR process. Even though the director may have to compromise his creative vision, at least the film won't go over budget due to unforeseen sound problems.
- ADR is a very tricky process and should be done in a professional sound studio with professional microphones. Avoid attempting ADR at home with a home editing system and a cheap microphone, because much of the prosumer software doesn't allow the level of finessing required to match ADR'd dialog properly into a scene.

Jason's Notes

When we recorded the sound for *Time and Again*, we took great pains to make sure that dialog was cleanly recorded on set, making the audio postproduction process a breeze. The bedroom scene in Awanda's trailer was a notable exception. When we shot Awanda's angle, the set was quiet and we captured her sound flawlessly. When it got time to shoot Bobby's angle, the skies opened up and we recorded every bit of a typical midwest thunderstorm over his lines.

Because I didn't have the money or the time to ADR the scene in postproduction, we took the sound of the rain falling on the roof that we recorded wild on set and laid it under Awanda's lines, making a continuous ambience throughout the scene. I then took the scene to Mike Farona at Neon Cactus Studios and, using sophisticated noise-reduction software, was able to practically eliminate the sound of the storm in the background. If you listen closely to the scene, you'll notice the actor's dialog is a little thin, because the software had to remove a pretty wide range of sound frequencies to eliminate the thunderstorm.

Even though we ran into some problems, the available technology helped me fix a scene that could have been ruined.

- Be aware that some actors are better at ADR than others. I found that actors who are musically inclined, especially drummers, are better able to match sync than those without a musical background. Less experienced actors can be more expensive because most audio studios charge by the hour.
- Remember that if you need to ADR a scene, you are replacing the original audio with studio-recorded audio. As a result, sound effects, footsteps, clothes rubbing, the handling of objects in a scene, and ambience all need to be recreated and laid under the new dialog, adding to the postproduction budget.

Track 2: The Foley Track

Foley is the sounds of an actor interacting with his environment and includes footsteps, clothing rustling, doors opening and closing, and the handling of props. Often these very quiet sounds are virtually unnoticeable by the audience, but are critical in creating a realistic environment for the characters.

Scenes that use the audio recorded on set can benefit from Foley to sweeten sounds the microphone may not have picked up. Adding Foley sounds can help punctuate critical moments and can be easily done in the editing process.

Foley is especially critical when a scene is ADR'd. Remember that ADR is intended to replace audio that was recorded on the set, so in addition to the dialog, all the Foley sounds must be rerecorded and mixed as well.

Foley is usually recorded at special audio studios in which the Foley artists watch the movie on a screen and use objects made of various materials, sizes, and shapes to record the sounds needed in the scene. Each sound is usually recorded separately and is then synced and mixed into the movie.

Foley sounds can be divided into several categories.

MOVES TRACK

Moves is the sound of an actor's clothing moving, rustling, and rubbing against other clothing and objects. It is virtually inaudible but critical in making the audio sound realistic. Foley artists use fabrics and materials similar to those of the actor's wardrobe and move with the actors on screen, recording the resulting sounds and mixing them into the movie.

FOOT TRACK

The foot track covers all the footsteps in the movie. Often, when dialog is rerecorded in ADR, it's necessary to add the sound of footsteps back in, matching the timing and pacing of each step. The Foley artist uses shoes similar to what the actor wore on a small square of floor that matches the make of the actual floor and mimics the movement, steps, and slides of the actor's shoes. She then mixes the foot track into the movie.

To record the foot track properly, try visiting a used clothing store and picking out pairs of shoes that match the shoes worn by the actors in the movie. Then, go to a flooring store and pick up a collection of wood, tile, marble, and stone floor samples that match the type of floor in each scene. It's also a good idea to have gravel, sand, grass, and concrete as well, if the scene calls for it. Position the mike two to three feet away from the floor sample, kneel on the floor with a shoe in each hand, and watch the movement of the actors. Try to hit the floor sample with the same rhythm and strength as the actors. Add reverb and EQ to the foot track and mix it into the scene.

SPECIFICS

Specifics are everything else beyond footsteps and clothing movement. Remember that you don't need to use the same object that appears on screen to create the sound. Part of the fun of creating the specifics track is creatively finding objects to mimic a similar sound.

Examples of the specifics track include the following:

Sound	How the sound is created
Bicycle riding over dirt road	Rustle hand in a thick paper bag of cat food
Horses galloping	Clap two coconut shells together
Bones breaking	Snap and twist celery stalks
Crackling fire	Twisting cellophane
Walking in leaves	Crushing egg shells
Bird's flapping wings	Pair of leather work gloves

Be organized before recording the specifics track. Make a list of the specific sounds needed for each scene, then gather the necessary objects you need to create the sound and record each sound effect separately so you can tweak them and mix them together later.

Track 3: The Ambience Track

Ambience is the sound of the environment. It's the sounds of waves, seagulls, and wind if you're on the beach; it's the sounds of car horns, people talking, brakes screeching, jackhammers, and radios playing if you're in New York City; and the sounds of copiers, phones ringing, background chatter, and music if you're in an office building. These ambience tracks add the final touch of realism to a scene and can be recorded on set, added using prerecorded sounds, or recorded anywhere after the fact in a similar location and laid down over the entire scene.

ROOM TONE

Ambience also includes *room tone*. Room tone is the background noise of the set you're shooting on. Even though it may sound very quiet, there are still signals being picked up from the microphone, whether they are sounds of the environment or simply the sound of the equipment operating. You can hear the difference the room tone makes by listening to a quiet clip both with and without the audio. Room tone is used to help bridge gaps between lines of dialog, in insert shots for which sound wasn't recorded, or to cover or conceal unwanted sounds.

One common way to record the ambience of a location is to record a few minutes on set. At the end of the shooting day, before you wrap production, ask everyone to stand still for a few minutes while the audio engineer records the ambience, or room tone, for at least a minute.

It may be necessary to edit the scene together and add room tone under some lines of dialog when there isn't any. Remember that the audience is more likely to notice a *change* in the ambience from shot to shot more so than they'll

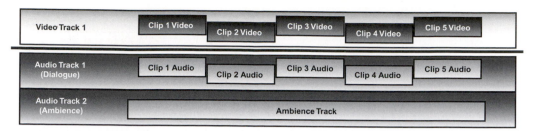

| Video Track 1 | Clip 1 Video | Clip 2 Video | Clip 3 Video | Clip 4 Video | Clip 5 Video |

| Audio Track 1 (Dialogue) | Clip 1 Audio | Clip 2 Audio | Clip 3 Audio | Clip 4 Audio | Clip 5 Audio |
| Audio Track 2 (Ambience) | Ambience Track |

Adding an ambience track under the edited dialog helps pull the scene together by helping cover the cuts between clips.

notice a consistent ambience track. Part of having room tone is so that it can be added to quieter shots for consistency. Once the room tone sounds consistent, then you can add the overall ambience such as people talking in the background of a restaurant or elevator music over the speaker in a store.

- When audio is recorded on set during a scene, the objective is to record only dialog – the ambience is put in afterward. Because the ambience track is several minutes long, it will add cohesiveness to the scene, pulling the edit together.
- The objective is to mix the dialog and sounds of the actors interacting with the environment all by itself on set. The native sounds of the environment are added in the editing room, where more control can be exerted over these sounds.

SOUNDS OF THE LOCATION

After the dialog is properly mixed with the room tone and the background sounds consistent, it's time to add the actual ambience track to the scene. Most ambience tracks can be pulled from sound effects CDs or even recorded on a similar location. If I'm shooting in an office, I may visit an actual office and record the ambience of the environment for a few minutes and then take that recording and lay it under the entire scene. Or if I shot in a closed-down grocery store, I may visit a grocery store later and record several minutes of the ambience to add under the entire scene.

Ambience is a great way to add production value to your movie. In the instance of sci-fi movies, the sounds of a spaceship can make the cheapest cardboard sets seem much more realistic to the viewer. Let the sound complement the visuals.

Another type of ambience is called *walla*. Walla is the indistinguishable murmuring of people in the background of a scene, for example, other patrons in a restaurant. Designed to blend into the background, a good walla track is recorded in such a way that a listener cannot pick out any one conversation, allowing the principal actor's dialog to be heard clearly.

High-quality sound effects libraries have several walla tracks, or, if you're on a budget, you can record your own walla track with friends or in an actual environment that matches the sound of your scene.

Track 4: The Sound Effects Track

Sound effects are non-Foley sounds such as explosions, gunfire, car crashes, and monster noises. These can be collected from sound effects CDs, downloaded from the Internet, or created and recorded in the studio. Sound effects help to establish key events in the film and establish the environment.

Be wary of cheap sound effects CDs from record stores or the Internet. They are often poorly recorded and contain a lot of background noise, which will make it difficult to edit in postproduction. The cleaner the recording, the better the mix.

Programs like Pro Tools and Digital Performer offer a wide range of tools to help you deliver the best possible audio.

Sounds effects can be sweetened or enhanced using software plug-ins in popular editing programs. Reverb, EQ, pitch shifting, speeding up or slowing down, noise reduction, and compressing are all examples of filters that can be used to help integrate a sound effect into the soundtrack. Pro Tools is one of the most common audio-editing programs available, although editing programs like Final Cut Pro and Adobe Premiere offer comparable plug-ins with slightly less control and speed.

Track 5: The Music Track

The music is the composed orchestral score in the movie. For more information on composing music, see Chapter 20.

MIXING THE AUDIO

When you are working in an editing program, I suggest creating a different time line to create a premix of each sound category. For example, one time line will contain only the dialog; the second is for Foley; the third for ambience; the fourth for sound effects; and the fifth for the music. This will not only help keep the potentially thousands of audio clips organized by category, but also help when it comes time to mix down the final audio. Using this process may even speed up your computer, because large numbers of audio and video clips in a single project can slow down the system.

When you are finished editing and mixing each sound category, open a new time line and import the mixed-down stereo dialog, Foley, ambience, sound effects, and music tracks. You can then easily mix the tracks together to achieve the proper balance between them, while making sure the audio never hits 0 db.

- When you are mixing the five tracks, dialog must *always* be the predominate and loudest of all the tracks. Even in the loudest battle scene in which music and sound effects drive the action, the dialog must always rise above the music and effects so the audience doesn't have to strain to hear what the characters are saying.
- When mixing the dialog track, make sure that all the dialog, from shouting to whispering, falls between 6 and 3 db. Even though this doesn't match how the spoken word sounds in real life, movie dialog is roughly the same volume throughout so that the audience doesn't have to constantly ride the volume with the remote control in hand.
- Play the movie while watching the VU meters. Every time the audio clips, or hits 0 db, use the rubber-band tool to isolate the part of the audio that peaks, and reduce the volume so it doesn't peak. You should be able to play through the entire movie and never hit 0 db.
- Try applying a light compressor to the entire dialog track to bring up the quiet spots and crush the loud spots, making the dialog much more even. In addition, a limiter prevents the audio from hitting 0 db by bouncing the peaking audio away from 0 db, much like a giant spring. The harder the audio approaches 0 db, the harder it's pushed back down. Although a slight limiter is useful, heavily limiting peaking dialog causes distortion.
- Once the dialog is ready, it's time to choose which of the four remaining audio tracks will be brought into the mix. A common mistake that many novice filmmakers make is to muddy the soundtrack by bringing up the music, sound effects, ambience, and Foley so loud that they become indistinguishable. Unlike real life, in which we hear hundreds of different sounds all around us, movie audio is much more sparse and the audio that is put into the film strategically focuses the audience on what they should be watching in the frame. For example, let's say we have a scene on a busy New York City street in which a woman is struck by a car and our hero rushes up to save her. Before she is struck, we hear the ambience of New York City, with the sounds of the cars passing by. We don't need to hear the Foley of her walking, or any substantial sound effects, so at this moment, the ambience is brought up. As she crosses the street, a single car horn blasts out at her. This horn must stand out from the rest of the ambience because it is coming from the car that will soon hit her, so we would bring up the sound effect of the horn over the ambience in the mix. Once the woman is struck by the car and our hero runs to her aid, we bring the ambience down to make room in the mix for our hero's dialog as he tries to save her and the music score that's fading in. At this point, we don't need the ambience of the city street. It's already been established and this moment in the scene is about our hero and the woman, not the surrounding traffic.

Mixing the sound effects, ambience, Foley, and music is like a dance. In any given moment, two tracks step forward while the other two are mixed down so that they don't all compete with one another. Balancing the ever-strong dialog track, this approach to mixing yields clean, easy-to-listen-to audio that will not distract the audience, but draw it into the moment on the screen.

Once all the tracks are edited, add light compression and a limiter to the entire soundtrack and be sure to listen to the audio on different speakers to make sure that the mix is clear and clean.

Mix the audio in a properly designed sound studio. The acoustics are specifically balanced so you can hear the broadest range of frequencies in as quiet a space as possible.

- Audio in a movie can be categorized into dialog, sound effects, Foley, ambience, and music. Be careful not to mix them too loudly, but in each scene, choose which of the five should take priority and make sure it stands above the other four. Dialog should *always* stand out above sound design or music.
- Make sure none of the audio elements exceed 0 db or the audio will peak and distort. Be careful when mixing your sound to leave enough headroom for the louder scenes. The dialog, though, should be of the same volume during the entire movie so the audience doesn't have to strain to hear lines during quiet moments.
- If you're mixing the audio tracks together, be sure to listen to the mix through different speakers. Remember that some people will listen to your movie on an expensive home theater system, and others will listen on a small mono-speaker 1970s fake wood–sided television with knobs to change channels. The audio needs to sound good on every system. When I produced *Time and Again*, I edited most of the movie on my Apple Final Cut Pro system and then took the final mix to a nearby audio studio to clean up several scenes. We listened to the mix on both $100,000 speakers and a pair of $20 speakers from the local electronics store. When the mix sounded good on each set of speakers, I knew we had found the correct balance.

M&E TRACKS

When a foreign distributor picks up a movie, they often require a DigiBeta or HD master tape with four tracks. Tracks 1 and 2 contain the stereo final mix of the movie audio, and tracks 3 and 4 contain a stereo mix of the music and effects, or M&E tracks.

M&E tracks are a complete mix of the movie audio minus the dialog, so that foreign countries can dub in the dialog in their native language. Keeping the various audio tracks separate makes it easy to generate an M&E track for distributors.

If you're planning on submitting your movie for distribution, be sure to keep the tracks separate during audio postproduction. If you don't, the distributor will require separate tracks and you will have to go back into the studio to remix the audio, racking up a bill for thousands of dollars in the process.

Jason's Notes

I had approached Mike Farona at the Neon Cactus Studios almost three years earlier for another film I had directed called *Clone*. We met at a party one night in Cleveland and began talking about my business as a filmmaker and Mike's business as a recording engineer of bands and live events. As we were both interested in getting into movie audio, we began to talk about my need for an audio studio to provide postproduction services for the film.

After meeting with Mike several times, I checked out the studio and he watched the rough cut of *Clone*, and we decided to work together. The arrangement was that Mike would do all audio postproduction services for free just for the experience of working on a movie. The result was a two-year collaboration that resulted in a film that won numerous international awards for artistic and technical achievement.

When I began working on *Time and Again*, I wanted to work with Mike again, but decided to perform the bulk of the audio work myself so as not to take advantage of his time and talents. Using Apple's Final Cut Pro, I was able to edit the dialog, sound effects, and music together into a 95% complete mix. I then converted the audio files to OMF and took them to Mike, who was able to perform light noise reduction, clean up some problem scenes, and master the final audio mix. Within eight hours, the audio was finished and ready to go. We burned the final mix to a 48-kHz 24-bit stereo AIFF file and I took it to my Final Cut Pro system and laid it back into the movie. He agreed to do the work for free and, again, added a few more awards that we won for *Time and Again* to his shelf.

CHAPTER 20
Music

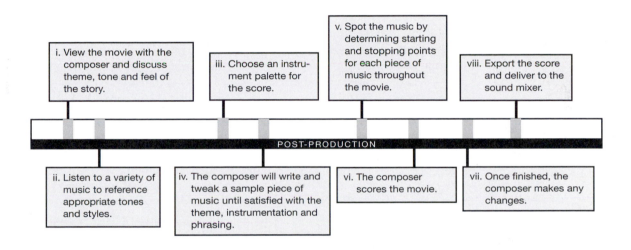

i. View the movie with the composer and discuss theme, tone and feel of the story.

ii. Listen to a variety of music to reference appropriate tones and styles.

iii. Choose an instrument palette for the score.

iv. The composer will write and tweak a sample piece of music until satisfied with the theme, instrumentation and phrasing.

v. Spot the music by determining starting and stopping points for each piece of music throughout the movie.

vi. The composer scores the movie.

vii. Once finished, the composer makes any changes.

viii. Export the score and deliver to the sound mixer.

POST-PRODUCTION

INTRODUCTION

Music is an important component of a movie and can help craft the feel and emotion of each scene. Considered the final dramatic player, the music is added after all the other dramatic elements – the acting, cinematography, sound design, and visual effects – have been completed. Music is also one of the most misunderstood and misused elements of the production, as first-time filmmakers often piecemeal music tracks without properly integrating them into the story.

Music needs to be directed in much the same way an actor does. The tempo, rhythm, timing, and phrasing of a musical score can be specifically written to bring out an emotion or feeling, filling in the last piece of the dramatic puzzle.

When I talk about directing the dramatic potential of a scene, I liken it to a pie that the director has to cut into pieces and divvy up among the departments. The actors get a piece, the cinematographer gets a piece, the sound designers get a piece; essentially, every department receives a piece. The size of the piece is entirely dependent on what the scene calls for. The final piece of the pie is reserved for the

Filmmaking.

© 2011 Jason J. Tomaric. Published by Elsevier Inc. All rights reserved.

music, and for the music to be just right, it needs to be crafted so that it perfectly completes the drama and fits with the rest of the dramatic elements.

Music can be added to a movie from any one of several sources. The music can be originally composed for the movie, it can be published and copyrighted material that has been cleared by the copyright owner for use in the movie, or it can be stock music. Each type of music has its own benefits and drawbacks, from creative control to cost.

- **Stock music.** There are companies that produce entire music libraries and license their unrestricted use to you when you purchase the library. You can use the music in any project you wish, from commercials to trailers to feature films, even if the project generates a profit. Once you buy the library, it is yours to use as if it were your own.
- **Music loops.** Popular software programs such as Apple Soundtrack come with thousands of simple musical loops, melodies, and rhythms that you can combine in an almost infinite number of combinations to create an original piece of music. Much like buying stock music, you have the right to use the music in any production you wish, even if it generates a profit.
- **Original music.** Local bands or artists who haven't been signed to a record label are usually willing to give you the rights to use their music in your film. It's free promotion for them and doesn't cost you anything. You can find local bands online or in any club that features local artists. Make sure that the CD recording is studio-quality.

Jason's Notes

Adding the music is unquestionably my favorite part of making a movie. I may be admitting a little too much to you, but the first time I hear the score played against my movie, it makes me cry . . . not because I'm exhausted from too many sleepless nights working on the film, but because feeling the emotional power of the music and seeing it complete my vision is one of the most unbelievable feelings an artist can experience.

- **Composer.** The best way to score your film is to have a composer write an original score specifically for the movie. Although this a time-consuming process, the resulting music will fit exactly what the movie needs. Composers will often work for free if they feel that the movie will be a viable launching pad for their career. Composers can be found in collegiate music programs, in orchestras, on the Internet, and at churches. The best part is that you and your composer own the rights to the music at the end of the project.
- Be aware of how music can change the overall theme of a scene. Although a particular mood may not be conveyed through the actors' performances, music can help add the underlying emotion, giving the scene its emotion. Play with different styles and emotions of music and see how it gives the scene a different look and feel.

Creating original music can be time-consuming, but the result is a musical experience that evokes the exact emotions you want from the audience.

STOCK MUSIC

- A variety of companies compose original music and license the unrestricted rights to use this music. From vast catalogs, you can choose virtually any genre and style of music, and whether you buy a single track or a compilation

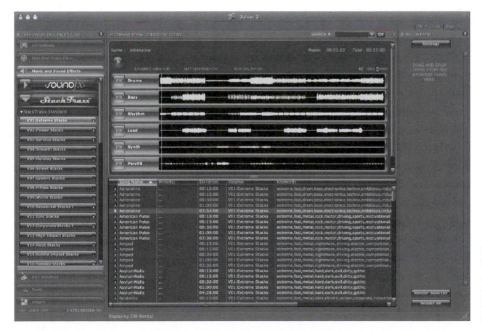

Some stock music libraries, like Digital Juice Stacktraxx, allows you to turn individual instruments on and off to customize the song.

CD, purchasing the music grants you the rights to use the music in any production you like.

There are a number of benefits and drawbacks to working with stock music. Benefits include:

- It's easy to listen through the music library to find the perfect song for your movie, and when you find it, you know you already have permission to use it.
- The music is finished and ready to be edited into the soundtrack.
- Provided you legally purchased the library, you have the right to copy, distribute, exhibit, and profit from any production that has stock music.
- Many stock music libraries feature rich, orchestral sounds that are perfect for a movie soundtrack.
- They are quick to work with and are of great help in a time crunch.

Drawbacks include:

- The music cannot be edited for timing or feel, although you can edit the music to shorten or lengthen it by slicing the sound file between verses or refrains or at the bridge.
- You are stuck with the melody and instrumentation of the music, which makes it difficult to adopt a musical theme for your movie. Most movies have a theme that runs throughout the movie as well as individual themes for the individual characters. The musical arc follows the characters along the story, changing as the characters change. With stock music, you only have one or two pieces of music with similar instrumentation and melody, making it difficult to maintain a recurring theme throughout the story.
- The music you use is not unique to your project. Because anyone can own a stock music library, your movie music may appear in anything from car commercials to industrial projects.

Ultimately, stock music libraries are terrific for television and radio commercials, industrial projects, and even short-form narratives for which you need music quickly and for which the music doesn't need to fit to the action on the screen. If you're working on a feature film, I would recommend staying away from stock music, as the lack of flexibility may hurt your movie more than help it.

Jason's Notes

Even though I worked with a composer who wrote an original score for *Time and Again*, I still used stock music in a number of scenes. The diner is one example: in this location, the music playing over the radio in the background came from a stock library I bought from Digital Juice. I needed an upbeat 1950s rock-and-roll tune but didn't need it to change with the changing drama of the scene, so I ran it though a high-pass filter to make it sound a little tinny and then compressed it so it wouldn't detract from the dialog and main audio. The result was a great piece of music that sounded like it came from the radio. The even better part is that I had the rights to use it!

USING COPYRIGHTED MUSIC

If you like the soundtrack written by a Hollywood composer or a popular artist, you can secure the rights by contacting the publisher (the publisher is always named on the CD case). Understand that the cost of leasing the rights to the song is dependent on the nature of your project, what the distribution plan is, how many copies of you movie will be distributed, and what the exhibition format will be (film festivals, theatrical, DVD release, foreign or domestic). These licenses are often very expensive, sometimes costing tens of thousands of dollars.

Most music rights are handled through the two following organizations:

ASCAP: www.ascap.com
BMI: www.bmi.com

Any work produced after 1920 is copyrighted and cannot be reproduced in any way without expressed written permission from the author, publisher, and copyright holder. This means you cannot add your favorite artist's music to your movie, even if it's ten seconds of a song, or use classical music or use an existing movie soundtrack.

Music written and performed before 1920 is in the public domain and can be used in your movie without any legal consequence. It's a difficult and time-consuming process to determine whether a composition is in the public domain, but visiting the Library of Congress is a great way to start.

When looking for works that are in the public domain, be careful of the following:

- **Classical music.** Although the written piece itself may be in the public domain, the performance of it may be copyrighted and cannot be used without permission of the musicians that performed it. If you have the written music, you can always perform the piece yourself or hire a musician to perform it for you under contract. You then become the owner of the performance and have the right to incorporate it in your movie. For example, Chopin's "Nocturne No. 9" is in the public domain, provided that you perform it yourself or contract a pianist to play it. But using a recent recording by the Cleveland Orchestra would be illegal unless you secure permission from the orchestra and from the pianist who played it.
- **Pop music.** Permission must be secured from the publisher to use any portion of the music in a film or video production. A majority of music licensing is handled through ASCAP and BMI.

On a cautionary note, if your movie is picked up by a major film festival or a distributor, you will be required to show proof that you've obtained the necessary permission for all music, or the festival or distributor will refuse to exhibit your movie.

Although the composition itself, like Chopin's "Nocturne No. 9", is in the public domain, a recorded performance of it is copywritten.

Jason's Notes

Do not use music in your movie without securing the rights from the copyright holder. Distributors will require you to provide proof that you have obtained the rights to a copyrighted piece of music before accepting your project. Many film festivals, especially the larger festivals, may also require similar proof. Remember that once you pick up a camera and begin to shoot, you are a producer who is making content. If you are looking to make a living as a filmmaker, you will be paying your bills with the money your movies and creative content make.

People who steal movies and music are not only hurting the industry, they are also hurting you. One of the reasons the record industry has stopped paying for the development of new artists is because there's no money left to pay for new artists. Piracy of music and movies has seriously cut into the development funds that used to allow large media companies to discover and develop new talent like you! Support the industry you're trying to work in. Support yourself and protect your future. Don't encourage piracy of movies or music.

MUSIC LOOPS

A new alternative to working with stock music is working with loop-based music creation software. Programs like Apple Soundtrack, Adobe Soundbooth, and Sony ACID give you unlimited flexibility to create original music by providing thousands of sound loops. A *loop* is a simple recording of a beat, a rhythm, or a melody from hundreds of instruments that you can piece together to make a complete piece of music. These programs give you the freedom to change the tempo, pitch, and phrasing of the music by using complex algorithms to conform each recorded loop to your project settings.

Much like stock music, purchasing the software gives you the rights to use the music you write in any production you want, even if it makes a profit. Many of the programs even allow you to record your own instruments to mix into the score. You can even import the QuickTime version of your movie into Apple Soundtrack Pro so you can watch the movie while you score, ensuring that the score matches the pacing of the movie.

Although loop-based music creation software affords filmmakers a wide rage of options and creative flexibility, you're still limited to working with prerecorded loops. One excellent option is to lay down the basic percussion and rhythm tracks and then record live instrumentalists playing an original melody. By using a combination of techniques, it's possible to make a beautiful, original score that you have the rights to use in your movie.

WRITING ORIGINAL MUSIC

Working with a composer is a rewarding and challenging task. An artist in his own right, the composer must write each piece of music so that it meets the director's vision, serves the emotional subtext of the scene, and yet allows him to explore his own musical creativity.

Finding a Composer

Finding a composer is easy; however, finding a composer with a compatible style, musical taste, and personality, and the time to dedicate to your project can be difficult. I recommend "auditioning" your composer the same way you might audition an actor. His initial score may be terrific, but you have to determine how easy it is to work with him once you begin asking for changes. You don't want to get stuck in the position of having to edit the movie to the score, simply because the composer was unwilling to change it.

There are plenty of ways to find a qualified composer in your area.

- The **Internet.** With the advent of Craigslist.org, community bulletin boards, and Google, searching the Internet will yield dozens of composers, small orchestras, and music aficionados in your area. If you live near a major city, I recommend posting a listing on Craigslist.org. The listing is free and you'll be surprised how many responses you'll receive.
- **Churches.** Many exceptionally talented musicians play at local churches every Sunday. Feel free to approach them after a service or call them during the week to discuss your project. I met my composer, Chris First, through a friend who attended a church Chris played at.
- **Universities.** Local universities often have music programs. Call the dean of the music program and ask to speak with a professor who might be able to refer talented students to you. If you live near Los Angeles or New York, keep in mind that several universities offer music courses specifically for writing movie music. Students will jump at the chance to have their work attached to a movie, even if it is independent.

Once you have a list of potential composers, take the time to meet and get to know them before deciding to work with them. Although their musical ability is important, it's even more important to find a composer with whom you feel comfortable working. Make sure the composer understands your vision, is excited about the project, and is willing to try new approaches if the current approach isn't working. The relationship between a filmmaker and a composer is a very special one, so be sure to choose the right person.

When working with the composer, remember that he is an artist as well and enjoys a certain creative freedom. As a director, paint the picture of what you want the music to accomplish and then allow the composer to do her job. Overdirecting the composer is a surefire way to limit the quality of the resulting score.

Working with a Composer

Now that your movie has been locked and the dialog and sound effects are in place, it's time to begin working with the composer. It's important to have as complete an audio track as possible so that the composer understands what is happening in each scene and how to write the music so it works in conjunction with the existing sound elements.

- **The overview.** Sit down with the composer and watch the movie from beginning to end a few times and talk about the story, the character arcs, and the plot points to give him a solid idea of what the movie is about. Even thought the visuals are complete and the audio track is finished, you'll still be watching an incomplete film. Because the missing music will heavily influence the emotional tone of the story, it's critical for the director and composer to be perfectly clear about what the story is about. Talk about why you felt inspired to tell this story, what emotions you want it to stir up in the audience, and what the theme is. Understanding these intangibles is the first step in composing an appropriate score.
- **Musical tone.** Discuss how you envision the music's role in the movie as if the music were a character. What emotional support should it provide, how should it support the characters, and how much should it lead each scene? It doesn't matter if you understand music or not. As a director, you should talk about what the music should do emotionally in each and every scene. Give the composer a "motivation" for the music as much as you'd give each actor a motivation for his character. For example, in *Time and Again*, I talked with composer F. William Croce about the scene in which Bobby Jones is walking through the wheat field during the opening title sequence. Even though the visuals establish a warm sunny day, I needed the music to imply that something was wrong by having an ominous, almost disconcerting, feel. Regardless of what the instrumentation is, the end result needed to be unsettling.
- **Choose the instruments.** After you discuss the overall feel of the music, think about the types of instruments you hear in the score. Orchestral instruments or synth sounds have an array of different tones and will heavily influence the sound of the score. Do you hear heavy percussion, light woodwinds, or emotional strings? Are the instruments native to a certain region of the world, or do you hear a traditional orchestra? I often spend hours with my composer listening to instruments from around the world, either in her sample library or in other pieces of music, to find the perfect "voice" for the movie. The job of writing the first piece of music becomes much easier once you've selected your musical palette.

Once the composer and director share a common vision for the music, how it should sound, and what it needs to accomplish, it's time to begin planning the details of the score.

Spotting the Film

An important step in the composing process is *spotting* the film with the composer. Spotting involves going through the movie and writing down when,

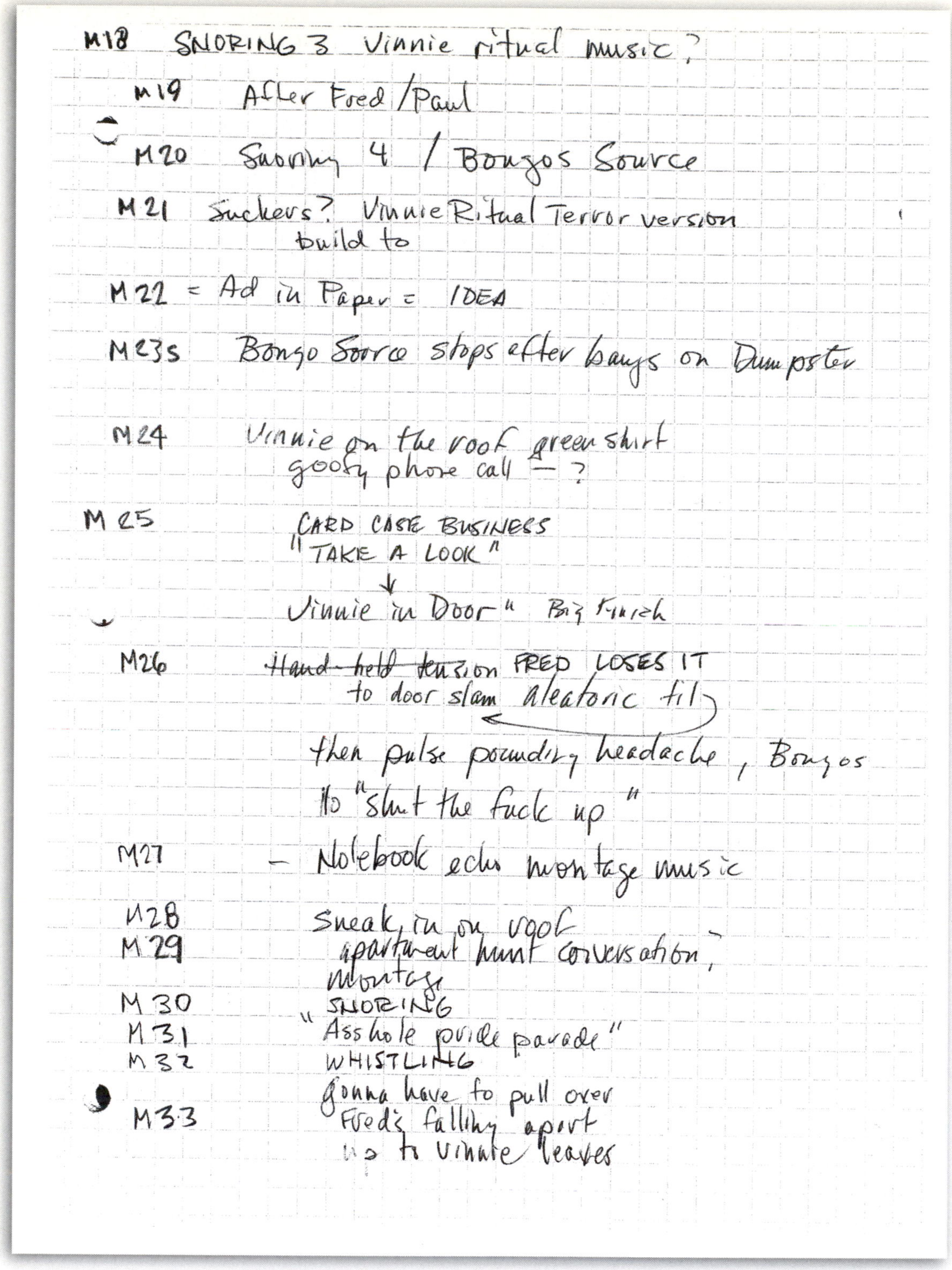

M18 SNORING 3 Vinnie ritual music?

M19   After Fred / Paul

M20   Snoring 4 / Bongos Source

M21   Suckers? Vinnie Ritual Terror version
            build to

M22 = Ad in Paper = IDEA

M23s   Bongo Source stops after bangs on Dumpster

M24   Vinnie on the roof green shirt
            goofy phone call — ?

M25   CARD CASE BUSINESS
            "TAKE A LOOK"
                    ↓
        Vinnie in Door " Big Finish

M26   ~~Hand-held tension~~ FRED LOSES IT
            to door slam aleatoric fil⟩
        then pulse pounding headache, Bongos
        to "shut the fuck up"

M27   — Notebook echo montage music

M28   Sneak in on roof
M29   apartment hunt conversation,
        montage
M30   "SNORING
M31   "Asshole pride parade"
M32   WHISTLING
M33   gonna have to pull over
            Fred's falling apart
            up to Vinnie leaves

Composer Jim Lang's spotting notes for the feature *Fred and Vinnie*.

to the frame, each piece of music needs to start and stop, and then discussing what the music needs to accomplish during that time. At the end of the spotting session, the composer will know how much music is needed, where it goes, and what style of music is required.

I often sit down in front of my editing system and use the timecode as a reference as we scrub through the movie. The composer usually has a sheet of paper and I literally give him the starting and stopping timecodes for each segment that needs music. Sometimes the music needs to be only a few seconds and other times, the score will be seven or eight minutes long. For each piece of music, we discuss how it needs to fit into the movie, how it will carry the story.

For example:

> 01:01:34:12 to 01:02:07:25—Bobby Jones escapes from prison. Driving percussion, action, sense of urgency and fear. Heavy on drums, but not too brassy. Should crescendo to the point at which the vortex opens.
> 01:02:07:25 to 01:03:12:18—Bobby Jones exits vortex and enters field. Music suddenly shifts. Ominous, creepy. Something's wrong. Try synth strings and unusual sounds. Not too "in your face." Let music work in the background and support the scene.

By the end of the spotting session, you will have a list of the number of songs that need to be written for the movie so the composer can go off and begin writing.

- Be as clear and concise as possible about the starting and stopping points of each piece of music when talking to the composer. Tell her *why* the music is starting and stopping and what type of emotional feel you want the music to invoke. Explaining *what* you want the music to do is sometimes better than trying to explain specifically what you want it to sound like.
- Be careful not to overscore the movie. Using too much music will hurt the movie by overdramatizing the action. Use music sparingly and carefully. Music in the right place will help a scene soar, but overscoring will draw the audience's attention away from the scene itself to the music, defeating its purpose.

Sample Scores

For larger, more complicated projects, I like to have the composer write a series of sample pieces that use different instrumentation and phrasing so we can find the right sound before beginning the actual work on the scene. Problems arise when a composer begins scoring a film and the results aren't what the director is looking for. This can be avoided by writing test scores before the actual scene work begins. My composer Chris First and I find this to be a very liberating process that allows us to try out a number of ideas, sounds, and styles before committing to using any one of them for the film.

Temp Tracks

If there are two words that strike fear into the hearts of composers, they are "temp track." A *temp track* is a musical track the director edits into the movie using a preexisting movie score or classical music. Directors like temp tracks because it helps them see how the music affects the movie in the editing room. The problem with a temp track is that the director often falls in love with it and asks the composer to replicate it – a difficult and very uncreative job. Most composers don't have the resources to recreate popular music like *Carmina Burana* or Beethoven's *Ninth Symphony*, often favorite choices for many directors. And even worse, a director may fall in love with the temp track so much that the composer's score doesn't compare.

Composers would prefer that you leave all music out of the movie and allow them the creative freedom to write a score that fits the film. It's all right to listen to other music to get ideas or to share a feel you like, but don't lay it into the movie, fall in love with it, and expect the composer to write something comparable.

WORKING WITH MIDI

Most Hollywood movies employ orchestras and choirs comprising musical freelancers who are able to read the composer's music on their first read-through. These musicians and the recording facilities often cost hundreds of thousands of dollars a day, placing them well outside the financial reach of most independent filmmakers. Fortunately, today's technologies give filmmakers access to original orchestral music through MIDI-based computer systems.

MIDI information records the duration, attack, and decay of each note hit on the keyboard. Then, by mapping a prerecorded sound to that key, the composer has an unlimited array of sounds at her disposal.

MIDI (Musical Instrument Digital Interface) is a computer interface that allows a composer to map various sounds, both prerecorded and digitally created in a computer, to individual keys on a keyboard. MIDI is the ideal alternative, providing realistic orchestral performances with less cost.

With a MIDI system, the composer can buy sound packages ranging from orchestral instruments to synth sounds to sound effects. Once loaded into the computer, he can program a certain sound set to his keyboard so, for example, if he were to hit a C key, it would play a recording of a violin playing a C note or a trumpet playing a C note. The sounds samples are also touch sensitive, so the harder a keyboard key is pressed, the stronger the attack on the instrument.

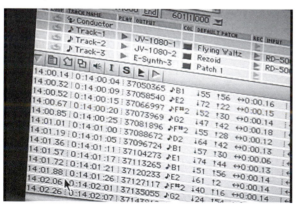

Instruments can be layered, much like audio tracks in Final Cut Pro, to build a massive orchestra or an array of sounds. Because it's nonlinear, any instrument can be changed at any time, tempos can be changed and pitch raised or lowered to meet the demands of the movie. MIDI is the best way to produce outstanding music for a fraction of the cost of recording it live.

For *Time and Again*, Fred Croce purchased several orchestral samples he used for the score. The result is a lavish score made up of real instruments, all mapped to the keys on the keyboard. Like Fred, most composers have their own composing suite and sound samples.

One added benefit of working with MIDI is the ability to load and sync the movie into the recording program. By importing the movie, the composer can write the music to frame accuracy.

FINISHING THE SCORE

Once the composer has finished writing the score and all changes have been made, it's best to output each piece of music separately as an AIFF file. If you're working in DV or HDV, output the files in stereo, 16-bit, 48 kHz. For HD movies, you can output stereo, 24-bit, 48 kHz. You can then either import the music into your editing program to mix into the final movie or give it to an audio studio so they can mix them together.

It may be necessary to add a compressor and some EQ to the music so it doesn't peak the levels. Refer to the instruction manual of your editing software for directions on how to do this.

- When the composer scores the movie, she should not adjust the volume of the music when scoring, but rather give the score to the audio engineer to mix it into the movie.
- A common problem in independent films is a music track that is too loud and overwhelms the dialog. Pull the music back in the final audio mix so that the dialog can be prominently heard.

UNIT 5
Distribution

i. Assemble press releases that detail the production, screening or release information, production stories, cast and crew bios and a story synopsis.

iii. Find a reputable sales agent who can represent your movie to distributors.

Distribution

ii. Contact the local media and arrange interviews for magazines, radio and television stations. Generate a buzz around your project.

iv. Apply to film festivals with the help of the sales agent.

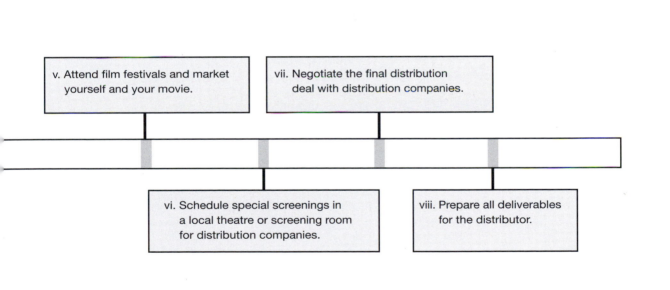

v. Attend film festivals and market yourself and your movie.

vi. Schedule special screenings in a local theatre or screening room for distribution companies.

vii. Negotiate the final distribution deal with distribution companies.

viii. Prepare all deliverables for the distributor.

DIGITALLY MASTERED
COLLECTOR'S EDITION
Time and Again
A JASON J. TOMARIC FILM
"A superbly-crafted suspense story!"
- Bill Martin, FOX News
WINNER OF 3 TELLY AWARDS
BEST DIRECTOR, BEST CINEMATOGRAPHER, BEST LOW BUDGET FILM
WIDESCREEN

CHAPTER 21

Distribution

INTRODUCTION

Distribution is the duplication, advertising, and promotion of a film to theatrical, television, or home video markets, both domestically and internationally. Securing foreign distribution is increasingly important due to the escalating worldwide demand for movies. Many distributors seek out new product at film festivals and film markets in search of quality films – in some cases, offering substantial advances.

Jason's Notes

There are two stages of moviemaking: making it and selling it. Many filmmakers spend all their time and resources on the former that they don't think about the latter until it's too late. The marketability of your movie begins all the way back to the development process, long before the script is even finished.

Every filmmaker dreams of having his film premiere to a sold-out theatre of excited, supportive moviegoers, but the reality is that very few actually get this opportunity. Distribution is a complicated and somewhat mysterious part of the process that many filmmakers seem to ignore until it's too late.

The process of making a movie is the same as the process of manufacturing any other product. Research the market, the audience, and what the distributors are looking for before you undertake a production. Most filmmakers spend massive sums of money and time on a movie only to discover that there's no market for it.

Smart moviemaking means figuring out a marketing and distribution plan before you begin preproduction:

- Set up meetings with domestic and foreign distributors and ask to talk to a sales rep.

Filmmaking.
© 2011 Jason J. Tomaric. Published by Elsevier Inc. All rights reserved.

- Ask them what genres are selling and what genres they feel will be hot in a year. For example, the horror genre is generally a consistent seller in the foreign market, is cheap to produce, and doesn't require big name actors in the cast.
- Find out which actors you should approach to help increase the marketability of the movie. Which actors are bringing in the largest sales of independent movies in the foreign market?
- Find out what format distributors prefer: 35 mm film or an HD format?
- What is the ideal length for the movie?
- What marketing materials should you collect during production to help in the distribution of the movie?
- What are the average sales prices for the type of movie you're making? This will help as you calculate the budget and determine how much money you should spend.

Jason's Notes

Many filmmakers consider it a sellout to design a film around what distributors are looking for, rather than letting the movie stand on its own merits. Before you begin a production, you need to make a very important decision as to whether you want to make a commercial film or a film for art's sake. If you want to make a commercial film that gets distribution and makes a profit, you have to produce a movie that is a viable product in the world market. If distribution is of no interest to you and you don't care if anyone sees your movie, these guidelines do not apply to you.

The rules of producing and selling a movie are a lot like the rules governing the game of basketball. Each player must acknowledge and understand the parameters, the size of the court, the height and diameter of the hoop, the number of players on each side, and the time restrictions for an organized game to take place. Whereas some may find these rules limiting, many talented athletes have excelled at the game, even when playing within the guidelines. The same philosophy applies to the production of a movie, in that filmmakers must follow the distributor's strict guidelines governing the content, format, casting, and genre for the film to be commercially viable. Using a little creativity and talent, filmmakers can certainly succeed within a distributor's rules. Remember that the film industry is a business designed to make a product that sells and makes a profit.

So what are distributors looking for and how does a movie become a commercially viable product?

- **Who's in it?** The first question most distributors will want to know is what name actors are in the film. Recognizable names help sell the film in foreign territories and command larger profits. Unfortunately, the stature of the actors involved overshadows practically every other aspect of the movie. If you want to sell a film and make good money, hire name actors.
- **What is the genre?** Horror and action films sell best in foreign territories because they're not overly reliant on translated dialog like dramas or comedies. These genres have a longer shelf life and are universally top-sellers in the global market.
- **How long is it?** Most movies need to be between 90 and 100 minutes long. If you're producing a low-budget movie, keep the length to as close to 90 minutes as possible to stretch the budget as far as possible.
- **Production value.** Quality cinematography, special effects, and production design are all-important factors in helping sell a movie. Regardless of how low the budget is, all that matters is that the film looks expensive.
- **The buzz.** Movies with a bigger buzz tend to fetch higher dollar amounts. Be sure to drum up as much publicity as you can to attract distributors.

Begin the marketing of the movie before you start production:

- Build a web site that teases the audience and builds interest in the project. Post trailers and behind-the-scenes photos to build a buzz so that when the movie is finished, people will already be familiar with and anxious to see the film.
- Take lots of publicity and behind-the-scenes photos during production. The distributors will ask for these to help promote the movie. They are also helpful to distribute to newspapers and magazines when critics write articles about the movie.
- Get as much media coverage as possible during production. Newspaper clippings, television news stories, and magazine articles are all powerful ways of building a buzz around the film and attracting distributors.

FOREIGN DISTRIBUTION

Foreign distribution is the licensing of the film to theatrical, home video, and television buyers in over 65 countries. Most independent movies make more money in the overseas market than in the Unites States, which is why careful planning and casting are critical in making a film with the broadest appeal.

Jason's Notes

Be very, very careful when working with distributors; with the exception of a handful of reputable companies, many distributors know the industry and how to shape contracts in their best interest, often leaving you with nothing. Even with an airtight contract and sharp legal advice, most filmmakers never see a single penny from the sales of their film. Distributors are truly the Great White sharks of the entertainment industry.

Most independent movies are picked up by a foreign sales company that serves as a middleman, brokering deals with individual distribution companies in each country. The foreign sales company does not replicate or distribute the movie itself, but markets the film to television stations, home video distributors, and theaters in foreign countries. The distributors in each country will pay a flat rate to the foreign sales company for the exclusive right to sell the film in that country, keeping the resulting sales and subsequent profits for themselves. The more recognizable the names and the more popular the genre, the higher that rate.

Foreign sales companies will sell films to international distributors at film markets. Held six times a year, these markets are high-profile events that may occur during notable film festivals. Using advertising, posters, and movie trailers, the distributors lure potential international buyers in an effort to showcase and sell off their library of films. Buyers include home video distributors, theatrical exhibitors, and television station owners looking to purchase programming for their companies.

There are six major film markets:

- The **American Film Market (AFM)** is held every November in Santa Monica, California, for eight days. Nearly 300 buyers attend the hotel-based market and can screen films on sale at local theaters.
- The **Cannes Film Market** occurs in May in Cannes, France, during the Cannes Film Festival. The festival is a showcase for screening films and the market is a venue for selling films.
- The **MIFED Market** occurs each October in Milan, Italy.
- **MIPCOM** takes place in October in Cannes, France, and is mostly focused on television productions such as series and made-for-television movies.
- The **European Film Market** occurs in Berlin, Germany in February and runs in tandem with the Berlin Film Festival.
- The **Hong Kong International Film & TV Market (FILMART)** takes place in March and provides a sales opportunity for film and television programming.

Distributors pay the costs of traveling and representing the film at these markets, although market costs and additional marketing expenses such as posters, trailers, and press kits will be taken out of the gross revenues generated by the movie.

If the movie is shot on 35 mm film, or the distributor chooses to transfer the movie to 35 mm film, the distributor may set up a screening at a nearby theater for potential buyers. Transferring a 90-minute digital movie to 35 mm film will cost on average $30,000–$90,000, depending on the lab and the quality of the transfer. This may be a necessary move to sell the theatrical rights to a movie, although with the proliferation of high-definition (HD) broadcast and theatrical distribution outlets, HD masters are becoming more widely accepted.

Foreign sales companies usually require a filmmaker to assign them the rights to sell the film to all foreign (meaning outside North America) territories in all theatrical, home video, and television media.

- Do not try to market a film to foreign territories yourself. Part of the job of a foreign sales company is to collect the monies due to them from individual buyers. The larger the foreign sales company, the easier it is to leverage their position to make sure each distributor pays.
- The foreign sales company will also make sure that the movie is sent in the proper format and within proper technical specification as required by each distributor.
- The foreign sales rep will represent and pay for the up-front costs of marketing and promoting the movie, although these costs will be deducted from your movie's gross income.

DOMESTIC DISTRIBUTION

Domestic distribution is the licensing of the film to theatrical, home video, and television buyers in North America (United States, Canada, and Mexico). Unlike foreign distributors, domestic distributors will create the product, the artwork, and the marketing materials; replicate the product; and broker the distribution deals with stores in North America. Domestic distributors often have connections with large retail stores, video rental stores, and online stores and will push to sell large quantities of the movie through these outlets.

DISTRIBUTION CATEGORIES

Distributors specialize in one or more markets, such as theatrical, television, direct-to-DVD, or video-on-demand. The salability of your film and profit-generating potential will often dictate how much of a financial risk a distributor is willing to accept. Given that the distributor will pay the high costs of advertising and replication up front and will see a return on only the gross revenues, many distributors choose the movies they purchase carefully. Subsequently, only those movies that have the commercial appeal will be considered for larger markets.

The primary markets throughout the world include the following:

- **Theatrical release.** The film is released in theaters in the United States and in foreign territories. Independent films are rarely picked up for mainstream release, as screen availability is already extremely competitive among Hollywood films. Most independent films are released in small art-house theaters to small audiences who enjoy nonmainstream movies.
- **Home video.** The most likely distribution outlet for low-budget, independent films, home video, and DVD distributors sell the movie to video sales and rental stores.
- **Television.** A sale to a television station or cable outlet can gross from $10,000 to $750,000 for the television rights of a film. Television sales can be divided up into broadcast, cable, pay-per-view, video-on-demand, satellite, and closed-circuit television (airplane screenings).

ATTRACTING DISTRIBUTORS

Attracting the attention and interest of a distributor is like trying to sell a book idea to a publisher. It's critical for the distributor to understand the value of the product and see a potential market for the film before agreeing to distribute it.

Make a Movie Poster

First impressions, as the old cliché goes, are lasting. This couldn't be more true than when talking about the movie poster. Also called key art, the movie poster is the first and most important marketing tool in gaining the interest of audience members, distributors, and producers.

The movie poster for *The World Without Us*, a feature-length documentary I shot in 20 countries with Mitch Anderson.

DESIGN

When creating the key art, remember that it will be used for the movie poster, web site, DVD cover art, DVD label, DVD menu design, and even the trailer. This key art will be the unifying thread in the visual campaign to market your film, so make sure it's right.

Jason's Notes

I find it really helpful to consult with a professional designer for my one-sheet, and always include that cost in the budget. Low-budget posters indicate a low-budget production and can adversely impact distributor interest.

When creating the key art, keep the following tips in mind:

- **The style of the key art should reflect the style of the movie.** The key art should reflect the tone, mood, and visual style of your movie. As much as a pitch should encapsulate your plot in a couple sentences, so too should your marketing art be clear on the genre, tone, and theme of the movie.
- **Present a dominant image.** Most good art features a central subject or object that draws the eye, followed by smaller design elements that support the central feature. Remember that sometimes less is more, so keep your visual message simple and clear.
- **Use color.** Color can be a fantastic tool for conveying a message or tone in your art. If your movie is a moody sci-fi movie, then perhaps dark blues and blacks are best. A romantic comedy may call for brighter, pastel tones, much as a horror film calls for shades of red.
- **Design it large.** When designing the key art, remember that it will be used in a variety of applications, so be sure to make the initial design image a large enough resolution that it works for all your needs. Standard movie posters are 27″ × 41″ at 300 dpi, so it may be wise to create your key art to these specifications and down res for other uses.
- **Create a tagline.** Taglines are catchy phrases or sentences that convey the premise and tone of the movie. Taglines are printed on the movie poster as a setup or to compliment the images on the poster. Some examples include:
  - "In space, no one can hear you scream." (*Alien*)
  - "How much can you know about yourself if you've never been in a fight?" (*Fight Club*)
  - "In a world of 1's and 0's, are you a zero, or The One?" (*The Matrix*)
  - "The Story of a Lifetime." (*Forrest Gump*)
  - "He's the only kid ever to get in trouble before he was born." (*Back to the Future*)
  - "Fear can hold you prisoner. Hope can set you free." (*The Shawshank Redemption*)
  - "He's having the worst day of his life . . . over, and over." (*Groundhog Day*)

- ■ "They're as straight as can be, but don't tell anyone." (*I Now Pronounce You Chuck and Larry*)
- ■ **Include credits.** Be sure to include the movie credits at the bottom of the poster. Use a font like Helvetica Narrow.
- ■ **Include the web site.** Always include the URL of the movie's web site. The intent of the poster should be to attract interest for the movie, ultimately pushing people towards the web site to see the trailer.

The poster for my feature *Time and Again.*

Produce a Trailer

If you ask any distributor what are the most important aspects of your marketing campaign, they will tell you they're the poster art and the trailer. A trailer is a 1.5- to 2-minute, tightly edited pitch designed to engage the audience and make them want to watch your movie.

As an independent filmmaker, your audience is the distributor you are trying to convince to license the rights to your film, the financiers who may be interested in investing in your next project, and the producers who may want to hire you. This audience is much more demanding than the end-moviegoer. Industry professionals will be assessing your capacity to produce industry-standard creative and technical content.

Jason's Notes

Few producers will watch your entire movie, making a strong trailer and poster even more important. If you are not 100% sure of your ability to cut a strong trailer, hire a professional editor. Remember, the trailer is the gateway to your movie. No one will be interested in a movie if the trailer sucks, regardless of how good the film is.

If you're shopping your movie to distributors or promoting your talents to producers, remember that in Hollywood, few people will actually watch your entire movie. They will, however take the time to watch half your trailer. If they like what they see, they'll take the conversation with you to the next level. Short and concise is the best way to reach people in the industry because there simply isn't enough time to read all the scripts and view all the movies filmmakers submit.

TRAILER EDITING TIPS

When you edit the trailer for your film, keep the following tips in mind.

- **Make sure the story is clear.** Audiences should walk away from the trailer with a good idea of the story you're telling. All too often, novice filmmakers edit a random assortment of cool images that tells no story. Conversely, the trailer should never be a shortened version of the movie. The trailer should entice people to want to watch the story – not tell them the story. Always set up the story and main character, clearly present the problem, then intercut various conflicts that *make the audience want to see how the character gets out of.*
- **Build a story arc.** Your trailer, just like a movie, should have a beginning that sets up the story, a clear presentation of the conflict, and an increasingly intense montage of visuals that present the problem in the story. The only thing missing is the resolution. That's what you want the audience to watch your film to see.

- **Include the best shots.** The audience is going to judge the production value and acting in your movie by what they see in the trailer. Always put the best shots and performances in the trailer.
- **Consider hiring an editor.** Most independent filmmakers edit the trailer for their own movie. This can be a problem because they know the story so well that it might not translate well in the edit. An objective editor can assemble the best shots to ensure a sensible, logical storyline.
- **Use original music.** Avoid using recognizable movie scores or classical music, as audiences already identify the music with other visuals. If you rip off a Hollywood soundtrack, you will probably never be able to compete with the visuals, production value, and performances of the scored movie. Using copywritten music is also illegal.
- **Make sure the trailer reflects the tone and style of the movie.** How many times have you watched a Hollywood movie and felt duped in a bait-and-switch marketing campaign where the movie doesn't resemble the trailer? Although the Hollywood publicity machine may be able to get away with this to a certain extent, independent filmmakers don't have this luxury. Make sure your trailer is true in style and tone to your movie.
- **Tweak every edit.** Comb through every shot, every edit, and every transition to ensure the trailer is as flawless as you can make it. Make sure audio is properly mixed, dialog can be heard, and the music doesn't overwhelm the other audio tracks. Make sure the black level is set properly and the whites don't exceed technical requirements. Overall, the trailer should be the best part of your movie because you and your film will be judged by the quality of the trailer.
- **Strong motion graphics.** Spend extra time to create compelling titles, especially a memorable title reveal. The choice of fonts and use of animation can really add production value to the trailer.

MARKETING YOUR TRAILER

Make preparations to distribute the final trailer as widely as possible, taking advantage of as many free outlets as possible. Distribute the trailer for free to the largest possible audience – but always make sure a link points viewers to the film's website. The goal, especially early on is to build a loyal fan base to whom you can later sell the final product.

- **Produce a web site.** Create a very simple web site that includes the trailer and the key art for your movie. A link to the trailer should be included in all emails, letters, and printed on all materials related to the movie.
- **Include the trailer on the DVD.** When you produce the screening DVDs, be sure to include the trailer as well. When you're authoring the DVD, consider setting the trailer to loop so it can be run continuously at film markets.
- **Keep it mobile.** Consider loading the trailer on your iPod or mobile phone. You never know who you'll meet that may be interested in seeing it.
- **Load it onto YouTube.** One of the fastest ways to distribute content to the masses it to post the trailer on YouTube. Be sure to post a link to your web site so people can learn more about your film.

Build a Website

One of the least expensive yet most effective ways of marketing your movie is to set up a web site. Although there are a number of ways to set up the site, carefully plan what you want the web site to accomplish. Is your intention to build awareness of your project? Perhaps you want people to buy your movie if you're self distributing. Are you using your web site to attract distributors? Whatever your goal, be clear on your objective and make sure your site reflects that objective.

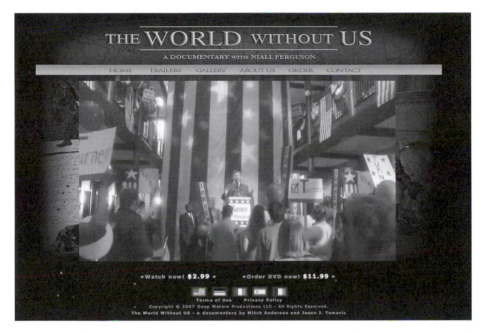

The web site for *The World Without US*.

- **Create a buzz** - Web sites are often used as a way of building a fan base so that once the film is complete, there is already knowledge of and interest in the movie. This slow and steady marketing approach is ideal for small-budget productions where time can be spent nurturing a fan base. There are several ways to do this. *The Blair Witch Project* employed one of the most successful uses of a web site by leaking news stories that "real footage" had been found that purported to tell the story of a group of doomed documentarians. By creating a buzz around the story, potential audience members who learned of the setup were further intrigued to see the outcome.

Other movies, such as *King Kong*, attempted to build a fan base by posting blogs and behind-the-scenes videos, in *King Kong*'s case, from director Peter Jackson. Bringing the audience in and making them feel a part of the making of the movie increases the likelihood of converting them to paying audience members.

As an independent filmmaker, think about a way to hook the audience early on. What can you post or how can you present your project to build a fan base?

There are a number of features you can add to your web site, depending on what you want it to accomplish:

- **The trailer.** Quite possibly the most important part of the web site, the trailer should be cleanly encoded using the Flash, QuickTime H264, or Windows Media codecs. Offer three different sizes for the user to choose from and make sure the trailer is easy to find.
- **Key art.** Especially critical when approaching distributors, always include the key art, or a variation of the key art on the web site. Stylistically, the site should reflect the tone and genre of the movie, enticing the audience to see it.
- **Cast and crew bios.** Consider including a brief description of the key cast and crew, especially if they are recognizable names. By promoting name actors, you add legitimacy to your film and make it even more attractive to distributors.
- **Production stills.** Include high-resolution stills from the movie. You can make them available as simple screenshots, or brand each still with the name of the movie so people can use them as desktop images.
- **Behind-the-scenes photos.** Include photos of the making of the movie. Audiences love seeing the actors and crew in a production environment amid the cameras, lights, and rigging equipment.
- **News coverage.** Include scans of newspaper articles or clips from local television coverage to add excitement and validity to the project.
- **Media downloads.** Consider making a password-protected page that contains four or five high-resolution photos from behind the scenes, a downloadable electronic press kit, and downloadable press releases for any media outlets interested in writing a story on the movie. By making everything available online, information is quickly and readily accessible.
- **Take the traditional approach.** You can build a web site simply as a way for people to view the movie trailer. Using the poster art as a background, use a simple one-page design that includes the movie trailer and contact information for the producer. The interface is quick, simple, and draws all the attention to what's most important: the trailer.

This is the most effective web site design when pitching your movie to distributors and producers who usually don't have the time to go through an elaborate site.

This is the approach most studios take when developing a site for a movie. You can view dozens of examples of this type of web design by visiting www.apple.com/trailers.

Tips to Getting a Distributor

- **Hire a sales representative.** With the complexity of the distribution process, hire a reputable sales rep who, for 10% of the gross revenue, will negotiate with distributors on your behalf, arrange festival screenings, assemble press kits, implement marketing efforts, set up private screenings with distributors, and try to secure the best distribution contract possible.

- **Submit your film.** Try sending the film, trailer, press kit, and a cover letter to a distributor and ask them to review the movie. Be sure to send a thank-you note and follow up with any questions they may have.

- **Enter the film into festivals.** The easiest way to get your movie in front of distribution companies is to screen at major film festivals. Distributors often attend top-tier festivals looking for projects to acquire. Major film festivals receive thousands of entries each year for only a couple dozen slots, so take the time to assemble the highest-quality submission materials to help increase your chances.

- **Get positive reviews!** If audiences and critics like the movie, distributors are more likely to view the film. Positive word-of-mouth, critical reviews printed in newspapers and online, and news coverage of your project are all outstanding ways to attract distributors' attention.

- **Present the movie to distribution companies once it is finished.** Avoid circulating rough cuts, works in progress, and unproduced concepts. Unless you already have a proven track record, unfinished works may actually hurt you by wasting the one chance you had to impress a distributor. Always present your movie in its most polished form.

- **Arrange private screenings** in New York and Los Angeles, where most distributors are based. Renting a screening room can cost around $500–$1,000 per showing, but you can help manage the screening by pitching the film before and after it runs, filling the screening with your friends and supporters of the movie to increase the excitement for distributors, and talking to distributors in person.

- **Hire a good entertainment attorney** who can read through and help negotiate the distribution contract. Distribution contracts can be long, complicated documents that, if unchecked, can provide loopholes for the distributor to write off profits so you may never see a dime, regardless of the number of copies they sell of your movie.

- **Begin assembling and organizing distribution materials during pre-production.** On-set pictures and copyright notices are easy to generate while in production and are often required elements of a distribution agreement.

Before signing with a distributor, contact the producers of other films picked up by the distributor to see if the distributor has behaved ethically, paid the residuals, and kept honest bookkeeping records and how well their sales numbers met the projections.

PAYMENT

In addition to residual payments based on the number of sales, distributors may pay you an advance, or up-front money, if they purchase your movie. The advance is intended to help you cover the costs of deliverables and the distributor will recoup the advance from the gross earnings of the film before paying you additional residuals.

There are a number of terms of a distribution deal, each of which can be negotiated in the contract. Distributors will usually take $25,000–$35,000 out of the gross sales to cover advertising and marketing costs, in addition to a budget for replication, distribution, and recoupment of the advance before paying you any additional profits. In most instances, the only money you will ever see is the advance, because low sales, creative bookkeeping, and exceedingly high marketing costs keep most of the gross revenues in the pockets of the distributors.

The amount of the advance, percentage of royalties, and payment schedules are often affected by a number of factors:

- **Who is in the film?** Recognizable actors not only help secure distribution for a film, but also increase its value. Audience members and customers at video stores are more inclined to purchase a movie if they recognize an actor on the box cover. When producing a film, spending $50,000–$100,000 on a recognizable actor to play a small cameo role may substantially increase the sales of the film, especially if that actor has international appeal.
- **What genre is the film?** Typically, genres like action, horror, and animation are easier to sell in the international market than comedies and dramas because action works much better when the dialog is translated and dubbed in a foreign language.
- **What is the technical quality?** High production values will increase the amount of money a distributor is willing to pay. Distributors will be hesitant to purchase a film with poor lighting, sound, special effects, and production design. Distributors usually buy only films shot on 35 mm film or HD formats.
- **What types of films are popular at the time?** Current box office successes have a great impact on what types of films distributors buy. At the height of *Titanic*'s popularity, dozens of movies about the doomed luxury liners, boats, and shipwrecks appeared on video store shelves.
- **Is the film good?** If your film can hold an audience's attention and is entertaining, distributors will be willing to pay more money for the right to distribute the movie. Word-of-mouth advertising and reviews are just as important as purchased advertising.

DELIVERABLES

When a distributor agrees to distribute your film, you will be required to provide a number of materials, including the mastered movie, chain-of-title, music cue sheets, dialog transcriptions, and split audio tracks. Begin gathering these materials at the beginning of the production to simplify the distribution process and minimize your out-of-pocket costs.

- **Delivery of the film on 35 mm film, high definition or digital betacam.** The technical requirements of movies released on DVD, on television, and in theaters are very carefully regulated and must meet or exceed stringent technical guidelines. Most distributors require that you master the movie in the best possible format and ensure brightness and color values, audio levels, and picture resolution meet broadcast specifications. Producing an HDCam master alone can cost upward of $1,000 per tape and a conversion to PAL (for overseas sales) can cost an additional $1,000–$1,500 per tape. If your film was shot on HD or 35 mm film, you may need to provide a pan-and-scan full screen as well as a letterboxed version, which can additionally cost thousands of dollars.

It takes a lot of work and money to get your movie to this stage.

- **Stereo mix on tracks 1 and 2—M&E on tracks 3 and 4.** When a film is distributed to non-English-speaking countries, the distributor will often dub the dialog in the audience's native language. To do this, you are required, when mixing the audio in postproduction, to separate the dialog and provide a clean copy of the music and effects tracks. When the master copy of the movie is made, the complete English version stereo mix must be placed on tracks 1 and 2 of the master tape and the music and effects tracks, minus dialog, must be placed on tracks 3 and 4. This is an easy task if a majority of the film is ADR'd, but if the original on-set dialog is used, consider making a Foley and ambience track during audio post so when the dialog is stripped away, the M&E track still exists.

- **Dialog script.** Distributors require a word-for-word transcription of every spoken word in the movie so that dubbing houses can rerecord the dialog in a foreign language and closed-captioning services can quickly type the dialog for DVD and television markets.

- **Music cue sheet.** Distributors require a detailed list of every song used in the film, proof of the copyright holder's permission to use the track, label, and artist information.

- **Song lyrics.** Distributors require a complete list of all song lyrics so they can be translated into different languages.

- **Advertising materials.** Include photographs, behind-the-scenes photos, and any and all print materials for use in the advertising of the movie. It is extremely important to generate on-set photos of the making of the film as well as promotional photos of the cast and crew during production so the distributor can create press kits and sales and marketing literature.

- **Movie trailer.** If a trailer has been edited to promote the movie, the distributor will ask for a copy of it, either to use it to promote the film to potential buyers or to include it on the DVD. If the distributor deems the trailer to be unsatisfactory, they will produce a new trailer for around $10,000, to be deducted from the film's gross revenues.

- **Chain-of-title.** Be prepared to provide copyright notices and proof of ownership of the movie. Registration with the U.S. Copyright Office is required.

M1S	Pizza Source	00.01.20	S	3:03	J Tomaric	Hiraeth Music/100	ASCAP
M2	Main Title	00.04.27	MT	:36	Jim Lang/ 100	Hiraeth Music/100	ASCAP
M3	Box O Tapes	00.07.42	BGI	:39	Jim Lang/ 100	Hiraeth Music/100	ASCAP
M4	Restaurant Photo Montage	00.11.02	BGI	:44	Jim Lang/ 100	Hiraeth Music/100	ASCAP
M5	"Today's the Day"	00.12.58	BGV	1:34	Andy Paley/100	Twilight Tunes/100	SESAC
M7	"Each Other"	00.16.23	BGV	1:31	Patrick Tuzzolino/100	Mamaronek Roofing Music/100	BMI
M8S	Bongo Willie 1	00.17.50	S	:35	Jim Lang/ 100	Hiraeth Music/100	ASCAP
M9	Bathroom Ritual	00.20.33	BGI	1:21	Jim Lang/ 100	Hiraeth Music/100	ASCAP
M10	Look At My Cards	00.22.49	BGI	:30	Jim Lang/ 100	Hiraeth Music/100	ASCAP
M11	Cigarette Search Montage	00.26.05	BGI	:52	Jim Lang/ 100	Hiraeth Music/100	ASCAP
M12	Snoring #2	00.30.56	BGI	:25	Jim Lang/ 100	Hiraeth Music/100	ASCAP
M13	Bathroom Anxiety	00.31.58	BGI	:27	Jim Lang/ 100	Hiraeth Music/100	ASCAP
M13a	"Takin' A Dump"	00.32.28	OSV	:22	Scott Chernoff/100	Hiraeth Music/100	ASCAP
M13b	"Middle Age Losers"	00.33.24	OSV	:27	Fred Stoller/50/Scott Chernoff/50	Hiraeth Music/100	ASCAP
M15	Vinnie Goes Hollywood	00.35.08	BGI	1:00	Jim Lang/ 100	Hiraeth Music/100	ASCAP
M16s	Movie Lot Source	00.36.28	S	:29	Jim Lang/ 100	Hiraeth Music/100	ASCAP
M17	After Audition	00.37.34	BGI	:24	Jim Lang/ 100	Hiraeth Music/100	ASCAP
M18	Asleep on the Floor Snore#4	00.39.00	BGI	1:08	Jim Lang/ 100	Hiraeth Music/100	ASCAP
M19	Suckers?	00.40.29	BGI	1:10	Jim Lang/ 100	Hiraeth Music/100	ASCAP
M20	Ad In Paper	00.41.55	BGI	:15	Jim Lang/ 100	Hiraeth Music/100	ASCAP
M21s	Bongo Willie 2	00.46.48	S	:17	Jim Lang/ 100	Hiraeth Music/100	ASCAP
M22	Vinnie On The Roof	00.47.59	BGI	:13	Jim Lang/ 100	Hiraeth Music/100	ASCAP
M23	Take A Look	00.49.51	BGI	1:00	Jim Lang/ 100	Hiraeth Music/100	ASCAP
M24	Shaky	00.53.52	BGI	1:42	Jim Lang/ 100	Hiraeth Music/100	ASCAP
M25s	Bongo Willie 3	00.55.20	S	:04	Jim Lang/ 100	Hiraeth Music/100	ASCAP
M26	Headache	00.55.30	BGI	2:43	Jim Lang/ 100	Hiraeth Music/100	ASCAP
M27	Notebook Echo	00.58.12	BGI	:18	Jim Lang/ 100	Hiraeth Music/100	ASCAP
M28	Sneak In On Roof	1.01.04	BGI	:16	Jim Lang/ 100	Hiraeth Music/100	ASCAP
M29	Hollywood Pad	1.02.28	BGI	:20	Jim Lang/ 100	Hiraeth Music/100	ASCAP
M30	Snoring#5	1.04.25	BGI	:18	Jim Lang/ 100	Hiraeth Music/100	ASCAP
M31	Off the Edge	1.05.56	BGI	:43	Jim Lang/ 100	Hiraeth Music/100	ASCAP
M33	Avoiding Vinnie	1.07.20	BGI	1:21	Jim Lang/ 100	Hiraeth Music/100	ASCAP
M34	Got My Life Back	1.10.00	BGI	:49	Jim Lang/ 100	Hiraeth Music/100	ASCAP
M35	"On The Mound" Card	1.15.11	BGI	:21	Jim Lang/ 100	Hiraeth Music/100	ASCAP
M36	Friends Again	1.16.56	BGI	:26	Jim Lang/ 100	Hiraeth Music/100	ASCAP
M37	Vinnie Passes	1..20.01	BGI	3:48	Jim Lang/ 100	Hiraeth Music/100	ASCAP
M38	"Each Other"	1.23.29	EC	3:39	Patrick Tuzzolino/100	Mamaronek Roofing Music/100	BMI
M39	The Vinnie Tapes Remix	1.26.22	EC	2:52	George Calfa/100	Calfaco Music/100	BMI

The music cue sheet for *Fred and Vinnie*, music composed by Jim Lang.

- **Errors and omission insurance.** Required for almost all domestic distribution in the United States, E&O insurance protects the distributor from any third-party lawsuits stemming from the production of the film, such as theft of the idea or unauthorized use of copyrighted material in the film. E&O insurance can cost anywhere from $4,500 to $15,000 and must be paid before a distributor will accept the movie.
- **Additional materials.** A distributor may ask for behind-the-scenes clips, videos, news reels (copyright-cleared, of course), director commentary tracks, making-of specials, or any other additional materials to put on the DVD to increase sales.

The cost of deliverables can quickly add up, and wise producers include a line item for distribution in the budget. If the distributor doesn't offer an advance, you must personally bear the costs of producing the deliverables yourself. Ironically, the cost of distribution can be more than the cost of producing the movie.

FILM FESTIVALS

Producing a film is a tremendous amount of work, and although many directors dream of receiving a million-dollar check for their film, many are content just to have their work screened in front of an audience. Regardless of your

Time and Again
premiered to sell-out
crowds. It was certainly
an exciting day for the
cast and crew . . . and
me, too!

intentions, film festivals are a terrific way to exhibit your movie and start down the path toward distribution.

- Most major cities around the world have film festivals. Check out www .filmfestivals.com or search for "film festivals" on the Internet to find dozens of guides to festivals, the dates they run, cost of application, and the genres they are soliciting. An outstanding tool is www.withoutabox.com, an online submission site that identifies relevant festivals and allows you to quickly submit your movie to multiple venues from one account.
- Film festivals are outstanding venues for meeting other filmmakers, agents, managers, attorneys, distributors, film executives, and financiers. Because the purpose of the event is film-based, most attendees are approachable and willing to talk about the business.
- There is a difference between the film festival and the film market. Film festivals are places to screen your work, gain recognition, vie for prizes and awards, and generate reviews and publicity for your film. Film markets, such as the Cannes Film Market in France, the American Film Market in Los Angeles, and MIFED in Italy, provide an opportunity for foreign buyers to screen and purchase films already represented by distributors.
- When applying to a film festival, follow the application instructions closely and *apply early*. Many filmmakers wait till the last minute to submit and the judges are often overwhelmed by the number of late submissions.
- Check the submission format. Does the festival require a DVD copy or a VHS copy of your movie? If it's a short film, can you upload it to their web site?

- Most film festivals require a nonrefundable application fee that averages between $25 and $150, payable by check or credit card.
- Although film festivals may accept rough cuts, or works-in-progress, send the most complete – if not the finished – version of your film possible. Only you know what the final quality will be, not the judges. They will see only what you present them, and the better the presentation, the better the chances of your film being accepted.
- Send a detailed press kit that describes the history of the project, anything unusual about the production, or any other information that will help distinguish your film as being worthy of special attention. The film festivals are always looking for something new and exciting.
- Generate as much publicity and press during the production of the film as you can. The bigger the buzz, the more likely the film festivals will be to accept your film. Don't go to the festival – get it to come to you.
- Know the exhibition formats supported by the film festival. Although most festivals support digital projection, some festivals may still require a film print. Film prints can be extremely costly, running into the tens of thousands of dollars for a feature film.
- If your movie is accepted, arrive at the festival armed with postcards and posters to advertise your movie and its show times. Much like a Hollywood release, potential moviegoers will be more inclined to see a film if they know about it and find it interesting.
- Bring lots of business cards. Film festivals provide the opportunity to network and build contacts in the filmmaking community.
- When planning to attend a festival, secure hotel reservations as early as possible, especially for larger festivals. Rooms fill up quickly and the hotels sometimes charge a higher price, so book early.
- Purchase festival tickets in advance, as popular films will sell out quickly.

SELF-DISTRIBUTION

Self-distribution involves replicating, marketing, and selling the movie yourself without the aid of a distribution company. This gives you complete control over all aspects of the film – how much to charge, where to sell it, and how the monies are dispersed. The drawback of self-distribution is that you must front all the money to produce, replicate, advertise, sell, and ship the film.

Producing and Selling DVDs

As is the case with practically any business model, producing and selling your own product will give you the most control and provide the highest profit margins. One viable option for selling your movie is to build a web site and using credit card processing companies like 2checkout (www.2checkout.com) or PayPal, accept, charge, and fill orders as they come in – essentially managing the entire distribution process yourself. Post trailers and marketing videos on YouTube, MySpace, and Facebook for free to draw traffic to your site and increase sales, or purchase advertising through Google AdWords. Online ads for

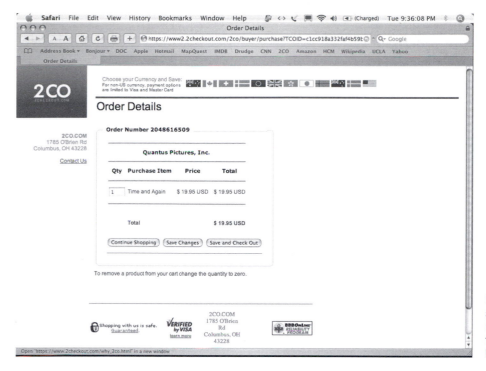

2checkout.com is a shopping cart site I use to process orders from my web site, FilmSchoolonDVD.com.

your movie will appear on any AdWords-supported web site bearing similarities in content and users who click on your ad will be routed to your web site.

Online sales outlets like Amazon and eBay can bring in additional sales, and although the number of sales probably won't be as high as if a distribution company were involved, profits per unit will be higher and you can produce the product on an as-needed basis.

If you opt to manage your own distribution web site, it will be necessary to keep an inventory of DVDs to ship out as orders come in. DVDs can be replicated either commercially in bulk, with on-disc printing, black Amaray case, and full-color insert cover for around $1,400/per 1,000 copies, or using a DVD burner at home, producing single copies on an as-needed basis. Take note that discs burned in DVD burners are read on only about 92% of DVD players and may not reliable enough for commercial sales.

On-Demand DVD Fulfillment

A second option is to hire a company to produce and ship DVDs on an as-purchased basis, allowing you to focus on marketing the movie. These fulfillment companies will setup a web page for your movie and take a percentage of each sale. Though the cost of making each DVD is higher, you don't have to worry about replicating, storing, and shipping large numbers of DVDs. The biggest benefit of on-demand fulfillment is that you retain the rights to the movie should you ever be offered a traditional distribution deal.

Streaming and Download Distribution

With the increase of bandwidth and more powerful computers, online distribution has become a viable option for audiences to download or stream your movie directly from a web site, generating revenue from fees or through advertising. With audiences becoming more accustomed to viewing content online, content isn't limited to feature films, but a new genre of TV-show style, short-format episodic series called "webisodes," that are intended to be viewed solely online. Regardless of the type of content you are selling, online distribution has several strengths and drawbacks:

- **Charging customers.** The first way to generate revenue is to charge customers who want to watch the movie – either as a pay-per-view or as a one-time charge for unlimited viewing. There are several pros and cons to this approach.
  - **Aversion to paid content.** Audiences and internet users have grown accustomed to viewing content for free. With the explosive growth of YouTube and Hulu, viewers are generally hesitant to pay for any content, choosing instead to visit a web site with free content.
  - **Minimal costs.** As the distributor, your costs are minimal – setting up the web site, paying for the setup and monthly charges of the payment gateway and credit card processing service and the cost of hosting service. By streaming content online, you are saving the costs of producing a physical product and eliminating the cost of DVD authoring, DVD replication, cover design and printing, storage, shipping, packaging and fulfillment.
  - **Online content can be stolen.** Any media product, regardless of its delivery mechanism can be stolen, but online movies can be easily copied and distributed. The least safe method is to simply encode your movie in a QuickTime or Windows Media file, both of which are easily copied to the user's hard drive. Use a codec that supports streaming video and draws the video from your host's servers as the user watches, preventing the movie from ever being downloaded onto the user's hard drive. Although choosing the streaming option provides the greatest protection from casual piracy, it requires working with a hosting company that can support streaming video – and they usually charge based on the amount of data being streamed. The more people stream your movie, the more you pay – good problem to have, especially if customers are paying to watch your movie.
  - **Advertising is still costly.** As is the case with any self-distribution method, you still need to advertise and market your movie to prospective audiences. Although pursuing the free options of posting the trailer on YouTube, writing blogs, and creating a marketing web site will all help, unless your marketing campaign goes truly viral, you may need to spend money on advertising to increase the traffic to your site.
  - **Some audiences still want to physically own the movie.** As great as streaming movies are as a new distribution form, there is still a substantial percentage of people who refer to purchase a DVD, download

the movie, or otherwise own the content they paid for. Although audiences are becoming more accustomed to accessing and watching content online, consider online streaming as a one of several distribution options.

- **Advertising.** The second option is to provide the movie to viewers for free, generating revenue on a per-view basis through the display of advertising on your site. Advertising can take many forms – users can be forced to watch video advertisements before the movie begins, online ads can be generated through Google AdWords, or advertisers can post banner ads on your web site.

  - **The content is free.** In general, you will see increased viewership by providing content for free. With the advertising model, it's important to generate enough traffic to encourage advertisers to pay for ad space, a task that can be difficult without a prior track record.
  - **Finding advertisers is difficult.** As content creators and distributors, we are facing an interesting problem – the number of advertising dollars is constant, yet the number of distribution outlets fighting for them is increasing. A decade ago, the only media outlets capable of attracting big advertisers like Coca-Cola, Honda, and BMW were the national television networks, large newspapers, and big radio stations. Now, these advertisers are finding value in reaching small, niche markets through small web sites. Because the amount of advertising dollars is constant but the number of outlets perusing those dollars is growing, less money is being spent at any one site, and those dollars will only be spent if you can prove a return – a high number of viewers. One technique used by production companies today is to partner with an advertiser, work out a financial deal, then create a show that revolves around the advertiser's product. For example, you may be able to secure Blockbuster Video as an advertiser by producing a movie or a web series that takes place at a Blockbuster store – essentially soft-selling Blockbuster's services in each episode. Often times, large companies pay to have web series produced to provide the veneer of "entertainment," all with the intention of selling their product or service.
  - **There isn't a lot of money in advertising.** Although it is possible to generate revenue through advertisers, it generally isn't enough to pay for production costs and generate a substantial profit. The only way to increase the profit potential of a web-distributed series is to reduce the overall production value by shooting more footage each day, minimize the number of crew members, forego lighting and complicated camera moves, keep the postproduction simple, and shoot as much content as possible each day. Reality television grew from this formula, which can also be applied to web-distributed content.

Tips for Marketing Your Movie Online

Online marketing is a fairly new and ever-evolving practice that adopts many rules from traditional marketing while introducing a number of new guidelines and techniques. The greatest benefit of online marketing is anyone can do it fairy inexpensively. When marketed properly, an online campaign can go viral and viewers will self-perpetuate your ads, helping word of your movie spread farther than you could ever have achieved on your own.

- **Know your audience.** Know specifically who you are targeting through your advertising both demographically (age, economic status, geographic location, gender, and ethnicity) and psychographically (hobbies and interests). As you craft your advertising campaign, think about how you can best reach and speak to that audience.
- **Keep content freely accessible.** Make sure users have easy access to your content. Don't require users to register, enter email addresses, log in, or type in a password to see your materials.
- **Make marketing content easy to share.** Encourage users to email, forward, and refer your content to their friends. The easier it is to forward content, the faster your audience will grow.
- **Use social networks.** Creating a page for your movie on social networking sites like MySpace, Facebook, and Twitter is an outstanding and almost necessary way of building a fan base for your film.
- **Give away freebies.** Audiences love free content – whether it's behind-the-scenes footage, sneak peaks of scenes from the movie, or blogs or photos from the set. The more you give the audience, the more they may want to see and be willing to pay to see.
- **Try something new.** Audiences tend to respond to something they haven't seen before – when *The Blair Witch Project* premiered, the marketing campaign selling it as a true story captivated audiences and launched the marketing to a new level. Audiences are more savvy now and are hyperaware of misleading advertising campaigns, making these techniques less and less effective. Try to devise a novel approach when packaging and marketing your movie.
- **Never give up.** Self-distribution of a movie is a slow burn – it takes time. Without the multimillion-dollar marketing resources of the studios, your marketing strategy will be largely word of mouth, so be patient and prepared for a long-term marketing campaign.

Staging a Theatrical Screening

You can choose to work outside the film festival system and organize your own screening in local theaters, either by renting the theatre or by making a deal with theatre owners to split the gross revenue from ticket sales.

Combining a smart advertising campaign with strong local support can attract a large public audience, and if your movie is profitable, the theatre owner may be willing to extend the run to another weekend. This can be a challenge in larger cities with competing films and entertainment venues where enticing audiences to buy tickets to an obscure independent movie can be expensive and unpredictable.

If you opt to simply rent the theater and self-promote the movie, there are a number of associated costs:

- **Cost of renting the theater.** Local community theaters and one-screen theatres may be more willing to work with you than large multiscreen chains, which are dependent on revenue from studio movies. Small theatres are generally more flexible for scheduling, rental rates, and show times and can benefit from the added publicity generated by and indie movie. Discuss either a flat rate to rent the theatre or a percentage of ticket sales.

- **Cost of equipment rental.** Unless the movie was shot on or transferred to film, it may be necessary to rent a digital video projector and/or appropriate sound equipment. These rentals range from $500 to $1,000 a day – costs that can be recouped through ticket sales. When we premiered *Time and Again*, we rented the screen, projector, a complete sound system for the weekend, and labor to set up and strike the equipment for $1,900. I played the movie off my MacBook Pro directly through a FireWire drive to the projector and it looked *awesome*!

Here I am before the premiere of *Time and Again* in 2003. It was incredible seeing the number of people interested in seeing my movie. The feeling in the air was electric that night.

- **Cost of printing tickets.** Local printers can easily print tickets for the premiere on a colored card-stock to make it more difficult for people to copy. A different color per show or date can keep ticket inventories organized.

- **Schedule multiple screenings.** Even if the theater is available for only a weekend, schedule as many screenings as possible, both matinee and evening screenings, to maximize the possible number of attendants. We held the Friday night premiere for *Time and Again* at 7:30 p.m. and then screened it again on Saturday, at 4:30 p.m., 7:00 p.m., and 9:30 p.m.. Our rental arrangement with the theater and the equipment rental company was for one weekend, so the more screenings we packed in, the more revenue we generated.

- **Advertising.** Contact the local media and distribute press kits promoting the release of the film. Schedule interviews on the local television station or radio morning shows to talk about the movie and generate hype. Always include press photos, bios of the cast and crew, and some quotes that the media can use in newspaper articles. Newspapers may ask for print-quality photos taken from the set or stills from the movie itself, so be prepared with these resources, as the newspaper writers are often under deadline.

- **Promotional materials.** Consider creating posters or DVD copies of the movie so the audience can purchase these souvenirs on their way out the door. It's a great way to make extra money and can help cover the costs of the premiere.

Quantus Pictures Inc.

Motion Picture Production Company

PRESS RELEASE-FOR IMMEDIATE RELEASE

Jason J. Tomaric premieres his latest film, "Time and Again" at Chardon's newly renovated, historic Geauga Theatre on June 20 and 21, 2003.

THE STORY

"Time and Again" is the story of Bobby Jones, a convicted murderer, who has been sentenced to thirty years in prison for a crime he didn't even remember committing. Bent on finding the real killer, he escapes from prison only to be thrown back in time to July 14, 1958... the day of the murder. With six hours to work, he must reconstruct a forgotten past to save himself... until he meets the sexy diner waitress, Awanda. It is only then that his true priorities are tested.

MAKING THE FILM

"Time and Again" was produced during the summer of 2002. Shot over fourteen days at dozens of locations, the filmmakers recreated the July of 1958 with nearly 75 period cars, hundreds of extras and the assistance of several local communities. Chardon and Chagrin Falls were the primary locations as the camera crew shut down several streets, including Chardon Square itself for the spectacular end of the film. But one of the most exciting scenes, the opening prison break, was shot at Grafton State Prison where filmmakers took control of the prison exterior for an entire night. Rigging spotlights, smoke effects and pyrotechnics, the director, Jason J. Tomaric, set the stage for Bobby Jones's journey back in time.

With the continued success of the digital medium, the filmmakers also produced a three-hour long documentary entitled "How-to-Make-A-Hollywood-Calibur-Movie-On-A-Budget-Of-Next-To-Nothing" which walks the viewers through every stage of the how "Time and Again" was made. Featuring dozens of interviews with cast, crew and local authorities, viewers learn everything from how to find actors and equipment to learning to read between the lines of a script to finding and using editing equipment. Cleveland weatherman Brad Sussman hosts the documentary which will be released with "Time and Again."

ABOUT THE FILMMAKER

Jason J. Tomaric, 27, has enjoyed national success as an award-winning director and renowned digital filmmaker. Winning six Telly Awards for his directing work last year alone, Mr. Tomaric owns and operates Quantus Pictures, Inc., a complete motion-picture production facility. In addition to directing films, Mr. Tomaric has produced and directed dozens of award-winning commercials and productions for clients such as McDonald's, Microsoft, Hitachi and RCA Records. His last feature project, "One," premiered to over 1,300 people at Cleveland's lavish Palace Theatre and attracted the attention of numerous studios including Sony Pictures who screened the film as part of the digital conference at the Sundance Film Festival. Mr. Tomaric currently resides in Chardon but will be relocating to Los Angeles at the end of the month.

ABOUT THE PREMIERE

"Time and Again" and another Tomaric short film, "The Overcoat" will premiere at the Geauga Theatre in Chardon on Friday, June 20th at 7:30pm and on Saturday, June 21 at 2:00pm, 4:30pm, 7:00pm and 9:30pm. Tickets are $8.00 and will be available at the door. The Geauga Theatre has special significance as it was used as a location in the film. The theatre is located at 101 Water Street, Chardon, Ohio 44024 right on Chardon square.

Press Releases

Catching the attention of the media by developing a strong press release is the first step in marketing a movie. Press releases are brief, one-page summaries of a news story that provide a reporter with all the information he needs to pursue and cover the event.

- **Story synopsis.** In a brief paragraph, describe the plot of the movie in the same way it would be written on the back of a DVD case. The newspaper will probably print the synopsis directly from the press release.
- **Cast and crew.** List the main actors and key crew members and include short bios of each person.
- **Quotes and funny stories.** Include a variety of quotes as well as interesting anecdotes from the set, especially those that may appeal to local audiences.
- **Premiere times.** Give concise directions of when, where, and how much tickets to the premiere will cost. Give landmarks as a reference if the theater is difficult to find.

Check out the press kit for the feature film "Clone" at Filmskills.com. See page vi for details.

- **Include photos.** Newspapers may ask for photos from the set or stills from the film. Have five or six pictures ready in a high-resolution, emailable format to send to the paper.
- **Clips from the movie.** If television stations express an interest in interviewing cast or crew members, prepare either a trailer or a series of short (10- to 15-seconds-long) clips to be broadcast on the air during the interview. We had the greatest response not only from viewers, but also the news anchors, when we ran part of the trailer. Giving the audience a chance to see clips from the film is the best way to market it.

Index

Note: Page numbers followed by *f* and *t* refer to figures and tables, respectively.